Where Is Abbas Kiarostami?

Where Is Abbas Kiarostami?

TOWARD A POSTCOLONIAL
FILM-PHILOSOPHY

Hamid Dabashi

UNIVERSITY OF CALIFORNIA PRESS

University of California Press
Oakland, California

© 2025 by Hamid Dabashi

Library of Congress Cataloging-in-Publication Data

Names: Dabashi, Hamid, 1951- author.
Title: Where is Abbas Kiarostami? : toward a postcolonial film-
   philosophy / Hamid Dabashi.
Description: Oakland, California : University of California Press, [2025] |
   Includes bibliographical references and index.
Identifiers: LCCN 2024017920 (print) | LCCN 2024017921 (ebook) |
   ISBN 9780520397170 (cloth) | ISBN 9780520397187 (paperback) |
   ISBN 9780520397194 (ebook)
Subjects: LCSH: Kiarostami, Abbas—Philosophy. | Philosophy in motion
   pictures. | Motion picture producers and directors—Iran. | Motion
   pictures—Iran—Philosophy. | Motion pictures—Iran—Aesthetics.
Classification: LCC PN1998.3.K58 D33 2025 (print) | LCC PN1998.3.K58
   (ebook) | DDC 791.4302/33092—dc23/eng/20240702
LC record available at https://lccn.loc.gov/2024017920
LC ebook record available at https://lccn.loc.gov/2024017921

33 32 31 30 29 28 27 26 25 24
10 9 8 7 6 5 4 3 2 1

For
Ramin Bahrani

Let us not touch the arrangements of the world. . . . My task is to watch and watching is so delightful. I have come to the feast of this world, and this world has come to my feast. If I did not exist, something would be amiss in Existence. If the branch of this willow tree in our house did not move this very moment, the world would be burning in anticipation. Everything is exactly how it should be. I have learned not to find fault with things. I love blossoming and I love the shriveling too. . . . Every second I am renewed, and I shall renew my surroundings. . . . Let us not ask any questions. Let us stay within ourselves—and sprinkle fresh water in our inner selves. Let us shine in our own sky. Let us expand ourselves. And if solitude was a bit too much, then let us open the doors and call on each other.

Sohrab Sepehri, from a letter to a friend, dated Tehran, 22 April 1963

Contents

Acknowledgments — xi

Introduction: Where Is Abbas Kiarostami? — 1
1. Mirror of the Invisible World — 49
2. Aesthetic Alienation — 86
3. Between Aesthetic and Nonaesthetic Reasons — 124
4. The Foreign Familiarity of Rereading Reality — 164
5. Toward a Critique of Postcolonial Aesthetic Judgment — 195
6. Surfacing of a Semblance of Subjectivity — 222
7. The Aesthetic Formation of a Nomadic Pilgrim Subject — 245
   Conclusion: When the Earth Is Shaken and People Wonder Why — 282

Notes — 299
Filmography and Selected Works — 321
Index — 329

Acknowledgments

Raina Polivka, Senior Editor at University of California Press, took an immediate interest in the detailed proposal that ultimately resulted in this book. She chaperoned the project through the process of acquisition with care, competence, and purpose. I am blessed by her vote of confidence in my work. Shaj Mathew saw an earlier draft of this book and gave it a thorough read and sent me copious notes gently urging me toward the expansion of some of the major thoughts I have shared in this detailed study of Abbas Kiarostami's oeuvre. An anonymous reviewer was equally generous and helpful with their comments. I am grateful to them. Words fail me to thank Ahmad Kiarostami, Abbas Kiarostami's son, who is in charge of the Abbas Kiarostami Foundation and who has generously given me permission to use the illustrations in this book and otherwise enabled my further archival research. I am equally grateful to Hamid Keshmirshekan, the eminent Iranian art historian and critic, for his particular help with illustrations in chapter 7, an earlier and shorter version of which he included in an edited volume he published. I am grateful to my research assistant when I was working on this book, Hoda Mohamed Elsharkawy, who helped considerably with bibliography research and other chores. During the final stages of production, my other caring and capable research assistant Rukhsar Balkhi was equally helpful. I thank her for her dedicated and efficient work. Procuring high-resolution copies of the illustrations in this book and the permission to use them are all indebted to her extraordinary capacities for research. I am grateful to the chair of my department, Gil Hochberg, and our director of academic administration and finance, Jessica Rechtschaffer, for facilitating much crucial research assistance when we work. The crucial task of copyediting the final draft of the book was in the capable care of Theresa Winchell. With a gentle but firm hand she made sure my sentences were behaving without marring the manners of my signature prose. Words fail me to thank her enough! Ramin Bahrani has been a solid friend and a steady source of confidence and trust in my life for decades. Dedicating this book to him is just a simple sign of how much his presence has meant to me.

Introduction

WHERE IS ABBAS KIAROSTAMI?

In bahr-e vujud	This see of existence
Amadeh birun	Has surfaced
Zeh nahoft /	From the unseen.

Omar Khayyam (1048–1131)

About a year or so before he released one of his masterpieces, *Taste of Cherry* (1997), I had lunch with the late Abbas Kiarostami (1940–2016). He was visiting New York for the screening of some of his previous films. As usual, my Columbia colleague Richard Peña, the program director of the Film Society of Lincoln Center at the time, was his host. On this occasion, like many others, Peña had a luncheon gathering in honor of Kiarostami to which he had invited me and a few other friends and colleagues. He sat me next to Kiarostami at the top floor of an Afghan/Persian restaurant near Lincoln Center. As we were waiting to order our food, Kiarostami and I began to catch up on our latest news, and one thing led to another until he began to share with me how he was waiting for the fall season to start in Tehran to shoot one remaining scene of his forthcoming film, *Taste of Cherry*. "What is the film about?," I asked politely. He did not directly respond; instead he told me he had once heard or read a quote from the Romanian philosopher E. M. Cioran (1911–1995) to the effect that "were it not for the possibility of suicide I would have killed myself a very long time ago."

The paradox of the phrase was extremely striking to me then as it is now—"Were it not for the possibility of suicide, I would have committed suicide a very long time ago"! The subject of *Taste of Cherry*, as you might know by now, is a man who seems to be determined to commit suicide. I never bothered to check if E. M. Cioran had actually said something like that or not—maybe he did, maybe he did not. He was fond of aphorisms of this sort and some had compared him to Nietzsche in this respect. I preferred to keep the genealogy of the phrase right as I just shared it, from what Kiarostami told me he had heard or read Cioran having said. By the time of this conversation in the mid-1990s, I believe, I knew Cioran's work quite well and had read him extensively and yet had never, to the best of my recollection, come across anything like that phrase. But it did sound like something he would have said in his pithy aphorisms. I was introduced to Cioran by my dear friend Farhad Mechkat, who in the 1970s was the music director and principal conductor of Tehran Symphony Orchestra. After the revolution of 1977–1979, Farhad Mechkat and his family moved to New York, where we became close family friends. Farhad is a deeply cultivated musician who was educated in Europe and the US and in his capacity as an artistic force at Rudaki Music Hall in Tehran was behind a major institution in Iran, and truly a gift to my generation of Iranians. Through him I had come to know of Cioran and read many of his works, including *The Temptation to Exist*, *History and Utopia*, and *The Trouble with Being Born*. Later when I learned of Cioran's love for Hitler and admiration for German and Italian fascism, I altogether abandoned any serious interest in his work.[1] Kiarostami's reference to Cioran in the course of that luncheon in New York was both surprising and quite intriguing. But I did not share any of these thoughts with Kiarostami at that time. I was just curious where he would be going with that phrase in his forthcoming film.

As exemplified by Mechkat's detailed knowledge and Kiarostami's one-sentence impression of Cioran, the manner in which European intellectual legacy had reached Iran very much defined the tangential place of the country in the vicinity of a Europe that had mitigated its relationship with the world at large. Kiarostami's impressionistic encounter with a famous European thinker was neither definitive to his cinema nor entirely relevant to what those impressions did with or to his cinema. On another occasion, after the screening of *Taste of Cherry* at Lincoln Center, I recall a member of the audience asked Kiarostami if at the end of his film he was

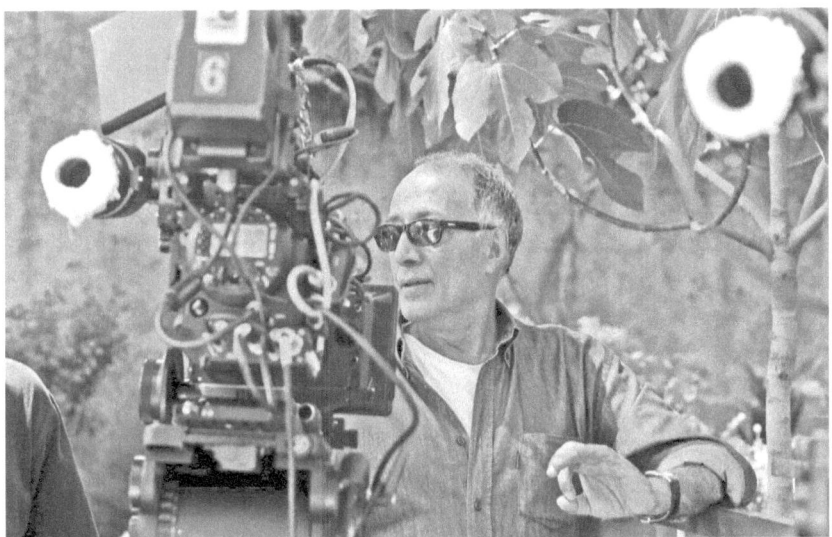

Figure 1. Kiarostami and his camera. Courtesy of Abbas Kiarostami Foundation.

appealing to Brecht's notion of "alienation." I could sense Kiarostami did not know what exactly Brecht's idea was but managed to come up with a response. Afterward I told him how in our sorts of performing arts we did not need Brecht's conception of "Verfremdungseffekt," or Viktor Shklovsky's *Ostranenie* (of which he was unaware) for that matter, because our kind of mimesis is not total identification of mimetic act as best evident in our Ta'ziyeh. Soon after that conversation, Kiarostami made a film about Ta'ziyeh and staged it in Avignon in France. The little that he managed to learn in casual conversations here and there were parts of a larger world of impressions and hearsay that eventually metamorphosed into the sublimity of his own artworld. To be sure, that sublimity is irreducible to the scattered remnants of such casual conversations, but they do point to the varied framings of the reception of his cinema in multiple cultural contexts.

I share these memories to locate perhaps the most iconic Iranian filmmaker of his or any other generation at the elliptical edge of the world he embraced in fragmented pieces and to which his own coherent cinema and artwork came in equally fragmented piecemeals. How do these two piecemeals from two diametrically opposite directions come together and gel in our understanding of the rich and effervescent artistic legacy Kiarostami has left behind? Where exactly, in other words, is Abbas Kiarostami located as an artist, a filmmaker, a poet, a painter, a photographer? What do such locations tell us and how do they help us understand his artworld and artwork? I am not here after a hidden treasure trove or a secret talisman of what his cinema "actually" means in total abstraction—a treasure trove and secret talisman that I have somehow discovered and now wish to share. Quite to the contrary: I am, rather, after locating his cinema in the open-ended crosscurrents of both his immediate Iranian surroundings and the distant global receptions that must come together to enable any and all readings of Kiarostami's cinema and other artworks. Is he an Iranian filmmaker, we might wonder, who became globally celebrated by making films for film festivals like Cannes, Locarno, Berlin, New York, and Tokyo—as some of his hardnose Iranian detractors have suggested? Or did he in fact make site-specific Iranian films that enriched and deeply diversified the otherwise provincial European and North American cinematic parlance? Are these two propositions actually mutually exclusive? Neither of these two propositions is entirely accurate or entirely false, as indeed neither of these questions is specific to Abbas Kiarostami, and one might ask them about any other renowned filmmaker from anywhere else in the world. But still, raising them about a specific filmmaker goes a long way toward situating, framing, and making such questions globally relevant. I am, in short, less concerned with what his cinema "actually" meant in abstraction (which no one knows) than with what the multiple locations of his cinemas have enabled the world to see, perceive, and comprehend in his artworld. If there is a meaning and significance to his artistic legacy today, it is located precisely on the "Borromean rings" of what we may simply identify as national, postnational, and world cinemas. It is impossible to parse and partition these Borromean rings.

For decades these Borromean rings of the varied receptions of Kiarostami's cinema have fascinated and preoccupied me—a fact that extends far beyond his specific artworld and embraces any significant artists from anywhere else in the world. This has something to do with the fact that my initial encounter with his cinema began as a young cineaste in Iran and then became more serious in Europe, the US, and eventually in Japan, Mexico, and Argentina, and finally the Arab world. I eventually came to identify these correlated Borromean rings in terms of *national*, *postnational*, and *world* cinemas. Filmmakers like Kiarostami initially emerge in the local context of their artistic traditions, and they eventually move forward in new directions and into new locales, ultimately becoming global products where no particular narrative (including or perhaps particularly their own) has any exclusive claim on them. This fact gives a renewed momentum to the "reception theory" as articulated by Stuart Hall, a process he identified as "encoding and decoding" a message.[2] This in turn raises the question of where exactly a filmmaker like Kiarostami is located and how we are to read him, which above all gives rise to an embedded alterity in the identity of this cinematic legacy, all staged within an interstitial space that contracts and expands organically. My concern has never been with which one of such decoding is better than the others, or more accurate, or more convincing, but with that embedded alterity that they entail and thus put a hermeneutic spin to any reading of Kiarostami's artistic legacy.

IRANIAN CINEMA AT HOME IN THE WORLD

"I have often noticed that we are not able to look at what we have in front of us, unless it's inside a frame." Kiarostami's final masterpiece, *24 Frames* (2017), starts with that citation. Suppose we opened that frame and asked ourselves in what frame Kiarostami's own entire oeuvre would or should or could be located? The answer is both very simple and yet quite complicated. Throughout his filmic career Kiarostami was received and perceived within multiple, concurrent, contradictory, and sometimes even hostile frames of reference. The task at hand, I believe, is not to decide which frame is more accurate. That would be going on a goose chase, with militant nativism on one side and vacuous globalism on the other. Far more insightful would be if we were to see what happens to an artist's oeuvre when seen through the kaleidoscopic crosscurrent of multiple frames—over which we have no control, about which we have ample space to think.

Let me go upstream from Kiarostami and place his artwork first in the immediate context of Iranian cinema, the fertile ground on which he first grew and flourished. Where exactly his cinema is located on the widening spectrum between national, postnational, and world cinemas is precisely the hermeneutic and aesthetic plane upon which we can begin to reread him more fruitfully. Two seminal theoretical perspectives on space, first by Henri Lefebvre and then followed by Edward Soja, have both socially and philosophically expanded our conception of space. Lefebvre's idea of "social space" and Soja's idea of "the third space," which (borrowing from architecture) I have already expanded into the versatile concept of "interstitial space," is crucial here.[3] We are not required to appropriate Kiarostami's artworld into either the national or the postnational or even world cinemas to read his artworld better. Instead, we need to articulate the third interstitial space on which his legacy is now most conveniently located and therefore best readable. What and where exactly is that third space?

Back in 2018, BBC Culture polled 209 critics in 43 countries soliciting their rankings of the best in world cinema.[4] "We asked critics," BBC Culture reported, "to vote for their favorite movies made primarily in a language other than English. The result is BBC Culture's 100 greatest foreign-language films." Four Iranian films had made it to the top 100 titles, one to the top 25: three by Abbas Kiarostami—*Close-Up* (39), *Where Is the Friend's House?* (94), and *Taste of Cherry* (97), and one by Asghar Farhadi, *A Separation* (21).[5]

Neither the fact that a number of key moments in Iranian cinema had made it to this illustrious list nor the particular films that these critics had selected was surprising. One might suggest any number of other films that could have been on this list, but no one could question the importance of these four films or the towering presence of Abbas Kiarostami among world-class filmmakers. Iranian cinema was by now at home in the world. The key conceptual framing here was of course "world cinema,"[6] which has been the subject of extensive scholarship, and the criterion that the films were selected was the fact that they were not in English. The two adjacent framings of *national* and *postnational* cinema were not of importance here.

By and large, the critics who had been consulted to make these selections knew little of Iranian or any other cinema except the cinema of the country of their own origin through major international film festivals, chief among them Cannes, Venice, Berlin, and Locarno—all of them European events and locations overshadowing other major festivals happening in the US, Japan, Korea, the Arab world, Africa, or Latin America. Their understanding of Iranian cinema was perforce limited to and channeled through these festivals, and there is much else in that cinema that is beyond their easy reach. But nevertheless, their selections are not entirely off the mark or contradicted by other masterpieces of Iranian or any other cinema. The key factor here is that the idea of "world cinema" (just like "world literature" or "world philosophy," etc.) are entirely European in origin, articulation, and destination. There is nothing necessarily wrong or right about this fact. It just is what it is. The Borromean circles of national, postnational, and world cinemas all therefore gather theoretical momentum on the sites of these European festivals, as does the embedded alterity at the heart of any national identity, and thus the crucial significance of the third, interstitial space this whole spectacle generates.

The path of Iranian films into these major festivals has been long and winding, its origin to its destination always rooted in the social history of Iranian cinema.[7] The fact that Iranian cinema (or any other national cinema) has found a global audience through these festivals is a crucial component of the aesthetics and politics of their widespread receptions, feeding back into the production lines of successive generations of Iranian filmmakers. Neither Cannes nor Venice nor others in and of themselves make these films global; the fact that around the world, festival curators in Asia, Africa, or Latin America (or even the US, Canada, Japan, Australia, and New Zealand) take their cues about any national cinemas from these festivals does.

The wider landscape of Iranian cinema over the last one hundred years plus has been a variegated topography of extraordinary cinematic events upon which major filmmakers have risen to global attention. Iranian cinema has been integral to Iranian social and cultural history, having a symbiotic relationship with the environment that has sustained and informed it and been in turn enriched and nourished by its visual and performing arts. More specifically, the historical formation of Iranian cinema took place on a transnational public sphere—both in its origins and its destinations—from the East India Film Company studios in India where the very first Iranian films were made to the Cannes, Venice, and Locarno film festivals where its global celebrations have created a new politics and aesthetics of receptions for it.[8]

There has never been a moment in the long history of Iranian cinema when it was confined to the postcolonial borders of its current frontiers. The very first Iranian sound film, *Dokhtar-e Lor/Lor Girl* (1932), subtitled *The Iran of Yesterday and the Iran of Today*, was produced by Ardeshir Irani and Abdolhossein Sepanta at the Imperial Film Company in Bombay. Not just in cinema but in every other aspect of Iranian social and cultural history, in the course of its encounter with the European colonial modernity we must think of a larger frame of reference extending from Europe to the Ottoman and Russian empires all the way to Egypt and India as the historical site of the rise of Persian prose and poetry, as well as Iranian visual and performing arts.[9]

In that long history one might emphasize a few landmarks when a transnational public sphere was crafted for both the production and the reception of Iranian cinema, with a number of iconic filmmakers having staged the best Iranian cinema has had to offer. The figure of Forough Farrokhzad (1935-1967), a leading poet of her time, shines over the history of Iranian cinema. With a singular short documentary, *Khaneh Siah Ast/The House Is Black* (1962), premiered and awarded at the Oberhausen Short Film Festival in 1963, Farrokhzad set the Iranian cinema on a creative path from which it has not since diverged. Shot on location in a leprosarium, *The House Is Black* defined the miasmatic fusion of fact and fiction in a unique and pathbreaking way. Before that fateful decade had ended, Dariush Mehrjui's *Gave/The Cow* (1969) was smuggled out of Iran and screened at the 1971 Venice Film Festival, where it won the critics prize (FIPRESCI). Its screening at the Berlin Film Festival further consolidated its global recognition as a defining moment in the emerging Iranian cinema. Based on a short story by the leading Iranian dramatist Gholamhossein Sa'edi (1936-1985), *The Cow* told the story of a villager and his unique anthropomorphic relationship with his cow with astonishing visual and narrative panache.[10]

Although much crucial development happened in Iranian cinema of the 1970s, the world's attention was drawn to the Iranian revolution of 1977-1979 and its regional and global repercussions. What brought the world attention back to Iranian cinema was Amir Naderi's masterwork, *Davandeh/The Runner* (1984), which was something of a revelation when it premiered at the Festival of the Three Continents in Nantes. Shot in multiple locations in southern Iran during the Iran-Iraq War (1980–1988), *The Runner* crafted a cinematic landscape of its own, where we follow the solitary life of a young boy mesmerized with running, to which Naderi gives a deeply moving allegorical significance. It was immediately after the global success of *The Runner* that the world took notice of Abbas Kiarostami, when his now classic film *Khaneh-ye Dust Kojast/Where Is the Friends House?* (1985) was premiered and awarded at the Locarno Film Festival. By this time Kiarostami was of course a known and fairly successful filmmaker in Iran.[11] But his reception in Europe suddenly placed him next to Vittorio De Sica of *Bicycle Thieves* (1948), Yasujirō Ozu of *Tokyo Story* (1953), and Satyajit Ray of the Apu Trilogy (1955–1959) and gave his work a global reception of unsurpassed power and significance. The introduction of Iranian cinema into the category of "World Cinema" as a result was crucial in facilitating a different reading of it far beyond the control or even intention of any European film festival—though they were the instrumental vehicles through which the world took notice of Iranian cinema.

Kiarostami was solidly established as the leading Iranian filmmaker on the global scene when the Makhmalbaf family came to put a particularly poignant spin on that reception, especially when the young Samira Makhmalbaf premiered her debut film, *Sib/Apple* (1998), at Cannes when she was barely eighteen years old. I was at Cannes that year and saw how the global perception of Iran changed overnight from a bearded angry man (Khomeini) to the bright, smiling face of a young filmmaker. That was a transformative moment in the global reception of Iranian cinema, and with it, Iran itself. By the following decade, Jafar Panahi had risen to the top of European film festivals, when his *Dayereh/Circle* (1999) was premiered and awarded at the Venice Film Festival. Jafar Panahi was a protégé of Abbas Kiarostami, but he pushed the cinematic prowess of his mentor into decidedly social and political domains far beyond the evident cinematic interests of Kiarostami himself. Initially he did so in measured and judicious strokes. But soon after, he was arrested because of his political activism during the Green Movement (2008–2010) and sentenced to suspended prison terms and barred from filmmaking, which he defied, smuggling his films to European film festivals, as he descended into a vindictive and angry prosody detrimental to his own earlier masterpieces. The world was changing and with it the place of Iranian cinema in it.

By 2010, the world had thought Iranian cinema had offered it all it had. The spectacular rise of Asghar Farhadi altered that perception when his family drama *Joda'i Nader az Simin/A Separation* (2011) was nominated for an academy award and won the Oscar. Farhadi has come to cinema from a theater background, and his films remain deeply dramatic in a theatrical sense. But the ingenious cinematography of his director of photography, master Mahmoud Kalari, has been instrumental in defining Farhadi's sense of cinematic drama. This first Oscar for an Iranian film placed a long tradition of cinematic history on a global scale never attained before. Farhadi's achievement was obviously predicated on a sustained body of work by many others before him. But still the national cinema he now represented was given a worldly disposition that even Kiarostami had not achieved, and yet with it Kiarostami himself was being re-examined too.

The global staging of Iranian cinema had by now offered it an audience upon which some of its best films solicited an international attention that aesthetically and thematically fed back to its cinematic repertoire. In the process, no doubt, some of the best in Iranian cinema never received the attention they richly deserve. Among its older masters, the cinema of Farrokh Ghaffari, Ebrahim Golestan, and Bahman Farmanara are chief among such neglect. Iran has also benefitted from some gifted women filmmakers like Rakhshan Bani-Etemad, Marziyeh Meshkini, and Manizheh Hekmat, who, too, have not received the attention they rightly deserve. Meanwhile, outside Iran, and from the fertile ground of its worldly origins, a new generation of Iranian filmmakers has emerged, chief among them Ramin Bahrani (*Chop Shop*, 2007) and Shirin Neshat (*Women without Men*, 2009) who, deeply rooted in the most enduring aspects of Iranian cinema, now carry its aesthetic dimensions into uncharted territories. Iranian cinema emerged from the fertile grounds of world cinema and came back to it already rooted in its masterpieces from the four corners of the world. This cinema has always been at home in the world, and the cinema of its globally most celebrated master Abbas Kiarostami was chief among the works that had the world as the frame of its reference. This does not mean its national framing is to be neglected or overcome but that we have more than one way of seeing the films this particular cinema keeps producing.

THE IDEA OF A POSTNATIONAL CINEMA

One can only grasp the significance of the steady hands of Kiarostami in his cinematic oeuvre, his unwavering vision, and his artistic world when we place them all against the background of the tumultuous vicissitudes of his immediate national and postnational cinemas.[12] Three ideas are at work here: The *national* into which he was born as a filmmaker, the *postnational* into which he grew, and the *world* cinema within which he was ultimately located. The specific disposition of these three modes of producing, seeing, and understanding cinema will have to be considered simultaneously in the work of any serious artist like Kiarostami. That trilectic, one might say, is the hermeneutic grid against which serious filmmakers might now be understood.

At the height of Kiarostami's cinematic career, there were signs of what we might call a *postnational cinema*, a proposition not so outlandish in the heightened age of transnational globalization. The idea is based on a conception of national cinemas, or any other national cultural movement, as predicated on national traumas.[13] Consider Kiarostami's protégé and leading Iranian filmmaker Jafar Panahi's film, *Taxi* (2015), which garnered the top prize at the Berlin Film Festival, and which pushes the idea of any national cinema even farther into the hinterland of European film festivals. It opens new frontiers of wonder as to the future of art and its relevance to the collective fate of a people in whose name these festivals brand their prizes. Fraught with political pamphleteering, award-winning Iranian film *Taxi* panders specifically to European film festivals. The in rise of this postnational cinema that overrides national traumas and waters it down to a festival audience in Europe does not make Kiarostami's cinema either exclusively national or postnational—but locates it on an interstitial space, which is precisely my point of investigation in this book. A filmmaker becomes postnational by virtue of the political and aesthetic parameters with which they are received, interpreted, and celebrated beyond the particularities of their national origins.

As the prize was announced in Berlin, high-ranking cinema officials in Tehran (all of them political ideologues at the service of the ruling state) denounced the festival for being too political, while Panahi himself retorted that no one was more political than these officials, as BBC Persian pitted the two positions against each other and thus dragged the top film prize even further into its ... well, politics. This politicking of course did not have to wait for Iranian officials who were not happy with this prize. "In a win for freedom of speech tonight," as Nancy Tartaglione, the international editor for the website *Deadline*, put it, "Iranian director Jafar Panahi was awarded Berlin's Golden Bear for his latest movie, 'Taxi', despite being banned from film-making in his home country and not being allowed to travel abroad."[14] All these are true, if not truisms, but the result remains the same: The active formation of a postnational cinema does not care if a film is even seen in the filmmaker's homeland, which for Panahi and many other filmmakers is almost impossible. The age of the digital and the internet (soon to be augmented by the global COVID-19 pandemic) no longer needs to wait for any in-person screening of a film in any given country. But still, the fact and phenomenon of cinema precisely in this age have perforce exited any and all assumptions of national frontiers.

Panahi is indeed one of the most globally celebrated victims of censorship and the wanton tyranny of the state in which he lives. He is also a world-class filmmaker. But have these two factors now crisscrossed to generate a condition where the making of national cinema is no longer plausible? The best evidence we can offer to elaborate this point are two diametrically opposed reviews of Panahi's *Taxi*, one in English by Kevin B. Lee of the highly influential *IndieWire* praising this film to the moon, calling it "a unique cinematic masterpiece," and another in Persian by Iranian film critic Mohammad Abdi for *Iranwire* politely but severely criticizing it, dismissing it as "having problems from the get-go."[15] Lee considers it "an essential film of the year, if not the decade," praising it as "thoroughly exciting, entertaining and ingenious work of cinema ... to the company of all-time greats." But Abdi has a drastically different view. "Almost all the actors, including Panahi, act astonishingly badly," he says. He considers the dialogues of the film "sloganeering, designed to give information to foreigners and not integral to the characters' persona."[16] One can dismiss neither of these two professional film critics. They both make their cases quite persuasively. We must therefore come to terms with the postnational reality that Panahi's cinema signals, and into which his mentor's cinema is surely located.

The film, Abdi believes, could have been a good parody, a joke, except it is not. Film critics of course are all entitled to their opinions and do in fact invariably disagree on the quality and significance of a film, though perhaps not quite as drastically opposed to one another. But the issue here is not just the difference of opinion between two film critics. The issue is something far more serious. Panahi's *Taxi* benefits from every potent technique with which he is known and praised—particularly his uncanny ability to thrive on that strange combination of fact and fantasy that in my book *Close-Up: Iranian Cinema: Past, Present, Future* (2001) I termed "factacy." While Lee might indeed see something in the film that merits the label "a masterpiece," Abdi makes a very persuasive case that it is fraught with political pamphleteering—and when that happens, for the benefit of the filmmaker's German and European audiences to whom a more subtle Persian prose and cinematic poetry would be entirely lost, then, alas, art has categorically collapsed into not just political counter-propaganda but, much worse, into anthropology. When we have to decide between anthropology and a cinematic "masterpiece," then we face an improbable space that has announced itself as "postnational" cinema—at once self-indulgent and literally outlandish, and yet not entirely irrelevant to the fate of a national cinema.

On merely technical grounds, the particular matrix of filmmaking evident in *Taxi* has been entirely exhausted and done to perfection by Panahi's own mentor Abbas Kiarostami in, among other films, *Ten* (2002). Panahi fails to push the idea anywhere farther than Kiarostami has already done. In the absence of any cinematic innovation like the ones we see in Panahi's real masterpiece *Crimson Gold* (2003), *Taxi* does indeed collapse into political pamphleteering, especially in that awkward moment when the leading Iranian human rights activist Nasrin Sotoudeh begins repeating almost line by line her legitimate political denunciations of the Islamic Republic—for listening to which we really need not have bothered one of the national treasures and masters of Iranian cinema. As evident in this film, therefore, something terrible seems to be happening to Iranian cinema when one filmmaker favored by the government, Majid Majidi, is given a multibillion-dollar budget to make a biopic trilogy on the life of the Prophet Muhammad, while another is censored and sentenced by the same government and has to struggle against unconscionable limitations when making a film, risking his own cinematic legacy and integrity. In other words, the censorial policies of the ruling Islamic regime are chief among the factors, though not the sole reason, that have conditioned the creation of this troubled spot called "postnational" cinema.

Panahi's latest films are watched, praised, prized, or else criticized on a lopsided analytical grid, within an asymmetric and convoluted hermeneutic circle, skewed in its cinematic concepts, cockeyed in its aesthetics, and yet quite persistent in the terms of its promotional power. People praise him, confused between their political solidarities and their cinematic judgment. Panahi is not the only or the first filmmaker to make a film while incarcerated. The gifted Kurdish filmmaker Yilmaz Yilmaz Güney, too, directed his masterpiece *Yol* (1982) from jail—though he gave detailed instructions to his assistant Şerif Gören to do the shooting. But as a magnificent filmmaker of unwaveringly progressive politics, he had the advantage of much simpler technical capacities. The postnational disposition of Güney's masterpiece therefore has more to do with the fact that as a Kurdish filmmaker he had to embrace the politics of Türkiye (a chief state tormenting the Kurds) putting a claim on his cinema.

Panahi's is a different world, and the new technologies of representation that digital cameras and cyberspace screening have enabled come as a mixed blessing when they make it possible for filmmakers like Panahi to make "films" while banned from making films, send them to festivals like Berlin and receive accolades, and from there to circulate it around the world, all rightly to celebrate Panahi's political courage, as it slowly dawns on us that when watching these films we may also be looking at the dying flames of a once glorious national cinema. The decline and perhaps even fall of national cinema as a bona fide concept does not mean magnificent filmmakers will no longer come around in that nation. Jean-Luc Godard once famously said, "Film begins with D. W. Griffith and ends with Abbas Kiarostami." The ending of cinema as we know it, to switch the register, with Kiarostami is a prospect at once exhilarating and pensive. In his own defensive response to this comment by Godard, Kiarostami retorted that Godard had actually changed his mind and did not think so anymore. But both the assertion and the retort mark the moment when Kiarostami himself considered the assertion plausible: "I do think I'm diverting cinema off its course a little bit, especially with Ten."[17] The question is precisely in what direction—a question that cannot be answered either completely endorsing or categorically dismissing Godard's tongue-in-cheek assertion, a judgment that in Persian rhetoric we call *Madh-e Shabih beh Zamm*, or *Zamm-e Shabih beh Madh*/Praise in the Form of Blame, or Blame in the Form of Praise. In that bold and beautiful rhetorical device, we have a precise place when resuming our reading of Kiarostami in, through, and beyond postnational cinema.

CINEMA AND THE CONDITION OF COLONIALITY

A key factor in our assessment of the interface between national, postnational, and world cinemas is the central significance of the condition of coloniality in cinematic production and reception.[18] The politics and poetics of reception and spectatorship at work in the dominant spectrum of European film festivals is very much determined by this condition of coloniality and its contingent Orientalism.[19] It is therefore not just the politics of tyranny in Iran, or anywhere else for that matter, that has occasioned the space of postnational cinema, but the condition of coloniality definitive to these spaces has been equally consequential.

The winners of top prizes during the Cannes Film Festival in May 2013 went to an Iranian and a Tunisian filmmaker—but both their films were set in France. The much-coveted Palme d'Or award went to Tunisian Abdellatif Kechiche's *Blue Is the Warmest Color* (2013), which had shocked some critics with its graphic sex scenes. *Variety* magazine described it as containing graphic lesbian sex scenes. Far from sporting any such racy claims to fame, and yet securing the award for best actress, Iranian filmmaker Asghar Farhadi's *The Past* (2013) tells the story of the return to Paris of an Iranian man to meet his estranged wife, played by actress Berenice Bejo. How are we to identify these films: French or Tunisian, French or Iranian? Both films are in the French language. But scarcely anyone asks the filmmakers why they made their films in France, or whether—having done so—the result is still a Tunisian or Iranian film.

The formation of national cinemas—and national cultural movements in general—are predicated on national traumas (as I have pointed out extensively). If so, what is the difference between a Tunisian and an Iranian filmmaker producing a film in France? Is the result still part of Tunisian and Iranian national cinemas or has it entered the realm of postnational cinema? The European press usually identifies the Tunisian director as "the Tunisian-born French director Abdellatif Kechiche." But Farhadi is always, and rightly so, considered "an Iranian director." Why? What's the difference? The two directors might travel between Paris and Tunis, or Paris and Tehran, as frequently or as infrequently. They may speak Arabic, Persian, French, or even English under one or another circumstance. So, the answer is not in which language they are more idiomatic or whether they are more at home in Paris, Tunis, or Tehran.

The answer must be elsewhere. To answer that question, we need to go upstream to the two different conditions of coloniality in which a Tunisian and an Iranian filmmaker find themselves. Tunisia was for decades a French colony: France occupied Tunisia in 1881, which remained a French protectorate until 1956, when it found its independence. As a former colony it has had a very close link with France, and as such is thoroughly caught up in its colonial and postcolonial history. Iran, on the other hand, was never officially a European colony, though it was entirely located in the geopolitics of coloniality from the early nineteenth century and was twice occupied during the First and Second World Wars by the Russian/Soviet Union and UK/Allied forces. These two similar but not identical colonial conditions are two among many other framing factors locating Tunisian and Iranian artistic productions.

As I have extensively argued in my previous works on Iranian and Palestinian cinemas, the formation of national cinemas—and national cultural movements in general—forms the narrative unfolding of national traumas. The Tunisian national consciousness today is integral to an entire history of aggressive French colonization, and even in the conditions of its postcoloniality, it has reflected that intimate relation. France is integral to that consciousness, even after the Tunisian revolution—or perhaps particularly in the aftermath of that cataclysmic event. During and in the aftermath of that extended period of colonization, a sustained circularity of labor and capital has kept Tunisia and France on a closed circuited loop, which has resulted, among other things, in France being as much a home to Abdellatif Kechiche as Tunisia. Nothing has changed in that intimate relationship of the colonizer and the colonized since Tunisia ignited the Arab Spring—to the point that today French is as much a Tunisian language as Arabic.

The close and even intimate link between France and Tunisia is not just due to obvious economic ties. It has a richer psychological disposition. From Frantz Fanon's *Black Skin, White Masks* (1952) over Albert Memmi in *The Colonizer and the Colonized* (1965) to Ashis Nandy in *The Intimate Enemies* (1983), postcolonial thinkers have extensively theorized the condition of coloniality and the manner in which the two sides of the imbalance begin to fade into each other in both degenerative and reproductive mutations. Consider two postcolonial novels: one by Sudanese writer Tayeb Salih, *Season of Migration to the North* (1962), and the other by Iranian writer Simin Daneshvar, *Savushun* (1969)—one flamboyantly racy and murderous and the other entirely sedate and subdued in their respective encounters with the conditions of coloniality.

Compare the vindictive, angry, and murderous escapades of Salih's protagonist Mustapha Saeed with the melodious and poised demeanor of Daneshvar's protagonist Zari, and you have a clear indication of two vastly different encounters with European colonialism. The same applies to Asghar Farhadi when compared with Abdellatif Kechiche. Farhadi comes from a cinematic tradition whose defining national trauma is formed by revolutionary uprisings against domestic tyranny, extended war against a neighboring Arab country, and the continued struggles of Iranians for a democratic future. In the formation of that national trauma, colonial forces such as France, Britain, Russia, and the US sport a very self-serving memory. Paramount are the towering tyrannies of monarchs and now mullahs. The respective characters of Abdellatif Kechiche and Asghar Farhadi may both speak French and live in Paris, but they exude the temperaments of two very different takes on our humanity. This is not to say that Iranians do not speak French, or that Tunisians do not have a pride of place for their Arabic, but simply marks the varied conditions of coloniality that occasions the habitat of a filmic consciousness. When today we talk about "national cinema," it does not mean that films made within the national boundaries of a nation-state are entirely nativist or immune from influence from the world of cinema. Quite to the contrary. There is no understanding of Kiarostami without seeing his lights in the towering shadows of Yasujirō Ozu and Satyajit Ray.

Every national cinema is deeply influenced by the world *of* cinema, even if a filmmaker never leaves their homeland. But the world they inhabit, the images they see, the sounds they hear, the dreams they envision, are the creatures of a different habitat. The question that the world *of* cinema faces today is in what direction postnational cinema is heading, when the rise of a range of democratic movements in the Arab and Muslim world has enabled a manner of visuality beyond the postcolonial limits and possibilities. We are at the very nascent moment of a critical artistic consciousness when both Kechiche and Farhadi are overcoming the traumatic moments of their creative consciousness, in what Walter Benjamin considered a "Copernican turn" in historiography: when history is remembered or forgotten only to the degree that it can alter the vision of the present. The colonial twist to national cinemas therefore places them in a postnational space that in turn becomes their entry thrust into world cinema: thus the interlinking of the Borromean rings that has planted the infinity of an *alterity* inside the totality of every cinematic *identity*. In that Levinasian phrase I place and rest my case as I pave my way toward a trilectic reading of Kiarostami's legacy.

THE WORLD WAS AT HOME IN IRANIAN CINEMA

We now need to come to terms with the fact that before a first-rate filmmaker has put one foot into the world outside their homeland, they are already embedded in world cinema.[20] That proposition introduces yet another key factor, the idea of "world cinema," onto the plane of the interface, the Borromean rings we encounter in the making of national, postnational, and world cinemas. Much critical scholarship has been produced on the idea of world cinema, modeling it on the ideas of "world literature" or world philosophy, on all of which, as I have detailed in my book on the Shahnameh, we might posit a critical stand.[21] I do of course very much appreciate the work that bold and brilliant scholars like Shekhar Deshpande and Meta Mazaj have done in proposing world cinema as polycentric, polymorphic, and polyvalent.[22] But still, I make a critical distinction between the *worldly* and the *world* cinema. Iranian like all other national cinemas has been worldly and gains little to nothing from being incorporated into the dubious domain of "world cinema"—which even at its most critical take remains squarely at the service of what European film festivals decide are to be part of this world cinema. Allow me to explain.

On Friday 16 March 2018, I had the distinct privilege of joining legendary Iranian filmmaker Amir Naderi and Dave Kehr, the curator at the Department of Film, on stage at the Museum of Modern Art (MOMA) in New York to launch a magnificent retrospective of his work. *Irresistible Forces, Immovable Objects: The Films of Amir Naderi* began with *The Runner* (1984), one of the last films he made in Iran, and continued with the rest of his oeuvre that he has directed in the US, Japan, and Europe. This was not the first time the cinema of Naderi was being celebrated in the US or anywhere else in the world. Over the last quarter century that I have known him and been involved in his cinematic adventures, I have been a close witness to numerous similar celebrations in the US, Europe, and Japan, marking the unfolding thresholds of his unique and inimitable visionary artistry.

How Naderi has navigated his illustrious cinematic career from a pioneering filmmaker in the rising moments of Iranian New Wave in the late 1960s up to such career celebrations around the world is the story of how Iranian cinema has transcended itself to become an unfolding drama in the course of what we know today as "world cinema." Naderi, just like his close friend and fellow luminary Abbas Kiarostami, is no longer pigeonholed within any national cinema—with all that this entails and all that it denies. He has, by the power of his singular imagination, assumed his unique signature. How did that happen and what does it mean?

I was born to the world *of* cinema (not "world cinema") with the cinema of Naderi (born in Abadan in southern Iran, 1946). Although he is not much older than I am, he was already an accomplished and widely loved and admired filmmaker upon my arrival in Tehran to attend college in the fall of 1970, the year he made his inaugural film, *Khodahafez Rafiq/ Goodbye Friend*. This was at the height of the Pahlavi dynasty—wealthy, powerful, luxurious, with no revolutionary cloud in the sky of the second Pahlavi monarch except for a handful of Marxist guerrilla fighters waging an ill-fated attack on a police station in northern Iran. The astonishing achievement of Naderi's cinema has been to stay attuned to the politics of his time but never succumb to its vagaries when he disappears behind his camera to discover the world for us.

Goodbye Friend told the story of a vagabond thief plotting his last heist. The most elemental forces of Naderi's cinema are already evident in his first film: a solitary man facing insurmountable obstacles for one final, definitive victory. Almost fifty years later, one of his latest films, *Mountain* (2016), tells the same story. This is not to say his films have not been political. His *Saz-Dahani/Harmonica* (1973) and *Tangsir* (1973) were definitive to the political upbringing of multiple generations. But no matter how politically accented, these and all his other films were still obsessively fixated on the struggles of one man against a mountain of odds. This singular theme has remained constant in Naderi's cinema and came to global attention in his towering masterpiece: *The Runner* (1984)—the story of a solitary boy in southern Iran turned into a sublime allegory of humanity surviving the odds stacked against him with steadfast courage, verve, and imagination.

The Sisyphus of Iranian Cinema, Naderi left his homeland and came to live and work in New York in the early 1980s, but his cinema did not become "American" or "postnational" after this move. His cinema became purer, more sublime, to the point that he has now completely shed any modicum of narrative storytelling his cinema ever had. It has now reached the zenith of the clean, visceral, undiluted visual realism that has always been definitive to his cinema, which has always thrived on a sustained and mute visuality—where no words compromise the vision. By now Naderi has transcended any claim of any national cinema on his art. He began his career in Iran, subsequently moved to the US, and more recently has made feature films in Japan and Italy. He then returned to the US and resumed making his films in Los Angeles. Would that make him an Iranian, an American, a Japanese, an Italian, or any other hyphenated filmmaker? No, it does not. He has become a worldly filmmaker, not a world filmmaker.

But the answer to that question, however we might formulate it, is much less important than the consistency of his cinematic vision that has steadily moved toward pure allegory. Naderi's cinema has always been unburdened by excessive loyalty to storyline. He is a minimalist storyteller. He has now become the quintessence of his own metaphoric cinema. Once a high-ranking Iranian official in charge of censorship, Naderi told me a while ago, laughing, asked him for his script to approve his next film. He took a pen and a piece of paper from the man's desk and drew a straight line from one end of the page to another and said to him: "There, that's my script—it's the story of a boy who goes from here to there," pointing to the two ends of the straight line on the page. That line was the script of his remarkable film *Water, Wind, Dust* (1989). That story always reminds me of the final works of the Spanish master artist Joan Miro (1893–1983), which I once spent weeks studying closely at Fundación Joan Miro in Barcelona. Toward the end of that collection of Miro's work, there is an alcove where three of his last works are ritually staged. On three huge white canvases, we see nothing but a singular thin black line drawn from one end of the canvas to the other.

I have had multiple occasions to argue how the formation of national cinemas—and national cultural movements in general—are predicated on national traumas. Filmmakers can either degenerate into political pamphleteering that caters to European film festivals or transcend those national traumas and cultivate their own signature art. The late Abbas Kiarostami and Amir Naderi are paramount examples of the latter case. In Naderi we are witness to the lifelong fixation of one artist, in his case now close to half a century of filmmaking, having seen a dream and then devoting his entire life to trying to show it. Much is, of course, biographical in Naderi's cinema, particularly his masterpiece, *The Runner*. But the question is what he does with his biography.

Few artists around the globe have managed to overcome the bizarre and ridiculous accident of their birth and upbringing and show the world what they have seen. Rooted as they are in their homeland, they spread their branches and blossoms in a world of their own, which we cannot but sit down politely to learn, admiringly to love, patiently to own. Yes, Naderi is an Iranian filmmaker. But in his cinema, he brought the world to his homeland, and in the very same cinema, he brought his homeland to a full worldly recognition—all in pure, beautiful allegory of what it means to be human—all too frightfully, solitarily, human.

My principal suggestion in this book, on which the rest of my unfolding prose dwells, projects the idea that Abbas Kiarostami happened at the conflating moments of the Borromean rings of the national, postnational, and world cinemas—when and where the defining national traumas emerge to meet and sublate into the transnational traumas of the globe. If national cinema is predicated on national traumas, then postnational cinema emerges out of global traumas such as deadly pandemics, transregional draughts, environmental calamities, massive labor migrations, refugee crisis, et cetera. Kiarostami had done the phase of the national fully when, facilitated by Cannes and other European film festivals, he became a global name, and then soon after the transnational took over to yield momentum to the idea of world cinema. Kiarostami's *ABC Africa* (2001); Mohsen Makhmalbaf's sojourn into Türkiye, Pakistan, and Afghanistan; Sohrab Shahid Sales's move to Germany and then the US; and Amir Naderi's presence in the US, Europe, and Japan are paramount examples of the national yielding to postnational and world cinemas, while filmmakers like Ramin Bahrani hit the ground running as postnational filmmakers and the widely commercialized artwork of Shirin Neshat on the model of Ai WeiWei began with the seeds of some crucial ideas speaking to the postnational, but alas eventually degenerated into a vacuous blip in the "Oriental" art industry, precisely in the opposite direction of Palestinian artists like Mona Hatoum or Emily Jacir, who never lost their feet on the battleground of their homeland. Yes, when Shahid Sales or Naderi left their homeland and began making films in Europe and the US, the world was already in their respective cinema. But as they began to work in their new habitat, the very texture of that world began to change. A dialectic of reciprocity thus began to form and disinform what it means to be an Iranian filmmaker facing the world.

ABBAS KIAROSTAMI: CLOSE-UP, LONG SHOT, AND CUT!

"You are something to behold!" I called Abbas Kiarostami the day after I arrived in Tehran in the summer of 1997 to tell him I had just landed. "How long have you been away from Iran?," he asked on the phone. "Almost twenty years," I responded abashedly. "Oh Lord, you are something to behold."[23]

Over the last half century, I have known, taught, wrote on, analyzed, synthesized, criticized, and theorized Abbas Kiarostami's cinema into the very fabric of my own sense of aesthetic sublimity and critical thinking. Born and raised in Iran during the Second World War, Abbas Kiarostami was the product of the liveliest period in Iranian artistic creativity. The rise of the Iranian New Wave in the 1960s was rooted in the effervescent history of modernist Persian poetry and fiction of the previous three decades. Kiarostami lived a professionally successful and productive life and eventually received richly deserved global recognition. When he won the landmark Palme d'Or at the Cannes Film Festival for his *Ta'm-e Gilas/Taste of Cherry* in 1997, he had almost three decades of spectacular masterpieces behind him. His Koker Trilogy (1987–1994) permanently placed him in the pantheon of world masters with a unique and uncompromising mode of "actual" (as opposed to "virtual") realism through a cinematic technique I have had occasions to call "factasy" (a portmanteau of *fact* and *fantasy*, inaugurated by the founding mother of Iranian cinema, Forough Farrokhzad) in her *Khaneh Siah Ast/The House Is Black* (1962). It was in his *Nama-ye Nazdik/Close-Up* (1990), however, that Kiarostami left students of world cinema with a masterpiece to behold and wonder at for generations to come. After his global celebration as a master filmmaker, art connoisseurs began to notice his other gifts.

By the end of his life, he had become a force of nature, trying his hand at poetry and photography, directing European operas, and experimenting with video installations. His latest films were shot in Africa, in Europe, and in Japan. He became the harbinger of a postnational cinema from the heart of his mastery of his own national cinema. Kiarostami had a distanced, judicious, and characteristically cool relationship with politics. As his cinema explored the deepest layers of our perception of reality and how to alter it, he remained mostly (but not entirely) aloof to the tumultuous politics of his homeland. But we must keep in mind that one of the most political Iranian filmmakers of our time, his protege Jafar Panahi, made some of his best and most successful films based on Kiarostami's scripts. Kiarostami was the master of long shots and long takes. When teaching his work, I usually tell my students only half-jokingly to compare his cinema with that of Oliver Stone and refer to his *Any Given Sunday* (1999), in which at times you see an editing rate of five cuts per second! In the case of Kiarostami, he places his camera somewhere he likes, gently says "Action" under his breath, goes home, takes a nap, comes back and says "Cut!" He never seemed as if he was looking for something. He always appeared to have already seen it and just wanted to show it well. As such, he always kept us on our toes when we thought we knew what he was showing us but particularly when we were uncertain of where he was taking us. I have had my share of frustration with some of his scenes—particularly, I now recall, in the troubling stable scene in *Bad Ma Ra Khahad Bord/The Wind Will Carry Us* (1999), when I was sure he was trespassing over some inviolable lines of gender and class violence. I never changed my mind about such scenes, but then again precisely such troubling scenes turned the labyrinth of his cinema into the philosophical anxieties of a world he had so carefully crafted and made so irresistibly enigmatic to us.

Done with the patience of a Sufi master with an eternity as his frame of reference, his long shots/long takes dwell on a vision of reality long enough to strip it of all its pretenses of meaning—before he assigns it a renewed significance. Once the absolutism of reality (as the German philosopher Hans Blumenberg would call it) begins to ooze out of our received conceptions of what is real, Kiarostami gently leads what remains into a whole new world of significance. His camera made the foreign familiar by making the familiar foreign. A luminous light that sparkled like a shimmering sunrise off the coast of the deepest layers of Iranian art and poetry, Kiarostami was a prophetic visionary of the sort that Iranian culture has produced only a handful to grace its pride of place in its contemporary history. Not that many of those masters are left behind: Kamran Shirdel, Bahram Beiza'i and Amir Naderi are now the living custodians of that national treasure that defines Iran for what it is. Among them all, Kiarostami commanded a self-assuring patience that guided his calming soul from one medium to another.

As fate would have it, I heard the news of Kiarostami's passing as I was reading Ramin Bahrani's script for his take on Ray Bradbury's classic *Fahrenheit 451*, throwing his gauntlet at Francois Truffaut's signature take on it. I remember the day Bahrani had screened his *Chop Shop* (2007) in Cannes, which Kiarostami had attended. Soon after the film had ended, Kiarostami came to him and gave him a big hug for the whole world to see. I remember Ramin called me from Cannes soon after that hug. "After this," he said, "I don't think I have anywhere else to go."

I did not think so. With that hug and many more loving memories of Kiarostami left with his immediate and distant protégés, he has left so many hidden cameras in the darkest corners of our souls. My last happy memory of Abbas Kiarostami is at a dinner party in his honor given by a mutual friend in New Jersey, across the Hudson with a view of Manhattan. Amir Naderi was there too. At one point a few of us were standing in the kitchen and I was busy giving a critique of Dariush Mehrjui's film *Pari* (1995) to a couple of friends. Before I knew it, Kiarostami was holding a camera and coming closer to my face, capturing my impromptu analysis and inadvertent gesticulations. It was a small digital camera. He and his camera made me fearfully self-conscious. I have no clue whose it was. Somewhere in that camera there are a few minutes of my thoughts as captured by Kiarostami for a posterity that will never see it. How did he see me, how did I appear to him, or more importantly, how did he hear, interpret, or perceive my thoughts? I have no clue. But as I write this book, I proceed with that ethereal moment when he was looking at me through the craftsmanship of his gentle, caring, and yet scarily perceptive and revelatory camera. The passing of Abbas Kiarostami on 4 July 2016 marks a moment when the sustained work of a master filmmaker became his lasting legacy. When he declared his very last "Cut," our work was cut out for us to begin the task of mapping out the varied domains of his signature as a floating signifier.

TOWARD A POSTCOLONIAL FILM-PHILOSOPHY

How are we to visualize that lasting legacy, what metaphor would best represent us at the moment of imagining ourselves at the receiving end of Kiarostami's artworld? Many European and American scholars reflecting on the prospects of film as philosophy have found Plato's allegory of the cave quite compelling—and rightly so. Nathan Andersen, for example, in his *Shadow Philosophy: Plato's Cave and Cinema* (2014) offers this analogy in particular reference to Stanley Kubrick's *A Clockwork Orange* (1971), where the lead character is forced to watch violent films.[24] Although now outdated in the current state of film-philosophy scholarship, that is indeed a good analogy, as far as it goes, and if we are all forced to reach for Plato as a kind of philosophical security blanket, of a sort, for philosophizing about cinema. An alternative image perhaps, one among countless others from around the world, equally or even more suitable for reflecting on film as philosophy, is the final scene of Farid al-Din Attar's

Conference of the Birds (1177) where the thirty surviving birds that make it to Mount Qaf face a mirror in which they see their own reflections—and thus figuratively meet Simorgh in the mirror of their own souls. Whereas in Plato's allegory the cave dwellers have to turn around to see the source of light coming from behind them, in Attar's image the birds have to look forward at the reflection of themselves in the mirror in front of them. In a movie theater, we ordinarily look forward to seeing the film—we don't look backward to see the projectionist's room. Plato's cave is the house of shadows, Attar's Mount Qaf is featured with a concave mirror. The top of a mountain with a mirror screen is a far superior metaphor for cinema than a cave wall with shady figures staring at their own dark shadows. What the thirty surviving birds see in that mirror on top of that mountain is just the truth of themselves, both literally and figuratively, individually and collectively. There is a truth and a creative consciousness in what they see—unlike the cave dwellers in Plato's allegory who are entirely cast in a self-deceiving exercise and thus the whole point of the Platonic allegory that someone from the crowd has to turn around and discover the source of the light coming from behind them.

In arguing his case for the relevance of the Platonic cave, Nathan Andersen, a professor of philosophy in Florida, goes to Stanley Kubrick's *A Clockwork Orange* (1971). What would be the effect and implications of Attar's image if we went to Abbas Kiarostami's cinema—in his immediate cultural neighborhood—and what would the comparison do, not just for film-philosophy but for a postcolonial take on the idea? Suppose we were to consider Kiarostami's entire cinematic oeuvre a meditation on the collective unconscious of a postcolonial person imagined in a cinematic universe that ipso facto posits a nomadic, migratory subject. How would that supposition fare with his lasting legacy? Suppose we consider a towering Iranian filmmaker who became a household name in arthouse cinema. Did he not reach the Mount Qaf of world cinema at Cannes, there to screen the fate of his people, the image of a world otherwise unseen, having had visions of that unseen—just as Omar Khayyam says: "This see of existence / Has surfaced / From the unseen"?

Whether Plato or Attar, or ideally both, still the key question remains Kiarostami's work itself and the towering place it has demanded from and in our attention. Whence and wherefore that significance? Kiarostami

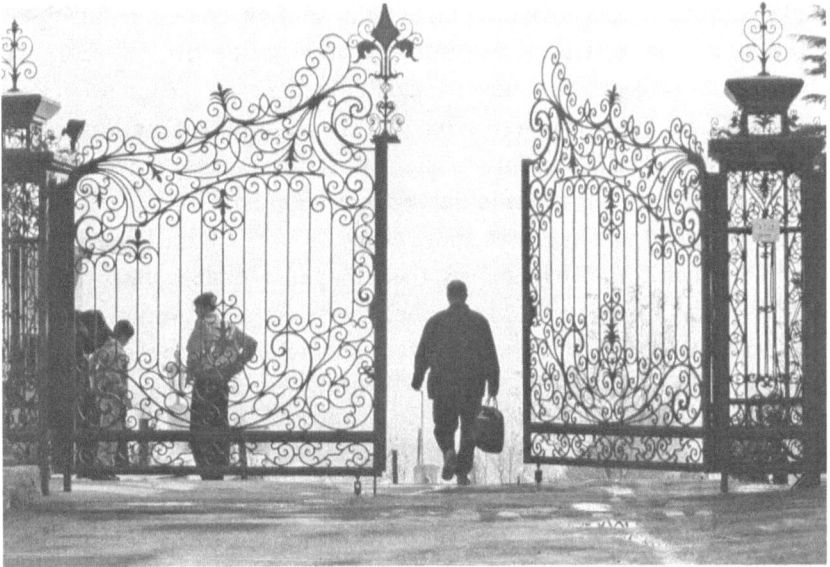

Figure 2. Abbas Kiarostami, *Taste of Cherry* (1997). Courtesy of Abbas Kiarostami Foundation.

emerged as an iconic figure in world cinema with a unique aesthetic signature. After he won the Palme d'Or award at Cannes Film Festival for his *Taste of Cherry* (1997), his recognition as a visionary filmmaker went global. Film festivals, film critics, film scholars, and even philosophers like Jean-Luc Nancy have ever since paid close and critical attention to his cinema. Kiarostami was also a gifted poet, painter, photographer, and theater and opera director. After his untimely death in 2016, the full spectrum of his artwork demands closer and more comprehensive attention. Over the last quarter century, Abbas Kiarostami's cinema has been the subject of extensive and erudite scholarship, in both Persian and European languages, to which I have already made my own pioneering but modest contributions. But today, more than half a century since the commencement of his cinematic career and almost a decade after his passing, it is time for a critical re-examination of his oeuvre, with a particular theoretical perspective as to where in the widening gyre extending from national to postnational to world cinema that legacy exactly rests, and what it means and entails. With detailed attention to the location of Kiarostami's work on that spectrum, in this book I intend to build on the existing scholarship in multiple languages and offer a radically fresh perspective on where we should place his legacy and how to read it. My more specific intention is to explore Kiarostami's oeuvre searching for the philosophical underpinning of his artworld.[25] That premise obviously requires a perspective on what such a philosophy in a postcolonial register might entail.

In his pithy but important short essay, "What Is Film-Philosophy?," David Sorfa writes: "We might say, then, that Film-philosophy is the past and future of film theory."[26] More concisely, he explains: "Arguments as to when film-philosophy may have started can stretch back to the early decades of the twentieth century. In the postwar era, which saw the rise of Film Studies as a discipline, American philosopher Stanley Cavell was perhaps the very first to do something that we might explicitly call film-philosophy as we now know it, in his *The World Viewed: Reflections on the Ontology of Film* (1971)."[27] That indeed is an apt demarcation. Cavell's by now classic autobiographical reflections on (going to) movies is indeed a crucial cornerstone to consider for philosophical reflections on the cinema that the American philosopher had experienced watching Hollywood films, as well as the work of a number of key European directors. But, and thus the point of my take on film-philosophy that would speak to Kiarostami's legacy more specifically, in his wildest dreams Cavell could not have fathomed a filmmaker like Kiarostami, from an outlandish (for him) place called Iran, which in fact raises another key issue that brings us to Edward Said's conception of "double vision," namely how we see the world and how the world might not even see us. If we were to borrow and expand (on the model of his "traveling theory") Edward Said's idea of "double vision," we might say Abbas Kiarostami, too, had occasioned a double vision of us as he saw us domestically and as he boldly staged his vision for the whole world to see us beyond its provincial limitations.

But "philosophy" for me is not just European philosophy, though European philosophy is not to be exempted from philosophy either. It needs to be historically located, provincialized to Europe, so that other theoretical reflections on poetic, literary, visual, and performing arts can also be considered legitimately philosophical. Much of the theoretical reflections on film-philosophy is almost exclusively limited to landmark figures in European or Eurocentric philosophy, even when the idea is extended to non-European cinemas, such as Kiarostami's. I have nothing against such projects. I in fact find them quite insightful. But as I have shown elsewhere, the idea of philosophy is in dire need of critical reflections to open the space for critical and creative thinkers outside the European provinces.[28] In expanding my own theoretical concerns into these spaces, I am not allergic to any aspect of European philosophy, especially those in the tradition of the critical theory of the Frankfurt School into which I have introduced a decidedly postcolonial spin.

Along with a whole constellation of stellar filmmakers from Asia, Africa, and Latin America, Kiarostami provincialized Europe, as it were, dismantled "the West," and thus effectively questioned the rampant Eurocentricity of film-philosophy as we see it today by envisioning us as if our condition of coloniality had been erased, that it had never existed—and yet (and here is the rub) he staged that vision in a world where the fact and the condition of that coloniality did indeed exist. Let us recall how Edward Said coined the concept of "double vision" in his *After the Last Sky* (1986) in reference to the photography of Jean Mohr, and how Said thought Mohr "saw us as we would have seen ourselves—at once inside and outside our world."[29] Said of course meant this double vision as an occasion of the self-estrangement of Palestinians, himself included. And it is precisely that sense of self-estrangement and alienation that I wish to borrow from Said to extend to Kiarostami's postcolonial disposition as a filmmaker. Kiarostami did not see us as the Cannes Film Festival saw us, contrary to what his detractors in Iran had accused him of doing. In his vast and variegated body of work, which includes his uncinematic works, he saw us as we were—as he saw us—though stripped of our condition of coloniality, bared to the bone of our quintessential angst. And yet when we saw ourselves thus staged on the grand scale of Cannes Film Festival, we were at once exhilarated and troubled, to be seen for what we were by ourselves, and yet to be staged in a world that was not ready to see us as we were, or hoped to be. In this double vision, in precisely the opposite direction of how Said meant it, Kiarostami spelled out both the terms of our aesthetic liberation and the world that we still had to set right to reach that distant vision. If Said's conception of "double vision" marked his and our entrapment under the postcolonial gaze in the condition of coloniality, Kiarostami's liberated vision occasioned and enabled a philosophy of liberation akin to the Argentinian philosopher Enrique Dussel's lifetime project to enable the world to see us beyond the terms of colonial conquests and their contingent projects of epistemicide and aestheticide, as the Portuguese philosopher Boaventura de Sousa Santos would say.[30]

Overcoming this condition of imperial coloniality is definitive to what is now emerging as "postcolonial cinema studies." Relying on the pioneering work of Priya Jaikumar, a professor of cinematic arts, Sandra Ponzanesi and Marguerite Waller, in their edited volume on the subject, write: "Cinema served both to consolidate empires and to dismantle them.... Cinema played a very paradoxical and ambivalent role on both sides of the imperial divide. The beginnings of cinema corresponded with the apogee of colonialism but also to the proliferation of anti-colonial independent movements."[31] That ambivalence remains definitive to the poetics and prosody of the cinematic prose we might examine in a quest for a decolonized film-theosophy. By the time we get to the work of masters like Satyajit Ray, Akira Kurosawa, Yasujirō Ozu, or Abbas Kiarostami, the legacy of that contested space has long since completely yielded aesthetically to what was once politically lost. It is therefore imperative to locate the cine-aesthetics of Kiarostami's legacy in a location where the contested space of coloniality has already yielded to a superior command of the cinematic parlance, far beyond the reach of the Eurocentricity of the imperial history of the craft. There is, to repeat, an infinite alterity internalized in this postcolonial cinema far beyond the reach of any totalizing identity that Eurocentric aesthetics might claim.

How we might reach that space is as much an aesthetic as it is an epistemic proposition. In the work of a philosopher like Jonardon Ganeri, especially in his *Attention, Not Self* (2018), we encounter a far more radical twist in philosophy of mind and epistemology that takes full advantage of classic Indian philosophy to bring attention to "attention" and away from the self-indulgent "self."[32] This is a much-welcomed syncretic move for, thus radically altered, our state of consciousness moves to the modularity of attention and away from the shape-shifting self—especially in its deeply compromised capitalist and psycho-pathologized renditions. What is cinema other than the art of redirecting attention to otherwise invisible sites? Ganeri's project is of course more directed toward a philosophy of mind and a phenomenology of consciousness than an aesthetic of seeing, but still his two main concerns with how attention first places and then accesses a specific direction in attention draw deeper toward the internalized alterity rather than totalized identity, which is precisely the character of Kiarostami's cinema most rooted in Sohrab Sepehri's poetry.

ABBAS KIAROSTAMI AS A FLOATING SIGNIFIER

I began publishing shorter and longer pieces on Kiarostami over a quarter of a century ago—and every time I thought I had him figured out, he managed to surprise and draw me back to his work. I published my first essay on Abbas Kiarostami in the fall of 1995, just a couple of months after his *Through the Olive Trees* (1994) had been premiered in New York, following its official release in the fall of 1994 at Cannes, and two years before he won the Palme d'Or and emerged as a household name in world cinema. Soon after, I began working on my first book on Iranian cinema, and almost a quarter of a century ago in the late 1990s I began writing what was soon to be published as one of the earliest comprehensive accounts of Iranian cinema, *Close-Up: Iranian Cinema: Past, Present, Future* (2001), in which I devoted a full chapter to the entirety of Kiarostami's cinema up until that moment. A few years later I published my other major work on Iranian cinema, *Masters and Masterpieces of Iranian Cinema* (2007), in which again I devoted a whole chapter to one of his masterpieces. Soon after the publication of these books, and as my attention was drawn to Makhmalbaf and other filmmakers, Kiarostami's cinema became the subject of about a dozen learned monographs and countless erudite essays, in multiple languages, primarily in French, some in Italian, a few in English, and of course a sizable body of critical work in Persian. Except for my book, most other studies of Abbas Kiarostami paid little to no attention to the Persian material, as did the Persian material mostly ignore studies in European languages. Thus thus emerged a varied body of otherwise excellent work on a seminal filmmaker of our time—divided across linguistic, ideological, and political lines. The more exciting these varied receptions of Kiarostami became, the more one would wonder where to locate his cinematic oeuvre.

Even a quick glance at the body of critical writing on Kiarostami over the last quarter of a century shows a palpable interface between those who pay close and insightful attention to his visual and cinematic aesthetics, and those who dwell on the politics of his cinema—while sometimes the bifurcation is equally sharply divided between works produced in Persian (mostly political) and works produced in Italian or French (mostly aesthetics). Far more useful would be if we were to collapse this false and misleading binary and create a tertiary interstitial space where we have to come to terms with both his aesthetics and his politics, as well as the critical works produced both in his native Persian and mostly in French, Italian, Spanish, Portuguese, or English.

Kiarostami was neither politically aloof nor was he shooting from the hip like his protégé Jafar Panahi or his nemesis Mohsen Makhmalbaf—who have been very flamboyant in their politics. Expecting Kiarostami to lead a column of opposition to the ruling regime in his homeland was as ludicrous as trying to parse his cinema along the lines of the short history of the Islamic Republic that rules Iran or against the backdrop of conspiracy theories about the Cannes, Berlin, or Venice film festivals, as some of his Iranian detractors have tried to do. All these sideshows detract attention from the substance of his cinema, which is a reality sui generis demanding critical attention. What his intentions were, how he read his own cinema, or what film critics and film scholars have made of his cinema all lead us back to the *location* of his cinema, where we place and consider his artworks. To succumb to the politics of ressentiment evident in some of his ardent Iranian detractors distracts our attention from Kiarostami's global spectatorship, while at the same time ignoring his Iranian critiques disregards the political and aesthetic differentials that are created between the multiple worlds a work of art simultaneously generates, sustains, and occupies. When we bring the two sides of this false divide together, the interface between aesthetics and politics generates a whole new vista onto a postcolonial semiosis where the intuition of transcendence evident in a work of art begins to generate its own aesthetic reasoning. We need to be, and in this book I am, concerned with the sustained legacy of his artworld, and what it has achieved, what it means, what sort of a knowing, feeling, acting subject it entails. To achieve that, we can neither disregard his Iranian readers nor can we privilege them with any interpretative priority or authenticity. Kiarostami's cinema emerged like an Alexander Lighthouse (here is another metaphor superior to Plato's cave) with a mirror on the top during the day and a fire at night to draw the attention of seafarers coming at it from left, right and center. As ships have now landed at its feet, as it were, Kiarostami's cinema itself has started revealing exactly what the nature of that mirror at daytime and that fire at night would be—helping us understand why was it that one way or another we were drawn to his cinema—and once that happened, what sort of worldly seafarer, what kind of nomadic subject, did it help us recognize dwelling in our own unknowing subjectivity, all invested in the visions of the invisible his cinema so confidently entailed and delivered.

Let me return to my Attar metaphor as conduit of doing film-philosophy in a postcolonial register. In *Conference of the Birds*, the central character of the Hoopoe is the visionary guide who leads an entire nation of cantankerous birds through seven valleys of hardship and insight to show them their truth and bring them to self-realization. Like many other legendary filmmakers, Kiarostami became the Hoopoe of an entire landscape of human predicament to stage the contingent sovereignty of a nomadic, unknowing subject. If we are, if I am, as I write, that very unknowing nomadic subject, then in effect I sit to watch his films and look at his paintings and photography with the visionary insights he has installed in me. As his artworld is a mirror to me, my critical thinking is a mirror to him. We are mirroring each other's artworld and philosophy. Plato's cave may have been a spot, a way station, on our way to Attar's Mount Qaf after all.

HE WAS ALWAYS SOMEWHERE ELSE

Abbas Kiarostami was a filmmaker, a screenwriter, a poet, a photographer, a painter, a graphic art designer, and a film producer who during his lifetime received widespread global recognition and celebration. Arguably not since Goethe's *West-östlicher Divan* (1814–1819), inspired by Hafez's poetry, and after that Edward Fitzgerald's translation of *Rubaiyat of Omar Khayyam* (1859), had an Iranian name or an aspect of Persian art been so globally loved and admired as Kiarostami's cinema and by extension his other works of art. His sudden and untimely death left much that is still to be said about what he has left behind.[33] But while Hafez and Omar

Khayyam were primarily known for their poetry (though Omar Khayyam was also a prominent mathematician), Kiarostami's legacy is multifaceted and much in need of a comprehensive understanding. The global import of Goethe's and Fitzgerald attention to Persian poetry was also the result of European imperial hegemony—for what matters to them turned out to become iconic for the rest of the world under their hegemonic influence, while Kiarostami's global reception is indeed indebted to European film festivals at its inaugural moment but then became domestic to multiple other moral and intellectual domains. What makes his location in the interstitial space of multiple worlds significant is therefore the fact that he was an artistic polyglot always mobile in both his aesthetics and the way his artworld solicited either complementary or contradictory attention.

In a career that expanded over half a century, Kiarostami had emerged as a towering figure on the global art scene, actively involved in some forty films—short, feature, and documentaries. His Koker Trilogy (1987–1994), *Close-Up* (1990), *Taste of Cherry* (1997), and *The Wind Will Carry Us* (1999) established his name and reputation as an iconic master of his craft. The Palme d'Or that he received at the Cannes Film Festival for the body of work that had culminated in *The Wind Will Carry Us* consolidated his significance as a master filmmaker definitive to world cinema. In the latter part of his long career, with films like *ABC Africa* (2001), *Certified Copy* (2010), and *Like Someone in Love* (2012), Kiarostami moved the location of his cinema outside Iran deep into Africa, Europe, and Asia. At the time of his death in 2016, Kiarostami's name was synonymous with the world he had received from other iconic masters, from Akira Kurosawa and Yasujirō Ozu to Satyajit Ray, Chen Kaige, Ingmar Bergman, Andrei Tarkovsky, and scores of others. He added a distinctly Iranian angle to the cinematic lore he had inherited from major filmmakers before him. Despite the remarkable consistency in his cinematic lore, he remained entirely unpredictable as to where he was taking the body of his work, for there was an equally consistent mobility in his artistic career in which long takes and winding roads with a camera inside and another outside his vehicle became emblematic of his visions. His persona as a filmmaker and his filmic visions came together to form a flawlessly floating signifier.

Kiarostami's oeuvre went extensively beyond his fame as a filmmaker. His cinema was deeply rooted in his career as a screenwriter, film editor, graphic artist, photographer, art director, producer, and designer for credit titles and even commercial advertising. He even directed an opera. Throughout his career, and as his global fame grew, his other works received more serious attention. Kiarostami's cinema was rooted in the pioneering generation of Iranian New Wave, which was in turn embedded in the postwar Iranian art scene and eventually reached a crescendo in the 1960s and included groundbreaking filmmakers like Amir Naderi, Bahram Beiza'i, Dariush Mehrjui, Sohrab Shahid Sales, Nasser Taghva'i, Ali Hatami, Masoud Kimia'i, and Parviz Kimia'i. In this company, Kiarostami eventually found his own singular signature—a signature that by virtue of receiving a global audience reached new heights of reception and interpretation. As a gifted photographer, Kiarostami was fascinated by winter landscapes and rainy windows—though he photographed any number of other subjects. At one point in his career, he also produced Mozart's opera *Così fan Tutte*, which premiered in Aix-en-Provence in 2003 and then at the English National Opera in London in 2004. He also published collections of his poetry. *In the Shadow of Trees: The Collected Poetry of Abbas Kiarostami* (2020) has brought together his published poems into one volume of English verse.

The kaleidoscopic character of Kiarostami's artworld has left a legacy that must take the entirety of his oeuvre simultaneously—manifested in every single item in that legacy. I am holding in my hand, as I write, a tiny little book, 5 × 3½ inches, with the name of Abbas Kiarostami on it as its author, titled *Dad az Gham-e Tanha'i/Alas the Sorrow of Loneliness* (published in Tehran in 2018). The subtitle of the book is "Loneliness in the Poetry of Old and Contemporary Poets." The publisher tells us at the very beginning that the book was collected in 2013 but was delayed because they were looking for a contemporary poet to write a preface to it, but both Kiarostami and that poet (we don't know who she or he was), passed away.[34] The tiny pages of the book are replete with selections of one- and two-liners from a gamut of Persian poets, from Hafez, Sa'di, Shah Ne'amatollah Vali, and Vahshi Bafghi to contemporary poets like Mehdi Akhavan-e Sales, Nader Naderpour, Simin Behbahani, and Forough Farrokhzad—all on the central theme of loneliness or solitude. This is a minimalist but quietly troublesome book. Why loneliness? What did he mean—his own loneliness, our loneliness, both, neither, perhaps loneliness in a generic and existential sense? The size and shape of the book, the echoes of its minimalist content, and the solitary power of one word, "loneliness." That solitary unit remains definitive to the entirety of Kiarostami's work. This book appears like a solitary dot in a vast and variegated landscape Kiarostami caringly cultivated and made his own. Inside every such dot, that entire universe is remembered and embedded. To read and watch and come to terms with Kiarostami, we need to see the entirety of his amorphous form forming from the epicenter of that dot to the farthest removes of those snowy landscapes he loved to photograph.

STATE OF THE ART

With this book I wish to reach a new generation of film and cinema studies thinkers, scholars, students, and cineastes, particularly in the emerging field of film-philosophy—in which Kiarostami's cinema has already attracted significant interest. But at the same time, given the global popularity of Abbas Kiarostami as a major filmmaker who was widely celebrated in his own lifetime, this book might very well be of interest to a wider nonspecialist reader as well. I intend to offer them a comprehensive understanding of a major artist with a distinct vision of our world. The new field of film-philosophy and the larger public sphere in which a filmmaker like Kiarostami has crafted a significant viewership is where I hope my book will reach a new conception of cinema as an artform that need not be exiled to the recondite seminar rooms of cinematic speculations by reciting the all but forgotten joy of cineastes who were film-philosophers *avant la lettre*.

Over the last quarter of a century, a considerable body of literature has been produced on Kiarostami's cinema—but very little on his poetry, painting, photography, or theatrical and operatic works. Most of these writings can be divided into two main categories: (1) spontaneous journalistic articles full of wonderful insights but limited in their thematic range, critical imagination, or analytical depth, and (2) longer academic and critical monographs by media and film studies scholars. Kiarostami has also drawn the attention of other seminal filmmakers as well as philosophers who have reflected on his oeuvre. The earliest reflections on his cinema were obviously produced in Persian, but soon after he won the Palme d'Or in 1997 serious European scholars and film critics began to produce more substantive studies of his works. Much of the critical literature on Kiarostami is in fact authored in Europe, mostly by Italian, French, Spanish, and Portuguese critics, followed by English critics, mostly in the US. Not a single one of these reflections on Kiarostami's cinema is devoid of some crucial insight, but still he and his artworld remain like Rumi's proverbial elephant in a dark room, people touching aspects of his work and speculating about the whole.

Among the earliest work on Kiarostami was an edited volume in Italian by Bruno Roberti, *Abbas Kiarostami* (1996). Soon after, in Persian we have the edited volume by the veteran Iranian film critic Zaven Qukasian, *Majmu'eh Maqalat dar Naqd va Mo'arrefi Asar-e Abbas Kiarostami/ Collection of Essays Introducing and Assessing Abbas Kiarostami's Works* (1997). Two volumes followed and were published in Italian—one, Marco Della Nave's *Abbas Kiarostami* (1999), and the other, Marco Dalla Gassa's *Abbas Kiarostami* (2000). Almost at the same time, two books followed in French, one by Yousef Ishaghpour, *Le réel, face et pile: Le cinéma d'Abbas Kiarostami* (2000), and the other by the prominent French philosopher Jean-Luc Nancy, *L'Évidence du Film: Abbas Kiarostami* (2001). In Spanish, meanwhile, we also have Alberto Elena, *The Cinema of Abbas Kiarostami* (2002), subsequently translated into English and published in 2005. By which time also, in English, we had Mehrnaz Saeed-Vafa and Jonathan Rosenbaum's *Abbas Kiarostami* (2003). This was followed by a book in Portuguese published in Brazil by Jean-Claude Bernardet, *Caminhos de Kiarostami* (2004). Italian critics were not yet done with Kiarostami. The director of the Venice Film Festival, Alberto Barbera, in collaboration with Elisa Resegotti, published their *Kiarostami* (2004) at this time. This was followed by the publication in Persian of a deeply controversial polemic against Kiarostami's cinema by two Iranian critics, Morad Farhadpour and Maziyar Islami, *Paris-Tehran: Sinema-ye Abbas Kiarostami/Paris-Tehran: The Cinema of Abbas Kiarostami* (2008). Precisely in the opposite direction was an insightful book in English by Mathew Abbott, *Abbas Kiarostami and Film-Philosophy* (2017). By now a younger generation of Iranian scholars writing in English had joined the fray, evident in a collection of insightful essays published in a special issue, "Abbas Kiarostami," in *Iran Namag* (2, no. 4, 2018), a quarterly of Iranian Studies. Meanwhile in English we saw the publication of an excellent monograph by Julian Rice, *Abbas Kiarostami's Cinema of Life: From Homework to Like Someone in Love* (2020). In Spanish this was followed by Alain Bergala's *Erice Kiarostami: Correspondences* (2022), which is an edited version of the correspondences between a major Spanish filmmaker and Kiarostami. Most recently we have a major essay on Kiarostami by Laurent Kretzschmar, "Is Cinema Renewing Itself?" (2022).

What is remarkable (in fact quite astonishing) about these books and articles is how insular they mostly are and that their stated purposes are without the slightest serious concern for what others may have said about the subject of their scholarship or speculations. These studies are also almost entirely about Kiarostami's cinema at the expense of disregarding all his other artistic engagements. My objective in this book, quite to the contrary, is to put forward the first comprehensive study written in the aftermath of Kiarostami's passing and therefore cast a complete look back at his legacy—fully aware of what others have said and done about Kiarostami. More to the point, not just those books written in English but in fact all other studies written in any other language are almost entirely self-referential in their scholarship and critical apparatus and mostly self-centered in their narratives—in a rush to tell the world what they think of Kiarostami without much critical attention to what others may have said. They scarcely care to look at the body of literature that was available to them when they wrote their books or essays—especially works in languages they do not seem to read. European and American critics scarcely pay any attention to Persian sources, while Iranian critics rarely read works produced in other languages—and when they do, they do so in a spirit of faux familiarity. The unique feature of my way of thinking in this book first and foremost is that I pay close attention to everything, and in fact I make a theoretical point about these vivid political and aesthetic differentials between and among works on Kiarostami.

I watch and read Kiarostami of course first and foremost through the entirety of his own work but also through the cacophonous dissonance and kaleidoscopic heteroglossia (to use a mixed metaphor) this chaotic body of critical writing has created around the name "Abbas Kiarostami." I may have affinity with one reading over another, or prefer one film or photograph over another, but the theoretical cast of my mind here is primarily concerned with that real and robust cacophony rather than offering a false and soothing harmony among them. In addition, the ambitions of my project here are geared toward a critical engagement with more philosophical reflections on cinema such as those of Gilles Deleuze's *Cinéma I: L'image-mouvement* (1983) and *Cinéma II: L'image-temps* (1985)—though not as a point of departure or theoretical scaffolding to enable my reading of Kiarostami, for which I have plenty of other exciting inroads. The same way that his cinema is to be placed within those Borromean rings where national, postnational, and world cinema (may or may not) meet, it should also be placed within various theoretical narratives that have been offered the world as to how to watch and read him, in multiple languages, effectively making him a floating signifier, but equally crucial, placing his cinema within other genres, such as photography, painting, video installations, and operatic works with which he engaged. From the cinema of Yasujirō Ozu to the poetry of Sohrab Sepehri—something in and about Kiarostami's cinema demanded and exacted and drew attention outside itself but through itself. That dialectic is at the heart of how I propose we need to re-enact our perspective of his cinema and artworld. Through an adaptation and expansion of what Edward Said called "contrapuntal reading,"[35] I place Kiarostami's multifaceted artworld and the dynamics of reading him in multiple languages and discourses by way of accessing the innate heteroglossia at work in the name "Kiarostami."

The result of that heteroglossia pivots toward a form of philosophical meditation on a towering Iranian filmmaker seeking gently to transform his global reception via an articulation of a frame of epistemic reference that places the rich Persian poetic and aesthetic sensibilities in a sustained conversation with a decolonial project at large. Kiarostami's legacy is the occasion of this film-philosophical project. Liberating a filmmaker of immense aesthetic energy and the philosophical culture that has enabled and framed him into the veritable field of postcolonial and decolonial theory is now an urgent task predicated on the solid scholarship of major historians like Hamid Naficy, who in his epic four-volume tome *A Social History of Iranian Cinema* (2011–2012) has paved the way for a much more theoretically probing prose, perhaps so far best represented in texts such as Negar Mottahedeh's *Displaced Allegories* (2008)—though both these classics are entirely inattentive to the rich possibilities of Persian aesthetic and philosophical heritage, and sidestep the epistemic urgency of the decolonial project. Such pioneering texts were crucial stepping-stones in anticipation of a theoretical twist bridging the hitherto untapped Persian philosophical prose in conversation with the larger project of decolonial film-philosophy. My preference for the term "postcolonial" in this book is in deliberate juxtaposition to the "precolonial" condition in order to historicize the European colonial interlude in world history and not to credit or blame or fetishize it for more than what it is. By definition, my thinking through the postcolonial is a decolonial project. Put in other words: postcoloniality is a condition, decoloniality a project. My postcolonial posture in and of itself is a decolonial project. Drawing on philosophical, poetic, and linguistic worlds hitherto untapped by students of Iranian cinema or film-philosophy deliberately stages the kind of decolonial film-philosophy I theorize by performing.

In doing so, I am fully aware of the significant progress that has been made in more recent years by a younger generation of scholars like Blake Atwood in *Reform Cinema in Iran: Film and Political Change in the Islamic Republic* (2016), or Nacim Pak-Shirazi in *Shi'i Islam in Iranian Cinema: Religion and Spirituality in Film* (2011), or Golbarg Rekabtalaei's *Cosmopolitanism: A Cinematic History* (2019). These studies have markedly improved our overall grasp of Iranian and, by extension, world cinema and opened up new vistas of critical thinking. Atwood has brought apt attention to the period of the reformist movement and its impact on Iranian cinema. Pak-Shirazi has crucially expanded our cinematic understanding of Shi'i politics and metaphysics. Rekabtalaei has opened up our eyes to the cosmopolitan disposition of Iranian cinematic experience—a crucial aesthetic take on the prodigious work of Ali Mirsepassi in the same domain. But there are also more crucial developments not directly related to Iranian cinema, like Dudley Andrew's "Atlas of World Cinema" that readjusts our reading of the phenomenon. "Any study of World Cinema," he rightly writes, "should . . . be ready to travel more than to oversee, should put students inside unfamiliar conditions of viewing rather than bringing the unfamiliar handily to them. This is the pedagogical promise of world cinema, a manner of treating foreign films systematically, transcending the vagaries of taste; taking the measure of 'the foreign' in what is literally a freshly recognized global dimension."[36] My dwelling on Abbas Kiarostami's artworld is also a step in that direction.

Beyond these immediate fields, a work like Jonardon Ganeri's "Blueprint for a Cosmopolitan Philosophy in a Polycentric World" or Bryan van Norden's *Taking Back Philosophy: A Multicultural Manifesto* (2017) has far-reaching theoretical implications that leave no study of any decolonial project insular to itself. In this latter work alone, van Norden has detailed the reasons why performing philosophy as usual will no longer suffice. Although his main point of contention is targeted against US campuses in particular, the implications of van Norden's arguments are global. The European canon may be necessary but no longer sufficient. This depth of provincialism is no longer cute or affordable. Van Norden brings his command of Chinese philosophy to bear on his liberated arguments. He has, to be sure, a decidedly political project, and rightly so: "Studying philosophy makes people more informed and more thoughtful citizens, more comfortable with the fact that others disagree with them, less vulnerable to manipulation and deception, and more willing to resort to discussion rather than violence."[37] But his arguments also have wider epistemic implications of which he is fully aware. Paramount in my book of course remains my preoccupation with Kiarostami and how I might help advance our reading of his cinematic legacy in terms rooted in his immediate and distant habitat. But my task is made much easier by the fact that critical thinkers from all over the globe have been hard at work overcoming the colonial legacy that has hitherto laid a false and falsifying claim on philosophy and a fortiori on film-philosophy.

WHERE IS THE FRIEND'S HOUSE?

To reach for that contrapuntal aesthetic reasoning, we need to go back to where we started—the rise of Kiarostami as a global figure. What happens to a towering filmmaker like Satyajit Ray from India, Akira Kurosawa from Japan, Hou Hsiao-Hsien from China, Andrei Tarkovsky from Russia, or Abbas Kiarostami from Iran when their respective cinema leaves their homeland and habitat where they were born and raised and where their aesthetic sensibilities first came to fruition and enters a global stage on which they face new and excited audiences? Where, in other words, would a filmmaker like Abbas Kiarostami's artworld be located? As a floating signifier, Kiarostami's cinema is located somewhere in the midst of the multiple but adjacent spaces of national, postnational, and world cinemas. My main purpose in this book is to argue neither of these received categories would singularly suffice as the first or final location framing Kiarostami's cinema, and that we must therefore place him on a multivariant plane of successive signification where a tertiary interstitial space is crafted that surpasses both the stagnant or suppressed nativist and falsely or forcibly globalized readings of his artworld. I propose this argument in order to commence the critical thinking of reading Kiarostami's work neither as an "aesthetic negativity," a space for the dissolution of nonaesthetic reason, as the post-Enlightenment European philosophers would argue, nor as an aesthetic positivity for that matter, but on the organic plane of a *deferred aesthetic difference* (with a nod toward Derrida's conception of *différance* or *deferment*, further articulated in Cixous' articulation of *écriture féminine*) that is best suited for coming to terms with his changing and alternating interlocutions with multiple worlds his artworld as the product of a postcolonial subject has both inherited and inhabited.[38] I make this argument through a reading of Kiarostami's cinematic oeuvre in the immediate context of Iranian, postnational, and world cinemas. I therefore dwell in the syncretic language, at once theoretical and yet site-specific, philosophical and yet self-transcendent, that is needed to read Kiarostami's enduring legacy. He was a floating signifier, a flying form that was itinerant, nomadic, like the Hoopoe flying us to Mount Qaf to have us look at the veracity of our own sublimity, and as such made a virtue out of the inevitable ephemerality of the work of art a postcolonial subject was destined to inhabit.

The central idea of "aesthetic negativity," from Adorno and Derrida to Christoph Menke, is predicated on the principle of aesthetic difference, or "the distinction between the aesthetic and the nonaesthetic." Here the basic supposition is that "only by conceiving of works of art in their negative relationship to everything that is not art can the autonomy of such works . . . be adequately understood." Art thus separates itself from its environment thematically while it paradoxically relates to it by making it intelligible against itself. "What art actually is, is contradiction, rejection, negation."[39] Add to that the reality of a post/colonial artist like Abbas Kiarostami, coming from the left field of the European cosmopolis, whose oeuvre will have to be deciphered through the thick incongruity of the aesthetic apparatus applied to it by multiple hermeneutic domains afforded it in the aftermath of its European reception. The result is a kind of aesthetic negativity that resides on the borderline between complete alienation and provocative appreciation. In other words, the aesthetic negativity of an artist like Kiarostami thrives on the paradox of being first mis/understood before it is appreciated. Misunderstanding is an understanding, and thus in trying to decipher Abbas Kiarostami, Europeans qua Europeans begin to misunderstand not Kiarostami but themselves. This vertiginous hermeneutic of misunderstanding is less harmful to Kiarostami than revelatory of Europeans. To the degree that the rest of the world begins to see and read Kiarostami through its European reception, then that hermeneutic of misunderstanding goes global. This means the idea of "aesthetic negativity" has always had global implications beyond the reach of Adorno's own initial articulation. My own theoretic apparatus, rooted in this aesthetic negativity, is therefore predicated on this tenuous borderline, banking and thriving on it. Like his winding "Roads" extending from the location of his camera to unknowing anonymity, our reading of Kiarostami must begin with the close-up assurances of where he is imagining he might be headed.

It is also here on the borderline of the aesthetic and nonaesthetic reasons that I place Kiarostami's disposition toward a postcolonial film-philosophy. This is in marked contrast but not in opposition to Mathew Abbott's recent work on the subject arguing that in Kiarostami we have a cinematic thinking sui generis, which is of course a truism.[40] But what kind of thinking—to which Abbott responds through the approximation and assimilating backward of that cinematic thinking to the works of some leading Eurocentric philosophers like Ludwig Wittgenstein, Stanley Cavell, John McDowell, Alice Crary, Noël Carroll, Giorgio Agamben, and Martin Heidegger? I have no objection to that. It in fact works well for Abbott and enables him to offer some provocative readings of Kiarostami's cinema. But I go upstream from those Eurocentric insights (exciting as it may seem to have crossed the divide between analytic and continental philosophy), effectively approximating Kiarostami to the way European and Eurocentric thinking allows, and do not take affinity between cinematic thinking and Eurocentric philosophy as a sign of Kiarostami's cinema-philosophy. There is a profound epistemic violence in that approximation that may indeed offer some serious insights into his cinema but at the cost of very serious damage to what it might otherwise contain. On that upstream, I begin with Kiarostami's existential condition of coloniality that effectively prohibits the kind of approximation and epistemic violence Abbott perpetrates. Let me begin with a key incident.

"Abbas Kiarostami, the Iranian filmmaker who is widely considered one of the world's greatest living directors, has been denied a visa to enter the United States."[41] The news astonished many but not others late in the fall of 2002. "Kiarostami had been invited to attend the New York Film Festival, where his new movie 'Ten' will premiere on Sunday, and then to lecture at Harvard and at Ohio State University," but American authorities both in Paris and Washington thought him dangerous to their national security. "Stringent new rules," we subsequently learned, "put in place after last year's terrorist attacks, now require a three-month background check on some applicants for United States visas, in particular those from Muslim countries."[42]

Kiarostami being denied a visa to come to the US to screen his films and discuss his cinema was the blunter and more vulgar testimony to his status as being designated a Muslim, a persona non grata, a suspect, a potential terrorist—in short, a postcolonial person at the mercy of the imperial order of American political reasoning. Neither did he need to come to the US nor did the officials at the US State Department denying him a visa lose any sleep thinking what the world thought of the vulgarity of their decisions. What mattered was the blunt edge of a relation of power that under the Bush administration had perhaps its rudest manifestation, before we reached the Trump era, of course. The solidarity of the Finnish filmmaker Aki Kaurismaki with Kiarostami underlines this truth. He was not denied a visa. He perhaps did not even need a visa. He, as a Finn, was most welcome without any suspicion that he might be a terrorist. The Norwegian mass-murderer terrorist Anders Behring Breivik would have had no problem entering the US. But Kiarostami did.

Let us now turn the lens in reverse. The condition of Kiarostami's coloniality is demarcated not just by the humiliation of denying him a visa to enter the US but by the contrapuntal staging of a Hollywood spoof called *Argo* (2012) directed by Ben Affleck telling the story of the US hostage crisis of 1979–1980. Denying the most globally celebrated Iranian filmmaker entry into the US and producing a lurid film about the US hostages come together to define what it means to be cast as a post/colonial filmmaker—whose very condition of coloniality now defines his postcolonial persona. The entire imperial and colonial history of the US and the UK in Iran culminated in the CIA-MI6 staging of the 1953 coup as the most vulgar episode in European and American imperial arrogance. Kiarostami was a teenager when this coup happened and the democratic fate of his homeland forever changed. Was his cinema at all affected by that fateful incident—reiterated in his adulthood when he was denied entry into a country that had viciously disallowed the prospect of a democratic future for him?

Kiarostami made his most political films through the scripts he wrote for his chief protégé, Jafar Panahi—such as *The White Balloon* (1995) and *Crimson Gold* (2003)—but those boldly political films are not the clearest manifestations of his politics. His most political act has been the effective suspension of the reality he has inherited as a postcolonial person—through a mode of filmic vision I have identified as "actual realism." His entire cinema, as I have argued in my *Masters and Masterpieces of Iranian Cinema* (2007), is a mode of actual realism in which reality is stripped of all its metaphysical underpinnings. He is political in that most radical way conceivable for an artist. But why would he and other masters of Iranian cinema want to strip reality of its inherited and dominant metaphysics? Because that reality has denied them agency, subjectivity, authorial voice and vision. The terms of his aesthetics are not political in the ordinary sense of the term but in the sense of a complete suspension and overcoming of the nonaesthetic reason—done in the shadows of his sublime and liberated aesthetic reasoning. The proclivity toward this aesthetic reason is rooted in the very simple fact that the nonaesthetic reason in which he dwells casts its debilitating spell on him when he walks into the US embassy in Paris and is denied a visa—which is the most decisive moment when the colonial reasoning of conquest and domination stages and asserts itself. In both its monarchic and clerical gestations, for or against the imperial umbrella, that condition of coloniality has spelt disaster for Kiarostami's nation. In scripts he writes for Panahi to shoot, he is naked in his politics of despair. In his own films he is upstream from that politics and thrives on dismantling its metaphysical underpinnings. On that spot, his cinema allows for a postcolonial philosophy of the unknowing subject.

What separates Kiarostami's artworld from its surrounding is therefore the serenity of his insistence on form as what demarcates it from its cacophonous political surrounding, which amounts to his most political act as a postcolonial person. This central normativity of form gives his aesthetic reasoning a pronouncedly destructive force against the colonial rhythm we have all internalized. When watching him, just as in the ending of his masterpiece *Where Is the Friend's House?*, we are lost in the uncertain darkness of a place we cannot tell exactly where it is. We have to go back home and do the homework ourselves, as it were, and the following day go back to the person of the friend (not his house) and gift him with what we were capable of doing in his absence.

When Abbas Kiarostami died on 4 July 2016, I was in Ocho Rios, Jamaica, vacationing with my children, entirely oblivious to the compelling reasons to keep him and other towering figures of Iranian or world cinema in mind. I was minding my own business, attending to my children, reading and writing other things. And boom: the news hit like a disorientating bang! My friend Marwan Bishara first texted me and soon after *Aljazeera* contacted me for a quick Skype interview, which I did give. But I was still dizzy. I sat down and wrote an obituary and sent it off to my *Aljazeera* editor. That night, I had a dream of Abbas Kiarostami. I do not remember the details of that or any of my other dreams. But I do remember he was in New York. I was picking him up from his hotel in midtown Manhattan, where he had just finished a series of interviews. I was driving, another friend whom I cannot remember was sitting next to me in the front seat. Kiarostami sat in the back seat—diagonal from me. I could see part of him in my rearview mirror. We were driving to New Jersey to a dinner party in his honor at a mutual friend's house. "Thanks for lending Hamid to us tonight," he said in Persian from the backseat so he could be heard on my car phone speaker. Who was it on the other side I was talking to? I could not remember. I woke up.

Just like through the reverse angle of my rearview mirror, Abbas Kiarostami's camera made the foreign familiar by making the familiar foreign. The moment we hear the news of the passing of a giant whom we knew at the time of his glorious achievements, time stands still, memories flood and overwhelm; words, pictures, feelings, phrases, glances, and snapshots of a lifetime all come together like a collage, a kaleidoscope, in which you cannot tell if you are a spectator or the spectacle. Last time I had this feeling was when my friend and colleague Edward Said (1935–2003) died. The full sense of incredulity is lessened with the dawning sense of unexpected loss and, moreover, the overwhelming recognition of the voluminous space occupied by another life adjacent to yours and yet so definitive to it.

The search for where Kiarostami's work resides and to wonder how we are to read his legacy are a search for the subtlest and most elusive soul of Persian culture and Iranian history casting an enabling spell on the texture of our worldly whereabouts. He was an Iranian artist of uncommon truth in a way that both staged and recast the legacy of a revered culture for a global audience. The philosophical twist to his cinema is radically real and yet mystical in its rootedness in a past he could not but possess. The global serendipity by which his legacy has been placed in the intersections of national, postnational, and world cinemas has been accentuated by his versatility to navigate and float into multiple aesthetic and hermeneutic domains and registers. In that undecidability of his location is precisely where we have a wide and enabling space to remake his acquaintances.

The obituary I wrote and sent to *Aljazeera* calmed me down for a few hours. But I remained restless. I talked to Ramin Bahrani on the phone. But I needed to talk to Amir Naderi and could not find him. He was in Japan. So, I began to write. I had a writing notebook with a blue plastic cover, and a whole thick stack of blank white pages were beckoning me. It was myself, the peace of mind of my children playing in the pool behind me, and the vast blue sea separating me from my active memories of a master artist the world had just lost. It was a shot straight out of Kiarostami's films. I was now fully in the pupil of his revelatory lens. I began to look for him through his own camera. I mapped out almost the entirety of this book in that little blue notebook in a small former colony island in the middle of the Caribbean. I now just need to decipher my own crooked scribblings. Kiarostami dwells somewhere in there. Through the rushed scrawl of my fleeting thoughts, I need to pause and decipher the calm and composed clairvoyance of a master meditating on the world beyond the cacophonous rushes of a colonized world we need aesthetically to decolonize before we might politically liberate it for our posterity.

1 Mirror of the Invisible World

Chon ohdeh nemishavad　　Since tomorrow
Kaasi　　　　　　　　　　Has not been
Farda ra . . . /　　　　　　Promised to anyone . . .

Omar Khayyam (1048–1131)

Half a century ago, the distinguished Polish scholar Peter Chelkowski published a selection of Persian poet Nezami's poetry he called *Mirror of the Invisible World: Tales from the Khamseh of Nizami* (1975). That auspicious title remained at the level of the intuitions of a gifted translator. But it also alluded to the manner in which visual imageries (*Suvar-e Khayal*) in Persian poetry point to a rich body of semiotic repertoire that we need to explore and extend as the aesthetic foregrounding of the cinema of Abbas Kiarostami. What this body of imageries marks is the vast gamut of poetic evidence in which we see the imaginative world of the Persian poet made visible by way of provocative allusions. These allusions work as the vision of an invisible world that the poet has seen (as if a blind person finding sight for the first time) and is now making that world poetically visible to the rest of us. This aesthetic foregrounding of Kiarostami's cinema in the poetic history of his homeland is therefore a metonymic deferral to that invisible world made cinematically visible. By and large, the aesthetically Europeanized reception of Kiarostami's cinema, particularly by his European admirers, exceptionally insightful in many other ways, has had no inroad into this poetic repertoire of his cinema. As textual evidence for this argument, I plan to work through Kiarostami's early

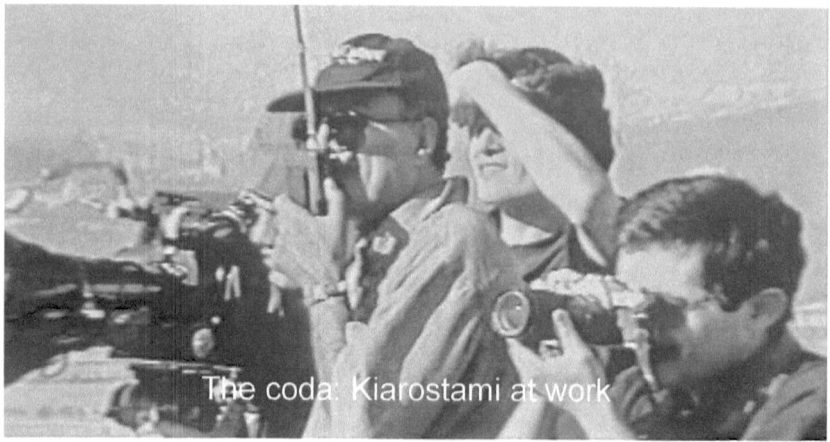

Figure 3. Abbas Kiarostami, *Taste of Cherry* (1997). Courtesy of Abbas Kiarostami Foundation.

shorts and features as he begins to discover and own his visual vocabulary. At this stage, long before the reception of his cinema goes global, we witness palpable evidence of his visual rootedness in Persian poetic imagination.

Understanding these metonymic allusions to a body of poetic repertoire otherwise hidden to the naked eyes is necessary because almost any time the idea of Kiarostami's cinema and "philosophy" has come together as a case of film-philosophy, his artworld has been assimilated backward into the European conception of "philosophy," in which Kiarostami's oeuvre of course offers a rich aesthetic glossary, commentary, or else case study. Even when critical thinkers have sought to explore philosophical aspects of his cinema as his cinema, they have done so in terms rooted in European philosophical terms. That limited critical apparatus should not by any means be discredited (for it has been exceptionally fruitful) but instead seriously expanded. The rich and diversified body of poetic allusions, or Suvar-e Khayal, in which I believe Iranian visual and performing arts are rooted, are by and large a terra incognita in the field of cinema studies and very much confined to the literary critical domains. We need carefully to explore that field and bring it to bear on Kiarostami's work, chief among all other serious Iranian filmmakers. To be sure, here we do not have iconic figures like Heidegger, Derrida, Deleuze, or Lacan to cite. Instead, we have a rich and fertile ground of theoretical speculations and poetic evidence that will help us tease out the philosophical disposition of Kiarostami's cinema in a more immediate but hidden habitat. This in effect is an attempt to encounter the texture of his filmic grammatology through the theoretical articulation of the ocularity of his evident Suvar-e Khayal.

IMAGINATIVE IMAGERIES IN PERSIAN POETIC LEGACIES

One of the most influential pieces of scholarship on Persian poetic imageries is *Suvar-e Khayal dar She'r-e Farsi/Imaginative Imageries in Persian Poetry* (1971) by the leading Iranian literary scholar Mohammad Reza Shafi'i-Kadkani. Subtitled "Critical Investigation on the Transformation of Imageries in Persian Poetry and the Course of the Theory of Eloquence in Islam and Iran," this groundbreaking work is the most solid piece of critical scholarship on the subject in any language.[1] The purpose of the author in this book, as he tells us, is to examine Persian poetry with specific attention to what he calls "*Bayan-e Honari*/Artistic Expressions," which he launches toward a renewed understanding of the aesthetics of Persian poetry. Exploring what he terms *Suvar-e Khayal*/Imaginative Imageries, Shafi'i-Kadkani pays close attention to Muslim theorists but begins with the Aristotelian tradition and other Greek philosophers. In the second part of the book, he applies his findings to various prominent poets, geared toward the evolution of these imageries, from the earliest periods coming all the way down to the Constitutional period in the early twentieth century. The two parts of the study are integral to each other, for his theoretical speculations in the first part are themselves rooted in his close reading of the entire history of Persian poetry, and when he turns to apply these findings to samples of that legacy, obviously there is a corresponding delight to see his observations closely verified. The result is an exceptionally rich and insightful understanding of the centrality of imaginative imageries, or imageries that are aesthetic constructs rather than physical observations on the very texture and disposition of Persian poetry. The work as a result is both speculative and archival, meant to unpack the way aesthetic imagination of the poets has enriched the history of Persian poetry.

What does Shafi'i-Kadkani exactly mean by "Imaginative Imageries?" Here is what he writes:

> Considering the fact that the word "Image," both etymologically and idiomatically, is equivalent to the word "Tasvir" of an object, whether it be a mental image or material, it is therefore appropriate that what in contemporary literary criticism and books on European rhetoric is called "Image" (and some among our contemporaries have considered it "Tasvir") be identified with the word "Khayal" as it has been used in Arabic and Persian poetry and literature, for not only the word "Image" etymologically means "Tasvir" and "Shadow" and "Khayal," philosophically too the domain of its usage is close to this idiomatic use among the literary critics.[2]

Shafi'i-Kadkani then turns to other thinkers who consider this idea of Khayal as the occasion of a vision one has in a dream, or imagines while awake, which is decidedly different from the things one sees with one's own physical eyes, for what we imagine we do not actually see, so there is a difference between what we actually see with our own eyes and what we imagine in our mind. Shafi'i-Kadkani then quotes the Shi'i theologian Allamah Hilli (1250–1325) to the effect that the difference between what we actually see and what we imagine is that our mind interferes or interjects into what we imagine, as for example when we see a scarecrow on a farm, for it resembles a human being; the image we see in the mirror is also an example of Khayal. Shafi'i-Kadkani then gives examples to show Khayal as Image or else as *Parhib*/Apparition, or *Shabah*/Ghost, and *Sayeh*/Shadow—after all of which he concludes that Khayal is the best Persian equivalent for Image.[3]

This approximation of the English/Latin word *Image* and the Persian/Arabic word *Khayal* forms the comparative theoretical grid for Shafi'i-Kadkani to fine-tune his opening up the vast spectrum of Persian poetry to contemporary philosophical and literary speculations about the nature and function of the elemental forces of creative imagination in a work of art. His theoretical speculations are almost entirely of and on poetic sources, and scarcely he mentions cinema, or painting, or photography. But the astonishing fact remains how he is writing about cinema without knowing he is writing about cinema—and that is perhaps the most crucial part of his insights for Kiarostami's artworld. One of the most fascinating aspects of Kadkani's insights is when he applies his ideas to specific poets; among them, and most pertinent to my purpose here, is the pioneering Persian poet Rudaki Samarqandi (circa 858–941), who happens to have been blind. The first crucial thing Shafi'i-Kadkani says about Rudaki is that in his poetry he never connects an abstract idea to another abstract idea, and that he is far more into comparing material objects to material objects, and as a result there is very little place for similis in his poetry. Related to this feature of Rudaki's poetry is the absence of any exaggeration in his panegyrics—which are otherwise prone to excessive exaggerations in this respect.[4] Shafi'i-Kadkani then connects all these observations to the report that Rudaki was born blind, and as a result had no visual memories of objects whatsoever. He then cites Rudaki's contemporary, the eminent literary philosopher Abu Hayyan al-Tawhidi, who reported that when they asked Rudaki what is color, he said it is something "like a camel."[5] Shafi'i-Kadkani also compares Rudaki with another famous poet, Bashar ibn Burd (714–783), who, too, was born blind and whose imageries are equally bold and material, though in Bashar there is an almost exaggerated emphasis on color. What is equally fascinating about Bashar is that what he could not have seen has become definitive to the ocularcentricity of his vision, as it were, that all abstractions come in the form of visualities.[6] But in Rudaki there is no such exaggeration of color, and his ocularcentrism remains entirely material.

The combined insights of Shafi'i-Kadkani on Rudaki and Bashar lead to a form of ocularity that is material and solid, stipulates the absence of color in one and the exaggeration of color in the other, but both overcome conceptual abstraction with evident materiality and leave behind a solid poetic repertoire of visual imagination that becomes exemplary in our understanding of the very nature of "seeing," now evident and staged in the artwork of Abbas Kiarostami. What I am proposing is not a one-to-one correspondence between aspects of Kiarostami's cinema and the visual grammatology that Shafi'i-Kadkani uncovers in Persian poetic imagination, but a common aesthetic repertoire that has been evident poetically in a vast poetic memory and its renewed gestations in a cinematic adventure carrying the signature of Abbas Kiarostami.

Kiarostami's cinema was deeply rooted in Persian poetic diction, and he was a poet himself. His verbal and visual poetries, in fact, come together into a singular act of visually staging what Shafi'i-Kadkani theorizes in this seminal work of literary criticism. There is therefore an "inaugural" aspect to Kiarostami cinema that does not just begin with the centrality of children in his early shorts but thrives on the wide-eyed innocence of children so that we see the world anew from the vantage point of a child as if to discover and see the world for the first time, as if we were a blind poet like Rudaki or Bashar full of stories to tell and telling them in a way as if we see the world afresh through them. This is to do philosophy *with* Kiarostami, avoiding the assumption that only if you hang his cinema on aspects of European philosophy as an appendix or an afterthought is it then philosophical, or when a European philosopher writes about him, then that is philosophy—again, to be sure, when a European philosopher or film critic writes about him, we should also bring that reflection to bear on his cinema. But that will not be the end of the story. I am not even sure there is any teleology or beginning and end to the way we might watch his cinema. But still the application of European thinking to his cinema is not even the beginning of the story. It is, though, part of the story. We must look for the inaugural moments embedded in his cinema. Philosophy begins with the sense of wonder worthy of the moment that in his "Art as Device" (1917) Viktor Shklovsky considered the making of the familiar foreign, and conversely, we might add, the foreign familiar.

RE-VISIONING THE WORLD ANEW

How does a blind poet like Rudaki or Bashar visualize things? It is not just as seeing them for the first time, for the blind poet has never "seen" anything. He just imagines them poetically—for his is the case of pure verisimilitudes. Suvar-e Khayal, in the entirety of their aesthetic registers, are mental constructs, imaginative visions of things, with or without the slightest connection to the real things, as if all poets were blind poets, as if all visual artists were seeing things for the first time. As the plural of *Surat*/Shape, *Suvar*/Shapes are mental framings or molds into which the otherwise amorphous mental image of things, or Khayal, are planted or perceived. Cinema is therefore a kind of mobile Suvar-e Khayal, ways of shaping and framing and seeing otherwise amorphous things as the imaginative reception of those things, of realities ushered into truth as if from nowhere. Watching Kiarostami is like working through that constellation of Suvar-e Khayal, like watching things for the first time, and the evidence of that comes from his tampering with other poets' work.

I am holding in my hand a tiny little book, 4 × 6 inches, with a white dust jacket and blue and black fonts—handsomely crafted, like a collector's item, pleasant to look at, and small enough to carry in your pocket. It is almost the size of an iPhone. In the digital age, this is a piece of antiquarian pleasure packed inside a small piece of nostalgia. It is Abbas Kiarostami's selection of a few poetic phrases of the towering Persian poet Nima Yushij (1895–1960), which he has titled *Ab/Water*.[7] Nima Yushij has no book by this name. This is Kiarostami's title for a selection of Nima's poems, an anthology, of a sort. The little book consists of 272 blank pages with a bit of poetry from the vast compendium of Nima Yushij's oeuvre, each page set in a blue frame, at the center of which we read a fragment of one of Nima's poems—for example, "*Man zeh vaqt-e kudaki / Sha'eran ra dust budam /* Since my childhood I have befriended [or loved] poets,"[8] or "*Mah dar abr nahan mi-amad /* The moon was rising hidden behind the cloud."[9] We thumb through the sparse wording and the elegant interior design of the book and we marvel at more than anything else its sleek minimalism—in form and content. It is as if Kiarostami is after discovering the quintessence, the DNA, of Nima's poetry—sparse, minimal, sleek, resonant with meaning but confined and ascetic with words. It is quite obvious he has had an aesthetic pleasure looking at these photographic "shots" of Nima's poetic mind, with minimal dialogue, as it were, like his films, snowy white pages, just like his photography, and the whisper-like murmuring of a few precious words.

There is no doubt that today we are looking at Kiarostami's oeuvre in the aftermath of his having achieved iconic significance in national, postnational, and world cinema. We are therefore looking for and we are therefore discovering that about his cinema which we would have probably never suspected or detected before. Instead of bemoaning the fact that we have forever lost the capacity of looking at Kiarostami as if he were still a little-known Iranian filmmaker, we in fact need to dwell on and map out and detail why it is that the very fact of his postmortem thinking is the very best way of looking at him afresh. Iranians takes their poetry very seriously. If before he had become a global phenomenon Kiarostami had butchered Nima's poems the way he does in this little book, *Ab/Water*, he would have been skewered in the reviews. But there is now a reticence, a fear even, of even wondering what he is doing with these snippets of Nima's poems. In trespassing into that domain, with a sense of confident self-indulgence he does open a space otherwise closed to any other literary or artistic figure. That trespass is crucial in our reading and watching him today.

Let us take his very first short, *Nan va Kucheh/The Bread and Alley* (1970) where we see a boy, having just purchased a piece of fresh bread, is on his way home when he runs into a frightful dog and has to negotiate his way past his fears. The boy finally throws a piece of bread to the dog and runs to the safety of his home, while the dog now rests comfortably monitoring the neighborhood where a young boy with a bowl of yoghurt now faces the same fear. The short film cuts and we are left to wonder what might happen next. The story is inconclusive and minimalist. From the tongue-in-cheek ambiguity of this filmic prose, Kiarostami eventually reached his first major film, *Mosafer/Traveler* (1974), where we encounter a young street-smart teenager who wishes to travel from his hometown of Malayer to watch a football match in Tehran. He goes through any number of tricks in the book, including cheating his way by pretending to take pictures of his friends, for a nickel and a dime, as it were, with a broken camera, to pay for his bus fare to Tehran, where, as he waits for the game to start, he falls asleep and misses the game. The moral ambiguity of the plot defines much that will happen in the rest of Kiarostami's cinema. Through these early films of the 1970s, Kiarostami consistently teaches his audience a new way of looking at things. His camera is revelatory, sardonic, sarcastic, prosaic but at the same time self-confident. By this time, far more accomplished films like Dariush Mehrjui's *Cow* (1969) and Masoud Kimiai's *Qeysar* (1969) have been made to major critical reception and celebration. Kiarostami's films at this point are quiet, somewhat lackluster and inconsequential, and yet there is something disquietly curious about his way of seeing things.

Let's take another one of these early short features, *Tajrobeh/The Experience* (1973), based on Amir Naderi's script, where we watch a collage of subdued filmic phrases about a young boy working in a photography studio and having a juvenile infatuation with a young girl. Shot and cut with minimalist phrases, the whole film looks like an assemblage of disjointed prose coming together to suggest a hidden poetry. Decades later he "cuts" Nima's poems the same way, reduced to their formal phraseologies. Iranians may not have noticed it at the time but, back in the 1970s, Kiarostami was busy discovering new ways of depicting reality, and against an entire cinematic culture that was going in other directions with Bahram Beiza'i's early masterpieces. Kiarostami was busy articulating his own visions, perhaps akin to Sohrab Shahid Sales's before he left Iran and resumed a whole new career in Europe. Kiarostami stayed put in Iran and hard at work trespassing into the filmic culture of his own time, seemingly confident with what he was about to discover: Revisioning the world anew.

HOW TO RAISE PHILOSOPHICAL QUESTIONS IN A POSTCOLONIAL WORLD?

What is it that enables a philosopher in one part of the world to question the very notion of "Being" while other thinkers are either silent on the question, raise it in a different register, or else take it for granted? How is it that one or two or few philosophers in German, French, Italian, or English get to ask the sort of questions that effectively recast the very mystery of existence, of our being in the world, while in no other language anywhere else in the world contemporary to those European philosophers is that mystery falsely presumed to cause similar, or perhaps even different sorts of wonder? There is a freedom, a joyous frivolity even, from Nietzsche to Kierkegaard, Heidegger and Derrida and a whole slew of similar philosophers, evoking the most absurdly serious questions that no one anywhere else in the world seems to have dared to ask, with laughter or dread at one and the same time. Why is that the case? Who has the claim on the word *philosophy* as a discourse, a language, an institution, and by what authority? Is philosophy something that only "White People" do?

European thinking, thus self-designating itself, procreates itself, from Plato to Heidegger—by first and foremost manufacturing a longevity of that continuity and constancy and self-citation and therefore decidedly disregarding the rest. What is code-named "Islamic philosophy" or even "Jewish philosophy" and thus distanced and furthered from what therefore becomes not "Christian philosophy" but "Western philosophy" is the doppelgänger of that longevity, the shadows that make the shape of this "Western philosophy" possible by repressing its evident alterities. The phrase "Western philosophy" claims not just a continent, its history, and its people, but it opens its wings into an eternity, an interiority and primordiality that claim the world, the universal, whether the world and the universal accepts or rejects that claim. Against these odds, what can the world do but oblige? Can we contemplate our being-in-the-world anymore, or have European philosophers already done it for us? Have we by being born an Iranian, a Muslim, an Arab, an African, an Indian, a Chinese, a Jew, et cetera, with all the bewildering baggage these troubled designations contain, not been robbed of any clear slate on which we might think and write something fresh? There must be something of a deliberate but benign neglect in us to afford us the possibility of thinking about our being, let alone about Being. Under these circumstances, how can we talk about Kiarostami and philosophy in one sentence without first and foremost reducing his legacy into an outlandish commentary on that philosophy, robbing him blind, as it were, of its own philosophical premises?

There is too much history about us. We have always thought of ourselves to have occurred at the end of things—not their beginnings. We have been put here, we seem to think, to make sense of things past, not of things just beginning. We always assimilate things backward to what we already know, and think we must offer an account of it. How amazing (it) would be to feel you are at the beginning of something. Can we contemplate our being in the world anymore, or have our thinkers cum poets already done it for us? I think being born an Iranian, a Muslim, an Arab, a Turk, a South Asian, with all the bewildering connotations these terms contain, has robbed us of any clear slate on which we can think and write something fresh—except if we at least strategically take the condition of our coloniality as a point of departure. What bold audacity did Heidegger have to ask the most elemental questions of "What is being?" or "Why is there something rather than nothing?" His elaborate answer to that daring question in *Being and Time* (1927) is far less important than the question itself—and the daring imagination to ask it. "An enigma lies a priori in every relation and being towards beings as beings. The fact that we live already in an understanding of being and that the meaning of being is at the same time shrouded in darkness proves the fundamental necessity of repeating the question of the necessity of 'being.'"[10] That kind of questioning is not alien to a Muslim or a Chinese or an Iranian. But asking it anew requires a temporary hanging hook upon which we might opt to consider the colonial moment when we were epistemically severed from the prolonged and varied traditions that had asked such questions before us.

It is hard to hear Heidegger clearing his throat before asking what is being but first wondering what "the first formal structure of the question of being" should be, as he stipulates "questioning has its own character of being."[11] Before you know it, the questioner, the question, and the very attitude of questioning are all integral to the very question of being. We wish to question, so the question of being is asked from within the question of being. Heidegger says even asking the question "what is being" is itself already compromised by the *fact* that we are obligated to ask this question using the verb "to be," which is meant to be the object of the inquiry. "We do not know," he says, "what 'being' means. But already when we ask 'What is being?' we stand in an understanding of the 'is' without being able to determine conceptually what the 'is' means—or even more provocatively what this 'is' is."[12] That sort of logical questioning from the ground up requires such an implied philosophical confidence that the last time a Muslim philosopher dared such questioning was back in the sixteenth century during the Safavid period in the writings of the towering Shi'i philosopher Mulla Sadra Shirazi. But suppose we wish to look at Kiarostami irreducible in his aesthetics either to Heidegger and his "Western philosophy" or to Mulla Sadra and his "Islamic philosophy." Then what? Suppose we take the radical contemporaneity of Kiarostami's art-world seriously, and then suppose in his cinema we find ourselves provoked to think of the world, his world and ours, philosophically in the simplest sense, then how do we do that? The condition we call coloniality is not an answer but a premise, precisely because it captures the moment when we had left Mulla Sadra behind and did not yet know how to read Heidegger with a sense of agential autonomy.

If we are not to become antiquarian and resort to Islamic philosophy or self-alienated to appeal to "Western philosophy," we then need to ask how people in a postcolonial setting might raise philosophical questions ex nihilo, not by appealing to a theological denomination of their own but by rethinking their aesthetic and poetic questions that are embedded in their own immediate worldly disposition and therefore philosophical urges to ask simple questions. We therefore need to separate thoughts that have been marked as "Islamic" (to demarcate it from "Western") and the domains of creative and critical thinking that are not thus pigeonholed and therefore free to commune with a contemporaneity that has the markers of its own aesthetic claims to truth. That contemporaneity is neither "Islamic" nor "Western," for it is both/neither Islamic and/nor "Western," under the condition of colonial duress that has brought the two false binaries together and forced them to think in radically worldly terms.

Let me dwell on a moment in one of Kiarostami's earliest films, *Labasi bara-ye Arusi/A Wedding Suit* (1976) where we see three middle-aged men reminiscing about their personal and private lives occasioned by the making of a new suit for a boy to attend his sister's wedding. The film is cast as a comedy and it starts when a woman has brought her young son to a tailor to have him make a new suit for him to attend his sister's forthcoming wedding. The setting is simply unreal in its realism. The tailor's apprentice and his neighborhood friends get themselves into some mischief with that new suit. But all ends well. Simple, a bit funny, very little drama, a lot of unintrusive camerawork, and then a conversation among three middle-aged friends. As one brags about his amorous and erotic memories, the other two try to be encouraging and good-humored interlocutors. The scene is shot with minimal cuts in about three to four minutes. Kiarostami graces the dialogues with multiple accents of his characters, and finally cuts the sequence when one of the three men breaks into a song he remembers from his youth. The whole scene becomes a snippet of undiluted realism bordering on its own truth-claim, of *being* without asking about being, as the three friends reminisce about a life otherwise lost in anonymity. Their lives remain anonymous, inconsequential, and almost haphazard, and yet precisely in those terms made significant in its unremarkable prosaicism. Before such films, we could not imagine how extraordinary the ordinary could be—that we could be the subject of our own philosophical wonder. So ordinary are Kiarostami's scenes, we want to walk into them and have a tea with his protagonists. This simple transformation of the ordinary into something to behold is where the sense of wonder in the ordinary begins to pose itself as a simple but compelling (philosophical) question. We, the desubjected colonial subjected, suddenly find ourselves in a position to behold our ordinariness as the subject of our own bewilderment.

SIGN, SIGNATURE, SIGNIFICANCE

But how could such ordinariness go global? Why Kiarostami, and not some very serious other filmmakers like Amir Naderi or Bahram Beiza'i? What happened to Kiarostami could have happened to any number of other Iranian filmmakers—from Forough Farrokhzad in the 1960s to Jafar Panahi in the 2000s. Kamran Shirdel, Ebrahim Golestan, Bahram Beiza'i, Dariush Mehrjui, and Amir Naderi are chief among others who could have come forward and received recognition at Cannes and beyond. But it so happened, and deservedly so, that Kiarostami and his cinema were placed on a global pedestal and suddenly given a transnational audience, and with that a rich, diversified, and unfiltered viewership of his cinema. This fortunate event created a hermeneutic triangulation among the evidence of his cinema, his authorship as a filmmaker, and his widely differentiated viewership. The famous Umberto Eco's triangulation of the *intention of the author, intention of the text*, and *intention of the reader* was here instantly translated into the intention of the auteur, the evidence of his cinema, and the diversity of his viewership.[13]

This fact in and of itself transformed Kiarostami's cinema—both in production and in reception. Had he not been so catapulted into the global limelight, this triangulation would have never happened to his cinema on this massive scale. Conversely, had this global triangulation happened to any other equally significant filmmaker, say Beiza'i or Naderi, a different, perhaps a radically different, triangulation would have resulted and ensued. In my earlier work I have termed Beiza'i's work as "mythic realism," or Amir Naderi's as "visual realism," as opposed to Kiarostami's "actual" or Makhmalbaf's "virtual" realism, each of which would have probably solicited a different response.[14] It is now perhaps useless speculation to think through the potential consequences of what would have happened if Beiza'i's mythic or Naderi's visual or Makhmalbaf's virtual realism had captured the global attention as Kiarostami's actual realism did. But the particular triangulation of his sign, signature, and significance around the motif of "actual realism" has put forward a particular mode of film-philosophy that remains specific to his artworld.

The fact is unless and until a work of art is staged publicly, it has no or very little innate meaning or social significance. There are a good number of excellent filmmakers whose audiences by and large have remained limited or nonexistent. Their art becomes the subject of local or regional speculations or else part of the limited national scene. As a result, their work never returns to their immediate public with a global spin—as has Kiarostami's. The same can be said of just about any other great artist. Was Satyajit Ray the only Indian, or Kurosawa the only Japanese, Bergman the only Swedish, Visconti or de Sica the only Italian, et cetera, filmmaker? What made them iconic was not just the significance of their cinema but the synergy that their cinema created and sustained once it entered the global stage. Kamran Shirdel would have given the Iranian cultural scene a whole different take had he entered the global stage; so would have Bahram Beiza'i or Amir Naderi. Having thus stepped into the global limelight, Kiarostami's cinema in and of itself finds itself under multiple spotlights at once rich and potent, and yet by the same logic increasingly distanced from the initial manner in which he was seen before that decisive moment.

The global limelight, however, could be as much a curse for rootless artists as a blessing for rooted artists. Consider the ill-fated trajectory of Shirin Neshat's photography and video installations that for a while enjoyed tremendous global popularity and rightly so when it began in the early 1990s. But the sudden fame finally exhausted itself under the weight of its self-Orientalizing persistence. Neshat was never an Iranian artist, but a postnational American artist who banked on projecting herself as an artist "in exile."[15] Exile, true for millions of human beings around the globe, finally became a vacuous and self-negating hook for Neshat, which eventually turned against its own logic, when a lucrative art market began to take her out to auction houses. In the case of Kiarostami, the exact reverse was evident in the totality and organicity of his deeply rooted cultural heritage that came to bear on the constellation of his artworks. If we are not careful about this dynamic of rootedness, suddenly the sustained creativity of an artist like Kiarostami and the passing fame of Shirin Neshat would become conflated and confused. Kiarostami was and remained an open-ended sign to which was drawn a constellation of rich and probing significance. Shirin Neshat's art gallery in New York placed a lucrative commercial hold on her sign and signature and sold it to the highest bidder.

To understand the full dimensions of this dynamic, we need to begin with the site of the national where art first and foremost happens and expand to the postnational and reach the idea of world cinemas—where the trilectic enriches rather than diminishes the artwork. The task of the critique is to infer the emerging universal from the particulars of that space, which is to say to show how the dialectic of all its others is in the very identity of the work of art. The task of the critique is to link this to the transnational public sphere where the turgid designation of "exile" or "diaspora" or "accent" are all distortions that remain blinded to the possibilities of multiple worldliness. To go back to the ground zero of that worldliness in our own time, to the contemporaneity of our worldly existence, we need to dwell on the condition of coloniality not as an existential truth but as a political and therefore epistemic contingency, and therefore as a philosophical proposition, a contingency that in aesthetic terms ought to be read against the prolonged poetic evidence of the Suvar-e Khayal (here, broadly understood as tropes of imagination) an artist like Kiarostami and the world have inherited, of the ability to resignify the ordinariness in specifically Persian and Iranian terms and yet made universal by virtue of the very colonial contingency that has connected the whole world together. Except as a commercial ruse to sell the artifact to the highest bidder, no one is in "exile" in that world, for the whole world has been made alien to the global robbery that has brought the colonizer and the colonized together.

INTUITION OF TRANSCENDENCE: THE PHILOSOPHICAL FOREGROUNDING OF KIAROSTAMI'S CINEMA

The condition of coloniality as a core of philosophical contingency overrides the inherited certainties that usher an artist onto the global scene.

Kiarostami was born to two different and opposing conceptions of philosophy: "Western Philosophy" on one side and "Islamic Philosophy" on the other. His cinema was alien to both—though over the last decade some insightful work has been done to assimilate his cinema backward to aspects of European (particularly Continental) philosophy, with some quite insightful results. In between those two stretches of philosophical imagination, however, there is plenty of space to meditate on the philosophical nature of his own cinema—without assimilating it either to "Western" or to "Islamic" philosophy. Where would that space be? To answer that question, we need to take a closer look at the social and intellectual disposition of his birth and upbringing in mid-twentieth-century Iran. His cinema, in all its aspects, particularly if we are to tease out its film-philosophy forcefields, is rooted in that social and intellectual history, embedded as it was in superpower rivalries between the US and the USSR, inheriting the colonial heritage of Europe and Russia.

Kiarostami happened in a very specific national consciousness. He was born on 22 June 1940, just about the tail end of a momentous decade with enduring impact on his aesthetic reasoning. The 1930s were defined by three seminal figures: As Reza Khan staged a military coup to dismantle the Qajars (1785–1926) and assume political power with the help of the British, Nima Yushij was busy recasting the poetic foundations of Persian consciousness, while Sadegh Hedayat was erecting the edifice of contemporary Persian literary prose. Reza Shah did not last, but during his reign the colonial influence of Russia and the United Kingdom eventually yielded to the imperial prowess of the US and the USSR. Nima and Hedayat survived these fateful periods and thrived in the creative imagination of the younger generation. By the time Kiarostami was born and raised in the 1940s, Iran was under the military occupation of the Allied Forces, when Reza Shah was forced to abdicate in favor of his son Mohammad Reza Shah, as the pro-Soviet Communist Tudeh Party was being established, and the poetry of Parvin E'tesami was the defining voice of the social consciousness of this time. In the 1950s, when Kiarostami was a teenager, Mosaddegh's aspirations for decolonizing the Iranian economy was roundly defeated by the US-UK military coup of 1953. Mohammad Reza Shah was brought back to power by the CIA and MI6 when Kiarostami was still in high school, while a new generation of the followers of Nima's poetics emerged—Forough Farrokhzad, Mehdi Akhavan-e Sales, and Ahmad Shamlou chief among them. In the 1960s, as Kiarostami was coming of age, the rise of Iranian cinema was as important as fiction and poetry—with pioneering figures like Ebrahim Golestan, Farrokh Ghaffari, and Forough Farrokhzad paving the way. The 1970s witnessed the flowering of all these developments with a wide constellation of leading poets, dramatists, novelists, and filmmakers. This cosmopolitan effervescence came to a closure with the Iranian revolution of 1977–1979, followed by the austere dictatorship of Ayatollah Khomeini for an entire decade, 1979–1989, until his death. A brutal eight-year Iran-Iraq War (1980–1988) followed, and the decades of the 1990s and 2000s saw the expansion of the public and parapublic sphere and the emergence of a potent reformist movement. The rise of Kiarostami to global significance happened during these decades when the expansion of the public and parapublic transnational space allowed for first his cinema and eventually for his other artworks to receive a global audience. By the commencement of the 2010s, his cinema had achieved a critical mass from which exuded an unmistakable intuition of self-transcendence.

Looking back at these decades, we can see how the period of 1900s–1930s was dominated by the poetic diction of the Constitutional period, deeply social and political, almost unconscious of its aesthetic innovations, while during the 1930s–1960s it was augmented by the momentous rise of modern Persian fiction. The two decades of the 1960s and 1970s, which led to the Iranian revolution of 1977–1979, also saw the active interface of poetry and fiction eventually yielding to the rise and effervescence of Iranian cinema. These successive moves were seamlessly interrelated. The violently Islamicized revolution that followed put an end to all these organic developments. Now emerged the noisy space of personal blogs and underground music—of which Mohsen Namjoo was perhaps the most potent force—targeting the recalcitrant corruption and backwardness of the ruling regime. While the decade of the 1980s was under the spell of the charismatic terror of Ayatollah Khomeini and the horrors of the Iran-Iraq War, the 1990s saw the flowering of Iranian cinema around the world, led by Abbas Kiarostami. This is when an aesthetic intuition of transcendence embedded in these experiences had found its global audience in its fullest maturity. In the aftermath of the 1977–1979 revolution, Kiarostami remained the most consistent vision relinking his postrevolutionary conditions to his earlier career in the 1970s and gently tapping into his subterranean roots.

I have already had multiple occasions in my writings to argue that in Iran (and perhaps even for the world at large outside the colonial cast of Europe), poets, novelists, dramatists, filmmakers, and artists in general are collectively the functional equivalent of our "philosophers," in the most generic sense—questioning the nature and purpose of being, and the means of understanding such existential issues. What they have lacked seriously, however, is a thick theoretical encounter with their work. Much analytical, historical, and insightful work has of course been written on these works in and out of Iran. Against this tacit and implicit background, Kiarostami's cinema has remained steady, while his other artworks have elbowed their way into Euro-American recognition, and not on the nativist grounds where Shirin Neshat and her Barbara Gladstone Gallery had already cornered the Self-Orientalizing market. While the work of Shirin Neshat was being actively appropriated in both commentary and commerce into a deeply and irredeemably Orientalist prose of Kiarostami's European and American proponents, his work remained true to the philosophical origins of its birth and breeding.[16] While the self-styled "exilic" conditions of Shirin Neshat's work dragged it deep into commercial success and aesthetic platitude, Kiarostami's cinema and artwork exuded a philosophical confidence that was rooted in his location in the social and intellectual framework of his homeland.

Based and framed in this context, soon emerged a cinematic intuition of transcendence in Kiarostami's work, predicated on but not limited to the condition of coloniality of his homeland over the last two hundred years. The poetic confidence of Nima Yushij, the fictional universe of Sadegh Hedayat, and the dramatic world of Gholamhossein Sa'edi eventually found their way into Kiarostami's minimal and liminal storytelling. The philosophical foregrounding of Kiarostami's cinema must therefore be detected in the immediate context of his social and intellectual history from which premise the aesthetic urge of his aesthetic intuition of transcendence takes shape. If we take Kiarostami's *Nama-ye Nazdik/Close-Up* (1990) as perhaps a defining turning point in the full-fledged maturity of his cinema, that intuition of transcendence finds its way in the interface between reality and fiction, between the fake and the factual, when an imposter becomes more real than the real, more theoretically insightful than the thing itself. Sabzian at one moment becomes more real than the real Makhmalbaf he was faking to see and show himself as a widely popular filmmaker. In this film, Kiarostami reverses the order of reality and truth.

There is a tongue-in-cheekness about *Close-Up*, a subdued sense of humor, where truth and fiction trade places right in your face, as it were, and in that exchange and interface, cinematic truth trumps factual distinction between fact and fantasy—forming what years ago I called "factasy." Sabzian does not just look like Makhmalbaf, in his mind he is Makhmalbaf, he is even better than Makhmalbaf, a fiction that has already overcome the truth that it belies. This tongue-in-cheekness is rooted in Kiarostami's own social history, with which he has always had a diagonal and tangential rapport. Within the world of that factasy, Sabzian the fake becomes the author of Makhmalbaf the real. Mohsen Makhmalbaf ultimately appears as a character in the movie Sabzian has promised the family he has fooled he is making, and in that fantasy Sabzian is truly a filmmaker of uncommon talent. He managed to seduce Kiarostami to lend him his camera, camera crew, and global reputation to have him screened at Cannes. In every success that both Makhmalbaf and Kiarostami have had ever since, Sabzian has had a vicarious pleasure. That vicariate metamorphosis of truth and narrative is the substance of Kiarostami's film-philosophy.

COLLAPSING FORM AND FACT:
ALTERING THE NATURE OF REALITY

If indeed that be the context, then what would be the text of Kiarostami's film-philosophy, where his cinema yields to philosophical meditations specific to his filmic vision? To state the simplest fact, in his artworld Abbas Kiarostami was busy altering the nature of reality as we perceive it. To be sure, any number of other iconic poets (like Nima Yushij), dramatists (like Gholamhossein Sa'edi), filmmakers (like Bahram Beiza'i), or painters (like Bahman Mohassess) also did the same and dramatically altered the way we perceive reality. So, the question we need to raise and answer is twofold: (1) in what particular way did Kiarostami alter our perception of reality, and (2) what happened when that perception of reality exited the limited but crucial site of Iran proper and entered a transnational public sphere with a global audience?

To answer the first question, Kiarostami's film-philosophy must be rooted in his mode of realism. As I have argued before, multiple modes of realism might be identified in Iranian cinema: The *actual realism* of Kiarostami is just one of them. In that mode of realism, form and fact coalesce and transcend the received perceptions of reality—to the point that the actuality of reality becomes its truth. To answer the second question, when that mode of realism enters the transnational public sphere in multiple languages, it solicits a variety of readings ranging from a cliché conception of "humanism" to more serious philosophical engagements— all of which have done their share of turning Kiarostami into a serious or playful philosophical issue, but at the same time robbed it of this actual realism as the cornerstone of its philosophical force. Resisting that philosophical turn, at the very same time, are the nativist readings of his oeuvre by his mostly Iranian critics. The trouble with the nativist reading of Kiarostami is that it forecloses his innately cosmopolitan cinema (where his actual realism is located) before even a shot of his cinema was released outside his homeland. Kiarostami's cinema was cosmopolitan in two complimentary senses: (1) he and his cinema were a product of world cinema, with, say, the Japanese Ozu or the Bengali Ray infinitely more influential on him than any other Iranian poet or filmmaker; and (2) he was born and raised on a transnational public sphere—which I have shown in detail to be beyond the current borders of Iran as a postcolonial nation-state.[17] Oblivious to both these facts, aesthetically blind to see the worldly disposition of his cinema, the nativist readings of Kiarostami either describe him as making films for foreigners or else celebrate him for being "totally Iranian."

A similar trouble afflicts the term *humanism* when it is appended to Kiarostami's cinema, at a time when after Heidegger's critique of Sartre's assumption that "Existentialism is Humanism" the term has marked a deeply troubled domain in European philosophy—where the initial reading of Kiarostami's film-philosophy was inaugurated. In that context, celebrating Kiarostami as a "humanist" in effect robs him of authorial agency and his visual idiomaticity and therefore of his signature cine-aesthetics. To salvage the idea of "humanism," we need to relocate the debate to the site of the Iranian encounter with colonial modernity—where concepts are epistemically rearticulated. The commencement of Iranian cinema on the site of a transnational public sphere has enabled an entirely different kind of "humanism" without understanding the parameters of which the term is lost in its Eurocentric entrapments, as evident in the Heidegger-Sartre debate.[18] The concomitant rise of Iranian public space, public reason, the public intellectual, public happiness (as Arendt would call and consider it) is specific to a particular kind of post/colonial gestation. On this premise, the social and normative condition of democracy has emerged without either its economic foregrounding or the political apparatus to sustain it. Upon this public sphere, phantom liberties have historically emerged and soon assumed an aesthetic intuition of transcendence, at once real and unreal, more in form than in fact. Upon the fertile ground of a simplified prose of the Qajar period also emerged the poetry of the Constitutional period (1906–1911) at the turn of the twentieth century, predicated on a robust and powerful prosody that ipso facto constituted and defined the public sphere, which it calls *Vatan*/Homeland. Poets like Iraj Mirza, Aref Qazvini, Mirzadeh Eshqi, Abolqasem Lahuti, Farrokhi Yazdi, Parvin E'tesami, and Ali Akbar Dehkhoda were the harbingers of that aesthetic intuition of poetic transcendence, which in turn became the *conditio sine qua non* of the philosophical foregrounding of visual and performing arts that came to final fruition in Kiarostami's cinema. The "humanism" that can be attributed to Kiarostami must therefore be squarely located in the anticolonial struggles of his people that ipso facto reverses the issue of *essence* and *existence* at the heart of the Heidegger-Sartre debate into an entirely different metaphysics, which is neither "Western" nor "Islamic" but specifically Iranian in the sense of a moral and imaginative encounter with colonial modernity.

If we were to put that humanistic tradition on the transnational public sphere it embodied and the intuition of transcendence it enabled, then we will have a specific inroad onto Kiarostami's film-philosophy. Here we might be able to read Kiarostami the way Adorno has read Kierkegaard, not as a philosophical model but in the same critical spirit. Kiarostami's is an aesthetic of our existence neither in idealist nor in entirely existential terms, where we see how the terms of our existence are wrested from reality but kept at the threshold of total abstraction. The European reception of Kiarostami, as Adorno surmised about Kierkegaard, has identified and secured a "bourgeois *interieur*" in his cinematic oeuvre that offers it a reprieve from its own late capitalist boredom—and thus the symbolic significances of Cannes in May, Locarno in August, and Venice in September as top vacation destinations for the European bourgeoisie. Liberated from that European limitation, Kiarostami could also be seen and watched and read embedded in the dialectic of a postcolonial existence from which his cinema has arisen, "not to forget in dreams the present word," as Adorno would say, "but to change it by the strength of an image."[19] That image, the entirety of Kiarostami's project, we might suggest, thrives on the borderline of existential angst and agitated formal abstractions, where the trilectic of his national, postnational, and worldly receptions might in fact work best to his advantage to enable a more liberating reading of both existential materialism and aesthetic formalism. Adorno's project was to go after the German reception of Kierkegaard to dismantle Heidegger's turn to existentialism. This is an entirely provincial feud among European philosophers—which we might watch with some healthy curiosity and intellectual entertainment. But the lesson from his feud for the world at large is the distinction Adorno inevitably has to make between *aesthetic formalism* and *existential angst*, which he wants to root in historical materialism, and which for the world at large assumes decidedly a colonial twist that was beyond all these European philosophical horizons. But it is within ours. That crucial distinction from that otherwise local disputation comes to a much fuller presence in Kiarostami's cinema whose aesthetic formalism was in tune, however camouflaged, with the existential angst his cinema always faced, perhaps most poignantly in *Mashq-e Shab/ Homework* (1989).

Homework is a study of tyranny, caught in the microcosm of school homework children and their parents must negotiate within an already tyrannical politics of the ruling states. There is no mentioning of any state interrogations. But Kiarostami's own inquisitive voice and vista plus the repeated cuts to the cameraman and his camera have become emblematic. The experience of shooting this film becomes particularly poignant when the cameraman and Kiarostami's voice and presence add to the overwhelming anxiety of the children summoned to be interviewed in a small dark room. Kiarostami crafts the form as he makes the film, so that there is no abstract or prefabricated conception of facts to which the documentary (so-called) molds. Both the existential anxiety of doing homework at the receiving end of a belt if they failed as the microcosm of tyranny and the form Kiarostami's own film assumes come together to dismantle the binary into a tertiary space. There is no formal idealism at work here to note or dismantle, for contrary to Kierkegaard, as Adorno reads him, Kiarostami does not make an abstraction from the lived existential anxieties he examines. For Adorno, by the "lead of knowledge over existence, the knowing subject participates in truth through semblance, a participation which imageless existence, in its empty depth, never achieves."[20] For Kiarostami that "knowing subject" becomes an unknowing subject precisely because of the collapse of form and fact, anxiety and aesthetics, coloniality and modernity, onto each other. The nature of reality is therefore altered here not by any formal pronouncement or aesthetic manipulation but by the aesthetic collapse of form and fact onto each other. This, we might add here, is an aspect of postcolonial formalism entirely alien to the European philosophizing about "construction of the aesthetic."

As one more evidence, we see this collapse of form and fact unto each other perhaps best in the series of photography Kiarostami created and called *Regardez-moi/Look at Me*, in which he stages visitors to the Louvre and other museums, making a spectacle out of spectators and what they are watching, something he had done in his film *Shirin* (2008) and also in his adaptation of Ta'ziyeh performances, where he films, edits, and screens faces of the audience watching a performance of the Persian "Passion Play."[21] In these series of photographs, he frames the reframing of the work of art with the spectator as part of his own frame. This is the signature recipe of Kiarostami for collapsing form and fact by way of altering our experiences of the nature of reality, and thus his proclivity toward an aesthetic intuition of transcendence where as an Iranian, a Muslim, a third-world artist, and all other such forms of framing and alienating him from himself under the colonial gaze, he overcomes them all by framing the framers, and that is precisely how we should see his work as evidence of a film-philosophy beyond the reach of European philosophy. I repeat: The epistemic violence done to his work by force-feeding him to the self-referential "European philosophy" has been insightful in a violent kind of a way. But ultimately, as the framer of the European frame, his artworld requires an entirely opposite mode of thinking.

TASTE OF CHERRY: VERFREMDUNGSEFFEKT AS BEING-TOWARD-DEATH

Let us take the collapse of fact and form into each other as one crucial cornerstone of his film-philosophy one step further—framing it within the dramaturgical impact of Verfremdungseffekt. *Taste of Cherry* (1997) is arguably one of Kiarostami's most complete, poetically most cogent take on being-toward-death, a self-conscious awareness of the contingency-of-being, actively conscious of itself by making the central character for the duration of the whole film seeking the impossibility of ontologically being-toward-death. The evidently suicidal man at the center of the story is not hopeless, or at least we have no indication of that. He is just at the moment of our encounter with him, as we look at him close-up looking away from us, in search of a dignified death, already there—of being-unto-death. He is in effect the personification of being-after-death—a dead man driving. He has died before his death as the famous prophetic statement ("Die before your death") would have it for Muslims. In that being-after-death, he is the walking, driving personification of his (and our) contingency-of-being visually evident, of fragility of being. At the heart of *Taste of Cherry* is therefore a Khayyamesque fear of death turned upside down into a celebration of a fragile awareness of life. The Khayyam at the heart of this poetic reflection on death links the archaic moment of the old Persian poet to Kiarostami's uncanny visual musings. Kiarostami in effect transforms Khayyam's jovial remembrance of death by way of celebrating life into sonorous long takes and long shots where we are free to follow the meandering of the man into the hidden dramas of his being-toward-death. Kiarostami prolongs that musing for exactly the entirety of the film, and then allows for only a postscript V-effect (Verfremdungseffekt) at the very end of the film, where we see the director, his cast, and his crew shooting the last shot of the film—of themselves, as if Kiarostami was contemplating his own mortality by framing it inside a V-effect breaking of the Fourth Wall we never knew was there.

But in *Taste of Cherry*, Abbas Kiarostami goes far beyond Khayyam in his posturing of being-toward-death. For here Kiarostami does not just celebrate life by pondering death, as in the glorious monologue of Mr. Bagheri who works at the taxidermic institute, he does something far more frightening, far more exhilarating. He, Kiarostami, for the duration of the film, exposes the totality, the infinity and yet also the perceptive fragility of life by way of placing it self-consciously in the bosom of being-in-the-world. Every time the man encounters a stranger, he inquires to see if the stranger would come to bury him where he seems to plan to be found dead; at the moment of his being-toward-death, he comes closer to being-in-the-world. Here his closest mystic approximation is the Sufi notion of *fana* as opposed to *baqa*—or *dying while still alive*. In the figure of his chief protagonist, Mr. Badii, Kiarostami brings the two opposites closest together, whereby ending being becomes momentarily evident in forever-annihilating by forcing us for the whole duration of the film to look, watch, and observe a dead man walking, persuading, cajoling while driving. At that moment, Mr. Badii is Sadegh Hedayat who committed suicide in Paris in 1951, and he is Forough Farrokhzad who died in a tragic automobile accident in 1967, and he is also Sohrab Sepehri whose poetry was a joyous submission to death. Compared to those three iconic figures, Badii is decidedly ineloquent, mostly silent, and has a poker face mostly indecipherable. Badii becomes an abstraction of himself, less lonesome than lost in the solitude of his own abstraction, and thus the self-alienating force that becomes only visually blunt in the final Verfremdungseffekt sequence of the film.

Paradoxically, or perhaps just by sheer fate, the sudden and tragic death of Kiarostami himself has occasioned a much more serious encounter with his artworld through a sustained course of encountering and reassessing his lifetime legacy. This encounter must now be predicated on the cinematic idiomaticity of his enduring work, now forever severed from his person and persona. The combined effect of that idiomaticity and the grammatological utterances of his cinema are now cast onto the two interwoven framings of *textual authenticity* and *contextual embeddedness* of the texts he has left behind. With his death, a whole world has ended—the world he had seen and envisioned and is now left to be deciphered in terms domestic to his artworld. Why is Kiarostami's sudden and tragic death from medical malpractice such an irreplaceable loss and such a significant turning point in Iranian cultural history?[22] He became the summation of the best possible outcome of an entire aesthetic adventure that commenced entry into the twentieth century, came to full fruition in the last quarter of the twentieth century, and in the figure and artistic legacy of Kiarostami was finally globalized and given as a gift to the world at large. There were poets, to be sure, novelists, dramatists, artists, and even filmmakers as excellent, important, and exquisite as he was, or even more profoundly influential than he in his own homeland. But the global reception and celebration of Kiarostami's work became a reality sui generis and enabled it to summon all before or contemporaneous with him up, uplifting them to a higher notch and taking the result to a hermeneutically rich and rewarding stage. No one before Kiarostami in the contemporary registers of Iranian cultural history had achieved that depth of exegetical promise. In both that summation and that global encounter, Kiarostami became the only Iranian artist history had destined for this grand finale. He thus became the Verfremdungseffekt to his own legacy, first building and then collapsing it into itself, morphing the form and the fact of his lifework together, as if his entire life were devoted to finding a resting place for his legacy and asking his audience to come and bury him in awe and with dignity, just like Mr. Badii in *Taste of Cherry*.

THE POETIC ONTOLOGY OF BEING UN/REAL

The Verfremdungseffekt framing of the form and fact at the heart of Kiarostami's cinema points to the poetic ontology of his cinematic visions—and to see that in context we first need to step back a bit from Kiarostami and look at him in his natural home and habitat, for there and then he and his entire artworld could have easily slipped under the global radar by forces of reactionary politics and diversionary intellectual subterfuge. Iranian culture in the aftermath of the Constitutional revolution of 1906–1911 is defined by a constellation of poets, novelists, dramatists, artists, and filmmakers canonized on the premise of a public sphere that that can be traced back to sixteenth-century Isfahan as the capital of the Safavid dynasty.[23] How did these poets, artists, and literati come together as a force with a renewed understanding of their own being-in-the-world? How does that being place itself in the world and confront reality?[24] Paradoxically, the revolutionary condition of 1977–1979 was emotively made inevitable precisely by this poetic ontology of being un/real. This ontology was never actively philosophized or theorized. It was just sensed and practiced. The Iranian Revolution of 1977–1979 brought that under-theorized ontic reality to a volcanic eruption. Before the organized brutality of Ayatollah Khomeini's charismatic terror categorically dismantled that public sphere and space and sent it into an internal exile, it was co-terminous with the moral imagination of the Iranian encounter with colonial modernity. The reactionary asceticism of Ayatollah Khomeini bred massive economic corruption and political tyranny and together with the military industrial complex and the garrison state that he enabled and that after him held his Islamist theocracy together sought to trample upon the active memory of that moral imagination with a gaudy "Islamism" that was itself the greatest invention of "the West" they thought they were combating.

The politics of the revolutionary momentum yielded to Khomeini's wanton violence and unbridled brutality in establishing his theocratic "republic." As he and his lieutenants slaughtered the members of the old regime, held diplomats hostage, prolonged a brutish war with Iraq, perpetrated mass execution of political prisoners, purged university professors, mounted obscene "cultural" revolutions, and put a price on world-renowned novelists, they created a fertile ground for the rise of a cadre of friendly thinkers that called itself "religious intellectuals" as the ideological officers of the new regime. These religious intellectuals, as they dubbed themselves, had massive official support and began to produce widespread Islamist thinking led by such institutions as *Halgheh Kian*/Kian Circle, with Abdolkarim Soroush, Mohamad Shabestari, Mashallah Shams al-Va'zin, Saeed Hajjarian, Mostafa Rokh-Sefat, Emad al-Din Baqi, Alireza Alavi Tabar, Arash Naraqi, Mohsen Kadivar, Akbar Ganji, and Yousefi-Eshkevari as their leading figures. They formed a neo-Islamist cadre of intellectuals that was in effect the offspring of Ali Shariati and Morteza Motahhari, the two leading ideologues of the Islamist revolt. The dialectical opposite of these religious intellectuals now emerged mostly in Europe and posed as militant secularists and modernists—without an iota of critical thinking about that "modernity." While religious intellectuals had a serious (though not solid) scholastic education, their secular counterparts led by Aramesh Dustdar had no serious academic training or discipline. They were amateurish pamphleteers on public aid from European governments where they mostly led a parasitical life. People like Aramesh Dustdar, Mohammad Reza Nikfar, Daryush Ashuri, et cetera soon emerged as the doppelgänger of religious intellectuals. No substance or purpose of their own, but the negative side of their take on the religious intellectuals—the scene had become quite banal. Both these opposing groups had aspects of their opinion in the pre-Islamist takeover but were in full fruition in the postrevolutionary time when the rise of the geopolitics of the region cast a long and lasting shadow over the cultural character and displacement of Iranian reality, its very poetic ontology of being real in the unreal. Kiarostami and his colleagues happened at this critical juncture and were it not for the global attention he and his colleagues received, their voices and visions would have been overwhelmed, silenced, and blinded by the ruling pathology of the religious intellectuals and their nemesis.

The false and falsifying brewing between the religious and the secular cast its mundane shadow over a long and lasting history and began to divide them into their own and their opposing camps. By the time of the Islamic Republic, the towering figures of Persian poetry and fiction, drama and cinema, had reached their crescendo zenith just before they were brutally censored and some silenced. Nima had died but Shamlou and Akhavan-e Sales were still alive. Forough Farrokhzad had passed away; Amir Naderi, Ebrahim Golestan, Sohrab Shahid Sales, and Bahman Farmanara had left the country; Bahram Beiza'i was there, though mostly banned from filmmaking. Eventually things began to change. In poetry, with the death of Shamlou no other great poet did or could ever emerge. With the death of Houshang Golshiri, Mahmoud Dolatabadi was still alive but had produced his most significant work in the 1960s and 1970s. His *Colonel* (1980s) was his last great work. Sa'edi and Shahid Sales drank themselves to death in Paris and Chicago, respectively. Iranian culture went into shock and a subsequent shutdown and played under the radar. Eventually a new generation of filmmakers emerged, unmatched by any new generation of poets or novelists. As this generation of filmmakers took off with Rakhshan Bani-Etemad, Jafar Panahi, and Bahman Qobadi chief among them, they took their cues mostly from previous generations of poets, novelists, dramatists, and of course filmmakers. Poetry and fiction from Nima and Hedayat gave their baton to filmmakers and joined eternity. With very few exceptions, like Ghazaleh Alizadeh and Abbas Maroufi, no great poet, no serious novelist, no major dramatist emerged over the last almost half a century to come anywhere near the old generation. Cinema, however, had a bold new life, with filmmakers like Mohsen Makhmalbaf, Jafar Panahi, Rakhshan Bani-Etemad, and Bahman Qobadi daring the elements and producing some extraordinary works. Their work, however, would have remained entirely under the radar and unnoticed were it not for the sudden global attention that Abbas Kiarostami rightly received and richly deserved. Unbeknownst to the rest of the world, Kiarostami's artworld was the tip of this iceberg, as he turned the aesthetic intuition of transcendence evident in this fertile ground into a visual sublimity that seemed to have appeared out of nowhere.

It is at this point that Kiarostami's poetic ontology of the un/real soars to define his cinema—as perhaps best evident in one of his earliest masterpieces, *Traveler* (1974), in the sequence where the resourceful Qassem uses a fake camera to pretend to take pictures of his friends to swindle them of the little change they have to go to Tehran to watch the football match. As Qassem assumes the directorial role of Kiarostami and tells his victims to do one thing or another, Kiarostami's own (not so fake camera) registers some of the most glorious examples of the un/real, as the children pose from their "normal" look to their fake postures. We have multiple layers of real and un/real at work here—first for us is Kiarostami's real but invisible camera that records all these events, second is Qassem's broken but visible camera which is fake but is the real cause of the gesticulation for the children, and third is the fusion of these real and un/real cameras that forms the layered lenses though which we see the gesticulations of the children, never certain if they are posing for the un/real but visible camera of Qassem or the real but invisible camera of Kiarostami, or both, or neither. This entire sequence is a virtuoso performance in staging the poetic ontology of the un/real, in the midst of which we completely lose sight and sense of what is real and what is unreal, for form and fact have morphed into a tertiary space and entered a different register.

THE REPRESSED AESTHETICS OF A POST-ISLAMIST THEOLOGY

One could look at Kiarostami's artworld, as I have, as the repressed aesthetics embedded in a post-Islamist theology that can only be articulated now in hindsight. In my *Shi'ism: A Religion of Protest*, I have discussed aspects of Kiarostami's cinema as a response to the politics of despair, and a bifurcation between reality and representation.[25] But the implications of that bifurcation are far-reaching and open up to an interface between an aesthetic of emancipation and a liberation theology beyond the militant Islamism in which Kiarostami's cinema became a potent antidote. For that link, we need to consider a major intellectual force that predates Kiarostami's rise to prominence. Kiarostami's first short film was made in 1970, almost the same year that the leading Iranian public intellectual Jalal Al-e Ahmad died at a very young age. The two major figures may appear as entirely irrelevant to each other. But they are not. Jalal Al-e Ahmad (1923–1969) was arguably the most important public intellectual of Iran in the twentieth century.[26] No other public intellectual comes even close to his fame and significance. To be sure, he was no poet commanding the power and significance of Nima Yushij and his followers. His works of fiction, bar a few exceptions, were mostly negligible. He was no dramatist like his close friend Gholamhossein Sa'edi, or a filmmaker like Dariush Mehrjui. He had no lasting influence in these or any other specific artistic or literary endeavor. But he had something that no one else had. He had public audacity. He had a global vision when all his other contemporaries were mostly domestic in their immediate purposes. He was bold, daring in his critical imagination, braving uncharted waters to compare, contrast, analyze, theorize, embolden, and push forward. He was Frantz Fanon, Aimé Césaire, Albert Memmi, Edward Said, and Noam Chomsky all wrapped up in one bold Persian prose and politics. He brought the world, Latin America and African revolutionaries, Asian and European thinkers, the US and its entire imperial project, for his nation to read. As such, I have seen and detailed his significance for a post-Islamist liberation theology that is worldly and self-conscious of that worldliness.

Al-e Ahmad knew Iran inside out, having literally walked it from one end to another, writing ethnographic monographs in places he visited. He traveled to the US, Europe, the USSR, and Mecca (the four "Qiblas," as he called them) and wrote detailed, powerful accounts of them. He revolutionized Persian prose with his own unique, fast, quick-witted prose that many of his contemporaries mimicked but no one matched. He brought his global vision to bear on the audacity of poets and literati on whom he wrote pioneering and deeply insightful essays. He wrote on Nima, on Hedayat, and on every major and minor cultural development of his time. Without him, none of his contemporaries would have, or could have, imagined themselves performing always already in a global context. This above all was his enduring contribution to prepare the stage for the arrival of Abbas Kiarostami.

Al-e Ahmad had created the discourse and crafted the premise for the understanding of a worldly self-confidence, as Abbas Kiarostami sublated that confidence in decidedly visual and cinematic terms. Poetry and fiction were very much untranslatable, as were drama and other literary arts—and this fact of untranslatability was as much an attractive theoretical proposition as it has remained a philosophical cul de sac. It was therefore only visual and performing arts that had the unique and uncharted possibility of taking the Iranian sense and sensibilities to a global audience. Modern and contemporary arts were limited and very much domestic in their reach—only in the career of Kiarostami, and even that toward the end of his life, did the international art scene come anywhere near the rich and diversified film scene. In art, there were accomplished artists like Aydin Aghdashloo, Hannibal Elkhas, Koorosh Shishegaran, and many others; in photography, the work of the late master Bahman Jalali had reached a global audience by the end of his life. The combined effect of modern and neoclassical theater (Beiza'i, Akbar Radi, and Gholamhossein Sa'edi) had much to appeal to the younger generation and yet was very limited to nonexistent global reach. In cinema in particular, a number of leading filmmakers had paved the way for the eventual rise and reception of Kiarostami as the chief aesthetician of the post-Islamist liberation theology Al-e Ahmad had foretold. If the culmination of these artists and filmmakers in Kiarostami was accidental, the preparatory intellectual scene that had a deep-rooted urban theology of its own was not accidental. Al-e Ahmad was chiefly responsible for articulating it.

In what terms might we talk about the aesthetic dimensions of a post-Islamist liberation theology? A major theological theme in Kiarostami's cinema, centered around the conception of soteriology, is to be detected in his Koker Trilogy, formed in the aftermath of a devasting earthquake in northern Iran, when he traveled there to detect and outline the contours of life in the midst of death and destruction. The central theme of this trilogy—*Where Is the Friends House?* (1987), *And Life Goes On* (1991), and *Through the Olive Tress* (1994)—is the meaning of life and death (and therefore a soteriological conception of worldly salvation) under the duress and despair of an earthquake. The Koker Trilogy (or Earthquake Trilogy, as it is sometimes called) took its name because the films were mostly shot around the village of Koker, at the site of the earthquake. The trilogy did not begin with that intention when *Where Is the Friend's House?* was made, but when the earthquake happened in Rudbar and Manjil on 20 June 1990, and Kiarostami made his *And Life Goes On*, it took that turn and concluded with *Through the Olive Trees*—in which he makes a reluctant Adam and Eve out of Hossein and Tahereh.

There is a tongue-in-cheekness about the trilogy and its underlying metaphysics of salvation that starts with the second of the three and thereafter dominates the whole set. This tongue-in-cheek filmic prose (you never know if he is really serious or just makes it up as he goes along) works through a suspended realism, where we think we are watching something quite serious and all the visual and emotive accoutrements of the films testify to that and yet things progress in a slightly incredulous if not altogether frivolous suspense. That borderline of irreality is where Kiarostami hangs his truth-claims on a metaphysics that is not foundational, it is not serious, in the sense that Nietzsche meant it in his *Beyond Good and Evil*, "suppose truth is a woman, what then?" That particular aesthetic suspense is best suited for a post-Islamic liberation theology of which Al-e Ahmad was a harbinger. Long after his death and now soon after Kiarostami's, the two have come together.

TOWARD A POETICS OF DIVINE IN/VISIBILITY

If so, if we can look at Kiarostami's cinema as the aesthetic dimension of a post-Islamist theology, then we need to attend to the immediate next question as to in what terms is that aesthetic cinematic. What in the simplest terms defines our disposition toward Kiarostami's cinema is the enduring issue of ocularity—what can we and can we not see, and that goes straight to the heart of a poetic of sublime visuality at the doctrinal center of the Islamic conception of the Prophet's nocturnal ascent to the heavens to meet with God, or Mi'raj. It is here that Muslim theologians, philosophers, and poets alike have had to answer a very basic question: Is God visible or invisible to the naked eye? The theological debate around the central question of whether God is visible to the naked eye or not has been a central issue in Islamic doctrinal history. But at the same time, this very doctrinal issue entails a deeply rooted question of ocularity, of what it means to see or not to see. As one of the most iconic articles of faith testing this question, Mi'raj posits the prospects of "seeing" God. Did he see him with his own mortal eyes? Was this a real journey or just a figurative allusion? One of the most significant poetic occasions of reflecting on the matter is in fact in the twelfth-century Persian poet Hakim Nezami's *Khamseh* where on multiple occasions when he is praising the Prophet he turns his attention to the question of Mi'raj. This occasion is the focal point of what is behind the whole spectrum of Suvar-e Khayal in Persian poetry, together forming what constitutes the nucleus of the ocularity of Persian aesthetics.

The debate of the in/visibility of God is not a mere theological issue for it is precisely here where the active poetics of visuality is also located—between reason and faith, between divinity and humanity, between the mortal and the immortal, which is where the world is seen through its invisibility to the divine presence—where in cinematic terms the camera in effect becomes the instrument of divine vision. Here is where the prophetic and the poetics come together and transmute—in poets like Nezami who thought the vision of God was physical and philosophers like Avicenna who thought it metaphoric—where the possibility of seeing God oscillates between reason and intuition, physical and metaphysical. But in the doctrine also dwells a meditation on the invisibility of the Derridean Transcendental Signified—as the reassuring certitude that the system actually coheres. As that invisible instrument, the "Transcendental Signified" that makes visibility possible, the camera becomes a meditation on the invisibility of truth—the God-term of a semiotic culture incarnate. Here, whether or not God can be seen with mortal eyes is tantamount to

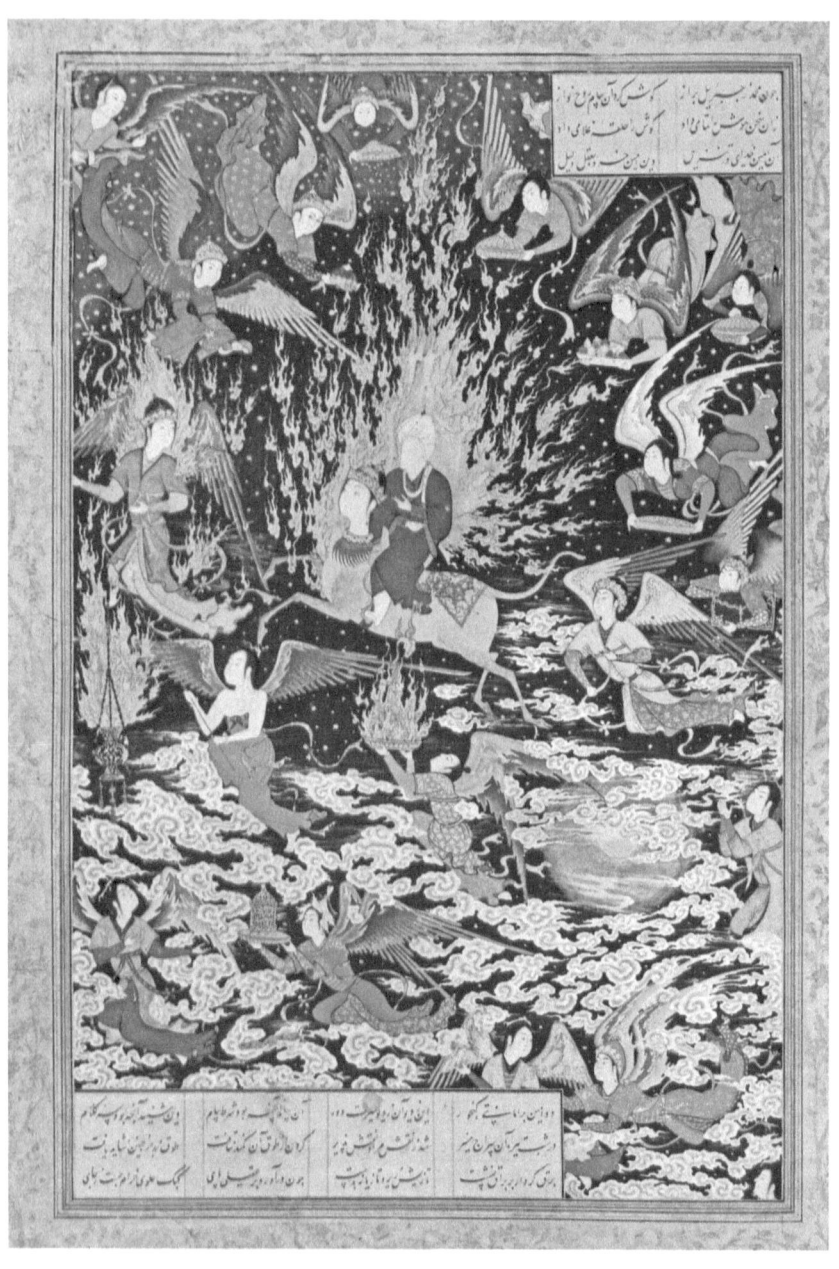

Figure 4. "The Ascent of the Prophet Muhammad to the Heavens" (Mi'raj) from a *Khamseh* of Nezami, Attributed to Sultan Muhammad, circa 1539–43. Reproduced with permission.

wondering if truth can be discerned through mortal means—the incompatibility of the immortal Truth to the mortal eyes. The two cannot touch except through the aesthetic mediation in poetry and pre-cinematic filmic meditation in a visual culture—and thus both the undecidability of the poetic diction and the translucence of the cinematic fiction become the interface between truth and representation.

If we were to collapse Avicenna's ontology and Derrida's deconstruction onto each other, as it were, we might suggest something like this: the Transcendental Signified or the unmoved mover becomes the simulacrum of an ultimate referent at the center of a signifying system as if it were, by necessity, outside that system. The dominant metaphysics of the system perforce relies on this foundational signification of its most indispensable factor to be inadmissible into its system. All other signifieds are, as Avicenna would say, *Mumkin al-Wujud*, or Contingent Beings, while the Transcendental Signified is the *Wajib al-Wujud*, or the Necessary Being, without which the whole system it implicitly sustains collapses. The in/visibility of the Divine Being is the *conditio sine qua non* of this metaphysics, for the Divine must always remain In/Visible—outside the system of signification. This premise might lead us toward a Mi'raj theory of cinematic vision, or the poetics of the in/visibility of God. The Transcendental Signified of the Persian poetics is where the world can be seen from God's point of view—though by necessity He Himself cannot be seen, for if He were seen, the whole system of signification, of seeing and being seen, of truth and all its varied narratives, will collapse.

Throughout the classics of Persian poetic discourses, we have a crucial segment about the Prophet's Mi'raj, when Muhammad is believed to have ascended to the heavens and visited with God, which means he is thought to have seen Him and then come back to earth. This of course is an article of faith that Muslims as Muslims believe in its veracity. Let us consider the basic outline of Mi'raj as we understand it in Qur'anic terms. Based on chapter 17: Al-Isra/The Night Journey and other chapters, Muslims believe God summoned the Prophet and moved him from Masjid al-Haram to Masjid al-Aqsa to show him His signs. "Glory to him who journeyed his servant by night, from the Sacred Mosque, to the Farthest Mosque, whose precincts We have blessed, in order to show him of Our wonders. He is the Listener, the Beholder" (17:1). There are also persistent reports by the Prophet's companions to that effect. Muslims believe the Mi'raj to be *Jismani*, or physical, and the narrative that Nezami uses in his poetic articulations begins at the house of Umm Hani, Ali's sister. From there, he mounts Buraq, a mythical steed, and thus he "flies" from Mecca to Masjid al-Aqsa in the company of Archangel Gabriel. From Masjid al-Aqsa in Jerusalem, he is then flown to Sidrah al-Muntaha, the tree that marks the utmost boundary in the Seventh Heaven, where all other prophets and planets are delighted in his company. At the Sidra al-Muntaha, Archangel Gabriel can no longer keep the Prophet company, at which point the Prophet changes his steed to Rafraf, and thus from Sidra al- Muntaha he reaches Qab-e Qusayn, or the span of two bows, and from there he finally reaches God, where Nezami specifically says Muhammad saw God with his own physical eyes. Some have interpreted this encounter as purely spiritual, others as entirely physical, and still others as part physical and part spiritual. This is what Nezami says:

> Since the Absolute is most desired,
> He saw God and God is visible—
> Seeing Him should not be denied to eyes,
> May He who has seen Him and not said so go blind—
> The Prophet saw Him not with any other eyes,
> But with these very eyes we have in our head—
> That vision though was not in any place—
> Nor going there took any passage of time.[27]

Here we may think of the camera as the instrument standing as the simulacrum of the visibility of the otherwise invisible, the site of the unseen becoming visible, from metaphoric to instrumental, in our reading of ocularity, just as Dziga Vertov would argue through his Kino-Pravda series and *Man with a Movie Camera* (1929), for through Kiarostami's or any other camera, we are approaching a vision of the sublime credibility of the evident otherwise hidden to our naked eye. To begin with Nezami's poetic of the Divine Visibility, the transmutation of the prophetic to the poetic allows for our vision of Kiarostami's camera as the instrumental enabling of an ocularity toward the sublime otherwise hidden to the naked and the mortal gaze. By and large the camera itself is the Transcendental Signified, the Unseen Seer, except for when as in the end of *Taste of Cherry* or throughout *Homework* and elsewhere he makes the camera visible to itself. The poetic of the Divine in/visibility that poets like Nezami enable defines the ocular disposition of the Persian aesthetic imagination. This is where Kiarostami's aesthetic articulation of a post-Islamist liberation theology thrives on the poetic ontology of being un/real and invisible, and this is how he has altered the nature of reality, as we perceive it through his camera, where an intuition of self-transcendence is made possible, where the contingency of the real is the location of Kiarostami's camera where he stands and declares himself, best rooted as he is in the condition of coloniality of his aesthetic imagination. This is precisely where we can raise philosophical questions in and about his cinema, deeply rooted in the repertoire of Suvar-e Khayal extending from the Persian poetic imagination into Kiarostami's poetically cultivated camera.

2 Aesthetic Alienation

Time was not passing through me—
I was a naked ecstasy.[1]

Sohrab Sepehri, "*Lahzeh-ye Gomshodeh*/The Lost Moment" (1332/1953)

History is the subject of a structure whose site is not homogenous, empty time, but time filled by the presence of the now. [Jetztzeit]. . . . A historical materialist cannot do without the notion of a present which is not a transition, but in which time stands still and has come to a stop.[2]

Walter Benjamin, "Thesis on the Philosophy of History" (1940)

The articulation of the Persian poetic premises of the invisible world that Kiarostami's cinema is making visible is necessary but not sufficient, for Kiarostami's artworld, crafted and coined in his homeland first and foremost, eventually goes global through a double semiotic gestation of "secular" (which for much of the world translates as "colonial") alienation that at once constitutes and yet disempowers its immediate postcolonial audiences. In between overtly politicized art and alienated spectatorship, the floating signifiers of his artworld remain full of unrealized possibilities. The global audience that European film festivals have fortuitously given to Kiarostami's cinema is both a blessing and a paradox in our encounter with his legacy—for that very first European and then global audience both affords it a very much welcomed worldly disposition and gives it an empowering interpretative space, and yet paradoxically affirms its place in a colonially compromised (mitigated) hermeneutic context. The theoretical task at hand is therefore to recognize and celebrate that global audience for the varied interpretative framings it has enabled and yet come to terms with its alienating effect on the legacy of Kiarostami's cinema and other visual and poetic works.

The global audience that Kiarostami's cinema richly deserved and aptly received entailed an element of aesthetic alienation, to the point that at least some of his immediate Iranian and other non-European spectators no longer recognized themselves in his cinema and became extremely suspicious of that reception and resorted to all sorts of bizarre conspiracy theories, which in turn resulted in much misplaced anger and animosity toward his cinema. I recall a heated conversation with the late Egyptian film critic Samir Farid (1943–2017) in Locarno in the late 1990s in which he was severely critical of Kiarostami's cinema and found it odd and based entirely on a hidden agenda that major European film festivals were celebrating him. He was appreciative of other aspects of Iranian cinema as, for example, represented by Dariush Mehrjui. But he adamantly dismissed Kiarostami's cinema as affirming Europeans' Orientalizing view of a Muslim society! That alienating effect, however, is itself a dialectically enabling force in a perfectly paradoxical way we need to decipher. This argument might be best worked out through Kiarostami's Koker Trilogy as the defining moment of his cinema as it exists today in its natural habitat in both known and still uncharted global territories. The soteriological dimensions of the Koker Trilogy, to which I just alluded in the previous chapter, here need to be seen in light of the aesthetic alienation it entails and conceals. But to bring these two forces together, we need to go upstream from such specifics and see what might be the cause of that aesthetic alienation. Abbas Kiarostami's artworld did not happen in a vacuum nor did its widespread reception, both inside his homeland and far away from it.

AESTHETIC ALIENATION AND ITS SELF-CENTERING BLIND SPOT

What exactly might the terms of this "aesthetic alienation" be? What does it mean if we were to say Kiarostami was "an Iranian filmmaker," or even at least nominally "a Muslim filmmaker?" What would such designation mean or do to our reception of his artworld? Here we need to dwell on the issue of "aesthetic alienation" upstream from Kiarostami and come carefully toward him.

In 1992, J. M. Bernstein published a seminal study of Kant, Derrida, and Adorno, in which he argued persuasively against the recent, post-Kantian distinction between the domain of the beautiful and that of the true, and therefore the good, thereby seeking to articulate, as these seminal European philosophers have, an autonomous domain for art. This articulation Bernstein considered a quintessentially modern phenomenon. This "aesthetic alienation," as he termed it, first separates art from truth and then seeks to articulate a relationship between them. To be sure, "this discordance of art and truth, in the face of which Nietzsche felt holy dread," he stipulates, "is as old as philosophy itself." However, it has become the constitutive feature of modernity: "Modern, autonomous art—the art whose form has become autonomous from the dominion of the metaphysical assumptions and orientations of Christian faith—has been expelled from modern societies, from the constitutive, cognitive, and practical mechanisms producing and reproducing societal modernity."[3]

Bernstein's designation of European "modernity" as the site of this alienation becomes doubly significant if we were to extend it from its ideological epicenter to what the rest of the world has experienced as "colonial modernity," where the sense of this partition between truth and the beautiful is entirely against the very grain of not just the received history but in fact the lived experiences of people under the political sway of European colonialism and its ideological foregrounding in its "Modernity," which Bernstein, like all other European and Eurocentric philosophers, falsely reads for global modernity. The issue becomes even more Eurocentric if we pay closer attention to Bernstein's designation of this schizophrenic partition specifically from the domain of Christianity, which makes it even more irrelevant to the non-Christian world, though hegemonic in its political implications. What is philosophically designated as "Modernity" is in fact *capitalist modernity*, which has an extended colonial shadow that engulfs the entirety of the human encounter with Europe. This Eurocentric partition between truth and the beautiful is of course entirely inimical not only with the history of Christianity itself (where art has been put to the service of the Christian truth) but with aesthetic domains like that of

Islam where the beautiful *is* the true—as evident in the famous saying attributed to Shi'i Imams: "Inna Allah Jamilun wa Yuhibbu al-Jamal/God is Beautiful and He loves beauty!" But the alienation caused by the condition of coloniality has radically overcome that fact too. The provincial Eurocentricity of such philosophical observations becomes particularly acute when the prose and politics of their delivery assume false universal claims.

At the core of this European (capitalist) modernity is what the German sociologist Max Weber (1864-1920) considered "disenchantment" with the world and what subsequently Jürgen Habermas re-emphasized as the quintessence of the experience of modernity:

> For Weber, the intrinsic ... relationship between modernity and what he called "Occidental rationalism" was still self-evident. He described as "rational" the process of disenchantment which led in Europe to a disintegration of religious world views that issued in a secular culture. With modern empirical sciences, autonomous art, and theories of morality and law grounded on principles, cultural spheres of value, took shape which made possible learning processes in accord with the respective inner logics of theoretical, aesthetic, and moral practical problems.[4]

From Weber to Habermas, the formation of "an autonomous art" is definitive to the project of European modernity—whether as a final fragmentation of human experience or else its opposite, preserving the domain of art as a camouflaged religious space for salvation.

How does this aesthetic alienation definitive to European modernity become manifest in Kiarostami's artworld? We need to address this question not in the insularity of any postcolonial artist, but precisely in terms that make them meaningful to the world at large. Reclaiming him either into his immediate (local) habitat or else catapulting him into his distant (global) reception will both do irrevocable damage to the totality of his aesthetic whereabouts. By virtue of his global reception, Kiarostami was the most significant cultural event of Iran in the twentieth century. He was to twentieth century what Hafez was to Goethe, Omar Khayyam to Fitzgerald, Ferdowsi to Matthew Arnold, Zarathustra to Nietzsche and before him to Mozart. All of these iconic comparisons are comparative, dialogical, bipolar. Hafez needed a Goethe to ride on the back of European colonialism and become a global phenomenon, as did Rumi need German Romanticism and American Transcendentalism, or the figure of Zarathustra did Nietzsche and Mozart.[5] This does not mean Hafez or Rumi or Khayyam or Zarathustra were not what they were to the worldly and imperial imagination of the Persianate world long before their European discoveries. What this means is the acknowledgement of the globality of the European imperial imagination making their Persian icons—as they did their Indian, Egyptian, African, and other "Oriental" icons—integral to their colonial iconography of culture and imperialism. From Zarathustra to Rumi, European Persophilia ushered the Persianate world into the imperial imaginary of Europe, while at the same time it enabled the shadow empire of bygone glories to reframe these iconic events in the Persianate world itself.

In the cases of Hafez, Sa'di, Ferdowsi, Rumi, and Khayyam, their European reception was not tantamount to any occasion for aesthetic alienation. Quite to the contrary: their European reception became a small part of the larger hermeneutic circle in which these seminal Persian poets were historically received. The same must be the case with Abbas Kiarostami. However, Kiarostami's reception at European film festivals and galleries and subsequently by European film and philosophy discourses happened at a different moment in the globalization of capital and culture—when in postmodernism, late capitalism had found its cultural logic, as Fredric Jameson would say.[6] The aesthetic alienation we detect at the reception of Kiarostami's artworld as a result becomes a double-edged sword whereby the aesthetic experience itself crafts the metaphysics of its own, irreducible either to the Islamic or Persianate logic of its past, or the colonial logic of its present, or a fortiori the postcolonial reason of its future receptions. In its encounter with works such as those of Kiarostami, the aesthetic alienation at its European epicenter discovers its own blind spots when that modernity that had caused it went around the globe colonizing peoples and their cultures, as it did their material resources and moral imagination alike.

AESTHETIC ALIENATION UNDER POLITICAL DURESS

Here it would be helpful to revisit a critical preamble that the distinguished American film critic Jonathan Rosenbaum writes on why and how Iranian cinema became a staple of a global scene. Here is how he formulates it:

> It is an unavoidable truism that any effort to nail down the specifics of a national cinematic "new wave" in an authoritative manner is doomed to a certain amount of mythmaking.... The Iranian New Wave, then, is not one but many potential movements, each with a somewhat different frame and honor roll.... I'd like to propose a lesser-known short film, ... Forough Farrokhzad's *The House Is Black* (1962).... More than any other Iranian film that comes to mind, *The House Is Black* highlights the paradox that while Iranians continue to be among the most demonized people on the planet (along with their neighbors to the west, the Iraqis), Iranian cinema is becoming almost universally recognized by critics as among the most ethical and humanist.... Two major factors appear to be at play: The most obvious one is the Iranian hostage crisis during the Carter administration.... The second major factor is that practically no other contemporary image of Iran has been available in the West to counter or even complicate the fundamentalist stereotype. It might be argued, indeed, that the emergence of the Iranian New Wave on the international film scene was motivated in part by a desire to fill in a blank page.[7]

In both its blindness and its insights, this passage encapsulates what I have proposed to be both a blessing and a curse and therefore a paradox in our encounter with Kiarostami's legacy—for the kind of critical assessment and reception that leading critics like Rosenbaum offer Kiarostami both helps detail his worldly disposition and yet at the very same time places him in a colonially compromised context. Rosenbaum is of course correct that since the US hostage crisis of 1979–1980, Iran as a country and a state has been systematically demonized, with some perfectly legitimate reasons—such as the barbaric act of taking the diplomats of another country hostage, even American diplomats who have had a history of plotting military coups in Iran. He is also right that in Iranian cinema there are indications of what he terms "ethical and humanist" dimensions. But the paradox that Rosenbaum detects and exaggerates—are Iranians really "the most demonized people on the planet" or just in the United States?—is itself exacerbated by the false binary that he posits between Kiarostami or Farrokhzad's cinema and the history of the country that had resulted in the hostage crisis.

Iranian cinema of Kiarostami or any other filmmaker is what it is not despite the Iranian history but because of it. So, Kiarostami's cinema is not a paradoxical humanism standing vis-à-vis the political criminality of the US hostage crisis—under which smoke screen the militant Islamists took the democratic aspirations of a nation hostage. There is therefore a tertiary space, an interstitial space, where the two events—a traumatic event in the history of a nation and the art that that very nation produces—stand not against but in fact right next to each other, where the separation that Bernstein, Habermas, and Weber detect in European modernity between the partitioned realms of the aesthetics and the truth-claims of a political culture has not taken place at the colonial consequences of that very same European modernity. In order to see that, we must insert the frightful fact of colonialism right into the fraught conception of European capitalist modernity—which results not in a global claim on a vacuous "Modernity" but in a colonially compromised and mitigated fact of aesthetic alienation. The aesthetic alienation of which Bernstein writes is doubly exacerbated by critical encounters with Iranian cinema (or Kiarostami) where this fact is consistently ignored, a cliché "humanism" is attributed to a national cinema, and thereby a false binary introduced between that humanism and the barbarity of those who rule over it.

To unpack this idea of "colonial modernity" and the spin that it puts on aesthetic alienation, we need to visit the issue of "comparative modernities."

"COMPARATIVE MODERNITIES?"

Early in February 2019, I was invited by the Institute for Comparative Modernities to give a lecture and participate in a subsequent seminar. Based at Cornell University, the Institute for Comparative Modernities "addresses a key problem in the study of modern culture and society: the transnational history of modernity and its global scope." As they see it,

> a broad range of scholarship over the last few decades has contested and complicated the two primary dimensions of the received narrative of modernity: that it arose strictly within the confines of Europe; and that its extension outside Europe was a matter of simple diffusion and imitation. What is emerging instead is an account of modernity as a global process in which deep and multifarious interconnections have created complementary cultural formations.[8]

Seeking to replace that Eurocentricity, "the Institute is dedicated to the study of modernity in such a transnational and comparative perspective. Its primary emphasis will fall on neglected or under-studied articulations of modernity outside of the historically constituted hegemonic spaces of Europe and the United States, but it will also give serious attention to conflicts and complexities within the West." They believe that

> inadequate understandings of the complex history of modernity have led to simplistic and untenable positions that unknowingly repeat colonialism's ideological juxtapositions of "us" and "them," with modernity (and all the positive connotations of historical progress that accrue to the term) all on one side and inscrutable backwardness all on the other. This results in ghettoized scholarship that is damaging to all. The standard equation of modernity with the West needs to be problematized and opened up to comparative examination. The Institute hopes to galvanize work in this direction by encouraging cross-disciplinary collaborative research that advances a genuinely global analysis of modernity that is also empirically faithful to geographical and historical specificity. By bringing attention to less frequently studied aesthetic and social practices from non-Western and immigrant communities, the Institute hopes to correct accounts of modernity as primarily Western in origin and dynamics.[9]

By the time of this invitation, my work against the grain of colonial modernity and in the direction of exploring not theories of alternative modernities but alternative theories to modernity had advanced far. In my *Persian Literary Humanism* (2012), I had navigated some fourteen hundred years of Persian literary humanism, from the dawn of the Islamic period to the present without once in need of the words *secular* or *modern*, *secularism* or *modernity*—for me, all ideological subterfuges for European colonialism—colonizing even the tempo of our historical imagination. This critical position had allowed me to explore the inner dynamics of Persian literary humanism in terms domestic to the world in which it was born and came to fruition. In my *Persophilia: Persian Culture on the Global Scene* (2015), I did something different but complementary. I mapped out the transnational public sphere that included Europe but was not limited to Europe and was structurally linked to the world of capitalist modernity and its colonial shadows, where the bourgeois public sphere had become a global phenomenon. In my *Shi'ism: A Religion of Protest*

(2011), I made another complementary move, which was to map out the transmutation of revolutionary reason into public reason. In *Iran without Borders: Towards a Critic of the Postcolonial Nation* (2016), I took the whole idea of the "nation" to be a matter of public sphere—and therefore rooted in the transnational public sphere that had collapsed the colonial and the capital and perforce categorically against the interests of the state.

In these and other works, I have argued the idea of the transnational history of modernity is mitigated through the colonial apparatus that gave itself a European center and a global periphery. Any attempt at "comparative modernities" or "alternative modernities" is therefore an epistemically compromised exercise to yield to that condition of coloniality—thereby robbing people of their own historic experiences. In its global scope, this European modernity worked through the circular rhetoric of a center and a periphery that gave capitalist logic of production and all its ideological foregrounding a false conceptual assurance as it robbed nations of their own repressed, denied, colonized, and denigrated histories. Modernity in and of itself was a colonial project—colonizing both time and space, categories and concepts, facts and phenomena of other cultures resisting its corrosive powers, casting a cannibalizing gaze at the history of the world while conquering the planet as the teleological logic of its metaphorical centrality.

Consider the sublime aesthetic assurances of a short film like Kiarostami's *Take Me Home* (2016)—one among many others. Forget about its habitually minimalist "story" and just look at the aesthetic confidence of the shots that frame and form the film. This is not European modernity—and this is not "Iranian humanism." This is not colonial "Westernization"—and this is not an anticolonial gesture either. This exudes with a kind of poetic depth that comes from the hidden layers of an aesthetic legacy of a confident imperial imagination—no longer a territorial empire of lands and monuments but an aterritorial royalty of creative imagination. Yes, the history of European colonial modernity is there too—but the reality and truth of that poetic event is irreducible to any particular trace of "modernity" or "modernism." The paintings of Kamal al-Din Behzad (circa 1455–1535) are there and so are the designs of Persian carpets; the lyrical poetry of Hafez is there and the gnostic assurances of Rumi. Once we allow for such traces, the generic history of colonial modernity is no longer sufficient to account for the truth of this artworld.

I therefore believe "the standard equation of modernity with the West" should not be "problematized and opened up to comparative examination." Quite to the contrary: We should categorically abandon the secular project of comparative modernity for it is an unmitigated recipe for the colonial conquest of lands and minds together. The futile exercise will in fact colonize the entire history of human experiences and assimilate them backward precisely to that illusion that calls itself "the West" or "Western Modernity." We would be cloning this European modernity and casting the rest of human history into cookie-cutter versions of Europe. "A genuinely global analysis of modernity that is also empirically faithful to geographical and historical specificity" will in fact dismantle the universal applicability of the category of modernity—and seeks alternative theories of and for the prose of our historicality in terms other than European modernity. "Attention to less frequently studied aesthetic and social practices from non-Western and immigrant communities" will do precisely the opposite of recentering "Western modernity" by finding global replicas for it. The world was not created with and through European modernity. The world had and continues to live through no alternative but repressed universalities of entirely different gestations and genealogies—liberating and potent visions that are yet to be seen and theorized. The opposite of "Modernity" is not the "Traditions" it has imagined to corroborate itself. The opposite of "the secular" is not "the religions" it has invented to cross-authenticate itself. The task at hand is not to find alternative modernities but to discover the rich complexities of the worlds European secular modernity has concealed by the power of its hegemony—and see their artifacts in terms domestic to those universalities. This is how works of art are de-alienated from their own aesthetics. A "film-philosophy" that must assimilate everything about Kiarostami to what calls itself "western philosophy" is a recipe for such deeply alienating colonization. Neither Eurocentric nor Europhobic, we need a liberated critical imagination that embraces the totality of our world today and is equally at home in the aesthetic sensibilities that are not forced to self-alienation under the blinding insights of "Western philosophy." Thus liberated, we will see Kiarostami waiting for us at the threshold of his artworld.

AGAINST COLONIAL MODERNITY

The dominant and false assumption that modernity arose in Europe and that through its civilizing mission this Europe went around the world modernizing it will have to be understood in the colonial context of its conception and spread. Modernity was materially a global process via an aggressive cannibalization and exploitation of the world at large—its mineral resources, cheap labor, and moral imaginations alike. A transnational study of modernity exposes the colonial character of the project and the liberal gentility of imagining comparative perspectives will conceal and camouflage the brutality of that historical fact. Materially global and ideologically Eurocentric, modernity pacified resistances to its colonial logic whether domestic to its presumed center or foreign to its colonial conquests. Modernity slaughtered Native Americans, enslaved African Americans, and dropped the atomic bomb on Hiroshima and Nagasaki with the same logic that it "exterminated the brutes" in Asia and Africa, before it came back to roost in Europe and slaughtered six million European Jews without blinking an eye.[10] This is what Adorno and Horkheimer feared and fathomed in their *Dialectic of the Enlightenment* (1947) and Ernst Cassirer traced back to the rise of European Romanticism in response to Enlightenment Modernity in his *Myth of the State* (1946). But as Aimé Césaire and others had fully recognized, the colonial ravages of the same Enlightenment Modernity was fully on display in Asia, Africa, and Latin America long before it came back to haunt Europe itself. That full picture of Modernity from its presumed European center to its farthest colonial reaches is what we need to keep in mind when discussing its alienating effects of the artifact imagined and delivered outside the unreal centers of European modernity.

As a globalizing project, European modernity was and remains a capitalist ideology and as such always had a dark shadow and we, the world outside Europe, are it, we are that dark shadow from where some of us have come and received a PhD in our Ivy League universities to dismantle that false and falsifying paradox.[11] Capitalist modernity was the modus operandi of European Enlightenment that, long before Adorno and Horkheimer had detected its dialectic in the aftermath of the Jewish Holocaust, created multiple global holocausts in Asia, Africa, and Latin America and in the materially and morally violated migrant and enslaved communities within its own boundaries. We therefore need to think theories not of, but alternative to, modernity—certainly when we begin to look at the artifacts produced and staged in the shadow of that modernity. But first we must rescue them from the trap of the Orientalist and Third World-ist straitjacket of the alienating modernity and reactionary traditions into which they have been falsely incarcerated, and then explore them theoretically.

We must use the occasion of meditating on Kiarostami's artworld by way of reimagining repressed and relegated alterities to the European philosophical identity colonially imposed on the world and retrieve their universalizing contingencies and theorize their current relevance—not assimilating them backward to the chronological, epistemological, geographical, and perforce philosophical imaginaries of the colonizing cultures. The trouble with assumptions of comparative or even alternative modernities is precisely this assimilating varied world and worldly cultures backward to the dominant epistemologies while contesting their mere narrative articulations. The opposite direction of opting for nativism, obscurantism, Orientalism, exoticism, remedial romanticism, and perforce toward "alternative modernities" preempts the far more urgent task of thinking through an alternative theory *to* modernity—which I did in my *World of Persian Literary Humanism* (2012) more than a decade ago. European modernity ended and was buried in the colossal calamity of the Holocaust. If following Adorno and Foucault we were to consider this modernity as the epistemic tyranny of Reason by the constitution of the Unreason in asylum houses, here in the case of the fusion of fact and fantasy as factasy (as I have proposed about how to read Kiarostami) we are in a tertiary space where that tyranny cannot hold. Modernity was the primacy of Reason evident and excavated in varied forms of the technologies of selfhood and personhood and subjectivities. Adorno thought this instrumental reason ended up in Auschwitz and Foucault thought they posited technologies of repression, while Heidegger thought they culminated in a fake and falsifying humanism. The modernity of Reason for Europe was colonial treason to reason for the world at large. Colonial reason had turned the colonized person into a knowable object since Kant's three critiques and long before Heidegger wrote his "Question concerning Technology" (1954) when the entire discipline of anthropology had helped European colonialists by turning the world into knowable objects to the knowing European subject.

As many observers have pointed out, central to the rhythm of all the three films in the Koker Trilogy is the element of repetition, or *tekrar* in Persian, which instead of any modernist or postmodernist reading of it (or perhaps adjacent to it) we might in fact see rooted in the famous quatrain of Khayyam about the fragility of life—which of course makes sense in the context of the trilogy:

> When life is over what difference does it make
> If it were sweet or bitter—
> When a cup is full what difference does it make
> Whether it is in Baghdad or in Balkh—
> Drink for after you and me
> The moon will keep waxing and waning to no end.[12]

But instead of an either/or reading of the rhythmic repetition of the narrative formalism of the trilogy, we may think of a tertiary space where modernity will have made accommodation for both its colonial disposition and the repressed narrative alterities it has disabled.

The case against comparative modernities starts right here—where the knowable things cannot become knowing subjects with an oversight over the knowable worlds without dismantling the whole European project. Once we abandon the false promises of "comparative modernities," then the real issue surfaces that, if not a theory of comparative modernity, then what alternative theory to modernity might emerge—what other syncretic worlds have been hidden under the rubric of European colonial modernity? How can we begin to look at a work of art—Kiarostami's, Satyajit Ray's, or Kurosawa's, et cetera—without assimilating them backward to European philosophy or aesthetics—without altogether abandoning that project but making it integral to alternative emerging worlds? The critiques of colonial modernity and postcolonial reason are necessary of course—but not sufficient. Dwelling too much on these two adjacent stations preempts the possibilities of a postcolonial thinking subject beyond the colonial modernity of the primacy of reason and progress. Here's where the bugbear of "tradition" is plastered against "modernity" and the historical retrieval of "precolonial" thinking is first branded as such and thereby aborted. Few civilizational sites are capable of such critical thinking beyond the condition of European coloniality. China, India, Egypt, Islam in general, and in this particular case Iran, are among the civilizational contexts that have the longevity of culture, the density of history, the richness of creative and critical thinking that can offer sites of alternative theories not *of* but *to* modernity. The fields of knowledge called "Oriental" or "Area Studies" or Anthropology are all remnants of such ghettos of colonial knowledge production at the service of an imperial imagination that has long since exhausted its paradigmatic claim on our credulities. Eurocentric theories of modernity do epistemic violence, generate false and misguided insights, sustain useless and abusive thinking that does epistemic violence to other visual and performing cultures, whereby the postcolonial scenes must make themselves understood to the currency of the colonizers' exchange rates.

The safest place to start to imagine the existing but hidden worlds upon which the postcolonial person can become a knowing subject is from the fertile soil of the work of art itself, when Kiarostami picks up his camera and whispers to himself or those near him "Action!"

ALTERNATIVE TO MODERNITY: ALLEGORIES
OVER CATEGORIES

Let us now be even more specific and see how an alternative theory to modernity might look. How would a renewed pact with the primacy of the work of art affect our reading of Kiarostami in terms rooted in his artworld—a cosmovision at once embedded in the world and yet transcending it? Let us first consider three crucial moments in European philosophy that have in fact punctured its preoccupation with "Modernity" long before we reach the triumvirate of Heidegger, Foucault, and Derrida—when Reason and Progress are no longer decoupled from Unreason and Allegory. These moments are Nietzsche, Kierkegaard, and Dostoyevsky—whose collective work dismantles the sovereign Kantian subject casting his (and knowingly his only) gaze upon the world. The next triumvirate of Adorno, Horkheimer, and Benjamin is the negative dialectics of the selfsame Enlightenment Modernity having perforce ended in Auschwitz. It took the mighty force of Heidegger, Derrida, and Blanchot to bring European philosophy and literature back together—and thus question the sovereign European Reason and the knowing subject it had posited and empowered. In this poststructuralist collapsing of the philosophical and the literary, still the towering figures of Nietzsche, Kierkegaard, and Dostoyevsky map out the contours of a European moment of epistemic deliverance from all-powerful "Modernity" with profound implications for the postcolonial liberation of the sign of art not as alienated but in fact as emancipatory. In Nietzsche, Kierkegaard and Dostoyevsky, the postcolonial thinker sees solid philosophical and moral allies. But among them all, and by virtue of his self-consciously Jewish messianic disposition, the figure of Walter Benjamin towers closest to the heart of a postcolonial Muslim. Here, as a Muslim thinker, I have consistently pulled Benjamin (and after him Levinas) away from his European habitat, in which he was driven to suicide, underlined his Jewish messianic proclivities, and pulled him toward my own home and habitat where I find him speaking Persian to me.[13] The exercise has been exceedingly liberating in learning how to overcome Modernity in terms exercised by the most potent forces within European thought and yet actively othered by it. The farther we pull Benjamin and Levinas from their European habitat, the more actively they become conscious of their Jewish heritage and thus the more conversant with a Muslim thinker. Such strategic alliances, based on factual and evident philosophical and moral affinities, are crucial if we are not to fall flat into the dead-end of nativist thinking.

Such divergent points of contact or near misses (or elective affinities) between a Muslim and a Jewish (European) thinker are necessary to note if we are not to fall into the trap of reading "the non-European," thus self-alienated, into the humdrum of so-called Tradition that European modernity invented to justify its colonial conquests and in reality never was. The colonial world, by virtue of the power of coloniality, was all cast in the shadow of European modernity—and if incompatible with their profit margins were dubbed "traditional." When in figures like Nietzsche, Kierkegaard, or Benjamin that European modernity self-destructs and thus articulates its own philosophical moments of crisis, we have a window into our own colonized worlds too—where we can no longer be turned into native informers. There is a difference between Hegel and

Kierkegaard, between Kant and Benjamin, between Heidegger and Adorno, between Habermas and Derrida. We dwell postcolonially in the fractures of those differences, for those moments of divergence point to our colonial conditions, which even that Algerian Jewish philosopher Derrida could not quite see, for he was too much in the sun of his European identity.

Let us now see how we can overcome this European modernity. In "Abbas Kiarostami Remembered: Why He Was Iran's Essential Filmmaker," Robert Koehler writes: "Kiarostami was the free filmmaker par excellence, since he managed to find his ever-developing acute approach to modernism through whatever system in which he might find himself working."[14] We have to see the genealogy of that "modernism" next to the realism where Kiarostami could be equally placed. Koehler further explains: "It was a particularly rigorous modernism, which Kiarostami embraced and adapted to suit his own ends."[15] Others have linked Kiarostami to what they have already called "modernist Persian poetry," and thus by association a modernist filmmaker.[16] Others, however, including in my own previous work, have opted to think through his cinema in terms of realism. In my *Masters and Masterpieces of Iranian Cinema* (2007), I examined twelve seminal Iranian filmmakers by navigating through a variety of multiple *realisms* in order to stay clear and complicate the habitual assimilation backward of Iranian cinema to European "neorealism" of the Italian vintage. In this oscillation between modernism of one sort and realism of many other sorts, Kiarostami's cinema has been the subject of a mixed blessing, at times insightful and at others disorienting. The task of complicating his realism was perhaps necessary but not sufficient. Something far more serious was needed—by way of coming to terms with the invisible truths of his own artworld.

Placing Kiarostami's artworld outside this European dichotomy between *modernism* and *realism*, without altogether dismissing their respective aesthetic domains, yields entirely different sets of insights into his cinema. In what I have called *an aesthetic intuition of transcendence*, I propose an affinity between an artist like Abbas Kiarostami's masterstrokes in his films and photography and a concept in Shahab a-Din Yahya Suhrawardi's (1154–1191) epistemological cosmogony that he called "Na-Koja-abad," a term we usually associate with the Arabic philosophical concept *"Alam al-Mithal*/Mundus Imaginalis" corresponding (but not entirely identical) with the Platonic idea of the "World of Ideas," or the "World of Forms." In its original Persian, the term that Suhrawardi uses is perhaps best translated as "Nowhereville." In Nowhereville, we are at the moment of the aesthetic remembrance of things past, and therefore of inexplicability, though with a nostalgia that self-destructs as it narrates itself. The factual evidence of Kiarostami's cine-aesthetics visually alludes to what Suhrawardi called *"Na-koja-abad*/Nowhereville," , somewhere that is nowhere but that is perfect and thriving in its whereabouts. We are sure that it exists, for it is a locus of civility, civilitas, and urbanity, or *Abad*/ Ville, but we cannot locate or even point to it. As such, as both speculative metaphysics in Suhrawardi and ocularcentric visuality in Kiarostami's art-world, they both allude to things that we sense but cannot see. This Nowhereville is therefore more *allegorical* than *categorical*. We can sense and imagine it, but we cannot locate and map it.

To be sure: I am not suggesting any causal relationship between Suhrawardi's Illuminationist Philosophy (*Falsafah Ishraq*) and Kiarostami's ocularcentric cinema. But I am thinking of a theoretical insight into Kiarostami's work that Suhrawardi's concept of "Nowhereville" offers as far more pertinent than the European binary of modernism and realism—or a fortiori, a philosophical reflection on Kiarostami's cinema, as best evident in Mathew Abbott's *Abbas Kiarostami and Film-philosophy* (2016), entirely alien as it is to Islamic or Iranian philosophical traditions and taking European philosophy for "Philosophy." How could the visual art of a twentieth-century artist, you might ask, possibly be related to the ideas of a twelfth-century Muslim Iranian philosopher? Fair question. The easy answer: The same way that Plato and Aristotle have cast a lasting shadow over every serious philosophical issue in poetics and aesthetics of domains code-named "Western." The same way that Plato's allegory of the cave still rules supreme over our philosophical reading of cinema. So much so that today, the term "philosophy" just means the European reception of these Platonic or Aristotelian traditions, at the serious cost of any other kind of philosophy, including Islamic or Iranian that is equally rooted in the Platonic and Aristotelian, plus other sources. But the more wholesome answer is somewhere else: Here I propose not a causal but a circumstantial relationship, something of a collective unconscious but not entirely of the Jungian transhistorical disposition, more of a mitigated space where the renewed knowledge of Suhrawardi's philosophical work through contemporary scholarship was made immediately available and accessible to Kiarostami's generation. The philosophical circle around the French Iranist Henry Corbin and his Iranian counterparts Seyyed Hossein Nasr, Seyyed Jalal Ashtiani, and Allamah Tabataba'i in the mid-twentieth century had generated quite a fashionable environment at the time of Kiarostami's emergence as a major filmmaker of his generation. The same is with a host of other Iranian and Muslim philosophers, mystics, poets, visual artists, whether dead or alive, Iranian or otherwise, that had created a powerful imaginative landscape around any given work of art of the period.

Let me give another example for those unfamiliar with the Iranian literary and artistic scene to see how the contraction of time and space works as a theoretical trope. Shahrokh Meskub (1926–2005) was a renowned literary scholar, and one of his most beloved books is *Dar Ku-ye Dust/In the Friend's Neighborhood* (1978), which is a reflection on Hafez's poetry.[17] In the introduction to this text he says he initially wanted to work on Zarathustra's *Gathas*—seventeen Avestan hymns believed to be composed by the Persian prophet himself—to place his mind in an "eternal atmosphere" when reflecting on the material circumstances of his contemporary life. But he soon abandoned that idea and instead opted to work through Hafez's poems. This is how he puts it:

> A few years ago, I wanted to write a treatise on the trilateral relationship among Humans, the World, and God. If there is the idea of God, what would be the nature and disposition of humans with themselves and with the world, and if there is no such idea then what? . . . I wanted to work primarily through the Gathas, in other words I want to shape my own thoughts based on the weltanschauung of these songs. . . . But when I started I was stuck. But Zarathustra's songs reminded me of Hafez's poetry, both of which have similar presence in pre- and post-eternity, the same desire to see the Friend.[18]

The result of this meditation is an exquisite disposition on the nature of our moral and philosophical imagination in communion with our past while living our contemporary lives. My turning to Avicenna and Suhrawardi in reading Kiarostami has a similar disposition to it. I, too, am after that contraction of time and space where a contemporary technological gadget is epistemically plotted in a distant creative soul.

When we place Kiarostami on that trans/historical terrain, others come to locate him in a more fruitful, worldly environment where we see him map out his visions of the invisible far more *allegorically* than *categorically*—whether in modernist or realist terms. I habitually place Kiarostami next to the Japanese master Yasujirō Ozu to be able to see them both better—one acting as the allegory of the other, as we see in the case of Kiarostami's *Five Dedicated to Ozu* (2003). This pairing can also be extended to the literary and philosophical domains. The dialogue and contestation between two major theorists of allegory, Walter Benjamin and Paul de Man, one a victim of the Nazis and the other a Nazi sympathizer, open up the hidden vistas of "allegory" as a literary device that they both read and theorized. Being a reader of that implicit dialogue is insightful, but it is in the Arabic-Persian dialectic of Avicenna in the eleventh and Suhrawardi in the twelfth century that we can bring the matter closer to the theoretical sensibilities of our postcolonial world. This rapprochement occasions a reading of Kiarostami through Suhrawardi and Avicenna that is far more *allegorical* than *categorical*, the way the two distant Iranian philosophers and their present echoes in Kiarostami's artworld have been read by leading scholars of the field like Henry Corbin or Taqi Pournamdarian, among others.[19] Reading Kiarostami allegorically, rather than categorically, is to overcome the overbearing terms of the modern, the modernist, or the triumphant modernity that is always in a rush to overcome the stagnant "Tradition" it had invented to become the vehicle of European colonialism. Allegorical reading, or reading Kiarostami as alluding to something other than what he shows, or what in Persian and Arabic poetics we call *Tamsil*, is the vehicle of having him show and tell in a language liberated from the colonial modernity he had always already overcome. What I am suggesting here cannot be violated by being branded "traditional," for the allegorical twists in the enduring works of Avicenna and Suhrawardi in fact place Kiarostami's work beyond the reach of European philosophical modernity—both spatially and temporally more radically contemporary than modern art can fathom.

In the series of pictures and the short film Kiarostami made titled *Roads of Kiarostami* (2005), landscape photography sublimates to pure formal abstractions and becomes a prime example of these allegorical readings of reality that yield neither to modernism nor to realism—though they can obviously be assimilated backward to them. But left to their own visual evidence as solid allegorical allusions to things that are too obvious to be seen, these photographs remain defiant of any and all categorical assimilations into known things—even before they are looked at with a Eurocentric set of eyes. From their actual landscape all inside Iran, to the light and composition that are deeply local, nostalgic, and proverbial, these allegorical snapshots in and of themselves become parabolic, forming the elemental forces of Kiarostami's cinematic imagination. Yes, there are the prospects of theoretical sublimations of these parabolic forces into far-reaching universalism of their own genesis, but for that to happen they will have to resist being force-fed into a European visual imagination. Again, this is not to deny them entry into a Eurocentric reading, which is beyond anyone's control, but to map out the preliminary theoretical force-field of a reading beyond the cliché "modernism" that we have been force-fed when standing in front of a work of art that may be yearning for a different read.

REASON/UNREASON, FACT/FICTION

This primacy of the allegorical over the categorical reading in turn points to the evident hyperreality of Abbas Kiarostami's photography through which we approach a heightened reality where the surreal leads back to the visions of the invisible and preempts the prospects of exacerbated aesthetic alienation. In Sohrab Sepehri's poetry, too, this hyperrealized signifier points back to the invisible sign and restores the strangeness of things. This is a Verfremdungseffekt that brings back the fiction of things to their irreducible Dasein or ontic thingness. Let me take this proposition through Suhrawardi to see how the prose of his colloquiality is playfully uplifted to the metaphysical. In his allegorical writings, Suhrawardi sees in the ephemerality of the material world the evidence of the sublime, just as Kiarostami does. They make the familiar of the prosaic foreign and thus make the foreignness of the invisible plausible—both through simulations of the similar and the rearticulating of the tension between the same and the other of Levinas. The total is therefore fragmented, and precisely in that fragmentation the infinity is seen in it, just like this crucial stanza in one of the famous poems of Mehdi Akhavan-e Sales:

> *Ba kodamin jadu'i tadbir...*
> With what kind of magical tricks
> With what kind of deceit is it or gimmick
> Oh you the righteous tell me in earnest—
> That appears unbroken on a broken mirror the image?[20]

I resort to Akhavan's poem because the fact is you will hear both Heidegger's German and Levinas' French in my English prose—but you will hear the Persian of Suhrawardi and the Arabic of Avicenna there too. That mélange or assemblage is the existential fact of a postcolonial mind that cannot and should never be censored. This is the diffusion and osmosis of reality into truth and truth into reality in fluid and amorphous ways. The diffusion and osmosis between the material and the moral, between truth and reality, between fact and fiction—or better yet, between hope and despair—is where the aesthetic alienation of Kiarostami's work liberates itself in healthy and productive ways. In this case, the active fusion of fact and fantasy generates a different perception of Reason or *Aql* where *nomos*, *logos*, and *mythos* come together to create a magnetic field of meaning that is not just dialogical but in fact heterological, not categorical but allegorical—namely a truth that always already points to other than itself, a heteroglossia that gestures at once toward denoting and connoting its alterities. When it is logocentric (as in philosophy), it is very much aware of the nomocentricity (legalism) it faces, and when it is theological, it is conscious of its philosophical or even theo-erotic urges that have been code-named Sufism.

This is the theoretical premise of my proposal that in Kiarostami's film and photography we in fact have a visual reconfiguration of Avicenna and Suhrawardi's visionary recitals, as Henry Corbin rightly called but wrongly Christianized them. De-Christianized and restored to their own Iranian and Islamic contexts, Avicenna and Suhrawardi and the whole visionary recitals they occasioned have far-reaching implications in how to read contemporary visual and performing arts, as indeed our reading of the *Suvar-e Khayal* does in reconfiguring poetic devices for cinematic purposes. But whereas in Avicenna and Suhrawardi we have a fusion of fiction and philosophy, in Kiarostami we have a synthesis of fact and fantasy—which in my earliest work on Kiarostami's cinema I have called "factasy." In Avicenna and Suhrawardi's visionary recitals, literary fiction sets the philosophical discourse free into an open-ended mimetic gestation. In the same vein, Kiarostami's vision of the invisible facts exude their fictional properties, as reason does its unreasonable repressions. Such border-crossings are procreative and generate and sustain a tertiary state of seeing, knowing, being. Let us remember Foucault in *Madness and Civilization*, where he says: "The language of psychiatry, which is a monologue of reason about madness, has been established only on the basis of such a silence. I have not tried to write the history of that language, but rather the archaeology of that silence."[21] Between language and silence, reason and unreason, we have the condition of all received categories yielding to become allegorical. Now consider the entire event in *Through the Olive Trees* (1994), and with it the rest of the Koker Trilogy, where there is an active fusion between the cast and the crew—the cast is the crew and the crew the cast. Sabzian, the chief protagonist, serves tea to the crew and the cast, and when he serves it to his fictional object of desire, Tahereh, it is both as a cast member and a member of the crew. Let us also remember Foucault's final assessment of the unreason: "And if, now, we try to assign a value, in and of itself, outside its relations with the dream and with error, to classical unreason, we must understand it not as reason diseased, or as reason lost or alienated, but quite simply as reason dazzled. Dazzlement is night in broad daylight, the darkness that rules at the very heart of what is excessive in light's radiance."[22] This is also the way we might think of the dialectic between reason and reason in the transmutation of categories into allegories, where what we see is the very surface of what would have been otherwise impossible to see. This border-crossing between fact and fiction is where the aesthetic alienation of Kiarostami's artworld is made allegorically impossible.

To understand the way this transmutation of capitalist reason into colonial unreason paves the way for the transmutation of categories into allegories on the colonial edges of that Eurocentric imagination, we need to remember a quick snapshot of what happened in Europe to occasion its Enlightenment as an ideology of global conquest. Enlightenment modernity was the ideological foregrounding of capitalist revolution in

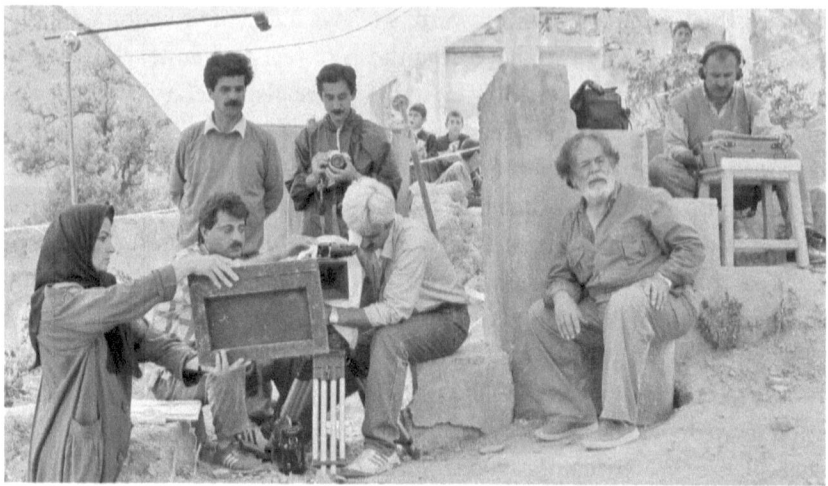

Figure 5. The cast and crew of *Through the Olive Trees* (1994). Courtesy of Abbas Kiarostami Foundation.

culture and industry. It was a formidable intellectual and philosophical movement that turned Europe upside down and determined the course of its colonial domination around the globe with a self-serving notion of Reason and Progress. The French Revolution of 1789 and the subsequent European Spring of Nations in 1848 radically altered the character and culture of Europe and universalized its bourgeois public spheres—revolutionaries and reactionaries alike took Europe for the world. Sometime between the death of Louis XIV in 1715 and the commencement of the French Revolution in 1789, the ideological self-perception of Europe began to change radically and assume a colonial significance beyond European borders.[23] These dates should be pushed back to 1492 and the commencement of the Reconquista and the Conquest of the Americas, to the Protestant Reformation initiated by Martin Luther and continued by Huldrych Zwingli, John Calvin, and other Protestant reformers in the sixteenth century, to the industrial and scientific revolutions that followed. It is after these cataclysmic events that *Les philosophes* began circulating their ideas in scientific academies, Masonic lodges, literary salons, and coffee houses, and in printed books and pamphlets—all visibly or invisibly rooted in European colonial possessions.

These revolutionary ideas eventually weakened the two adjacent institutions of the church and the monarchy, unleashed the power of bourgeois mercantilism and remapped the world in decidedly colonial colors. Without a colony or two to its name, no European nation could have had a claim to nationhood. We are the people of Nigeria and the rest of Africa, Asia, and Latin America who have dwelled on the real life of Paul Wilcox while stealing our lives and dignity to enable his Victorian and Edwardian morality. Take Paul Wilcox, the youngest son of the Wilcox family in E. M. Forster's *Howards End* (1910), and his African colonial business out of the picture and the whole narrative collapses on its domesticity. His brief flirtation with Helen Schlegel—before he dashes off to Nigeria, then England's lucrative colony, to attend to the family business in African rubber—is the main plot spin that makes the whole novel spin. That is not just a staple of E. M. Forster's novels, but the spirit of the entire age. What Europeans sometimes call their Age of Discovery, or the Age of Exploration, from the beginning of the fifteenth until the end of the eighteenth century, is actually their age of barbaric colonial conquest of the world. This is the hallmark of European colonial modernity with which the world at large was made alien to the terms of its own encounter with the world, and overcoming this colonial modernity is the singular task of the movement embedded in postcolonial thinking—aesthetic, philosophical, or a fortiori political.

The next stage after the rise of anticolonial struggle and postcolonial epistemic defiance against the combined forces of European conquest of the earth and the entrenched domestic patrimonialism it had put to its advantage—all to the detriment of the rising nations—is when these nations find the terms of their own liberations not in modernist or, as they say, "Western" terms but in terms integral to the global uprising against the new order of things. If anticolonialism was a veritable political project, postcolonialism is a decidedly moral, imaginative, aesthetic, and philosophical project. Theorization of the artworld of iconic artists like Kiarostami articulates the terms of that aesthetic and philosophical liberation. This is how we overcome the echoes and shadows of the European aesthetic alienation—not by taking European philosophy for "Philosophy" on one side of the spectrum or moving into entrenched nativism on the other, but by positing a tertiary space, a syncretic space, where visionary philosophers like Suhrawardi and Avicenna sit comfortably next to Walter Benjamin and Paul De Man without any sense of theoretical dissonance. The fusion of the false binary between East and West, on which the aesthetic alienation takes place, becomes the pharmakon that cures rather than kills, not despite but in fact through coming to terms with alienation.

THE POETIC "NOW"

Let us go back to the point of reading Kiarostami allegorically rather than categorically. A leading Iranian social scientist not usually known for her writings on cinema, Susan Shariati once wrote a short essay she called "Ba man beh zaban-e Ishareh Sokhan Begu/Speak to Me Allegorically." In this short essay, she cites Kiarostami as having once said, "I hate language, the bitter language, the harsh language, the language of the grammar, speak to me with the language of allusion, language of allegory."[24] In this essay dated Mordad 1395/July–August 2016, Shariati speaks of her youth in the decade of the 2000s, when she spoke with the language of harshness and grammar, as she admits, whereas now she is trying to stay away from Iran but Kiarostami's cinema comes to her in a small French town near Cannes, at Aix-en-Provence, where she lives. She speaks of having seen Kiarostami's films in that town and then joining a small gathering of the audience conversing with him about his cinema, including censorship in his homeland to which he responds that some issues in Iran are what they are and thus demand and exact a symbolic language, and that perhaps is good for it defines a particular kind of cinema. Shariati concludes this essay by saying she appreciates that sentiment but does not believe we are all artists who can speak that allegorical language—and that it is a good thing we are not all artists but that there are artists among us.

Here is where the balance between speaking the political truth and sensing the aesthetic of emancipation from and through that truth becomes evident. To be sure, Shariati is particular about her age and maturity and also about being away from Iran to reach that point, not to have abandoned the political truth or thought it overcome in art, but that it dwells with art simultaneously. The simultaneity of art and reason, or logic and rhetoric, points to the inaugural moment of "the Now" that is evident in the instantiation of Kiarostami's cinema. That aesthetic "Now" is the birthplace of the hermeneutic horizons of where and how to read a work of art against all prospects of its aesthetic alienation. Let's start with how Benjamin understood that "Now" in a historical frame of reference:

> History is the subject of a structure whose site is not homogenous, empty time, but time filled by the presence of the now. [Jetztzeit]*. . . . A historical materialist cannot do without the notion of a present which is not a transition, but in which time stands still and has come to a stop.[25]

In his note to this translation, the translator writes: "Benjamin says 'Jetztzeit' and indicates by the quotation marks that he does not simply mean an equivalent to Gegenwart, that is, present. He clearly is thinking of the mystical nunc stans. What is 'nunc stans'? The eternal Now that represented the consciousness of the Supreme Being in mediaeval thought." We have variations on these themes in Islamic mysticism too, of which Rumi, for example, speaks as Sufis being *Ibn al-Waqt*, creatures of the time, meaning now, not tomorrow, but not just in temporal sense, for the phrase is used against *Vaqt-e Digar*, another time, to which the response is right now. Let us see how Benjamin's "now" is read by Benjamin scholars:

> Redemption, as Benjamin here talks about it, is meant most prosaically: a redeeming (Einlösung) of possibilities, which are opened with every life and are missed in every life. If the concept of redemption points towards a theology—and it does so without doubt and a fortiori in the context of the first thesis, which mentions the "little hunchback" of theology—then this is not straightforwardly Judeo-Christian theology, but rather a theology of the missed, or the distorted—hunchbacked—possibilities, a theology of missed, distorted or hunchbacked time. Each possibility that was missed in the past remains a possibility for the future, precisely because it has not found fulfilment. For the past to have a future merely means that the past's possibilities have not yet found their fulfilment, that they continue to have an effect as intentions and demand their realisation from those who feel addressed by them. When past things survive, then it is not lived-out (abgelebte) facts that survive, facts that could be recorded as positive objects of knowledge; rather what survives are the unactualised possibilities of that which is past. There is historical time only insofar as there is an excess of the unactualised,

the unfinished, failed, thwarted, which leaps beyond its particular Now and demands from another Now its settlement, correction and fulfilment.[26]

If as Hamacher rightly proposes we have to think of the "Now" in the frame of a redemption that points toward a theology beyond its Judeo-Christian gestations, or Judeo-Islamic for that matter, then Benjamin's theological prelude points to a lived aesthetic possibility that frames that "Now" in an almost mystical suspension of the temporal passage of time. This is when the "Now" becomes embedded in History but not in that History. Hamacher points to "a theology of missed, distorted or hunchbacked time" where the postponed promises of yore remain at the heart of this suspension of all other theologies. These missed times, unfulfilled wishes, hover over the cortical and creative consciousness of History, and haunt it. Hamacher thinks "what survives are the unactualized possibilities of that which is past." This is what in my work I have marked as a post-Islamist theology, how we can reach the point to see "there is historical time only insofar as there is an excess of the unactualized, the unfinished, failed, thwarted, which leaps beyond its particular Now and demands from another Now its settlement, correction and fulfilment. This is pushing Benjamin's scant thinking into potent and palpably political domains, and rightly so. But the aesthetic implications of those "unfulfilled wishes" remain equally potent.

To see these aesthetic prospects evident in the "Now" at the heart of Kiarostami's cinematic moment, we need to move from the philosophical speculations of Walter Benjamin to a space closer to Kiarostami's poetic neighborhood. I have proposed to look at the oeuvre of the towering Persian poet Nezami Ganjavi (circa 1141–1209) by way of a poetic occasion where we can locate Kiarostami's work reflecting on itself, not just because one of Kiarostami's major works, *Shirin* (2008), is based on one of Nezami' romances, but because I am proposing that poetic moment as the location where we can place the creative disposition of Kiarostami beyond the vagaries of his own contemporary time, a time that is chronological, temporal, and spatial, rather than aphoristic and allegorical. My suggestion, for example, in the last chapter was to look at the manner in which Nezami articulates Mi'raj is to posit a theory of visuality beyond the mere cinematic rendition where Kiarostami reveals the invisible. In the

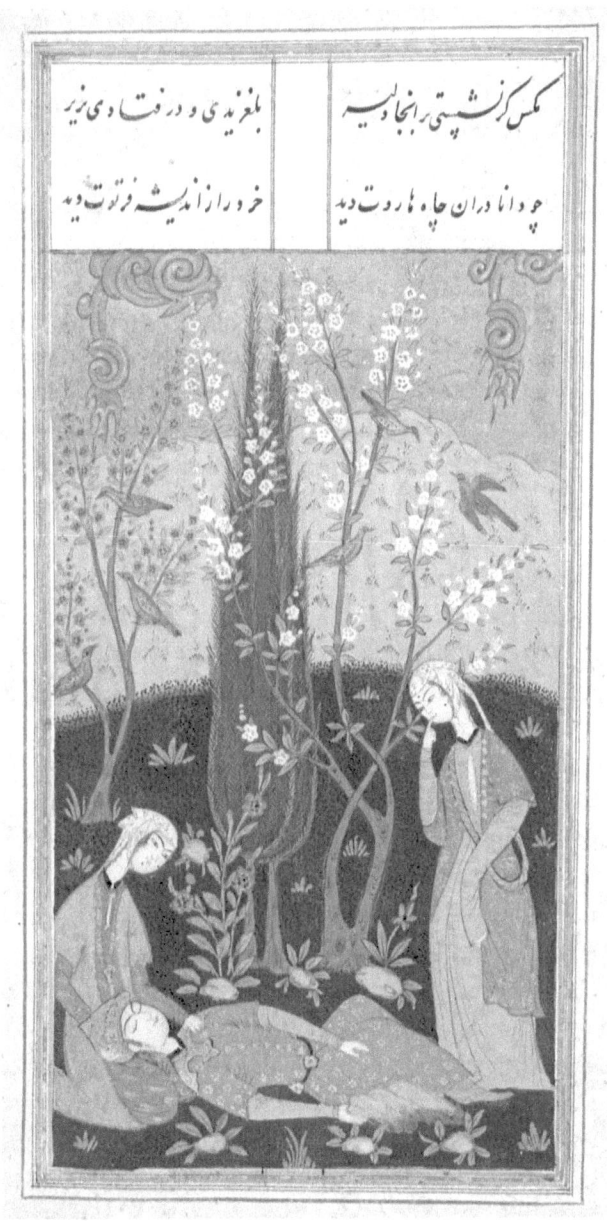

Figure 6. An illustrated leaf from the *makhzan al-Asrar/ Treasury of Secrets*) of Nezami: "The Disputing Physicians." Persia, Tabriz, Safavid, circa 1525–35. Public domain.

same vein, I might here offer the structural disposition of one of Nezami's masterpieces, *Makhzan al-Asrar/Source of Wisdom*,[27] by way of seeing what safeguards Kiarostami's cinema from self-alienation.

Let us look at the narrative disposition of *Makhzan al-Asrar* and how it is put together. It is divided into six distinct sections: First, Praising God Almighty and laying out the theological disposition of the poet; second comes an extended praise for the Prophet and detailing his Prophetology, how he perceived the very idea of prophethood; third comes the praise of his patron prince, Fakhar-Din Bahram Shah ibn Dawud; fourth comes a magnificent praise of poetry and eloquence, and a discussion of the superiority of poetry to prose; fifth comes a succession of passages in praise of solitude; and finally, sixth, is the body of the book which consists of twenty articles on various human virtues, such as respect for the royal subjects, superiority of humans to animals, renouncing the pleasures of this world, the nature of the virtuous life and preparations for the life to come, and then the book ends. There is no temporal passage in the book. Everything happens as if in one instance. There are corroborating historical pieces of evidence of the period, particularly in the section in which he praises his patron prince; and there are personal allusions, such as in the section in which he praises poetry. But all these temporal signatures fade into the totality of the poem and sustain its atemporality, its being in the Now of the poem itself.

The poetic Now evident here in Nezami becomes ethereal in Persian paintings illustrating episodes of his *Makhzan al-Asrar* where the event happens in a Sarmadi moment, a moment with no beginning and no end. Can we then look at the long shots of Kiarostami on those long winding roads, or vacated long shots, as if we are looking at a Persian painting of a manuscript illustration?

The time of Kiarostami's cinema is the poetic "Now" rooted in Persian poetic and visual imagination in which all masterpieces of aesthetic sublimation take place, before they are rushed into the marketplace of ideas and sentiments and film and art festivals. The temporal adjustment to atemporality effectively delocalizes the spatial too. Kiarostami's *Shirin* is rooted in Nezami's two romances, *Khosrow and Shirin* and *Leili and Majnun*, but even more in his poetic sublimation of time and space throughout his *Khamseh*/Quintet. During Kiarostami's own time, the two heroines became the subject of Ali-Akbar Sa'idi Sirjani's (1931–1994) iconic treatise, *Sima-ye Do Zan/Portrait of Two Women* (1988). Sirjani was a dissident political activist who died while in prison, many suspecting foul play. Before his untimely passing, Sirjani was also a master prose stylist and a literary scholar whose *Portrait of Two Women* became definitive of two radically opposed iconic figures in Persian literary imagination, favoring Shirin over Leili. Sirjani's timely version was potently contemporary, Kiarostami's atemporal and poetic by virtue of its capturing the very soul of Nezami's poetic Now.

OVERCOMING THE AESTHETIC ALIENATION

The overriding paradox of aesthetic alienation must be removed from the atlas of colonial bifurcation between a presumed center and a condemned periphery and relocated onto the poetic moment of the "Now" of the work of art itself—and thus to rescue and liberate it from the imaginative geography of colonial modernity created by the dominant narrative of "the West and the Rest," of European film festivals and "Third World" arts. The alienating location of "the Rest" is where all works of art are self-alienated and subjected to a gaze that, while praising them, robs them of their momentous spontaneity. Restoring to the work of art its own moment of the poetic "Now" brings out its inaugural poetic moment.

The Koker Trilogy is perhaps the best location of this liberation for it dwells on that "Now" precisely because it tells its story in the purgatorial moment of an earthquake when life has ended and the afterlife has not yet started. The soteriological aspect of the trilogy, or what in Persian we might call *Rastegari*, or salvation, frames this purgatorial moment, or passage. The Koker Trilogy details that moment for the duration of three films: *Where Is the Friend's House?* (1987), *Life, and Nothing More . . .* (1992), and *Through the Olive Trees* (1994)—to which we might thematically add, as has Kiarostami himself, *Taste of Cherry* (1997). But by the time of *Taste of Cherry*, the specificity of the event of the earthquake has both thematically and narratively disappeared. The trilogy does not become a trilogy until the second item, *Life, and Nothing More . . .*, when the Manjil–Rudbar earthquake of June 1990 happens and "the director" goes back to his location to find out what happened to his nonprofessional actors. The trilogy is consolidated as a trilogy with the third item when the fact of death has yielded to the urge to live.

Failing to see the centrality of death and bodily resurrection (*Ma'ad-e Jismani*)—a deeply rooted metaphysical issue in Islamic philosophy—around the budding courting by the lead actor in *And Life Goes On*, both Mathew Abbott and Jean-Luc Nancy, whom Abbott cites, dwell on the surface of "the many-faceted" aspects of reality, which is of course a truism if not even a cliché in Kiarostami's cinema. But still, based on that nonstarter Abbott raises a crucial question: "How do these techniques—which in theory should produce distancing, alienation, *Ostranenie, Verfremdungseffekt*, etc.—manage to draw us further into the films?"[28] This indeed is a key question—though I am not sure if Abbott is completely aware how his own writing on Kiarostami actually exacerbates that sense of alienation he wishes to rectify. He rightly turns this question into the cornerstone of raising serious philosophical issues:

> What is film's connection to the real world? What happens to reality when we screen it? How does film create problems of knowledge? Might it help us solve it? How can film make moral or political claims on us? What is the difference between documentary and fiction? . . . What does it mean to say a film is "philosophical"? This book uses philosophy and the films of Kiarostami for their mutual illumination, turning to the Iranian director in an attempt to finding and clarifying a form of cinematic thinking.[29]

But, and here is the rub, philosophy for Abbott is what calls itself "Western philosophy," though it casts itself as "Philosophy." Abbott's philosophical reflections are predicated on two sets of mutually exacerbating alienations: taking Kiarostami out of his moral and imaginative geography, and universalizing the particulars of what calls itself "Western philosophy." This anthropological gaze, Abbott acting as a Malinowski in the "New Guinea" of Kiarostami's cinema, turns Kiarostami's artworld into a field to be explored for the benefit of western philosophy, thus further giving this western philosophy further false assumptions of universalizing its particulars, while casting Kiarostami's cinema as the oilfield of a distant alien culture worth exploring for the benefit of the First World philosophy. You get hold of Kiarostami's films, catapult them from their natural and immediate habitat onto this "Western philosophical" domain and call it

"Philosophy," and start making some very insightful observations, to be sure, while entirely oblivious to the fact that this very exercise is working precisely against the crucial question of alienation you had raised to start with. That act itself, Abbott's own prose, is the profoundest mode of aesthetic alienation for any Iranian or Arab or Indian or Chinese filmmaker being thus "philosophized." If what European philosophers do is "Philosophy," and nothing else somewhere else might also be philosophy of a different sort, then we have emptied a work of art of its vital organs and turned it into an object of "philosophical" curiosity. Abbott is perfectly right when he says we need not look for philosophical reflections by the characters specifically or by plot more generally. "This not to deny," he further adds, "the importance of narrative and character; nor is it to ignore the political and cultural contexts of films. It is simply to say that these are not the domains in which the medium-specific philosophical propensity of film does its work."[30] But, by the same logic and the same insight, Mulla Sadra in philosophy or Nezami in poetic composition are not "cultural context" either. They are site-specific philosophical and poetic context that make that "medium-specific philosophical propensity of film" meaningful.

A major theological issue in Islam that has become a potent philosophical point of contention is the question of physical resurrection on the Day of Judgment/*Yawm al-Qiyamah*. Most major Muslim philosophers have dealt with it in one way or another. But it is in the work of the seminal Shi'i philosopher of the sixteenth century Mulla Sadra Shirazi's philosophical school of al-Hikmah al-Muta'aliyah (Transcendental Philosophy) that this issue assumes its most potent theoretical disposition, for he has a solid theory of body that changes its physical disposition toward the soul in physical, purgatorial terms, and on the day of judgment fosters a resurrection disposition.[31] It is therefore possible to look at the cinematic universe of Kiarostami as that purgatorial space where the dead bodies of those perished in the earthquake have been resurrected in the bodies of their loved ones, and in the urgent love affair of Hossein and Ladan, the urge toward procreation is the passage from this purgatorial space through Harakah Jawhariyya toward a metaphysical resurrection.

My quick excursion into the thinking of a seminal Muslim philosopher, to repeat, is not to suggest if Nancy, Heidegger, Levinas, Benjamin, Derrida, or in fact Abbott himself venture into Kiarostami's work they might not have something indeed serious to say. They often do. Kiarostami became a global phenomenon, and the world at large, including European and Eurocentric philosophy, has every right, reason, and occasion for insights into his work. As a postcolonial thinker, I am the by-product of many of these thinkers (*by-product* I say intentionally, for my thinking is not a direct descendent of their thoughts nor did they in their wildest dreams have imagined an Iranian, Arab, Indian, or Chinese encounter with their worlds). This encounter is inevitably predicated on an epistemic violence that thinkers like me are bound to perpetrate on the totality and infinity of what calls itself "Western philosophy," for we do not read them the way they are intended to be read for we are not their intended readership. We read and understand and interpret them with an entirely different set of sensibilities than their intended purposes. We have never been their intended purpose, we were never thought to be knowing subjects, because we were already assigned to be part of the knowable world, the object of their colonial gazes and anthropological investigations. But I am also the product of an archive of philosophical thinking outside the domain of these thinkers' comfort zones. I sense "death and resurrection" in the Koker Trilogy and I hear Mulla Sadra Shirazi. They do not. This is neither their fault nor my fault. The issue is surgically removing Kiarostami from his own creative and critical bread and butter, as it were, which certainly includes non-Iranian filmmakers and even thinkers, but not at the expense of gutting his cinema out of his more natural habitat simply because we do not know them. That is alienation galore. Mulla Sadra is not "cultural and political context" either—as Abbott suggests. He is the philosophical context. The grandest master of Shi'i philosophical thinking about the prospects of physical resurrection might perhaps bring as much relevance in our reading of the Koker Trilogy, or the favorite of physical reflection, *Taste of Cherry*, especially that famous encounter of Mr. Badii with the taxidermist.

The kind of thinking that Abbott or Nancy offer Kiarostami is indeed insightful but at the heavy expense of pushing his artworld further away from the world in which he lived and created—a world with the poetic (if not with the philosophical—if we were to make a distinction here at all) impulses of which he was deeply connected, and offering him like a piece of philosophical relic excavated in a faraway land to the examination table of an anthropological lab in Sydney or Paris. Read a page of Abbott and compare it with a page of the nasty things that an equally serious philosopher like Morad Farhadpour says about Kiarostami. They are not just comparable. They are almost violently opposed to each other. We cannot entirely dismiss Abbott as colonized gaze nor dismiss Farhadpour as entirely hostile. The two diametrically opposed readings of Kiarostami are the result of having placed his cinema on the atlas of the colonial center and periphery rather than the rooted space where he lived and created. The point and purpose of this relocation I propose from the atlas of the colonial gaze onto the moral and imaginative moment, the poetic moment, of aesthetic creativity, is the liberation of the postcolonial work of art from the condition of coloniality where the sublime moment of the philosophical meditation of the work of art survives its alienating circumstances to rediscover itself in terms specific to itself. My choice of invoking the classical moment of a sublime work of art such as Nezami's *Makhzan al-Israr* is to place Kiarostami's aesthetic urges and poetic panache for his own cine-aesthetics, enriching that Now with the Now of its own origins.

PALIMPSEST AND PENTIMENTO OF THE "NOW"

The moment of the "Now" as Benjamin understood it is still too solid—too entrenched in the materiality of the world it must transcend. It needs to be let loose. Kiarostami's Koker trilogy shows a way out.

There are at least three claims on the origin of the script of *Where Is the Friend's House?*—one perfectly obvious and legitimate and the other two not so obvious and rather unsavory. The title of the film, and perhaps its general sentiments, we know for a fact comes from the most famous line of perhaps the most famous poem of the iconic Iranian poet Sohrab Sepehri (1928–1980), "*Neshani*/Address" (1967):

Khaneh-ye dust kojast
Dar falaq bud keh porsid savar?

"Where is the friend's house"—
The rider asked early at dawn—

> The passerby threw the branch of light he held within his lips
> To the darkness of the sands—
> Pointed with his finger to a poplar tree and said . . .[32]

This much is obvious and rather innocuous. It links Kiarostami's film to a trajectory of Persian poetic diction and gives it a more cinematic twist. But there are at least two other claims on the authorship of the script—rumored for years and then uttered in detail by Niki Karimi (for years Kiarostami's intimate companion) when Kambuzia Partovi (1955–2020)—an Iranian filmmaker and scriptwriter—had died. Partovi is believed to have been the actual author of the script on which Kiarostami had made *Where Is the Friend's House?* The other is a short story called "Why Did Ms. Teacher Cry?" by Behruz Tajvar.[33] Kiarostami is accused of having had these two sources for his script of *Where Is the Friend's House?*, which he never officially acknowledged. Instead of jumping to the conclusion of plagiarism or any other such troublesome accusation, we have the opportunity to think of something more important about the Koker Trilogy. If these accusations have a legitimacy to them, then the whole trilogy becomes predicated on a composite "urtext," as it were, a multiauthored master text that never was, but Rashomon-like has had to be re-created by multiple accounts. There are other similar rumors about other films of Kiarostami, such as *Close-Up* or *Taste of Cherry*, that they, too, have had unacknowledged sources in other filmmakers' ideas. Such accusations and rumors raise the prospect of considering *Where Is the Friend's House?* as a composite or an "ur" text in the sense of being the result of a final artifact like a critical edition of a classical text based on multiple and variant manuscripts. What such persistent rumors suggest does not come together to question Kiarostami's authorial claim on his film—no matter where he may have chanced upon the ideas for his famous films. They do something far more important. They point to the formation of a palimpsestic text—an evident artifact on which a previous writing had been written but eventually effaced to enable the final product, and yet traces of the previous works are still somehow evident as persistent rumors—or perhaps more accurately we may suggest the metaphor of a pentimento where in a painting traces of earlier images are still present—again in this case in terms of oral rumors buzzing in the Iranian film community.

Either as a palimpsest or a pentimento, the rumors and testimonies hovering around Kiarostami's masterpiece posit the script of *Where Is the Friend's House?* as the evidence that exacerbates the moment of the "Now" in the oral innuendos accompanying the written text and the celebrated film on which it is based. This moment needs to be articulated in such details so as to place the particular mode of thinking philosophy through his films to become site-specific to his cinema, for the question is what is particular about Kiarostami's film-philosophy as opposed to, say, the cinema of Ingmar Bergman, which has also been the subject of meditations like Irving Singer's *Ingmar Bergman, Cinematic Philosopher: Reflections on His Creativity* (2007) or, say, the cinema of Andrei Tarkovsky, which, too, has been the subject of similar studies. This composite disposition of the Now at the inaugural moment of Kiarostami's cinema turns the work of art itself into the simulacrum of its troubled past, geared toward an uncharted future, and thus makes the possibilities of reading it liberated for a posterity yet to come when the film and the trilogy itself turn into an engine that is yet to exhaust itself, to drive itself home, never totally actualized.

Let us carry this emboldened moment of the Now into the inspiration that for a fact placed Kiarostami's film on a hermeneutic plain closer to his home and habitat. What does Sepehri's "Address," from which Kiarostami borrows his title, do to *Where Is the Friend's House?* Sepehri was a material metaphysician of the Now like no other poet in his immediate vicinity, which has promoted some to see a mystical disposition in his poetry, though that has to be seen in a very physical sense, deeply influenced by Zen Buddhism. Let's read the rest of the poem: Where exactly is the friend's house? Before the Rider in the poem gets to the tree, as it were, there is a little street lined with trees, "greener than God's dreams," where love is bluer than the wings of honesty. The Rider has to go all the way to the end of that street, where he will reach beyond adolescence, at which point he must turn toward the flower of solitude. Two steps to that flower, however, he must stop by "the fountain of all the mythologies of the earth," where suddenly a translucent fear overcomes the Rider. At that point, the Rider hears a hissing sound, and there and then he sees a little boy who has climbed a tall pine tree to pick a chick from the nest of light—there and then he asks the boy where the friend's house is.[34]

One can almost see Kiarostami's film in this poem—though with a "mystical" twist perhaps not so evident in the film itself. One might even say that the character of Babak Ahmad Pour is the personification of that Rider in Sohrab Sepehri's poem, and the whole story the visualization of what Sepehri outlines as the process of reaching a distant destination where we and the rider reach illumination. The journey starts at the dawn of the Now of the poem, passes through the street that is greener than God's dreams, with the wings of honesty, where the Rider is in pursuit of a loving task, through which he reaches adolescence, beyond which much of the journey is performed in the solitude Sepehri articulates. By now we have reached the fountain of all the mythologies of the earth, beyond which awaits a translucent fear. The hissing sound is the conversation with the carpenter, and the Rider himself now becomes the little boy who has climbed a tall pine tree to pick a chick from the nest of light. He no longer even needs to ask for direction, for by now he is already there.

If this story, the way I narrate it here, sounds and feels and reads like one of the visionary recitals of Suhrawardi or Avicenna, it is neither intentional nor accidental. It is by elective affinity. Thus read as a palimpsest or pentimento of the "Now," the masterstroke of Kiarostami has radically liberated itself from an aesthetic of self-alienation if we were to allow it to breathe in its own natural home and habitat before we drag it into any "Western" philosophical trajectory, which might be equally insightful but only after we have had a chance to see it flower on its own soil. Let's test this idea by reversing the angle and looking at one of Suhrawardi's visionary recitals as if it were a Kiarostami film.

Let us look at the treatise of the *Aql-e Sorkh/Red Intellect*. The narrator tells us that one of his friends once asked him if birds talked. He responds affirmatively—"Yes, birds talk."

> "How do you know," the friend inquires.
> "Because I was a bird, I was initially created as a falcon."
> "A falcon? Really? Then what happened? How did you become a human?"

Thus, the story begins. The narrator says once as a bird he and his friends were trapped by a bird catcher, blindfolded, and taken to some strange land where eventually his blindfold was lifted. He eventually finds himself in a desert where he encounters a youthful old man who has red hair and introduces himself as the first person created, and he is here on this earth to discover strange things such as Mount Qaf. The rest of the story is the accompaniment of the narrator with this Red Intellect discovering the mysteries of the universe. The language of the treatise and the search is dominated by Zoroastrian symbolism and various other stories we know from the Shahnameh, including the battle of Rostam and Esfandiar, to all of which the narrator gives a deeply philosophical interpretation. The story ends pointedly, leaving it to the readers whether they believe it or not.

How to read the cinematic power of this story Suhrawardi composed more than a thousand years before cinema was invented? But even more pointedly, what sort of a philosophical language is this?

3 Between Aesthetic and Nonaesthetic Reasons

We must wash our eyes—
A different kind of seeing we must learn:
We need to wash the words—
The word must be the wind itself,
The word must be the rain itself—
We must fold the umbrellas
We must walk into the rain—
We must take our thinking and our memory
Under the rain.[1]

Sohrab Sepehri, "Seda-ye Pa-ye Ab/The Sound of the Footsteps of Water" (1964)

Cinema—its screen, its sensitive membrane—stretches and hangs between a world in which representation was in charge of the signs of truth, of the heralding of meaning, or of the warrant of a presence to come; and another world that opens onto its own presence though avoiding where its thoughtful evidence realizes itself.[2]

Jean-Luc Nancy, *L'Évidence du film: Abbas Kiarostami* (2001)

My discussion of aesthetic alienation in the previous chapter points to the fact that on the colonial edges of European Enlightenment modernity the link between art and truth, between aesthetic and nonaesthetic reasons, is more tenuous and amorphous than it has been presumed to be on its European centers, for here any claim on philosophical truth and aesthetic judgment is site-specific, transitory, and spontaneous, neither generic nor espousing any claim on false metaphysical universality—and as such, the dialectic between art and reason generates a different conception of aesthetic sovereignty—and therefore a different mode of subjection and agency dwelling within that sovereignty, which we might call and consider an "unknowing subject." The aesthetic alienation at the heart of European modernity is rooted in what Marx identified in the first volume of *Capital* (1867) as commodity fetishism, and later Weber specified as the process of the disenchantment of the world. That commodity fetishism and that subsequent disenchantment become doubly alienating on colonial sites where it is exacerbated by both material and moral dispossession of the product of colonized labor. Through Marx's alienation effect and Weber's theory of disenchantment of Modernity, we might also see how the commodification of Kiarostami's own artwork at European film festivals and the prose it has perforce attracted can only be addressed through the moment of "the poetic Now" that suspends the opening of time through the purgatorial passage of the suspended prose of history. On such postcolonial sites, no fully knowing subject can be presumed to be the spectator of Kiarostami's knowable artworld—unless it is aesthetically entailed, implicated, and enabled. We might consider one of the masterpieces of Kiarostami's oeuvre, *Nama-ye Nazdik/Close-Up* (1990), as the primary evidence of such an aesthetically mediated sovereignty of the unknowing subject conditioned by the site of the sovereignty of the work of art—for in this film, Kiarostami's critical engagement with mimetic mis/representation between truth and fiction stages a radically altered state of exception that prefigures the dialectic between truth and narrative, between aesthetic and nonaesthetic reason, or perhaps best between categorical and allegorical mimesis.

KIAROSTAMI AS A CATALYST OF AESTHETIC SUBJECTIVITY

To arrive at that point where aesthetic sovereignty of the unknowing subject can correspond to the sovereignty of the work of art it beholds, first we need to clear the field in some significant ways. Let us begin from two opposite ends—first with a book in Persian that refused to take Kiarostami's work seriously and dismissed him as a fraud (and in the process scandalized itself), and then with a book in French that took him quite seriously and thought his cinema a turning point in our aesthetic imagination (and rightly so).

The publication of a strangely vindictive book denouncing Kiarostami as a fraud on one hand, and the composition of a sublime poem celebrating him and his art on the other—both in Persian—mark a crucial testimonial to the master filmmaker's significance as a catalyst of aesthetic subjectivity in his own homeland. First let us get one truly unfortunate book on Abbas Kiarostami out of the way. It is in Persian and is titled *Paris-Tehran: Sinema-ye Abbas Kiarostami—Dialog/Paris-Tehran: The Cinema of Abbas Kiarostami, A Conversation* (2008). It is an inexplicably hateful attack on Abbas Kiarostami and his entire cinematic existence, and indeed against the whole idea of Iranian New Wave, by two authors, Morad Farhadpour and Maziyar Islami, with little to no record of their having had any serious or professional engagement with Iranian or any other cinema except as translators of mostly European sources into Persian.[3] The book starts with a conspiratorial fallacy and concludes with an embarrassing display of undaunted ignorance. I attend to this book out of duty even though it is a document of impervious resentment and troubled prose that Kiarostami's cinema had caused among some of his own compatriots. Despite the embarrassment it causes anyone who reads this awkward diatribe, it had attracted much attention when it was first published in Iran back in 2008. The authors' claim to fame is not because they are known or respected film critics or scholars but because they are translators of some haphazard samples of contemporary European philosophy. They call their book a "dialogue." The dialogue between the two authors begins with a mixed metaphor of Shakespeare's King Lear and the Arabian Nights' character Aladdin—with Lear thinking royalty was embedded in his person, not in his royal circumstances (a seriously flawed reading of the play), and with Aladdin finding himself in the desert of the cinema world of the 1980s that was, our two authors tell us, devoid of any major filmmaker on the global scene, though the desire of French film festival directors for manufacturing such a major filmmaker was very much there and thus like Aladdin in that desert, Abbas Kiarostami found himself "crowned king" in

Cannes! The spectacle is so bizarre that I need to translate it verbatim so there is no misunderstanding:

> Kiarostami, too, just like Aladdin, was wandering in the empty and deserted space of the cinema of the 1980s, a space where as it happens was devoid of great and iconic filmmakers, although the wish to have that space occupied with new people was still there. The ultimate conclusion of this was the serendipitous sitting of Abbas Kiarostami on the throne of artistic filmmakers.[4]

The world of the 1980s had no major filmmaker? Seriously? It was a complete desert waiting for Kiarostami as a wandering Aladdin to be discovered and crowned? Akira Kurosawa was alive and well in the 1980s, as were Satyajit Ray, Stanley Kubrick, Margarethe Von Trotta, Peter Weir, Ousmane Sembène, Martin Scorsese, Krzysztof Kieslowski, Emir Kusturica, Rainer Werner Fassbinder, Shôhei Imamura, Jim Jarmusch, Bahram Beiza'i, and countless others. They were all happily busy making films. How many more should I add? Amir Naderi, Andrei Tarkovsky, Youssef Chahine, Souleymane Cissè, Agnès Varda, Abderrahmane Sissako, Moufida Tlatli, Ang Lee, Jane Campion, Chen Kaige, Hou Hsiao-hsien, Mira Nair, Wong Kar-wai, Jang Yimou? Kubrick alone made three of his masterpieces in this and the following decades—*The Shining* (1980), *Full Metal Jacket* (1987), and *Eyes Wide Shut* (1999). Ray continued to make his masterpieces well into the 1980s and 1990s. Kurosawa made *Kagemusha* in 1980, *Ran* in 1985, *Dreams* in 1990, and even more precious films well into the 1990s. Ousmane Sembène produced some of his masterpieces in the 1980s. Yilmaz Güney made his signature film *Yol* in 1982! The list goes on. What calamity people have lived under the Islamic Republic for these two characters to have been the best the Iranian intellectual scene could have produced! Ingmar Bergman produced some of his last masterpieces, such as *The Blessed Ones*, in the 1980s. It is simply embarrassing for two grown-up men sitting in the hallucinatory privacy of their delusions and thinking this decade or the decade after or the decade before that was just desert and Abbas Kiarostami a wandering Aladdin walking idly by and suddenly finding himself on the throne. That there was nothing in and about his cinema and his artworld except for the conspiracy the French cooked up to sell a lemon to the world!

What throne anyway? Kiarostami was not sitting on any throne. He was no Lear, no Aladdin, no monarch in any fantasy play. He was one significant filmmaker among countless others. Even when he received the Palm d'Or in 1997, he shared it with the Japanese master Shôhei Imamura. Was Imamura also a Japanese Aladdin? The "Dialogue" unfolds apace and concludes with even more senseless blather about "postcolonialism"—about which the authors evidently know next to nothing. The conclusion of the dialogue is a dismissive reading of not just Abbas Kiarostami's cinema but the entirety of Iranian New Wave as something deeply troubled and pathological—for which argument they turn to their amateurish impressions of Freud's essay "Mourning and Melancholia" (1917) via a dismissal of the entire field of postcolonial studies—from Edward Said to Spivak and any other name they could recall. The entire field of postcolonial studies in the four corners of the world for them is something not just "melancholic" in the Freudian sense but in fact psychotic and delusional in the Persian sense of the word M*alikhulia*, which is, of course, a cognate of *melancholia* but carries a whole different set of pathological connotations when used in Persian as these two bitter, angry men do. They begin by giving a flawed and abusive reading of Freud's argument in "Mourning and Melancholia." Freud never said some people do mourning and others do melancholia. He said mourning happens consciously and melancholia subconsciously. So, one person could do both. But our two translators-turned-film-and-culture critics confuse the two and attribute to the whole field of postcolonial studies a psychotic response to the loss of ancient glories of cultures! Failing to cite a single text by a single author in this field, Farhadpour and Eslami proceed to offer the most hackneyed reading of what is happening in the field of postcolonial studies, conflating and confusing all the major and minor figures of the field, including the late Indian Marxist Aijaz Ahmad (whose name they misspell) and who wrote the most potent criticism of Edward Said's *Orientalism* and they think he was a follower of Said! They think Aijaz Ahmad was an Indian so he must have been a postcolonial thinker too. He was a devout Marxist to his dying day. The utter hypocrisy of this position is also exposed when in the eighth chapter of the book the authors rely on the work of the selfsame Edward Said to argue the reason for the European interest in Kiarostami's cinema was in fact their Orientalism![5] The turn to this butchery of what postcolonialism is and what it does is to argue that the French and the rest of the Europeans turned to this Iranian filmmaker out of their Orientalist imagination, looking for an Aladdin to crown in the desert of the 1980s cinema and, lo and behold, here is a nativism of the Kiarostami they found and celebrated in line with the postcolonial search for resentful nativism and glory of their nonexistent past, out of a melancholic pathology to deal with their sense of loss. This is worse than conspiracy theory. This is conspiracy theory mixed with a delusional encounter with moral, intellectual, and political developments of which the two translators are woefully ignorant.

The prose gets increasingly hallucinatory, assuming the entire field of postcolonialism is after the goose chase of "ancient glories" and "forgotten selves" they have lost and they cannot cope with it and thus the cinema of Kiarostami becomes emblematic of the whole Iranian New Wave including Bahram Beiza'i and others who simply become nativist and in that nativism is the source of their appeal to foreigners. Particularly ignorant and nasty is their treatment of Africa, in which they say it is ludicrous for Africans to speak of their African identity for Africa itself is a colonial invention, "because in truth 'African identity' and even the term Africa itself are the product of European culture, and many people who live in this continent until this very day still find their identity by virtue of their membership in one tribe as opposed to another (such as Hutu and Tutsi), and do not even have a national identify [*sic*] let alone an African identity."[6] This brute illiteracy, ignorant of at least two hundred years of African art, culture, film, fiction, and philosophy, particularly of the towering work of the Congolese philosopher Y. V. Mudimbe in his monumental work, *Invention of Africa* (1988), is the sign of nothing but a deeply colonized, unabashedly racist, self-hating mind that is evident in the books these two not so self-respecting men have decided to translate into Persian—nothing from Asia, Africa, or Latin America, entirely mesmerized and obsessed as they are with Europe.

Paris-Tehran is a sad book to read—it is the sign of the moral and intellectual depravation of an entire country, where ideas and their location in history lack any serious provenance. A certain kind of intellectual perversity and thuggery is in the air of this book that is rooted in the Islamist theocracy that has enabled and benefited from it. The metaphor of Aladdin in the desert they use for Kiarostami may in fact be used for themselves, and the entire dialogue a self-projection, a deeply troubled inferiority complex turned visibly upside down against someone else. It deeply saddens and troubles me to write these words about a book I had to read out of nothing but professional duty toward a seminal Iranian artist who, like all other artists, could be the subject of severest criticism, but not out of sheer pathological hatred. This hatred is by no stretch of the imagination endemic or representative of a vast body of critical writing on Kiarostami in Persian, much of it highly appreciative and laudatory, where he is given the honorary title of *"Ab-e-ru-ye Sinema-ye Iran*/The Honor of Iranian Cinema." But still when such atrocities happen, and they do happen quite frequently, they need reading not for their insights, but for the puzzling pathology they document.

FROM THE RIDICULOUS TO THE SUBLIME

There is more to this hateful book than may initially meet the eye. I have closely read and briefly discussed it here not because it has anything serious to say about Kiarostami, but because it has something serious to hide about the condition of its own authorship. The problem with *Paris-Tehran* is much worse than its boldfaced illiteracy and seemingly incurable proclivity towards conspiracy theories. The problem is somewhere else. The problem is with the complete and deliberate abandoning of any prospect of aesthetic subjectivity—not just an inability to dwell aesthetically in the world of an artist the whole world has fully and happily and even critically embraced, but to foreclose any prospect of such aesthetic in-dwelling. The claim of the two authors that there is nothing aesthetically inherent about Kiarostami's work, and that Europeans just found him like an Aladdin wandering in the desert and choose him like a lucky ruffian to rule over them is the clearest indication that the authors themselves don't see anything significant or inherent in any work of art that any Iranian, or indeed any non-European, could ever produce. This is less a matter of their aesthetic blindness than a matter of the impossibility of an aesthetic subjectivity and authorship that they might fathom as violently desubjected colonial entities foreclosed for and unto themselves.

That these two people are primarily translators of almost exclusively European sources is not accidental or irrelevant to their violent attack on Kiarostami but is in fact definitive to this intentional blindness. In their minds, only Europeans are capable of thinking, knowing, building, and dwelling philosophically and therefore aesthetically. And only out of pity and haphazard despair these Europeans might pay a passing attention to an Aladdin wandering in the desert like Abbas Kiarostami—who is someone like them, incapable of producing or theorizing a sublimity beyond the political parameters of the postcolonial world—a world they dismiss and denigrate to be a joke. It is not just Kiarostami they angrily denounce, not even the entirety of the Iranian cinema they consider a pathetic nativist constellation of irrelevancies. It is not even the racist dismissal of Africa as a site of critical and creative intelligence. It is the impossibility of their own knowing, building, being, and in-dwelling aesthetically in the world that they both acknowledge, stage, and inexplicably hate all at one and the same time. Through a standard, even cliché, case of projection, it is themselves they deny and denounce for impossibility of knowing and being, but denouncing and denying there is anything to be seen or admired in Kiarostami. Their preoccupation with translating Giorgio Agamben, Alain Badiou, or Walter Benjamin is an act of flagrant self-flagellation, with each one of those translations a testimony to not just the inability but impermissibility to think, to dwell, to be—in this case, aesthetically.

To see this pathological impossibility of a colonized mind thinking clearly, and in order not to falsely generalize it to the entirety of a nation, we should move as far away as possible from these two translators in the opposite direction and toward their exact alterity: a magnificent Persian poet, a towering literary theorist, and a deeply learned textual critic farthest removed from the vicinity of their hateful prose. I have had occasions in the previous chapters to refer to Mohammad Reza Shafi'i-Kadkani (born 1939), who is no translator of European sources—though widely aware and conversant with those sources. He is a poet that Kiarostami deeply loved and admired and who, too, wrote one of his most powerful poems in honor and praise of Kiarostami—and dismissal of those who hated him. We move into a vast prairie of fresh and life-affirming domains when we run away from the conspiratorial dungeons of Morad Farhadpour and Maziyar Eslami toward Mohammad Reza Shafi'i-Kadkani's poem for

Kiarostami. The poem, titled "My Pigeons," starts with the image of a bitter old man who refuses to stick his head out of his tower to see birds flying:

> My neighbor could see
> Day and Night
> Their shadows and their guano droppings—
> And every day he'd be grumbling—
>
> Not even once did he stick his head out
> Of his bitter tower
> To see that Bleeding-heart pigeon
> In the glory of the turquoise-colored dawn—
> Or just to hear the flapping of their flight
> On the early morning rooftop![7]

The narrator keeps pleading with the bitter old neighbor, trying to entice him to open his eyes and see the beauty of the colorful pigeons flying. But the neighbor just looks at their shadows and their excrement and keeps grumbling in anger. The narrator finally takes his pigeons and moves them away to another town. Heartbroken, he comes back but much to his delight sees the pigeons have come back to his roof, and the bitter old neighbor, "the enemy of all beauty and grace," keeps grumbling. The poem ends with a praise and a curse:

> I buried myself under the ruins of disbelief,
> And as I was giving the birds seeds and drops of my tears
> I was thinking to myself:
>
> What a grace what a precious grace
> One can see in the demeanor and flight of these miraculous things
> That cleanse the soul in their pure currents!
>
> Oh God may those who see nothing
> But sin and excrements
> Under this sky
> Remain forever undignified and insufferable![8]

Now consider the way Kiarostami praised Shafi'i-Kadkani's poetry: "Kadkani's love for nature is unbelievable. It robs me of sleep. At night even when my window is completely dark, when I read his poetry, I feel it has dawned. It is as if I can hear the birds singing. Without even mentioning Nishabur, he does something with you that you want to get out and travel to Nishabur. He summons us back to nature."[9]

It is Shafi'i-Kadkani who through the metaphor of pigeons sees through the pathology of people such as Farhadpour and Eslami for whom ugliness and excrement and not flight of birds and beauty is all they see. When we put this poem and that book next to each other, the centrality of Kiarostami's artworld as a catalyst of aesthetic subjectivity in his own homeland becomes painfully clear. There is no reason that to be born in Iran, France, or Africa, or anywhere else in the world, is a sign of any clear-cut demarcation of how to read or watch Kiarostami, or any other artist. The fragmented fragility of the unknowing subject on the postcolonial site is self-evident. If a creative and critical culture can produce both a sublime poem and a pathological banality, then the crisis of the sovereign subject on the postcolonial site has a specific diagnosis beyond the haphazard location of a work of art, unless and until that work of art becomes conscious of its aesthetic sovereignty, to which prospect we must now turn.

TEHRAN-PARIS: A RETURN

Let us now turn our attention to a far more serious philosophical reflection on Kiarostami, this one by the eminent French philosopher Jean-Luc Nancy (1940–2021), who wrote a pioneering and influential essay on Kiarostami's cinema, *L'Évidence du film: Abbas Kiarostami* (2001), almost a decade before that infamous diatribe in Persian.[10] What is Nancy's philosophical take on Kiarostami—and why and how does it matter? I'd like to approach Nancy's text via a crucial review of it in the journal *Film-Philosophy* by a sympathetic reviewer, Laurent Kretzschmar, in order to read the French philosopher's meditations not in abstraction but within its immediate European context.[11]

Kretzschmar begins by making a crucial point about how among "those who have discovered film theory late in the twentieth century, . . . there has always been a feeling of arriving after the battle. We didn't take part in the major theoretical debates and were left studying retrospectively these theories at the university, hoping to find a way to look ahead and move on."

I could say that again, but from an entirely different angle evidently absent in Kretzschmar's point—the angle on film theory that has remained entirely Eurocentric. Kretzschmar proceeds and places a corrective lens over his objection and adds: "On the one hand, as film theorists absorb the shock of Deleuze's theories and get accustomed to its new concepts, this work no longer wears the absolute novelty it seemed to hold in the first place." Then comes yet another corrective lens: "On the other hand, the postmodernism debate is drying out, mainly because a consensus on its meaning for cinema and visual arts has not been found."[12] So far, so good, you might say—we are squarely within the domain of European and Eurocentric high film theory and robust film-philosophy. But how is Kiarostami to be seen and read better here than elsewhere?

These, to be sure, are crucial insights for those critical thinkers considering cinema with a philosophical archive not limited to Deleuze, Nancy, or the journal *Film-Philosophy* itself. This European archive has a rightful pride of place for everyone seriously interested in film. But at the same time, filmmakers such as Abbas Kiarostami, or Satyajit Ray, or Akira Kurosawa, or Ousmane Sembène, among others, have an equally if not more important location in their more immediate aesthetic and intellectual provenance that make Kretzschmar's thoughts on being late (already back in 2001, when Nancy's book had just come out, or 2002 when he reviewed it for *Film-Philosophy*) not just temporally plausible but in fact spatially resonant too. There is a spatial distance, in other words, that exacerbates the temporal distance that Kretzschmar correctly identifies. The temporal distance is a matter of generational timespans, whereas the spatial is a matter of colonial mentality, in which European critical thinkers enjoy a sanctioned ignorance (as Spivak called it) of material published in languages they do not read, or even if they do read it, it is by authors outside their archives and bibliographies. Kretzschmar is of course entirely oblivious to such issues, for his intended readership is entirely limited to those within a limited European provenance of philosophical meditation, even when they do so on the art-world of someone outside their provincial thinking. In short, we on the colonial edges of their modernity are duty-bound to read them. But out of astonishing colonial arrogance, they remain totally ignorant of the work others have done, which constitute a special differential adding to what he notices about the temporal lagging of engagement with film-philosophy.

Kretzschmar is fully appreciative of the significance of the crucial distinction Deleuze has made between the *movement-image* and the *time-image*—but more importantly he also observes

> these emerging time-images announce modern cinema and mark the end of the first period in the history of cinema that will be called classicism. Deleuze's central division brilliantly formalizes in the field of cinema the debate begun by Adorno's comments on the impossibility of representation after the Second World War, but leaves modern cinema as the only possible future, and therefore assigns to film studies the sole and infinite task to analyze the multiple variations of the time-image.[13]

This is a plausible periodization between classicism and modernism in European cinema—and in European or Eurocentric cinema only—and does not apply to any other artworld outside Europe. Filmmakers, artists, philosophers, literary critics, and historians outside the European provincialism must be allowed (not that we are waiting for any permissions) to think of their own varied and multiple periodizations—in plural. Kretzschmar's reference to Adorno and the "impossibility of representation after the Second World War" opens a whole different angle on film-philosophy outside its European provenance. For what he calls "Second World War," Adorno of course means the moral, aesthetic, and philosophical paralysis that the Holocaust had caused in European thought. When Adorno wrote "to write poetry after Auschwitz is barbaric," he put a loud and clear exclamation mark on that paralysis.[14] In the sentence just before that iconic phrase, Adorno wrote "cultural criticism finds itself faced with the final stage of the dialectic of culture and barbarism." Indeed—but that "final stage" the European philosopher saw in Auschwitz had started long ago in the Belgian Congo and British Bengal, or anywhere else under the colonial domination of European barbarism—to use Adorno's language. The entire school of critical theory ultimately reaches (or collapses) into postmodernism and thus creates a cleavage for the larger postcolonial world, the site of the real terror of European colonial modernity around the globe, to assert and insert itself and pave the way toward real "critical theory" (as Aimé Césaire began to do in his *Discourse on Colonialism* in 1950). The issue here, simply because we are dealing with an Iranian and not a European filmmaker, is to what degree Kretzschmar's periodization that comes to a crescendo with Deleuze in Europe is universally valid. European philosophers have this uncontrolled habit of thinking their thoughts are "universal" (they are not) and everyone else's thoughts "local" (they are not).

To a set of postcolonial ears, therefore, the entire postmodernist debate that Kretzschmar interjects here is nothing more than the chickens of European colonial modernity coming home to roost, as Malcolm X would say, dismantling its own manufactured sovereign subject and turning its instrumental reason against itself at one and the same time. When Frederic Jameson says postmodernism is "the cultural logic of late capitalism," we in the postcolonial world do as Fanon says, we pull out our knives, or at least make sure they are within reach.[15] Wake up and smell the roses! Late capitalism? Your late capitalism had begun much earlier in the savageries of European colonialism around the globe, where our naked bodies and denied dignities were the subject and the target of the violence that would come back to Auschwitz and paralyze Adorno's philosophy before collapsing into postmodernism. The only link between European postmodernism and global postcolonialism is the truth of colonialism, of which Palestine is to this day the prime suffering example. So, film-philosophy scholars like Kretzschmar ought to know what we hear when we hear European postmodernist debate about the image-time and such before they can come closer to see what a "postcolonial film-philosophy" might look like. We have entirely different sets of political and aesthetic sensibilities when we sit to watch a Kiarostami, or an Ozu, or a Ray.

It is precisely at this intersection between classicism and modernism that Deleuze and postmodernism left off—for Kretzschmar believes "both are fundamentally unable to overcome the limits of a certain conception of the history of film, for which the passage from classicism to modernity is the ultimate reference."[16] This is where he believes Nancy's short intervention on Kiarostami comes in and shows the way out of this European cul-de-sac. Kretzschmar is not fully satisfied with Nancy's intervention for "it is more an artistic draft than an academic sum, it requires many efforts to reap the full benefit of its propositions for film theory."[17] But how so? Kretzschmar is after "Nancy's underlying ambition for film theory," which is squarely located in one of Kiarostami's key films:

> In *Life and Nothing Else*, Nancy finds a perfect reflection of his own philosophy ... as the philosopher positions this movie centrally in Kiarostami's work, with Kiarostami as a "privileged witness" of the emergence of a new form of cinema. This positioning of Kiarostami ... at a cornerstone of the history and aesthetics of film is the starting point of Nancy's argument. But it is also a giant step as it conditions the interest of the book to the reader's willingness to accept that Nancy's comments on just seven movies can be extrapolated to cover film and visual arts in general. This demanding effort will constitute the main limit of this book.[18]

Despite this reservation, Kretzschmar still believes "the correspondence between Nancy's thinking and Kiarostami's filming proves to be a perfect match between film and philosophy and seems to carry enough convincing power to make reading *L'Évidence du film* an invigorating experience."[19] One cannot but share Kretzschmar's enthusiasm of this fateful encounter between a French philosopher and an Iranian filmmaker. Historically, we have had a few antecedents for such encounters, among them when Goethe discovered Hafez in his *West-östlicher Divan* (1814–1819), or Matthew Arnold Ferdowsi did so in his *Sohrab and Rustum: An Episode* (1853), or Fitzgerald in his *Rubaiyat of Omar Khayyam* (1859), or Emerson Sa'di in his poem "Saadi" (1899), or before them all when Montesquieu used Persian characters for his *Persian Letters* (1721), or one might even suggest when Nietzsche opted for Zarathustra as his dramatic persona in his *Thus Spoke Zarathustra* (1883–1885).[20] Today, those historical encounters are repeated in Nancy and Kiarostami, and all other antecedents could be quite insightful both for the European readers of Nancy and watchers of Kiarostami, and perhaps for the larger world above and beyond that limited domain. The difference, however, is on the state of European colonial hegemony in the world. When Fitzgerald translated Khayyam, for example, or Montesquieu wrote his Persian Letters, the British and the French were ruling the world; when Nancy watched and wrote a short essay on Kiarostami, the French could scarcely hold their own republic together.

What, then, is it exactly that Nancy has discovered in Kiarostami?

> What Nancy aims to achieve, therefore, is to define a new essence or form of film that has always been there but only appears now for itself in Kiarostami's work. The central idea of this new essence is that cinema is fundamentally

an art of looking at the world. To develop this unsurprising statement into an innovative path for film theory, Nancy uses two concepts. One is the concept of gaze or way of looking ("regard" in French); the other is a conception of the world. These two concepts are inextricably linked since the definition of film, as an art of looking is only made possible through the understanding of how Nancy conceives the world. And the latter is at the heart of Nancy's innovative purpose.[21]

To reach this insight into Nancy's work, perhaps the most insightful prose of Kretzschmar comes when he offers a taxonomy of successive periodization of cinema as an art form: "Modern and postmodern cinema are fundamentally reactionary as they are obsessed with the idea that the world no longer makes sense ... [while] classic cinema dealt with a pre-interpreted world and aimed at organizing every element of a movie toward a particular meaning, whereas modern cinema confronts a world that can no longer be understood, and aims at representing the loss of this meaning with the techniques of documentary and realism."[22] Based on this periodization, then comes perhaps the most potent insight of the essay: "Overcoming what we saw as a loss literally gives us the world, a world that Nancy describes through references to Heidegger's phenomenology as the neutral 'there-is' that comes ahead of beings and meanings and allows them to come to existence."[23]

This is a crucial insight we should take seriously and at face value, and not be tempted by the possibility that Nancy saw Kiarostami's films and could not make head from tail of it, perhaps could not link the Koker Trilogy and the films before and after them together and made a philosophical virtue out of his cinematic failure to follow the story—the story of a search in, and into, futility, of Kiarostami's camera (Khayyamesque at its best) celebrating life in the heart of misery and devastation, of the ability to look passively and patiently to discover the tempo of a world in despair. We have to bracket that temptation, for there is something serious that is the result of the Nancy-Kretzschmar's insight—namely, a world that refuses to be overwhelmed with the oversaturated significations narratively superimposed on it and has moved back from, again in Heideggerian terms, the ontological to the ontic thingness of things, or thereness of the world. This is a French philosopher reading an Iranian filmmaker with a German philosophic eye. Be that as it is, Kretzschmar is exceedingly insightful placing Nancy's philosophic perspective in this context: "Nancy argues that cinema is freeing itself from its obsession with the loss of meaning and begins to tackle the beings themselves. The natural posture of cinema is therefore not to represent a preconceived world, nor to represent the loss of this meaningful world, but to present the world itself."[24] Then comes the principal insight of Kretzschmar into Nancy into Kiarostami:

> Nancy concludes: "[T]he evidence of film is that of the existence of a look through which the world can give back its own real." In front of a world that is self-referential, and whose lack of meaning is no longer missing since it is rather a condition of existence, this new cinema is an art of looking and presenting the world and the beings for themselves, without organizing them towards a meaning (the limit of classic cinema), without consciously representing the lack of meaning (the limit of modern cinema), and without obsessively playing with the forms of the past (the limit of postmodern cinema). This short text proposes nothing less than a viable alternative in the attempt to go beyond the contradictions of modernity: a foundation and an opening for the cinematographic images of the twenty-first century.[25]

To drive this point home, Kretzschmar shows how Nancy theorizes Kiarostami's look or gaze—and here he wisely places Kiarostami's cinema beyond both classical, modern, and postmodern gestations as they are understood in European and Eurocentric periodization: "Where modern cinema often had a passive documentary way of looking (merely to record), Kiarostami's gaze is much more challenging for the spectators. Analyzing how Kiarostami uses distinction techniques, very selective framing, and the well-commented 'long cosmic shots,' Nancy shows how this cinema mobilizes the look of the viewer and acts as an eye-opener."[26]

Before concluding his essay, Kretzschmar curbs his own enthusiasm: "But if Nancy succeeds in convincing us that Kiarostami creates new and innovative pictures, how much of this novelty can be extended to the fields of film and visual arts at large? In other words, is this book simply an intelligent commentary of Kiarostami's movies, or does it contain the elements for a definition of an emerging new form of cinema and visual arts, as Nancy pretends? ... I could think of only a couple of film makers whose work may fall in this new way of filming: Hou Hsiao-Hsien and 'Beat' Takeshi Kitano." But he ultimately does with Nancy's philosophy what he says Nancy says about Kiarostami's films and just enjoys the view without any expandable body of knowledge: "After going back and forth in the text, trying to identify concepts and find a solid definition for them, I gave up, and kept on reading Nancy's fluent style with pleasure but with much less expectation regarding the final outcome of this book in regard to film, theory."

But—of minor concern here before we proceed—"the evidence of film is that of the existence of a look through which the world can give back its own real." Really? Suppose we take this insight as evident in the Koker Trilogy. Would this be equally evident in his other films? How reliable is this self-effacing look in other films of Kiarostami? Can we even trust what we are watching in a Kiarostami film—for the world he portrays to "give back its own real?" In *Close-Up* (1999), for example, Kiarostami tells the story of an obsessed cinephile named Hossein Sabzian who so closely and thoroughly identified with a leading Iranian filmmaker, Mohsen Makhmalbaf, that he convinced himself and a gullible family that he was indeed Mohsen Makhmalbaf. The question at the center of the film is not that he was lying. He believed himself to be Makhmalbaf. He had effectively metamorphosed into Makhmalbaf. This film was based on a real-life incident, which Makhmalbaf once told me he wanted to turn into a film himself but Kiarostami convinced him to let him do it. What immediately strikes the viewers watching this film is how all the "actors" in the film are the actual people who had originally been part of this drama. So, were Sabzian and his "victims" acting then or were they acting now—or both, or neither? They were re-enacting what they had acted in real life. The double take suddenly turns all actions into a simulacrum of themselves, whereby reality and fiction morph into each other and we are lost at the prospect of where exactly we are located and what exactly it is we are watching. If the world we see through Kiarostami's camera is "self-referential," then what exactly is it referencing? Where does the artistry, the playfulness, the trickery of the work of art come in to disturb the trust we might have in the world exuding itself out? What we are watching when we watch *Close-Up* is a radically altered state of being, of being as exception, of a topsy-turvy world that has ipso facto altered the dialectic between truth and narrative, between fact and fiction, between aesthetic and nonaesthetic reasons. Yes, "a look" exists—we can see that—

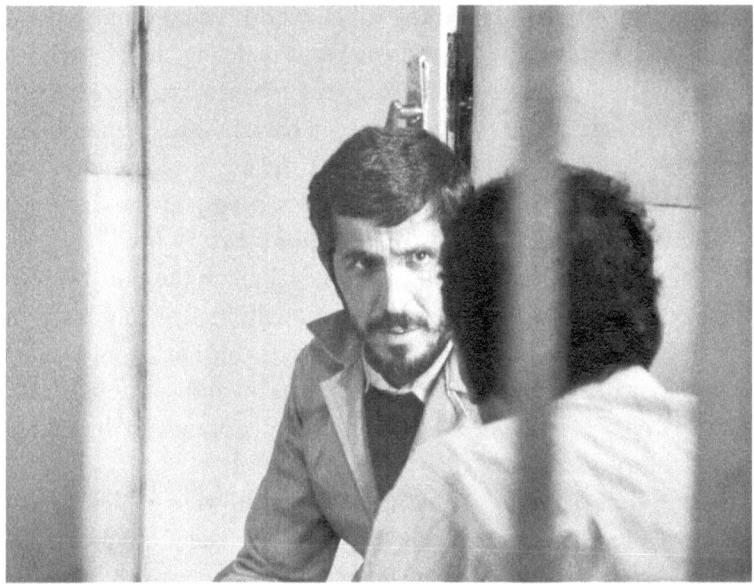

Figure 7. Hossein Sabzian in Abbas Kiarostami's *Close-Up* (1999). Courtesy of Abbas Kiarostami Foundation.

but through it the world we are watching could not possibly give us back its own real, for it is unreal. Here, we are not just watching an active and melodious fusion of fact and fiction—for the fusion has already crafted a tertiary space that since my first reflections on Kiarostami in my book *Close-Up: Iranian Cinema: Past, Present, Future* (2001) I have called "factasy." That factasy is not self-evident. It is aesthetically manufactured. The evidence of this particular film is not that of the existence of a look "through which the world can give back its own real." It is exactly the opposite of it.

BLINDNESS AND INSIGHT:
THE FICTIVE TRANSPARENCY OF THE REAL

What could we conclude from Kretzschmar's take on Nancy's engagement with Kiarostami? That there is no meaning to the world; that there is no lack of meaning in the world; and that there is no use manipulating the forms to prove there is no meaning to the world. There is only *gazing* at the irreducible ipseity of the world—without meaning. Just let the world reveal itself. This insight has an uncanny resemblance (but not entirely so) to what I wrote about Kiarostami's cinema back in 2001, when I had no clue what Nancy had said—reaching as I did for the "pre-interpretive moment of the world," which I said "becomes exactly the mode of operation in Kiarostami's cinematic."[27] Even before that, in my first essay on Kiarostami I published in the fall of 1995, just about the time Nancy was invited by Cahiers du Cinema to write about a filmmaker (but the volume for which it was intended never materialized). In that essay, too, I had termed this encounter with the naked world as operative through "the fictive transparency of the real."[28] But how did my reading and that of Nancy differ—and why does it matter?

The point here is not to suggest that I had said what Nancy published in 2001 back in 1997 in a slightly different way. The point is something entirely different. I had argued my point through a pairing of Kiarostami with the seminal Persian poet of Kiarostami's time, Sohrab Sepehri—and it is to Sepehri that we owe this insight both in his own poetry and in Kiarostami's cinema, decades before Nancy thought to write a short essay on Kiarostami. The difference between what I wrote and what Nancy wrote is not limited to the genealogy of my thought on Kiarostami, which is entirely independent of Nancy's. He had come to this conclusion about Kiarostami from the depth of his own philosophical preoccupations. I had come to it through the poetry of Sohrab Sepehri. Sepehri was as alien to Nancy as Nancy was to me when I was writing on Kiarostami back in 1995. But Kiarostami had in two different registers provoked almost identical insights by a French and an Iranian thinker because of his own rootedness in Sepehri, which I knew and Nancy did not.

But—and here is the far more serious difference between what I had written about Kiarostami before or simultaneous with Nancy, both of us unaware of the other—in what I had detected in Kiarostami, there was also a poetic artistry, an aesthetic manipulation of the real, to make it reveal its irreality. In response to Kretzschmar's question whether Nancy's take is exclusive to Kiarostami or more general, I might therefore add here that this is precisely the way I have always read Kurosawa's *Rashomon* (1950)—that the point of the film is not multiplicity of perspectives/representations and therefore relativism, but the visual fact of what we see—a woman violated and a man murdered—staring at us whichever way we look at it or however differently we may intercept what we hear the witnesses say. From Kurosawa to Kiarostami and from Kiarostami back to Sepehri, what we see is contingent on the artistry of the filmmaker and their making the world look other than it would have looked without that artistry—the "fictive transparency of the real."

We should not, however, be limited to only one reading of Nancy on Kiarostami, however potent and crucial. Two other related issues about Nancy and Kiarostami are important here: (1) We have a look at their encounter from a perspective halfway around the world from France and Europe by Moinak Biswas, professor of film studies at Jadavpur University, Kolkata, who reads Nancy for having said "Kiarostami does not primarily seek an image or a sign, he seeks a gaze. . . . To seek a gaze, to arrive at the eye to be set on what surrounds us, is for Nancy a fusion of the evidence that things are and that cinema is. For him this is a great renewal of the exhausted culture of the image. Kiarostami is no longer struggling with representation, but giving us presences, affirmations of a world";[29] and (2) the fact that Kiarostami was not the only filmmaker who had attracted Nancy's philosophical curiosities. He has been far more preoccupied with the renowned French filmmaker Claire Denis, who has even made a documentary on him, *Vers Nancy* (2002). There is a whole issue of the venerable *Film-Philosophy* journal dedicated to this encounter between Nancy and Denis.[30]

From Moinak Biswas's reading we may conclude the evidence of that gaze to be the defining moment of Kiarostami's cinema; and from Nancy's attention to Claire Denis, we may conclude the evidence of that gaze is not limited to Kiarostami's cinema. Kristin Lené Hole's major study, *Towards a Feminist Cinematic Ethics: Claire Denis, Emmanuel Levinas, and Jean-Luc Nancy*, reaches for a nonnormative take as she casts two philosophers (Levinas and Nancy) and a filmmaker (Denis) against each other. With feminist, postcolonial, and queer concerns at the center of her study, her film-philosophy has a potent claim on the field.

> Putting philosophy in contact with cinema gives flesh—both metaphorically and also literally, in the sense of centering the material body—to the concept

of ethics. This is not an ethics that is conveyed didactically or in a straightforward narrative manner, since Denis's films persistently avoid a moralizing tone. There is no "moral of the story" in a Denis film. . . . Instead, we are made aware of complexity, ambiguity and disjunctive connection. We are given a window into a world colored in shades of grey and left to sit with otherness, as opposed to feeling able to clearly distance ourselves from the characters and images on screen via moral judgements.[31]

Nancy's interest in Denis, as evident in Hole's study, is far more engaged and sustained than just a short essay and a quick chat with Kiarostami. From this more elaborate encounter of Nancy with Denis, Hole reaches for a common connection between Denis and Kiarostami when she cites this key passage of Nancy to "to show the real in its unrepresentability":

Evidence becomes that of passage rather than some epiphany of meaning or presence. Cinema is truly the art—in any case the technique—of a world that suspends myths. Even if it has put itself in the service of myths, at the limit, it finishes by taking them away; it carries off all epiphanies of meaning and of immobile presence into the evidence of movement. A world that links by going from one film to the next, and that learns thus, very slowly, another way of producing meaning.[32]

If the "real is unrepresentable," then the very same real is also accessible only through the camera that captures its conflated (embedded) truth, as in Kiarostami's *Close-Up*, where Sabzian's manipulative reading of reality (in which he himself is implicated) is enabled by Kiarostami's presence and the power of his cinematic gaze. This is what I have meant by "the fictive transparency of the real," for the real contains a fiction that makes it in and of itself meaningful. So, the world we see through Kiarostami's camera is one not of naked realities but of pure verisimilitudes—or more accurately, of realities that entail and exude their own verisimilitudes. "To seek a gaze," as Moinak Biswas reads Nancy to be saying, is to discover the constellation of the plays of the verisimilitudes always already embedded in the fictive transparencies of the real. Nancy's sustained reading of Clare Denis allows for that insight. His brief encounter with Kiarostami suggests such a prospect (as indeed Kretzschmar's reading has said so specifically) but does not sustain it. What the evidently unmitigated gaze of Kiarostami reveals is not pure reality but pure verisimilitude, a poetic of presence, of reality.

THE FRENCH PHILOSOPHER AND
THE IRANIAN FILMMAKER

If we were now to turn to the actual essay and the conversation between Nancy and Kiarostami, we would be in the presence of a different kind of meditation than these erudite takes by Kretzschmar, Biswas, and Hole may imply. I deliberately wished to separate the actual trilingual text of *L'Évidence du film/The Evidence of Film/Bedahat-e Film* (2001) from the way it has been hitherto received and interpreted by major film critics and scholars. The first issue that immediately strikes the reader of this trilingual volume is the translation of the word *Evidence* as *Bedahat*, which is strange and unusual to say the least, and perhaps even a flawed translation. The proper translation for *Evidence* is *Sanad, Madrak*, and words of that sort, and the translation for the word *Bedahat* is spontaneity, extemporaneously, speaking without thinking, or at best improvisatory, and such. One can guess where the translator went wrong with this choice when he took the Persian colloquialism of *badihi*, meaning *self-evident*, and made a verbal noun out of it as *Bedahat*, inattentive to the long history of this latter word, which does not come from that colloquial expression. There is therefore a discrepancy between the way Nancy uttered the word *Évidence*. which is the cognate of the English word *Evidence*, and the word *Bedahat* the way the Persian translator Baqer Parham, a perfectly capable and professional translator, has opted to place for it. This troubled translation extends into the text of Nancy's essay as well, where the initial reportage of the provenance of the essay is translated into a perfectly idiomatic Persian, but when Nancy gets into the thicket of his philosophical reflections, Parham's Persian prose becomes awfully mechanical and seriously flawed, not because of any misunderstanding of any particular French or English word but because the philosophical Persian prose that resulted is entirely outlandish and almost meaningless. The translation as a result shows a serious lack of knowledge about Nancy's philosophical system and the way he reads the world and visual arts of the sort Kiarostami represents as evidence of a world both bereft of metaphysical meaning and paralyzed with that loss but celebrating by dwelling on the presentation for the world itself. This simple underlying fact of Nancy's philosophical vision for the world is completely absent in

Parham's otherwise capable translation of the essay into Persian. The Persian translation is stylistically potent but fails to convey the rich philosophical prose of the original and sometimes is verbatim correct but organically meaningless. If a Persian-speaking person reads only that Persian translation without access to its French original or English translation, they would be completely at a loss as to what the big fuss is about this essay.

The original essay begins with two successive "histories" of how it came to be, initially by an invitation by the journal *Cahiers du cinéma* and subsequently by a Belgian publisher, after which the piece plunges into a succession of insightful meditations that are coded with such key words as "*Regard*/Look," "*Réel*/The Real," "*Prégnance*/Pregnant," "*Art surnuméraire*/Supernumerary Art," et cetera, until it reaches the key sections on "Regard/image/Look/Image" and finally "*Évidence*/Evidence." Each one of these sections is a rich and exciting meditation on an aspect of (Kiarostami's) cinema, facilitating a fresh way of looking at the sight of his filmic evidence. Here Nancy begins with the potent observation that "evidence always comprises a blind spot within its very obviousness: in this way it leans on the eye. The 'blind spot' does not deprive the eye of its sight: on the contrary, it makes an opening for a gaze and it *presses* upon it to look."[33]

As other readers of Nancy have suggested, we should read his comments on Kiarostami in the context of his follow up on Deleuze's idea of the emergence of the "time-image," when cinema ceases to pretend to represent the world. Nancy sees Kiarostami as the moment when we are equally liberated from the celebratory move of cinema to be freed from the postmodern preoccupation with this disappearance of the world. Now with Nancy, cinema comes to see itself as the primacy of the look, the efficacy of the movement, and the predominance of the real—whereby the world emphatically announces itself.[34] More specifically:

> Evidence refers to what is obvious, what makes sense, what is striking and, by the same token, opens and gives a chance and an opportunity to meaning. Its truth is something that grips and does not have to correspond to any given criteria. Nor does evidence work as concealment, for it always keeps a secret or an essential reserve: its very light is reserved, and its provenance.[35]

The final evidence is when cinema becomes its own truth irreducible to any other world that it may await interpreting: "Cinema—its screen, its sensitive membrane—stretches and hangs between a world in which representation was in charge of the signs of truth, of the heralding of meaning, or of the warrant of a presence to come; and another world that opens onto its own presence though avoiding where its thoughtful evidence realizes itself."[36]

Nancy's text is a choppy piece, not a coherent or even cohesive text, written on multiple occasions and times—between 1994, 1995, and 1999—and finally published in 2001 in the form of a volume in three languages. What as a result makes it cohere is the central idea of the text and not its elaborate argumentations—which it lacks. It is therefore a celebrated text because it is by a celebrated philosopher with a central and cohesive insight into the moment of what some have even called "post-postmodern" in European aesthetics—but does it have much to say to the world outside European provincialism? For that, we need to place Nancy's encounter with Kiarostami in the context of the French philosopher's larger concerns.

In his 1993 book *Le sens du monde/The Sense of the World* (1993/1997), Nancy dwells specifically on the sense of the world—a sense that is within the world itself.[37] This Heideggerian position strips the troubled European subject being in search of a meaning in the world other than the being of the world itself. Neither divinity nor any other metaphysical underpinning to our reading of the world other than the world itself exudes its senses. This is also what Nancy sees in Kiarostami's cinema—the naked evidence of the world exposed, celebrated, staged. In his other major work, *La creation du monde ou la mondialisation/The Creation of the World or Globalization* (2002/2007), he posits "mondialisation" as a "world-forming" process—exactly the opposite of globalization where the world is the object of conquest rather than the occasion for a renewed dwelling.[38] What anticipates his thought in Kiarostami is also his book *Les Muses/The Muses* (1994/1996), where in his piece on Caravaggio, painting is again not a representation of the empirical world but a presentation of the world, of sense, of existence.[39]

Placed in this larger philosophical context of Nancy, his short piece on Kiarostami extends and expands his central visions beyond the European reach to an Iranian artist and filmmaker who became part and parcel of the French artistic and intellectual scene, for it was at Cannes where Kiarostami first emerged as a global figure. The French as a result, and Nancy in particular, have every right to their philosophical reflections on Kiarostami, who is one of their own. But at the same time, the text of Kiarostami's own cinematic and artistic legacy, not the nativist proposition that he is "an Iranian artist," may also entail and enable alternative readings. If we were to compare the way Nancy treated Kiarostami seriously with the way two Iranian dilettantes, Farhadpour and Eslami, treated him with such disdain and denigration, the world must be grateful that at least the French took Kiarostami far more seriously than his own hateful and banal compatriots did. But neither does that ghastly volume, *Paris-Tehran*, represent the Iranian reception of Kiarostami nor does Nancy's philosophic encounter utter the last word on a multifaceted legacy of a major filmmaker who was born and raised on the fertile Iranian cultural soil but came to full recognition far away from his homeland.

THE NON-CONVERSATION

The "conversation" between Nancy and Kiarostami is something of a nonstarter if not an altogether mismatched embarrassment. Nancy starts by wondering if there is any connection between Kiarostami's filmic or photographic images and Persian manuscript illustrations (*Negar-gari*) that European Orientalists have called "miniature." Kiarostami says a graduate student once told him she was writing a doctoral dissertation on this similarity, but he was surprised by that comparison and unaware of it and was certainly not under the influence of "miniature" painting.[40] At this point, Nancy wonders if Kiarostami has any knowledge of "miniature painting," and Kiarostami says no, he does not, though in college he was exposed to it. Nancy then asks a poignant question to which Kiarostami offers a truly sad and unfortunate answer. Nancy says we in "the West" call this kind of Persian painting "miniature." What do you call it in your own language and tradition? "Incidentally," Nancy says, "do you say 'miniature' in Persian? Because I hear you're saying 'miniature'—surely, it is a Latin word that was recently borrowed? How does one say it in Persian tradition?"[41]

Kiarostami is dumbfounded by the question and says there is no word he could think of, and in fact *miniature* is what they call it in Persian too. He is of course right, and artists of his generation, deeply alienated from if not hostile to their own artistic traditions, would not be bothered to wonder what these Persian paintings were called in Persian. He could not think of terms such as *Negar-gari* and *Tasvir*, and like many others in his generation remains limited to the misapplication of the French word *miniature*, which is a confused and conflated European word mixing *minimum*, meaning "red lead," with *minimal*, as in "small," as illuminated manuscripts of Christian codices, that was later misapplied to Indian, Persian, and Ottoman paintings. The same is for the word *portrait*, for which again Kiarostami could not think of any Persian word and said in Persian we also used the word *portrait*. Of course, words such as *Shamayel* and *Temsal* are perfectly suitable for *portrait*, rooted in Persian poetic and aesthetic sources. The problem becomes confounded when the English translator of the conversation takes the sound "ch" in French for "sh" in English and transcribes the word *Chopoq* (a kind of pipe) as *Shopoq*! This part of the Persian, English, and French confusions between Nancy, Kiarostami, and their translators, confounded even more by the flawed application of the word *Bedahat* for the key French word of *Évidence* in the title of the book and the essay, makes the entirety of the book something of a freak show.

The fact that because of Kiarostami's ignorance of these terms, Nancy remained unaware of the word *Tasvir* or *Negar* for the terrible misapplication of *miniature* is particularly unfortunate, for these words would have alerted the French philosopher to the rich aesthetic traditions that have informed the visual vocabulary of all contemporary Iranian artists, including Kiarostami. The three-volume monumental work of Ruyin Pakbaz, *Da'erat al-Ma'aref-e Honar/Encyclopedia of Art*, or *Naqqashi Iran az Dirbaz ta Emruz/Iranian Painting from Beginning to Today*, is just the tip of the iceberg of the vast body of work available in Persian that could have been made available to Nancy and other Europeans who care to reflect on aspects of Iranian art. The word *Tasvir*, as it appears in the title of Shafi'i-Kadkani's seminal work, *Suvar-e Khayal dar She'r-e Farsi/Imaginative Imageries in Persian Poetry* (1971)—which I discussed in the first chapter—would have alerted the French philosopher to a far more serious allusion to his foundational idea in the essay and in fact in his philosophy.

The issue of translation for Kiarostami when he attended international events has been quite serious when he has been at the mercy of ill-prepared expat Iranians volunteering their services. The prominent *New York Times* film critic A. O. Scott recounts an encounter with Abbas Kiarostami in Cartagena, Colombia, where he was invited for a master-class, and where Scott moderated a conversation with the filmmaker, but they soon realized they had a serious language barrier that had to be negotiated among multiple interpreters trafficking in Persian, Spanish, and English, at the conclusion of which Scott observed: "But afterward many of us agreed that we had experienced something much stranger and more profound than a successful search for verbal equivalents. We swore that for a short but intense period, under the spell of the filmmaker's quiet charisma, we had all been thinking in Persian. But perhaps we had just been thinking in Kiarostami."[42] That "quiet charisma" phrase plus thinking "in Kiarostami" rather than any other language prepares A. O. Scott for an even more important note: "To an extent that we have only begun to grasp, movies invented a new way of thinking, and Abbas Kiarostami's movies are among the clearest and most challenging applications of cinematic thought."[43] That would be "film-philosophy" in a nutshell. But that the visual idiomaticity of a filmmaker completely overcomes the linguistic barriers among filmmakers, film critics, and philosophers paving their way toward the idea of film-philosophy is still a bumpy road.

The encounter between Nancy and Kiarostami ends, we read, with Kiarostami suddenly reciting the original Arabic of the Surah Al-Zalzalah/The Earthquake of the Qur'an out of the blue. Nancy asks if he knew the whole Qur'an by heart and he says no, but he likes this particular chapter of the Muslim Holy Book. Nancy says he knows this surah too. Kiarostami is surprised and Nancy says, well, he is interested in monotheism. So, no knowledge or interest in Persian manuscript paintings Europeans have miscalled "miniature," or even what to call it in Persian, just one chapter of the Qur'an to share for a filmmaker from an Islamic Republic. But in between these mishaps, a few fruitful comments emerge about Kiarostami's preference for nonnarrative cinema.[44] This is then followed by a collection of haphazard stills with no explanation or caption about their relevance to the text or the conversation—except this: "In this book, the relation between discourse and image should remain free—no commentary, no illustration."[45]

What makes the conversation relevant to the rest of the world, though in a roundabout way, is a series of exchanges where Nancy asks questions such as "I saw this picture in this film, what does that mean?" Here Kiarostami is at his best when he compares cinema to poetry and music and insists that a film must always preserve its mystery and not always be completely understood[46]—to which Nancy responds in kind and develops the idea of cinema as a relation to itself, not to the outside world. Except for such rare moments, much of the conversation is therefore neither here nor there—a casual chat between two erudite men—a French philosopher and an Iranian filmmaker, talking across each other into a polite vacuity. The crucial hermeneutic moment here relevant to Nancy's main idea is precisely the moment when he asks Kiarostami for his explanation of things. Had Nancy seen Kiarostami's *Close-Up* (1990) at this point—did he remember it? To what degree is a filmmaker able to unravel the mysteries of their own artwork? Was Hossain Sabzian a con artist, Nancy could have asked Kiarostami, or the very epiphany of cinema? Could Kiarostami have answered that question? Is any artist in full control of their artworld? Was Hossein Sabzian not more of a Makhmalbaf than Makhmalbaf himself—at the time that he was so successfully pretending to be Makhmalbaf that he had convinced himself and a respectable family that he was Makhmalbaf? When we meet Sabzian for the first time in Kiarostami's film, he is sitting in a bus with a copy of a published screenplay of Makhmalbaf's film *The Cyclist* (1987). Next to him sits another random passenger, later we learn a Ms. Ahankhah. A casual conversation ensues in the course of which Sabzian reveals to Ms. Ahankhah that he is Mohsen Makhmalbaf himself. Eventually, Sabzian/Makhmalbaf finds his way into the Ahankhah family house. He says he wants to make a film and use their residence as its location, with the Ahankhah family as actors. After a while, the family suspects that Sabzian is faking it. They alert a journalist, Mr. Farazmand, who corroborates their suspicion that Sabzian is not Makhmalbaf. The police finally intervene and arrest the Makhmalbaf look-alike. With that convoluted story, masterfully crafted by Kiarostami, where is the evident reality, and in what ways does the "evidence [refer] to what is obvious, what makes sense, what is striking and, by the same token, opens and gives a chance and an opportunity to meaning," as Nancy suggests? Nothing is obvious here, nothing is evident, everything is fake, and precisely in that falsity dwells the truth of the matter, crafted by a masterful play of Sabzian on Makhmalbaf, and Kiarostami on both of them.

But neither in that conversation nor indeed anywhere else is Kiarostami in any authorial position to unravel the "mystery," as he likes to say, of his own work of art. In *Close-Up*, as elsewhere, the varied intentions of the text override the intentions of its author, and *intentio operis*, as Umberto Eco would say, trumps *intentio auctoris*—which makes the conversation between Nancy and Kiarostami an exercise in futility.[47] But this is not specific to this conversation. Over the years, I have known and conversed with many filmmakers and other artists, Iranian and otherwise. I have never found it possible to talk to them about the substance of their work in any meaningful way. We talk about casual things, the weather, the politics, other filmmakers, et cetera. But never about the substance of their own work or what it means. I was vicariously imagining myself sitting next to Nancy and Kiarostami when they were talking and taking a picture to put on social media and say how cute it is that I could not think of anything more serious to say. From the distance of this safe location far away from both of them, now blissfully in the bosoms of eternity, as you see, I have much to say about both. Writing about a work of art is very different from writing about an artist. One thrives on a critical and meditative prose, the other feigns a biographical and public performance.

THE SOUND OF THE FOOTSTEPS OF WATER

Neither an ill-informed allusion to Persian "miniature" painting nor an irrelevant and off-the-cuff reference to a chapter of the Qur'an: What the encounter between Nancy and Kiarostami missed was where the French philosopher's philosophy and Iranian filmmaker's cinema come together on the glorious pages of Sohrab Sepehri's poetry. When it comes to Nancy's insights into Kiarostami's cinema, and the way those insights have been read admiringly by his readers, there is nothing in Nancy's essay, though delivered in his own philosophical diction, in the late 1990s that we do not read in the poetic Persian of Sohrab Sepehri back in the early 1960s, composed decades earlier in his seminal poem, "Seda-ye Pa-ye Ab/The Sound of the Footsteps of Water"—long before Kiarostami read Sepehri and ran with it toward his own camera. When Nancy says, "evidence refers to what is obvious, what makes sense, what is striking and, by the same token, opens and gives a chance and an opportunity to meaning," entirely unbeknownst to himself he is breathing in Sepehri's poetic universe, master poet of the obvious, the so obvious that is hidden in plain sight. Sepehri's entire poetry might be said to be this poetics of the self-evident, though lost in the thicket of the metaphysical. If he is a Muslim, he is a Muslim in the most evident, the most natural, the most accessible and immediate senses:

> I am a Muslim
> The direction of my prayer is a red rose—
> Prayer rug a fountain, I prostrate on light for a clay,
> The prairie is my prayer rug
> I take my ablution with the palpitations of windows
> . . .⁴⁸

When Kretzschmar reads Nancy's essay on Kiarostami as saying, "overcoming what we saw as a loss literally gives us the world, a world that Nancy describes through references to Heidegger's phenomenology as the neutral 'there-is' that comes ahead of beings and meanings and allows them to come to existence"—again, totally unbeknownst to himself, he is citing Sepehri and reciting his poetry in a philosophical prose:

> Our garden was in the shadow of knowledge
> Our garden was where feeling and plants tied together
> Our garden was the spot where the look, the cage, and the mirror met
> . . .
>
> Where we drank water without the need for philosophy
> Picked up berries without knowledge
> . . .
>
> Life was something like a thunderstorm during the Noruz—
> Like a poplar tree full of starlings
> . . .⁴⁹

In the poetry of Sepehri, we already have a suspension of representation and are in the presence of the presentation of the world itself—where we are invited to forego the illusion of reading the world for the pleasure of being it, where we drink water without philosophy, and pick berries without botany.

> I saw a book whose words were all made of crystals
> I saw a piece of paper made of the season of Spring
> I saw a museum far away from green grass
> I saw a mosque far away from water
> On the bedside of a disappointed Muslim jurists
> I saw a parch of water full of questions
> . . .
> I am close to the beginning of the earth
> I take the pulse of flowers
> I am quite familiar with the wet destiny of water,
> With the green habits of tree
> . . .[50]

When Nancy says, "cinema—its screen, its sensitive membrane—stretches and hangs between a world in which representation was in charge of the signs of truth, of the heralding of meaning, or of the warrant of a presence to come; and another world that opens onto its own presence though avoiding where its thoughtful evidence realizes itself," he is, again unbeknownst to himself, in the world of Sepehri:

> We must wash our eyes—
> A different kind of seeing we must learn:
> We need to wash the words—
> The word must be the wind itself,
> The word must be the rain itself—
> We must fold the umbrellas
> We must walk into the rain—
> We must take our thinking and our memory
> Under the rain
> . . .[51]

Sepehri revolutionized our perception of the introduction of things into thoughts, of plants into phrases, of fresh materiality of the world into legislating its evidence into any philosophy of it. From that evident materiality of the visible world, he crafted a material metaphysics, an intuitive contradiction in terms, that made perfect sense in his poetry. This is what I have called "the fictive transparency of the real" when translated into Kiarostami's cinema.

> Let us have bread and cheese for breakfast
> Plant a sapling at the turn of every phrase
> And scatter the seeds of silence in between every two syllabi—
> Let us not read any book where the air does not blow
> Any book where there is no wet skin of a dew
> Any book where cells have no full dimensions
> ...
>
> Let us go by the sea
> Spread our fishing net
> And catch freshness from water
> Let us pick up a pebble from the ground
> And feel the weight of being
> ...[52]

But this is not a self-evident world. It is a well-crafted world. It is not "out there." It is intuited and crafted. It is Sepehri's world, the world as he saw and sensed and depicted it, envisioned and poetically enabled it to reveal itself. The world was not just there to be revealed. This is the poetic instrumentality of Sepehri's poetic imagination that sensed and revealed it. Kiarostami's cinema is the visual sublimation of Sepehri's poetry.

THE UNKNOWING SUBJECT OF AN AGONISTIC PHILOSOPHICAL HERITAGE

What is the moral of the story here, as we read Nancy on Kiarostami? Above all, it is long overdue for European and Eurocentric students of philosophy to come to the bosom of the world, and to seriously complicate their notion of "philosophy" and question the way the word has been falsely appropriated and colonized by a certain westward trajectory of Platonic and Aristotelian thinking at the expense of all the others. The question is not whether other critical and creative thinkers around the world, and especially outside the Hellenic circle, have a claim on the word—of course they do. Nor is the question whether any kind of policing of the word becomes democratically available to all non-European philosophers. The question is not even the factual evidence of the trajectory of Platonic, post-Platonic, and non-Platonic philosophical traditions that have developed to the east of Plato's birthplace in the Arabic, Persian, or Urdu domains. Avicenna in Arabic, Naser Khosrow in Persian, Mohammad Iqbal in Persian and Urdu need not wait for any permission or generosity of a liberal European imagination to be considered philosophers. The question is the poetic and aesthetic recasting of the word *philosophy*, as we now see it rightly expanded to the domain of film but still holding its umbilical cord and security blanket (either of those two metaphors will do) of "Western philosophy." Time to cut that umbilical cord and deposit that security blanket in some safe museum closet for posterity.

This prevailing Eurocentrism in both "philosophy" and "film-philosophy" is no longer even cute or funny. It is seriously silly and embarrassing in this time and age. The issue is not to abandon "Western philosophy," if it so wishes to identify itself, and opt for "Eastern philosophy," whatever that might be, or else run toward "epistemologies of the South," as opposed to presumably the "epistemologies of the North." These are all false and deeply flawed categories. My concern here is not just the trajectory that Orientalists have dubbed "Islamic philosophy" and thus marked and alienated at one and the same time and that has in and of itself taken the Platonic and Aristotelian domains in directions decidedly different from those of "Western philosophy." My contention is also not limited by the varied schools within the Islamic philosophical heritage that have been historically identified as Peripatetic, Neoplatonic, Illuminationist, or Transcendental. My purpose here is rather to focus on Kiarostami's cinema itself, but instead of assimilating it backward into what calls itself "Western philosophy," or "Eastern philosophy" for that matter, each of which has suddenly discovered for itself a rich and fertile ground in aspects of world cinema without the slightest sense of hesitation or pause, allow for Kiarostami's cinema to breathe first in its own immediate natural habitat, which is the Iranian and Islamic aesthetic and intellectual history, normative and moral imagination, and cultivated intuition of transcendence. That, of course, requires a philosophical projection that begins in Kiarostami's own cinema, before we detect or speculate any other philosophical thinking contingent on it, of the sort that Nancy decidedly and fruitfully offers his cinema. The point is that if we are to take the encounter between a French philosopher and an Iranian filmmaker seriously, we then need a much richer and wider philosophical imagination that embraces them both and is irreducible to neither—and that by definition could not be an antagonistic space but certainly an agonistic domain. If we have received something that is now called "Western philosophy," and another thing that is called "Islamic philosophy," and now on top of that "the epistemologies of the south," we may take them all at face value but allow the oeuvre of a filmmaker and artist like Kiarostami to bring them all together into an aesthetic pluralism where they learn the significance of agonistic cohabitation.

The theocentricity of Islamic philosophy, replicated in Jewish and Christian philosophies, but all heavily Aristotelian, has been seriously complicated by the logocentric (*Falsafah*), nomocentric (Shari'ah), and homocentric (*Tasawwuf*) proclivities evident in the intellectual and doctrinal histories of Muslims, and in the larger domains it has had to cohabit with serious literary humanism (*Adab*) in multiple languages, with their own respective focal points of ethnos, logos, ethos, and chaos—as I have detailed it in my book *Persian Literary Humanism* (2012).[53] The result is a vastly rich and diversified philosophical diction that forms the world of its own, remotely resembling aspects of their Aristotelian proclivities but by no stretch of the imagination limited to it. That a filmmaker like Kiarostami is consciously alienated from that world and could not even think of what word to suggest for *miniature* or *portrait* is a clear indication that his aesthetic intuition of transcendence is in dire need of an active theorization beyond the reach of "Western philosophy." As a filmmaker and artist, Kiarostami breathed in the air and swam in the ocean of that moral and intellectual world even if he was not knowingly conscious of it. The issue is to place his legacy in that provenance.

We could also come to all these reflections through the critical thinking of the leading Iranian literary theorist Mohammad Reza Shafi'i-Kadkani, who has offered a bold and perceptive angle on how to read Islamic doctrinal history aesthetically. In explaining the hyperbolic prose of some seminal Sufi texts he has carefully studied, he opts to interpret them aesthetically, not on the presumption of how false or fanatical they might appear but on how beautifully they have been posed.[54] The veracity or falsity of such mystic reports of extraordinary experiences is not logical but aesthetic, he proposes. If they make aesthetic sense then they are true, and if they do not then they are false. In mysticism, he proposes, statements are uttered as declarative while they are in fact propositional, even if they are told as fact. Shafi'i-Kadkani then cites a phrase by the famous Persian mystic Abu al-Hasan Kharaqani (963–1033), who said when a mother tells her child "I die for you," she will not die no matter how many times she might say it. He then adds how he has always thought of Sufism as an aesthetic encounter with religion: "The rise and fall of Sufism, as I see it, is contingent on its aesthetic take of Sufism on religion."[55]

Is it possible to watch Kiarostami with a pair of fresh and curious eyes that see his work as an aesthetic encounter with the living or dead certainties of his received metaphysics, which he has succeeded visualizing? The thinking that this incursion into a philosophical imagination closer to the aesthetic home and intellectual habitat of Kiarostami enables an agency that is contingent on a postcolonial subject that is unknowable to "the West," knowable to itself, and unknowing in its hitherto contingent encounters with an agonistic philosophical tradition.[56] The key issue at this point is no longer any fictive or idyllic reconciliation among various philosophical traditions, East and West, as they have been colonially divided, which is an impossibility, but coming to terms with the fact of their agonistic cohabitation in a world that has willy-nilly produced a filmmaker like Abbas Kiarostami and attracted serious philosophical interests in his work, as perhaps best evident in Nancy's brief but still fruitful engagements with aspects of his filmic oeuvre. Agonistic philosophical heritage, as I propose it here, is conflictual, but not antagonistic, and the result of it is a negative dialectic (Adorno) that allows for a contrapuntal reading (Said) of "Western philosophy." Kiarostami's cinema offers the world a unique opportunity for this proposition, though it is not unique in that regard, and one can think of Yasujirō Ozu, Satyajit Ray, Akira Kurosawa, Chen Kaige, Nuri Bilge Ceylan, and eventually retroactively of European and US filmmakers too—if we are to take the ideas of world cinema seriously in a philosophical sense. The result of this is the articulation of a postcolonial unknowing subject that is made contingently sovereign by and through an agonistic epistemology that is required and occasioned in the primacy and veracity of a work of art crafted by Kiarostami's lenses.

AESTHETIC SOVEREIGNTY AND THE NOMADIC SUBJECT

What ultimately determines what sort of philosophical reflections or a syncretic (agonistic) disposition are most meaningful in any encounter with a work of art is not one philosophical discourse (exclusively Western, as we have seen so far applied to Kiarostami) as opposed to another (exclusively Eastern, as any nativist proclivity might suggest), but the work of art itself, its place in the world, and the aesthetic sovereignty that in and of itself it proclaims. Why does this aesthetic sovereignty matter? In his seminal study, *The Sovereignty of Art* (1988), Christoph Menke dwells on what he calls "aesthetic negativity" or "the distinction between the aesthetic and the nonaesthetic" and proposes "only by conceiving of works of art in their negative relationship to everything that is not art can autonomy of such works ... be adequately understood."[57] This position obviously leads him to a more fundamental position: "What art actually is, is contradiction, rejection, negation."[58] But how are we to place this conception of art in the domain of (colonial) modernity as a project? Menke calls this positioning "an unresolved ambivalence," which is to say art is to be seen as both one among other modes of experiences of modernity and yet as an experience that "exceeds the limits of reason of nonaesthetic discourses."[59] The tension is between autonomy and integrity, which Menke seeks to resolve via the proposition of "sovereignty"—which central idea he further explains:

> On this view, aesthetic experience is sovereign insofar as it does not take its place within the differentiated structure of plural reason, but rather exceeds its bounds. Whereas the autonomy model confers relative validity upon aesthetic experience, the sovereignty model grants it absolute validity, since its enactment disrupts the successful functioning of nonaesthetic discourses. The sovereignty model considers aesthetic experience a medium for the dissolution of the rule of nonaesthetic reason, the vehicle for an experientially enacted critique of reason.[60]

This "sovereignty model" demarcates the aesthetic experiences occasioned by and in the project of European modernity (for the world at large, colonial modernity) but not determined by it. The idea of sovereignty therefore safeguards the aesthetic experience from the presumption of autonomy that would be alienating, as we saw J. M. Bernstein has persuasively shown. The proposition of sovereignty, however, sets that experience apart from all other nonaesthetic reasons. Consider now the fact that this European nonaesthetic reason is coterminous with the logic of capital and therefore colonial modernity. The conclusion of Menke is quite critical:

> In truth, when the problems of a radicalized critique of reason are more deeply considered . . . it turns out that the potential for aesthetic experience to provide a critique of reason cannot be described as an implication of this experience, nor as contents separable from it, but only as an effect of it. Art is not sovereign in that it tears down the boundaries separating aesthetic and nonaesthetic experience, thereby proving itself to be the direct overcoming of reason. It is instead sovereign in that, as a discourse of merely particular validity, it represents a crisis for our functioning discourses.[61]

This for postcolonial art in general sets the aesthetic experience as such apart from the colonially instrumental reason of modernity—which for the colonized nation was a contradiction in terms. Menke's theorization of course is entirely within the European provenance, but its implications for the postcolonial scene become doubly important. Consider the following articulation of Menke:

> The aporias of the traditional romantic view of the sovereignty of art can only be resolved by combining two theses: (1) the deconstructive thesis that the aesthetic critique of reason is the subversion rather than the overcoming of reason; and (2) the thesis, which can be found in Adorno, that it is not the contents but the effects, consequences, or repercussions of art that are the foundations of this critique. Taken together, these two claims outline an understanding of aesthetic sovereignty—as an aesthetically generated critique of reason—that not only does not violate the autonomy of the enactment of aesthetic experience, but is actually premised upon it.[62]

By thus bringing Derrida and Adorno together, and making a case for the sovereignty of art, Menke makes his argument exceedingly relevant to the postcolonial scene—though this is nowhere in his own philosophical concerns or aesthetic imagination. For in this site, the sovereignty of the work of art entails and enables a corresponding sovereign but unknowing subject that cannot be but nomadic. This for the postcolonial world is not articulated by way of rebellious and defiant assertion of the postcolonial subject but by virtue of their public sphere, which is ipso facto a parapublic sphere, tangential to the presumed ideological centers of Europe, where the work of art, Kiarostami's cinematic oeuvre, becomes the locus classicus of the articulation of a postcolonial subject that is only sovereign to the degree that only through a nomadic subjectivity can one encounter the world of art as a knowable world.[63]

This unknowing nomadic subject is the sovereign agency that sits in front of Kiarostami's master stroke *Close-Up* with confidence. We might consider the commencement of *Close-Up* the moment when Kiarostami visits Sabzian in prison and secures permission to film his trial on charges of fraud. We know this is a fake trial, but we go along with it. While the whole trial stages the banality of the Ahankhah's son trying in vain to prove he was not duped, Sabzian basks in the opportunity that a leading filmmaker of his homeland has offered him the opportunity to explain to the world at large his love and theory of cinema—of art in general. From the bosom of his philosophy, Nancy would not be able to read the convoluted artistry at work among Kiarostami, the real Makhmalbaf, the fake Makhmalbaf, the real trial, and the fake trial and still call it the world presenting itself. For this is Kiarostami's artwork representing it in a tongue-in-cheek way. Kiarostami has made an art and a whole cinematic oeuvre out of this tongue-in-cheek take on reality, or "the fictive transparency of the real," as I have called it in a slightly more balanced and nuanced theoretical prose.

The event crescendoes into one of the most glorious moments in world cinema when Kiarostami brings "the real Makhmalbaf" to welcome Sabzian out of his legal predicament when he is forgiven and released. The two get on Makhmalbaf's motorbike and go buy a flowerpot and drive to the Ahankhah residence for him to apologize. The shots of the two Makhmalbafs embracing each other on the motorbike and becoming one person with two personae is truth manifest, a lie that has exposed the truth of the fake. The gimmick at the end that the recording equipment is presumably going bad is at least one way of making the filmic truth

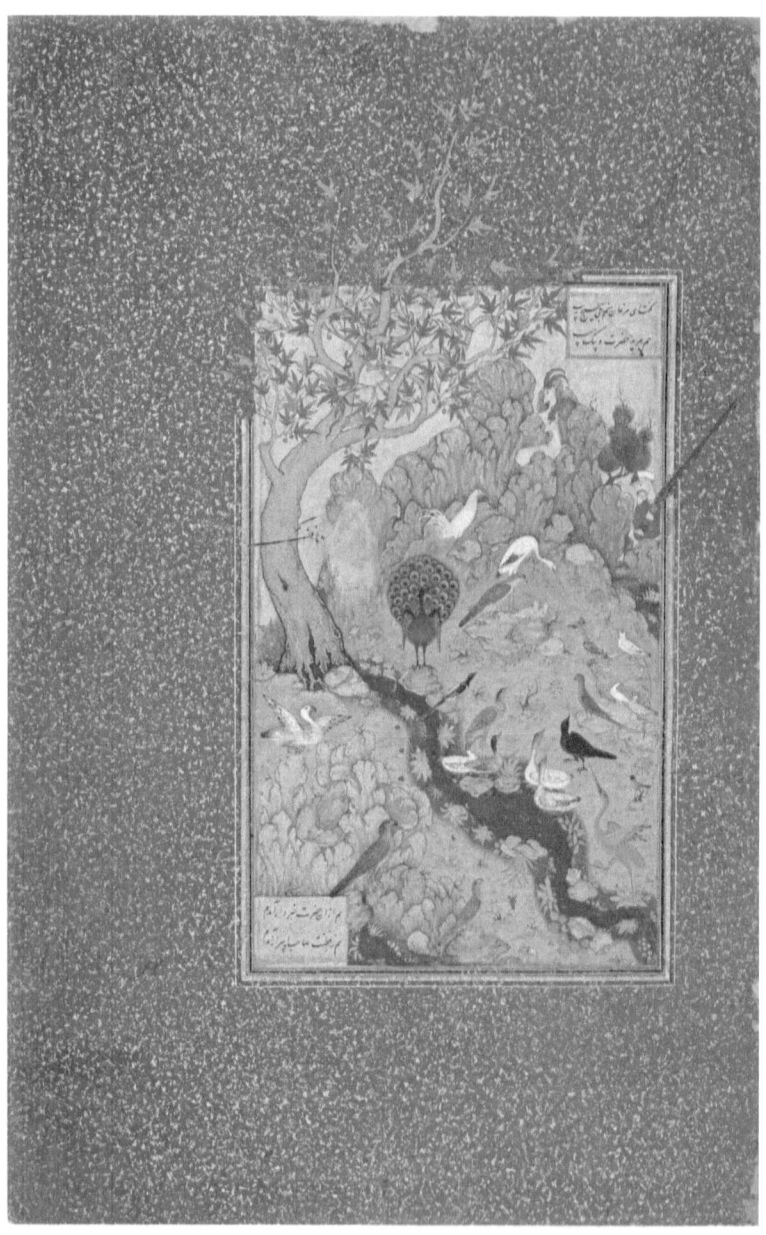

Figure 8. "The Concourse of the Birds," painting by Habiballah of Sava, circa 1600. Folio 11r from *Mantiq al-Tayr/Language of the Birds* by Farid al-Din 'Attar, circa 1177. Reproduced with permission.

self-evident. In Jamshid Akrami's house when we were both guests, Kiarostami told me the dialogue between Makhmalbaf and Sabzian was so forced and condescending that he opted to turn it into this moment of technical malfunction as a counter-alienating effect. When they get to the Ahankhahs, Sabzian goes to the speaker phone at the door to announce themselves and he first introduces himself with his real name, because Makhmalbaf is standing right next to him. There is a moment of pause and silence, he then moves closer to the speaker phone and says, "Makhmalbaf." Simply Platonic in its dialogical precision!

"A transcendent humanist in the tradition of the Italian neo-realists and the Indian director Satyajit Ray," the *New York Times* film critic Stephen Holden considered *Close-Up*, "Mr. Kiarostami has made a film that looks into the heart of a man accused of a crime and, instead of evil, discovers only sweetness, longing and a sad confusion."[64] Perhaps so, and if so, then the way Kiarostami has "looked into the heart" of a fake Makhmalbaf reveals the truth of his own cinema. The act turns all of us spectators into the mirror image of ourselves, just like those thirty birds (*Si-Morgh*) at the end of Attar's *Conference of the Birds*, and all of us the fully knowing subjects that have been presumed to be the witnesses to Kiarostami's knowable artworld. For here any critical engagement with mimetic representation between truth and fiction has ipso facto staged an altered state of being, an exception that has prefigured the dialectic between truth and narrative—where aesthetic sovereignty has met (has crafted) a corresponding nomadic subject. This is mimetically tricking the lemon of colonial desubjection into making lemonade of the postcolonial subject, where the artworld becomes the simulacrum of truth, not because it is "out there" and cinema just reveals it, but because it is not there and cinema crafts it. The truth is not self-evident. It is aesthetically poised and posited. From the categorical to the allegorical, the shift definitive to Kiarostami's artworld is how in between the aesthetic and nonaesthetic reasons he crafted his cinematic raison d'être.

4 The Foreign Familiarity of Rereading Reality

> It was past midnight
> And it was snowing—
> Falling just like forgotten fairies of one thousand legends
> Shedding their feathers off –
> Wind was blowing
> Just like a fierce commander—
> Though invisible—
> Issuing so many insane commands
> Ordering a tired, sad, and scattered army around.[1]
>
> Mehdi Akhavan-e Sales, "Barf/Snow" (1958)

In the previous chapters I have had occasion to offer the dramaturgical ideas of Bertolt Brecht and Viktor Shklovsky on what one called "Verfremdungseffekt" and the other "Ostranenie" as the aesthetic causes and consequences of the alienation effect that has defined much of Kiarostami's artworks—as perhaps best evident at the end of his *Taste of Cherry* (1997). Through stylistic and formal devices, Kiarostami has crafted a new way of rereading reality, which in my previous work I have identified as "actual realism." Mainly through a close reading of *Through the Olive Trees* (1995)—the last of his Koker Trilogy—and the contrast between its Iranian reception and global celebration—I now turn to a decisive moment in defining the specificity of his aesthetic alienation articulated between his familiar and foreign audiences. The Freudian idea of "the Uncanny" and Derrida's articulation of "Différance" are both at work here, making this edgy distinction between Kiarostami's Iranian and non-Iranian audiences (very broadly speaking) morally imaginative and aesthetically provocative. If we are not to dismiss one or the other of these two often diametrically opposed readings as either overtly nativist or unduly abstract, then we must bring the two divergent takes to work on a tertiary space where Kiarostami's radically postcolonial cinema transforms the aesthetic device of self-referential alienation into a potent theoretical affirmation of an itinerant, nomadic subject. Self-effacing, that itinerant, nomadic subject crafts a truth visible for the duration of a journey (or a walkabout) before discarding it in search of fresher and more inviting horizons.

"COMPLICATING ONE'S VIEW OF IRAN"

Kiarostami's *Through the Olive Trees* (1994) represents the coming to age of a new Iranian cinematic aesthetics. That revolutionary aesthetics, subversive of all absolutist terms of certitude, originates in Kiarostami's visual transformation of a reality he has relentlessly sought to bracket, to alter radically, to crack open and to redefine through the brilliance of his cinematic vision. The roots of Kiarostami's cinema go much deeper than this, perhaps his most globally celebrated film. From the early 1970s, he had been tirelessly at work crafting a vision of reality in which life is celebrated, death condemned, and the whole paradox of being underlined with a colorful crayon of irony. Be that as it may, it is in *Through the Olive Trees* that the entire cinematic vision of Kiarostami has come into full view.[2]

At its release in 1994, *Through the Olive Trees* was the most recent film of Kiarostami in a cinematic career that had spanned over two and a half decades. Much of this career had gone unnoticed by the rest of the world. But *Through the Olive Trees* suddenly led a global audience into witnessing the particulars of a sustained cinematic vision that has sought to reread a reality we have grown too accustomed to reading in old and tired ways. Watching and interpreting Kiarostami's films was now a global audience that includes Iranians inside and outside their homeland, friendly and hostile to the clerical rule in Iran. Attracted to Kiarostami's cinema are also European and American film critics, as well as those in Australia, Japan, and Latin America. That Kiarostami's cinema has found a global audience, and that Iranians respond with furious sincerity for or against his vision of things, are all integral to the cultural consequences of that cinematic vision.

Through the Olive Trees was first shown in the United States in 1994 in the context of the New York Film Festival, and the good news that emerged from that festival was that Miramax had decided to risk the outlandish idea of releasing "an Iranian film" in the United Sates. In the wake of Miramax's release in New York and Los Angeles in the winter of 1995, the American Film Institute had included Kiarostami's *Through the Olive Trees* among eleven Iranian features in a film festival it had organized at the Kennedy Center in Washington, DC. *Through the Olive Trees* was also the official Iranian entry for the best foreign film category for the 1995 Oscar. When the film was finally released in February 1995, it was hailed by the *New York Times* as comparable to Truffaut's *Day for Night*, while J. Hoberman of *Premier* enthusiastically identified Kiarostami as "an old-fashioned humanist film intellectual" and credited *Through the Olive Trees* with "[complicating] one's view of life in Iran."[3]

Stanley Kauffmann of *The New Republic* saw *Through the Olive Trees* and wrote enthusiastically about it. The review is generally positive. Perhaps the most ironic aspect of Kauffmann's review is that it begins with a reference to politics. Writing approvingly of Kiarostami's cinema, Kauffmann asked: "Do we still need reminders that human connections, conveyed in art, persist through political differences? We still can use such reminders, I guess, especially when they come through truly good art."[4] It is quite evident that by "political differences" Kauffmann refers to the sour (or even bitter) relationship between the Iranian and US governments. The irony of the statement is that Kiarostami's cinema is not only irrelevant to diplomatic relations between the United States and Iran but effectively subversive of any number of ideological forces at the roots of that hostility. This has been the plague of Iranian filmmakers who have chosen to remain in their homeland and continue to produce. While their fellow countrymen denounce them for making film for "foreigners," foreigners, and even some of their fellow Iranians in exile, continue to regard them as representatives of the Islamic Republic. Much less subtle than Kauffmann, for example, is J. Hoberman who in his otherwise positive review of *Through the Olive Trees* in *Premiere* could not resist a knee-jerk reaction when introducing Abbas Kiarostami as "the 54-year-old dean of Iranian (omigod) cinema."[5]

A FOREIGNER AT HOME

Kiarostami's cinema, however, has had a much more controversial presence in his own homeland. Not only *Through the Olive Trees* but the entire trilogy, of which *Through the Olive Trees* is the third, has been the subject of bitter controversy in Iran. The trilogy primarily is concerned with the transparent constitution of "reality," a concern that Kiarostami has elaborated on through a series of fictive and real events in and around the village of Koker, some 350 miles north of Tehran. *Khaneh-ye dust kojast/ Where Is the Friend's House* (1987) was the first in this trilogy set in Koker. When the village of Koker was devastated in the 1991 earthquake, Kiarostami returned there and made the 1992 film *And Life Goes On/ Zendegi va digar hich* (literally, "life and nothing else"), which is in fact about the director's search for the missing children who had acted in *Where Is the Friend's House?* The film *Through the Olive Trees* seeks to tell a love story in-the-making while Kiarostami's camera crew was busy making *And Life Goes On*.

Kiarostami's Iranian admirers have joined his European and American critics who have celebrated him as a new Satyajit Ray. His detractors, however, consider him a self-hating pseudo-intellectual and accuse him of any number of nasty things, even of being a talentless charlatan. The intense and ferocious nature of this controversy makes quite clear a number of critical issues in contemporary Iranian culture. First, while literary theorists have been busy debating the centrality of prose and poetry in postrevolutionary Iran, it is quite evident that film is rapidly assuming an upper hand in defining the terms of critical engagement with the dominant social issues. Second, it is virtually impossible to separate technical discussions of cinema from some crucial cultural and political debates that reach deep into the very metaphysical foundation of an "Islamic Society." Third, what one witnesses in Iran today is a cultural struggle with Kiarostami's Rostamabad Trilogy, as it has sometimes been called, as a major battlefield of this Kulturkampf.

The earthquake of 1991 in northern Iran and the film that Kiarostami made in relation to it constitute perhaps the most central battlefield in which the significance of his cinematic vision is being domestically assayed. *Through the Olive Trees* cinematically narrates itself as occurring while *And Life Goes On* is being filmed. Active hostility against Kiarostami's cinema in general took a particularly sharp turn after *And Life Goes On* was released. In a review of *And Life Goes On*, Farhad Golzar took strong exceptions to what he considered to have been Kiarostami's dismissal of the tragic depth of the earthquake in northern Iran. "This is a television genre," he objected, "it is only by mistake that it is being shown in theaters."[6] Golzar ridiculed what he took to be Kiarostami's banalization of a human tragedy. "This film is full of insult to life," Golzar concluded. It dehumanizes the human condition. It should not be called *And Life Goes On*, but something like "life is Nothing," or "Man is a Descendant of Monkey and Nothing More." The primary audience of Kiarostami, Golzar believes, are the international film festivals, especially the one in Cannes.[7]

Mas'ud Farasati, another critic, was equally harsh in his condemnation: "*And Life Goes On*, from the very beginning . . . is based on two big lies: (1) a representation of the earthquake, and (2) a claim to cinema."[8] Farasati finds Kiarostami's camera too neutral to the depth of tragedy it observes. That neutrality, Farasati believes, is not an ability but a failure to look, to observe, to see. Kiarostami's vision of life is too "bestial" for Farasati. There is no sense of tragedy in it, no depth, no sorrow. Farasati accuses Kiarostami of commercialism, even of charlatanism.[9] The film is custom-made, he believes, for the European film festivals, the French in particular. Farasati then proceeds to give a full political account of why he thinks Kiarostami's cinema is being received and celebrated in Europe:

> Indeed why is it that European film festivals and their juries . . . are so impressed by And Life Goes On . . . ? Why is it that they are trying to represent its poor, aborted, and fallacious technique as genuine and stylish? . . . It seems to me that [Kiarostami's vision] is the "neutral"—indeed bloodless, from-behind-the-closed-eyes, from-behind-sunglasses—vision of foreigners who have not seen the earthquake in Rudbar in a close-up, and they thank God that they were not there when it happened. For sure, they are neither Iranian nor from the East. This is the Western humanist vision that after watching a few minutes of news on television they feel a little guilty, as they

used to feel guilty about Hiroshima, etc.... Indeed the producers of And Life Goes On are these [Europeans], not an Iranian filmmaker who has character and identity. These people have commissioned the making of this film, and it is they who propagate it and give it prizes. Our filmmaker, like all other identity-dealers, is caught and humiliated in their trap, putting for sale himself and his forsaken culture. There is no honor in this, but shame. Kiarostami has enjoyed this historical-calendar chance that his film goes to the West—and then from there is exported back to our country—at a time when the Westerners are afflicted by "The New World Order" epidemic, the politics of eliminating the borders and creating a unified Europe, which itself is an attempt to confront the deep global economic crisis. This new politics demands its own culture ... a culture that engages in the elimination of ethnic and national boundaries. Lack-of-identity is the new strategy of the new world order.... But the self-lost and talentless culture-sellers will not benefit from this transaction and shall earn nothing but shame. All the prizes and praises will not last but a short time. Art shall be victorious once again. Because life, as art, continues. But not under the new cultural order; instead via a return, and proudly so, to one's origin and roots.[10]

All reactions to Kiarostami's cinema were of course not so negative in his own homeland. The journal *Film*, a monthly publication devoted to the minutiae of the subject, was extremely sympathetic to Kiarostami and enthusiastically reported his accomplishments at international film festivals. This journal has always given Kiarostami an opportunity to respond to his critics[11] and gave detailed, comparative assessments of his European and Iranian critics.[12] One positive and perceptive reading of Kiarostami's cinema has been given by Houshang Golmakani, who came valiantly to his defense and enthusiastically argued for the aesthetic integrity of his work. With a rare and remarkable insight, he observed that "an aspect of reality is that we [Iranians] are a people who in the course of our history have been more used to eulogy than songs of life. Whoever can describe a tragic event more lamentably we consider that person a more eloquent and capable orator."[13] Golmakani then proceeds to read every technical aspect of Kiarostami's camera virtuosity with a view toward the highest compliment that an Iranian aesthetician can give an artist: that his art is "impossibly simple."

Javad Tusi also has given a rather positive review of Kiarostami's cinema with certain reservations. Kiarostami's "realism" in particular is refreshing and healthy in Tusi's reading. He does take objection to Kiarostami's preference for Vivaldi's music as opposed to any number of jubilant melodies in Persian classical music.[14] Robert Safarian, Reza Dorostkar, and Majid Islami also have given positive responses to Kiarostami's vision.[15] In his theoretically informed *Point of View in Iranian Cinema*, Gholam Heydari included a positive reading of Kiarostami's camera work as a good and relatively consistent example of third-person singular narrative.[16]

Shahrokh Dulku, however, took strong exception to Kiarostami as a filmmaker, accusing him of not knowing the very alphabet of camerawork, while pretending to redefine the entire grammar of it.[17] Dulku describes how Kiarostami disregards the very rudimentary rules of "point of view" in camera work, but ultimately concludes with a moral condemnation of Kiarostami's cinema. Of *And Life Goes On*, he writes:

> I cannot disregard one crucial issue, and that is the moral lesson that the filmmaker [i.e., Kiarostami] wants to draw, following his previous film [i.e., *Where Is the Friend's House?*], and yet, just like in the previous film, because of weak execution, structural confusion, misconception of truth, and a convoluted vision of man and life, he reaches precisely the opposite conclusion that he wishes to reach. And Life Goes On wants to say that the "human" life is something precious and praiseworthy, but [actually] says that the "bestial" life is dear and lustful. It intends to praise and propagate human life, but in reality it propagates the bestial life. In order to give meaning to life, Kiarostami reduces it to the level of animal instincts (eating, sleeping, sex, and defecation). As opposed to noble, conscientious, and selfless men, the people in And Life Goes On are introduced at the end as base and mindless animals, ready to pull the dead body of the members of their family like carcasses, and spend their wedding night under a few feet of "palastik."[18]

Dulku then proceeds to denounce the European reception of Kiarostami's cinema and concludes with a sweeping condemnation of what he takes to be Kiarostami's arrogant view of his own country and culture:

> I could have finished this review right here. But one small item, perhaps even repetitious, is left which is troubling me badly and I am going to say it. Although I believe that content-criticism is not criticism at all, and a film that in form and structure has not yet reached the point of "speaking" does not deserve to be discussed in terms of its content, nevertheless I am going

to say what I have to say. There are things in And Life Goes On that are extremely troubling, so troubling that one cannot just pass them by. I will just mention them in a list and leave them to the readers' judgement: A man with a touristic appearance, a whitish hair and a "European" and "emotionless" look among the victims of the earthquake, the presence of a Renault automobile, the French poster of the film Where Is the Friend's House? ... The repeated appearance of the Red Cross cars, overwhelming emphasis on the instinctual (and not intellectual) aspects of life, and more importantly, a train of thought that looks at life not face to face and eyeball to eyeball, but from above (high on top), and with a pair of dark glasses. . . . This arrogant, emotionless, and calculating look inevitably represents an unreal picture of life, a picture about which (and in my view about Kiarostami's cinema in general) the judgement of Mohammad Hosain Ruhi [another critic] as an accurate doubt is applicable: "What kind of 'cinema' is this?"[19]

FOREIGN FAMILIARITIES

On many occasions, Kiarostami appeared troubled by this kind of criticism and sought to respond to them, directly or indirectly. In an interview with Omid Ruhani, Kiarostami tried to give an accurate description of his lead character Hossein Reza'i's perception of the earthquake which, I believe, is equally applicable to Kiarostami's own vision of an aesthetic resurrection of worldly signifiers:

> The young man [i.e., Hossein Reza'i, the lead character in *Through the Olive Trees*] has believed the earthquake. For him it is like the Final Day of Judgement. When all the houses are destroyed and everybody appears in an apparent and evident equality, it is only natural that in the face of this superior fate this futile thought should occur to the young and inexperienced mind of the young man that now, on the Day of Judgement, it is the day of salvation for those who have survived [the earthquake]. It is the day of equality and equanimity. But an experienced and worldly old woman corrects this illusion on his part and reminds him that the only thing that has happened is an earthquake and all the old and ancient principles and values continue to be valid. That people are still alive, and, so far as we are alive, we will not permit for these principles to be turned upside down.[20]

Kiarostami, however, runs all those ancient principles upside down. Perhaps the most enduring aspect of Kiarostami's cinema is precisely his principal discontent with "reality" as is. By bracketing it, and thus equally suspending our conceptions of morality, propriety, and political positioning, Kiarostami has been constantly at work in re-imagining a more enabling vision of reality. Judged by Kiarostami's detractors, however, that vision of reality either has not been registered successfully or else it has been judged morally repulsive. Javad Tusi, another film critic, wrote a devastating satirical piece on *Through the Olive Trees* in which he announced that he, for one, is not impressed by, in his judgment, Kiarostami's version of realism in cinema.[21] Mostafa Jalai Fakhr, however, has celebrated Kiarostami's "universal language" and sees nothing wrong, for example, with such "foreign" elements as a Red Cross ambulance or the French poster of *Where Is the Friend's House?* in Kiarostami's *And Life Goes On*.[22] In the midst of these ideological debates, however, occasionally a critic manages to concentrate on a scene and read it to the logical conclusions of its aesthetic promises. Naghmeh Samini, for example, has given by far the most insightful reading of the concluding scene of *Through the Olive Trees*, calling it a "magical long shot." She notes how the camera in the most sensitive moment, precisely at the instance when because of our previous cinematic experience we expect an answer for all our curiosities and thus share in the emotional climax of the work, the camera shies away from the focal center of contention, and authoritatively imposes its distance on us, too, as if it does not consider us intimate enough nor think us worthy of closely witnessing this love poem.[23]

On the same long shot, Ahmad Talebi-nezhad has offered a similar reading, emphasizing, however, that intimate expressions of love, of a sort that could persuade Tahereh to marry Hossein, simply are not permitted in Iranian cinema nowadays, and thus he accounts for the social and political imperatives underlying this hauntingly beautiful long shot.[24]

These occasional attentions to technicalities and what they might imply notwithstanding, the debate that raged over Kiarostami's cinema inside Iran invariably turned to questions of moral imperatives. Perhaps the most devastating review of *Through the Olive Trees* was written by Mas'ud Farasati, the editor-in-chief of *Naqd-e Cinema*, a periodical devoted to a technically informed and critical reading of cinema, published by the Islamic Propaganda Organization. Very bluntly, Farasati identifies *Through the Olive Trees* as a disingenuous and insulting film. An experimental and abortive film . . . in every plan of which exudes lie, artificiality, and clumsiness. . . . The film closes the same way that it opens, artificially and pseudo-documentary-like, and thus leaves open a path—an escape path—for all kinds of shallow, pseudo-intellectual interpretations and exegesis.[25]

Farasati's language very soon runs moral and condemnatory:

What is the use of these artificial dialogues, putting their heavy weight on the film and subordinating the scenes fully to their own advantage, other than denigrating and belittling the people? Why should they appeal to the audience? Could it be that by "audience" it is meant those few hundred spineless, rootless, and sick pseudo-intellectuals, natives and foreigners alike, who have discovered Kiarostami and are now putting him on a pedestal?[26]

Farasati is deeply contemptuous of Kiarostami's cinema:

A horrifying earthquake leaves thousands of people dead and much annihilation and destruction behind. Among all the problems and suffering of people afflicted by an earthquake, it is only a bestial marriage that attracts the attention of our filmmaker. And why? He himself puts the answer in the mouth of the "hero" of Through the Olive Trees, who says that "the earthquake was God sent" because now nobody has a house, and thus he is equal to everybody else. Is the sickly and psychopathic world of the peasant boy, who wishes every body's house destroyed, not part of our filmmaker's own inner world?[27]

Farasati proceeds to accuse Kiarostami of self-hatred, of being incapable of anything but disgust and denigration for his actors, his audience, and ultimately himself and his national and cultural identity. According to Farasati, Kiarostami's films are like remembering a nightmare while being awake. These nightmares are often distasteful, and in them one sees oneself as passive and incapable of doing anything. Kiarostami seeks refuge from one distasteful nightmare in one even more distasteful. Kiarostami's films, lacking both the pleasant aspects of some dreams and the painful fear and weight of nightmares—because he is incapable of facing either— tell us that he lives in such an insecure and torturous world. If at this late age he still has to learn the very elementary principles, the very alphabet, of cinema, it is because of this obvious reason that for him learning is equated with fear and denigration ... denigration, humiliation, fear, and escape are like a vicious circle that he cannot, and does not want to, break. He is accustomed to, and feels cozy within, it.[28]

Farasati's indignation and fury are matched by Behzad Rahimian's ridicule and banter. After an entirely dismissive review of Kiarostami's cinema, in which he observes, among other things, that

> to tell you the truth I feel quite embarrassed by Mr. Kiarostami's most recent films, which are considered to be ways for Europeans to get to know us Iranians.... We are not Czech, Greek, Japanese, or Latin American sharing certain cultural traits with Western nations. We are a nation with our own disposition, character, and ways, very difficult to be grasped by either Westerners or Westernized Easterners. So it is perfectly natural for them to have a strange interpretation of us. But it must be a source of shame to use their interpretation of us—just to appease them—to untangle Iranian life.[29]

Rahimian proceeds with a clever joke about Kiarostami's cinema implying that he has gained celebrity status in the world by virtue of a fake cinema, soon to be discovered for its embarrassing emptiness.[30]

THE GENTLER FOREIGNERS

Kiarostami's cinema has received gentler views outside his own homeland. During his lifetime, and even before he received the coveted Palme d'Or in 1997, he was one of the few Iranian filmmakers known and celebrated outside Iran. In August 1992, the François Truffaut Prize was given to Kiarostami for his *And Life Goes On*. Roberto Rossellini's award also was given earlier in the year to Kiarostami during the forty-fifth annual Cannes Film Festival in April 1992. Kiarostami has been recognized as a distinguished filmmaker in a number of other European film festivals.[31] European film critics could not praise Kiarostami enough. They lavishly compared him to Rossellini, Renoir, and Truffaut. This international attention to Kiarostami's cinema is extremely significant, not only for its domestic consequences but for the kind of critical attention that he as a filmmaker deserves. Because officials of the Islamic Republic naturally seek to take advantage of the global recognition that Kiarostami's cinema was receiving, the political opponents of the Islamic Republic, equally totalitarian in their ideological dispositions, deeply resented Kiarostami's success, not because they could not recognize the brilliance of his art but because the target of their political anger was taking advantage of that brilliance.

A good example of this debilitating problem is to be found in Reza Allamehzadeh's insightful account of Iranian cinema in the Islamic Republic. One of the most critical assessments of the propaganda policies of the Islamic Republic vis-à-vis international film festivals is to be read in Allamehzadeh's *The Illusion of Iranian Islamic Cinema*.[32] In this bitterly written book, Allamehzadeh, himself an accomplished filmmaker, argues that the most internationally acclaimed Iranian films have been produced not because of but despite official censorship brutally imposed by the propaganda machinery of the Islamic ideologues. Allamehzadeh argues that, except for Mohsen Makhmalbaf, none of the leading Iranian filmmakers is a particularly believing Muslim in the ideologically charged (or any other) sense of the term.[33] Even Makhmalbaf, Allamehzadeh proposes, "has exited the crowd of committed and devout Muslims" after the making of his famous feature *Dastforush/Peddler* (1987).

While preserving his critically positive judgment of Kiarostami, especially his *Where Is the Friend's House?*, Allamehzadeh condemns both the Islamic Republic and the Locarno Film Festival for having accepted this film, which was produced in 1986 but was included in the festival in 1989 against the specific stipulation of Section C, Article 6 of the bylaws, which states only those films produced during the preceding twelve months may be included in the annual festival.[34]

Allamehzadeh's criticism of the Islamic Republic—written in Persian, published in Germany—failed to have any effect on the enduring critical reception of Kiarostami's cinema throughout Europe, in France in particular. The French magazine *Positif* asked a number of leading directors to identify the previous generation of filmmakers who had had an enduring influence on them. Kiarostami was given the distinct honor of being included among these directors. His response was published in French, and its original Persian was published in the February 1994 issue of *Film*. A remarkable confession of Kiarostami in this statement is that for the last twenty-five years he scarcely had seen a film and that he cannot stand sitting through a film, especially his own. Fellini, particularly his *La Dolce Vita* (1960), had an enduring effect on him. Of *La Dolce Vita*, Kiarostami wrote:

> In my judgement, La Dolce Vita is a complete picture of moral and social collapse. People who had lost all their principles sat, with perfect intelligence and awareness, witnessing their own demise, wasting their lives in absolute passivity. La Dolce Vita was the celebration of incompetence and hopelessness. People . . . with no stability and in utter disappointment, followed endless events, while Fellini, a la Dante, through a poetic disorder and a sagacious vision, informs of an obscure and dangerous future, that we can now feel after some thirty years. Some thirty years before he spoke of the corruption of modern civilization and the collapse of all principles, of the absolute and utter destruction of moral virtues, he spoke of a rejection of the pseudo-intellectual bourgeois world.[35]

Kiarostami's take on Fellini, and on *La Dolce Vita* in particular, is quite revealing in terms of his own reading of the reality he feels desperate to change and renegotiate with his received culture. Film appears to be the most effective artistic medium through which he can engage in that renegotiation. As Yann Tobin has noted in his reading of *And Life Goes On*, this film "is also a grand film on cinema, its powers and its dangers, its magic and its artifice, its truth and its lies."[36]

RECASTING THE REAL

Between his admirers and his detractors inside and outside his homeland stands Kiarostami's cinema, constitutionally irreducible to any propaganda for or against any Islamic, or any other kind of, Republic. If Kiarostami is successful in holding our attention constant for a while and thus teaching us to see differently—he has endured so far (by the time he released *Through the Olive Trees* in 1994) for some twenty-five years, through an imperial dictatorship, via a gut-wrenching revolution, through the eight years of the Iran-Iraq War (1980–1988), in the thaws of an Islamic theocracy, and perhaps most challenging of all braced by the paradoxical forces of having been catapulted into a global limelight—he mapped out the principal contours of a postmetaphysical mode of being in which no ideology, no absolutist claim to truth, no metanarrative of salvation, ever will monopolize the definition of our "identity."

To renegotiate that identity, Kiarostami has had to enter into a no-man's land twilight zone of flattened-out reality in which things can begin to signify nothing, persons and animals and trees and emotions and colors can again fade into a tapestry of a pre-significatory state so that Kiarostami's camera can begin only to imply the possibility of another mode of reading reality. In a conversation with Philippe Piazzo and Frederic Richard, Kiarostami once was asked about the nature and function of the trip in *And Life Goes On:* "Is it ultimately real or fictive, lived or dreamed?," they asked Kiarostami. "You put me in a difficult spot," Kiarostami answered,

> The perception of reality is such a complex and nuanced phenomenon that we cannot really give a definitive answer to this question. The best of all positions undoubtedly consists of being ceaselessly in motion between dream and reality: this is a place of ideal life, my space of preference. My attitude is to refuse all convictions of reality, it is to sit between the two chairs of the real and the dream, to stay in motion and alive. My perception of reality is always the source, the mobilizing force, that pushes me to make movies. The real always has a power of fiction and of poetry that excites me and stimulates my creativity. This is the way I stay always faithful to reality.... It is a constant rule that animates all my films.[37]

This is a crucial clue as to how one is to read Kiarostami's cinema. For what we see in *Through the Olive Trees* is Kiarostami's mastery of his own version of "truth" that he detects and places between a reality he intensely dislikes and a vision he only can demarcate cinematically. The "intensity" of Kiarostami's rejection of reality as it is, however, is quintessentially modified by a mode of looking that in and of itself subverts all "intensities." At his best he lacks all convictions and yet manages to subvert, via a splendid sense of irony he has taught his camera, all passionate intensities. As a master ironist, Kiarostami crafts an absolutely meticulous labyrinth of subtle negotiations between fact and fantasy, thereby radically suspending the whole conception of what really is "real." There is a studied unstudiedness, a deliberately loose logic and rhetoric to Kiarostami's preferred modes of narrative, as also evident in his *Nama-ye Nazdik/Close-Up* (1990).

Kiarostami is fascinated by that nebulous borderline where reality submits to fantasy. In *Close-Up*, he had the same concern when he told the (real-life) story of a man who out of love and admiration for a leading Iranian filmmaker, Mohsen Makhmalbaf, pretended to be him, and went so far as fooling a whole family into believing that he was Makhmalbaf and that he intended to make a film about them. *Close-Up* turns this (real-life) story into a disturbing, yet endearing, tale of fantasy as reality.

In *Through the Olive Trees* Kiarostami has precisely the same fixation with that shadowland where reality and illusion begin to renegotiate their boundaries, give and take their respective anxieties. Toward that end, Kiarostami's camera is alternatively documentary-like passive and post-structurally agitated, yielding to the shaking movements of a truck on a country road in one sequence and masterfully creating a long shot of green pastures and olive trees studded with the colorful dresses of women and young girls in another. The lyrical roughness of Kiarostami's narrative is both a function of and a necessary angle to the story he wants to tell, to the received reality he wants to subvert.

Throughout this film, Kiarostami tests the blurry boundaries of facts and fiction, of that no-man's land twilight zone of the (un)real where facts fear fantasy, where fantasies brace and muzzle reality. In this, his latest and aesthetically most compelling version of his fixation with the nature of reality, Kiarostami narrows in on the traces of a would-be love story off and on camera. A camera crew and a director from Tehran have landed in the paradise-like, Northern Iranian village of Koker, recently devastated by a massive earthquake. What one sees is thus an operative precision in the making of a docu-fiction that has become the defining language of Kiarostami's vision.

The fictive/real camera crew has jammed the front door of a young couple who are to be the central characters of the would-be film (a scene from Kiarostami's pervious film, *And Life Goes On*). The husband is to come home in this scene, drop a masonry bag he has been carrying at the door, exchange greetings with his wife, and then change clothes and leave. That is the non-event of the film-to-be-made (*And Life Goes On*), which Kiarostami in turn takes and weaves into the love story he now wants to tell. Kiarostami's alter ego is Mohammad Ali Keshavarz, who early in the film introduces himself to us as such and says that "in this film, I play the director." It is on the premise of that oxymoronic shot, the director in front and not behind the camera, that *Through the Olive Trees* begins to tell its (hi)story. There is a scene later in the film where Keshavarz-cum-Kiarostami addresses a group of young schoolboys, who have been cordoned off in a corner to watch the making of the film, and says, "Children, you are not supposed to cross this line to come over here where we are making the movie. Do you mind if I come to your side?" Then he proceeds to go to their side, as Kiarostami himself transgressing the visible line—a rope—which separates reality from fiction. He takes one of their reading texts and quizzes them on their knowledge of local geography. Here for the first time, the director is doing something for the locals that actually matters. These kids need a teacher, which they obviously lack, otherwise they would not be sitting there watching a film being made. The same self-parody is evident when the assistant director is taking Hossein to the set and runs into a construction site barring her access to the shooting site. The mason in charge of construction bluntly suggests that instead of taking an able-bodied construction worker like Hossein to make an actor out of him, she should let him come and work on the making of this building. There is much local logic that either is missed or sabotaged by the intruding camera crew. When the director finds out that the local cook in his camp recently has been widowed, he suggestively asks him why he does not get married again. "It is unconscionable," the sixty-odd-year-old cook responds. "I was married to my wife for a lifetime, we have six children together. It is not fair for me to get married again now that she is dead." The director of course recognizes his intruding presence. Early one morning, he confides to one of his crewmen that if he were to shout at Koker village from a distance, "the soul of the people" would answer him back. There were only two words that when shouted out loud were echoed in the landscape: "hello" and "goodbye." After the "goodbye," the next "hello" would not even be answered/echoed.

   Hossein and Tahereh are the two central characters whose story holds the film together. Hossein is a construction-worker-turned-actor who is ambitious and upwardly mobile, having sworn to never again touch a brick. Tahereh is the young daughter of a couple who perished in the recent earthquake and who now is living with her maternal grandmother. Tahereh is selected by Kiarostami's alter ego (played by the veteran of Iranian cinema, Mohammad Ali Keshavarz) because of her mute beauty,

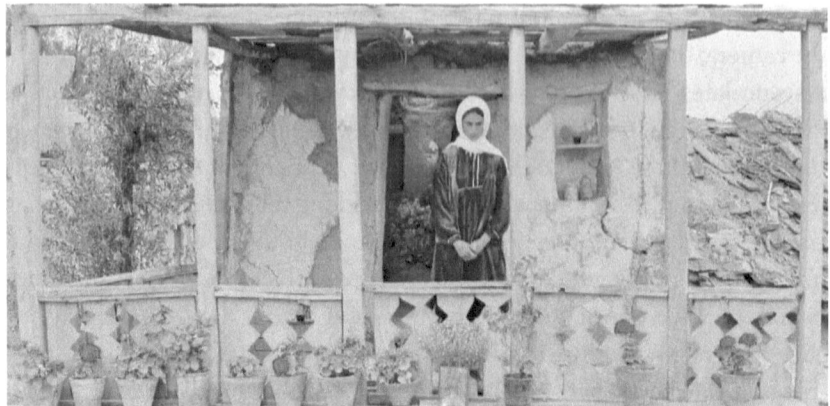

Figure 9. Tahereh Ladanian as Tahereh in Abbas Kiarostami, *Through the Olive Trees* (1994). Courtesy of Abbas Kiarostami Foundation.

sustained by a piercing gaze that drives the poor Hossein to the border of madness and does not leave the audience entirely unaffected either. She is selected from a handful of equally beautiful young girls, braced by a sea of less gifted classmates.

The opening shot, a pre-credit sequence that sustains the whole narrative, is what holds a postrevolutionary audience in awe of an emerging aesthetic. Imagine an open space in the middle of an olive garden in which stand some one hundred young girls all garbed in what the Islamic Idealogues call "Islamic dress": dark color, baggy coats, topped by an equally compelling dark scarf, tightly set, leaving all but the roundness of the face covered. The heavy wind blows the long robes and the flying scarves into the agitated branches of the olive trees. Dark and light studs on olive green is the contrasting vision with which Kiarostami's camera makes love from this to the very last moment of the film.

Tahereh Ladania had that rare, quiet beauty with which Kiarostami's camera could grace the unsuspecting background of a village devastated by an earthquake. Her understated charm, her bewildered gaze, and ultimately her budding sensuality become the subtextual energy of a love story that reaches for the most elemental forces of nature.

A shaky camera that is never quite sure where to stand, a story line that cannot resist going off on tangents, a dialogue that oscillates between the

Tehrani accent and the local Gilaki dialect, a fiction that is prohibited by a reality it cannot control, a paradise-like village ravaged by an earthquake, no less than invaded by this outlandish camera crew, a director who while waiting for a new leading man casually leaves his set to mingle with the local boys or chat with the cook in his camp, and scores of other, similar ends that release this film and all its potential narrative boundaries into the surrounding hills of the village, are the defining moments of Kiarostami's deliberately poststructural mode of storytelling. He dwells comfortably, deliberately, and with an ease that disarms all concocted readings in that ironic space he crafts for his camera between fact and fantasy. One should not see this film with any set expectation of where the lines of demarcation are drawn between fact and fantasy, between the real and the concocted, between the received and the staged, between location and studio, between living and acting. One has to let oneself loose and permit Kiarostami's camera to work its magic and reveal a mode of being carved between any dual set of binary opposition. He has been hard at work to cut and perfect this aesthetic space and *Through the Olive Trees* is by far his most successful version of it.

Hossein Reza'i is pure catharsis. He exudes a real/fantastic aura of unexpurgated zest. Kiarostami manages to extract from a man with no acting experience a performance so full of verve and sensitivity that one cannot imagine a professional actor being able to concoct that unique chemistry of factual fantasy.

Kiarostami's shaky camera, however, is kept steady by his assistant director (played with remarkably deceptive ease by Zarifeh Shiva.). She is addressed by her real name, "Ms. Shiva," throughout the film. She is the central axis of an otherwise perfectly confusing cross-breeding of fact and fantasy. Her clapboard opens every shot of the film within the film (*And Life Goes On* within *Through the Olive Trees*). Kiarostami cannot pass any chance for irony and double-erasure: while the clapboard is ostensibly for the filming of *And Life Goes On*, the actual wording on it reads all the details of *Through the Olive Trees*. Within that double-erasure, the cross-breeding of two films quoting each other, "Ms. Shiva" is the very image of determined order while the whole world seems to plunge into a bottomless pit of confusion. She is as Mother Earth herself restoring order to a life devastated by an earthquake.

182   CHAPTER FOUR

THE ADAM AND EVE OF THE NON-EVENT

Every non-event in *Through the Olive Trees* works toward the creation and the sustaining of this fictive transparency of the real. Hossein in real life is in love with Tahereh, but Tahereh does not as much as answer his "hello." Yet, in the film the Tehrani director is making, she plays his wife. In that electrifying span between the liberating command of "action" and the brutal abruptness of "cut," Hossein lives a fantasy for which his entire being yearns. Between the brutal abruptness of "cut" and the next liberating command of "action," he has to live the debilitating anxieties of a life cut short by an "acting career," a love left brutally unreturned. In fantasy, Hossein shouts at his wife for having inadvertently dropped water on a stranger while watering her plants. In reality, he offers her tea on a tray adorned with a freshly cut flower and tells her, between the two takes of the same scene, "I never will scream at you when we marry. For me marriage is this. I offer you tea and flowers, and you'll do the same for me." In "action," Hossein is the happy husband of a beautiful wife and the proud owner of a gorgeous house, perfectly confident in the ability of all his bodily movements. After every "cut," he is commanded by the camera crew to water the plants or serve them tea or attend to one chore or another.

The fictive transparency of the real, thus narrated by Kiarostami's camera, puts forward a radically subversive reading of a culture of inhibition brutally institutionalized by a theocratic revolution. No young woman speaks to a young man in this film. Tahereh, in fact, epitomizes the forbidden speech, elsewhere equally present. Young men do not fare much better. There is an absolutely debilitating scene where the first local man who was supposed to play the lead role after a number of tries finally concedes to the director that he cannot talk to the lead woman, "because whenever I talk to a girl, I stutter." This is the castrating sign of a culture of inhibition in which an unarticulated sense of fear and shame prohibits the most natural of acts.

As much as Azim stutters, Hossein is eloquent, rhetorical even, with an abundance of philosophy coming very naturally to him. In the truck ride sequence, he begins to share with the director his frustration with Tahereh and her family. They refused to let him marry their daughter simply because he did not own a house. He has been a construction worker since he was eleven, and yet he still does not own a house. "Well," Hossein reflects with noticeable irony, "then there was an earthquake and nobody had a house." The earthquake Hossein takes as a sign of divine justice for his broken heart. He refuses the director's suggestion to marry an illiterate gypsy girl because what would be the point of an illiterate man who does not have a house marrying a girl who is equally illiterate and does not own a house. "Those who are literate, rich, and own a house should marry those who are illiterate, poor, and do not have a house," he proposes. That way things would be distributed equally. Otherwise, "what's the point of those who already have a house marrying those who also have a house. What would they do with their extra house?" The director's rejoinder on the logic of capitalism entirely escapes Hossein's philosophical disposition.

The real love of Hossein for Tahereh, however, solves the director's fictive problem, because under the warm gaze of Tahereh he defies the culture and speaks his mind and heart to his real love. As an animalesque occasion, film is a subversive moment in the otherwise repressive modes of a routinized culture. Precisely because of that subversiveness, *Through the Olive Trees* has a phenomenal success in portraying the suppressed and denied sexuality of a whole culture. There is a beautiful scene in the truck ride sequence when the director starts to engage in a conversation with an older woman. She says she does not understand a word he says because she only speaks the local dialect. The director does succeed in engaging another older woman in a banal conversation about where they have been and where they are headed. In the meantime, he notices a stunningly beautiful girl sitting next to the older woman with whom he is talking. He makes a futile attempt to ask her name, when he is cut short by Hossein's admonition "Here strangers do not ask young girls what their names are." During this entire episode, the young girl hides her beautiful face, especially her gaze, behind her mother's back. She never as much as utters a word.

Tahereh's grandmother does speak loud and clear though, as do other older women and the young ones only when in the company of each other, excepting the presence of the grandfatherly director. The only other time that the young girls speak is when they are off camera. This culture of inhibition narrows in and closes up on the young men and especially young women, with their innate sexuality thus accentuated and denied.

CHAPTER FOUR

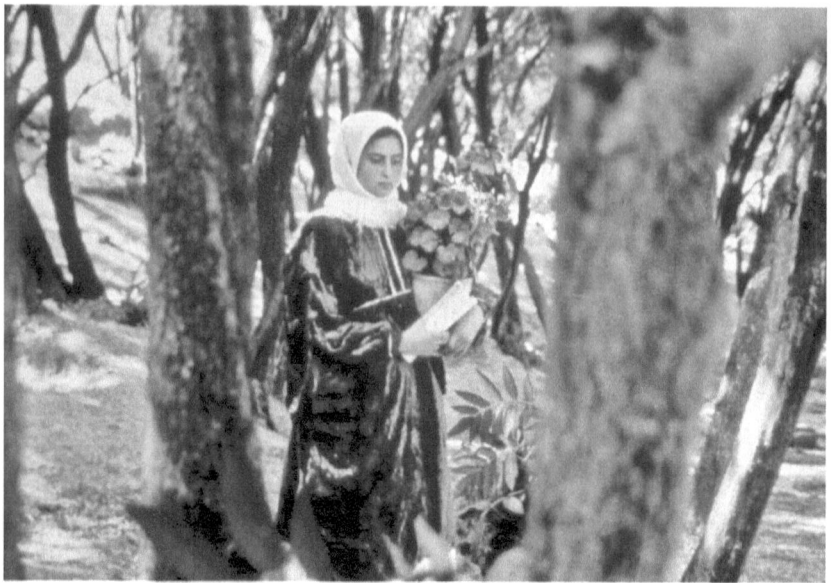

Figure 10. Tahereh Ladanian as Tahereh in Abbas Kiarostami, *Through the Olive Trees* (1994). Courtesy of Abbas Kiarostami Foundation.

The penultimate sequence, a brilliant tracking shot that weaves the gracious walk of Tahereh into the winding path "through the olive trees," is the silent scream of this denial. Throughout this penultimate scene, Hossein talks incessantly in a desperate attempt to persuade Tahereh to marry him. Tahereh walks fast yet graciously, with her young body adorning every turn of the camera, but never pausing for an instant to say a word. Kiarostami is ferociously conscious of the utter brutality of this silence. He, in fact, makes a brilliant point of it when Hossein and Tahereh are waiting between two takes and Hossein resumes his ceaseless verbal supplication, all to no avail. When he talks, she pretends to read from a book. "I understand if in front of all these people you don't want to say anything," Hossein interjects. "But if you care for me, would you just turn the page in your book?" The camera waits desperately on Tahereh, the book, and her hesitant hands, with her fingers holding the tip of a page. She does not turn the page. Hossein reformulates the same question yet another way, as if in a second take, and this time the camera oozes with the anxiety of an almost turned page.

Kiarostami defies all the logic and rhetoric of narrative strategies by alternating successfully and incessantly between the expected familiarity of the factual and the promising suggestions of the fantastic. This is what gives his cinema its specific signature. The story of the film in the film (thriving on its fantasy) is thus never anything more than a would-be sequence of innumerable, mostly unsuccessful, cuts. The fictive transparency of the real is plotted and achieved via an injection of an almost real sequence into the fabric totality of a life momentarily interrupted first by an earthquake and now by this bizarre group of intruding filmmakers. We might think of this state of factasy conducive to the condition of the fictive transparency of the real as the filmic version of Latin American magic realism or else as a rendition of the evident notion of "*Alam al-Mithal/ Mundus Imaginalis*" of Shihab al-Din Yahya Suhrawardi (which I briefly introduced in chapter 2). If we go through his oeuvre, the truth of the real becomes evident through its fusion with fantasy, and if we go toward it through Suhrawardi's Mundus Imaginalis, we go upstream from an aesthetic fusion of the two incongruent factors and see it as the evident materialization of a world of archetypes already conflated at the mythic moments of the philosophical tradition in which Kiarostami is located.

The strategic necessity of this "interruption" of the real by the unreal is evident throughout Kiarostami's vision of this paradise-like village. "Intrusion" and "interruption" are the operative modes of this vision. If that be the case, then how can a story be told, or even more important, how can a story be started and ended? Kiarostami tries to achieve narrative closure, as much as such a "closure" may be permitted in a non-genre he has encoded successfully in a lifetime of self-conscious filmmaking, via a long shot, the sheer beauty of which simply defies description. After a pause of momentary disappointment when he sees Tahereh first disappear into the olive garden and then emerge from it into the wide pasture, Hossein chases her down a slope that ultimately takes him to her side. The two tiny creatures, now mere spots on the vast, fruitful, and ripe olive green, begin to abandon the intrusive gaze of the camera and almost disappear into "real life" when an instant of hesitation on Tahereh's side sends Hossein jubilantly running up the track, toward the camera, as the most subtle suggestion that he may have received a positive answer. At this moment, the camera has the instructed decency of standing on the hilltop, leaving the young couple alone to the privacy of their emotions. The camera, of course, does not blink. It simply stands there, gazing through a long, sustained, submissive, and singular look, perfectly content with the reading of a jubilant Hossein climbing up toward it. Kiarostami has crafted this long shot—with only one master shot, no coverage, and only a suggestion of mise-en-scène—with impeccable control. The long shot is almost identical with the penultimate sequence of *Close-Up*, where Kiarostami again instructs his camera and sound to stay out of private, and supremely beautiful, moments in people's lives. Right before the last long shot in *Through the Olive Trees*, Keshavarz/Kiarostami appears from behind the olive trees, un-directing his two protagonists but this time not for his fictive camera, of whose whereabouts we remain blissfully ignorant, but for Kiarostami's, which must cast the last, long, and loving gaze. Gary Dauphin of the *Village Voice* has captured the very essence of this hauntingly beautiful shot:

> How Kiarostami weaves together these disparate threads is the film's closing gift to its audience. The last scene is less an ending about Hossein and Tahereh than it is a revelation of what Kiarostami has been doing throughout the film, the image comprising a cinematic gesture so in keeping with his always gentle intrusions that to even reveal its existence is to do Kiarostami something of a disservice. Let's just say that much like Hossein's final trip through the grove of the film's title, getting the point of Olive Trees's ending requires a certain measure of faith, not so much in Hossein's blind love for Tahereh as in Kiarostami's love of all of them.[38]

In the necessary distance of this essay from the initial screening of *Through the Olive Trees*, I have had the luxury of reading that last shot without the reservation that had constrained Dauphin as a conscientious reviewer. The closing shot also needs to be read in conjunction with the opening shot of the film. The last shot is even more perceptive if one remembers that Kiarostami's camera has learned to know its limitations and to keep its nose out of people's business only after its very opening shot when the camera literally opens into a wall, from which both it and the car that carries it have to turn away as they begin their journey into people's business. The delicate crafting and extremely careful construction of this early sequence inadvertently is known by the fact that the initial version was damaged in the laboratory, and Kiarostami had to reshoot them later.[39] The camera and the cars of the director and the assistant director in fact have similar intrusive functions throughout the film. They always have to negotiate an uncomfortable passageway for themselves into a life and space to which they do not belong. Throughout the film this renegotiation works toward the final resolution of a new man and woman that Kiarostami so tenderly seeks to create. Thus, in that very last scene of *Through the Olive Trees*—the "Garden of Eden" Kiarostami so magnificently has planted—walk a new Adam and Eve, cleansed in green showers of love Kiarostami so generously has poured over them.

To be able thus to reinvent a new Adam and Eve, Kiarostami must be quietly violent. The violent act of "intrusion" is the principal target of quiet subversion in Kiarostami's cinema. There is an eyewitness report from Kiarostami's location in *Through the Olive Trees* that is worth noting. Houshang Golmakani reports that Kiarostami's sets are remarkably quiet and peaceful:

> The few scenes that I witnessed being shot lack any sign of professional acting as it is understood in other films. It is as if nobody is filming anything. The serenity of Kiarostami's films [is] also evident on his sets. There is no screaming "sound, camera, action!" nor is there any sign of the usual hustle-bustle of shooting. It is as if on one side people are going about their ordinary business, and on this side a group of people are gathered around a camera, doing something or another with it. There is no shouting of "Cut!" either. Kiarostami and Ja'farian [the director of photography], who is even calmer than him, whisper to each other about the beginning, the end, about some technical issues, whether or not a retake is necessary. Occasionally, there is not even a whisper, just a signal or a look.[40]

A POETIC GENEALOGY

To detect the aesthetic origin of this mode of looking, we might trace *Through the Olive Trees* back to its poetic genealogy—as I have sought to do with the rest of Kiarostami's cinema. Kiarostami's cinematic vision is best represented in what Houshang Golmakani in jest, but accurately, has called the Rostamabad Trilogy—later code-named the Koker Trilogy. This cinematic vision rests on a visual reading of a poetic phrase from Sohrab

Sepehri, the stunning simplicity of whose poetry is served brilliantly by Kiarostami's camera. It is not accidental that Kiarostami finds in Sepehri a kindred soul. He is doing visually what Sepehri sought to do poetically with words. Sepehri was to the New Persian Poetry (*She'r-e No*) of the 1960s and 1970s what Kiarostami became to Iranian cinema of the 1980s and 1990s. They both deliberately revert to an irreducible simplicity as a narrative strategy to subvert the configuration of a reality they dislike and dismantle. They both use a mode of "weak thought" (*il pensiero debole*)—a postmetaphysical subversion of all absolutist certainties, as the late Italian philosopher Gianni Vattimo (1936–2023) called it.[41] They oppose "violent thinking" not by proposing their positions violently but by gently subverting the very foundation of violent thinking. Sepehri's poetry and Kiarostami's cinema are in and of themselves aesthetic manifestoes against a complicated reality that has progressed exponentially to unbearably ugly and heavily coded proportions. They both intensely dislike politics, as they do ideology, and the historical realities that go with them. Their poetic and cinematic cosmovisions are a joyous celebration of life in its irreducibly material and uncoded configurations. When one reads Sepehri's poetry, it is as if he had a poetic premonition of Kiarostami's cinema:

> I am from Kashan.
> My life is rather well:
> With a piece of bread, a little bit of intelligence, a smidgen of taste.
> I have a mother, better than a tree leaf,
> A few friends, better than the flowing water.[42]

It is very instructive to compare Sepehri's relentless fixation with nature to Kiarostami's similar attraction to trees, flowers, rivers, stones, mountains, et cetera:

> I am a Muslim.
> The direction of my prayer towards a red rose.
> My prayer-cloth a fountain, I prostrate on light.
> The prairie is my prayer-rug.
> I take my ritual ablution with the pulse of windows.
> The moon and the shadows roll in my prayer.[43]

A return to the irreducible simplicity of nature and all the glorious restrictions it imposes on being became Sepehri's Dionysian "mystic" way out of the miserable constellation of reality as he sought to find his way out of its debilitating negations. Much more than the mere title of Kiarostami's first film in the Rostamabad Trilogy is evident in Sepehri's poetry:

> Love was visible, so was the wave.
> Snow was visible, so was friendship.
> Word was visible.
> Water was visible, and the picture of things in it:
> The cool resting place of cells in the heat of blood.
> The wet side of life.
> The Eastern sadness of humanity.
> The season of wandering in the alley of woman.
> The aroma of solitude in the street of season.[44]

There is something remarkably similar about Kiarostami. His fixation with children, however, is a cinematic device he has found much more operative than Sepehri's love for nature. The two poet/painters (both Sepehri and Kiarostami were accomplished painters as well) are identical in seeking visual and poetic ways out of the engulfing configuration of the heavily coded reality via a subversive redefinition of it. If not read carefully, Sepehri could have been dismissed as a pessimistic and disengaged poet, tired and angry with the world as is and thus seeking to live a life diverted from it. There is no misunderstanding Kiarostami, however. He is relentless with his disquieting and subversive gaze: That is precisely what deeply angers and frustrates his critics, by and large the violent ideological metaphysicians of moralizing imperatives. Under Kiarostami's gaze, reality is reread backward to a material irreducibility—decoded, bold, defiant. At the moment of that material recognition, Kiarostami holds his camera constant and tries to negotiate a new definition of reality.

One of the crucial impacts of Kiarostami's repeated takes of the staircase shot in *Through the Olive Trees*, whether in conversation with Tahereh or with Kheradmand, is precisely this gaze at the service of a way to renegotiate reality. That act of renegotiating reality, contrary to the criticism of many of Kiarostami's hostile critics, rests on a brutally accurate conception of it. It is not that he arrogantly defies or belittles reality; it is that he passionately, but quietly, dislikes what he sees. Because of that moral and aesthetic rejection, Kiarostami seeks to alter our vision of reality, and through that vision reality itself. He proceeds by altering the reality he rejects morally and aesthetically via a camera that must learn to keep a strategic distance—thus his (in)famous long shots that his critics cannot stand—from what it must represent. The distancing representation is a strategic mechanism Kiarostami has mastered. The strategy works very well in managing at one and the same time to represent and not to represent, to be real and to be fictive, to be present and to be absent. This is the strategic counter-essentialism (to borrow and rephrase a critical proposition of Gayatri Spivak)[45] that Kiarostami has done extremely well at the service of his theoretical renegotiation of reality. To miss this necessary angle of Kiarostami's camera is to see him as an arrogant man, deeply distanced from people he does not represent, a charge that his hostile critics never tire from bringing against him. However, neither Kiarostami nor his camera are arrogant. On the contrary, he frames and evades realities he passionately, but softly, dislikes via a strategically counter-essentializing camera that seeks to subvert those realities and supplant them by others—visions and realities of which our modes of reading them yet are to be assayed. Kiarostami's cinema is the midwife to a whole new way of envisioning not only reality as it is, but more importantly, as it should be. He is not an idealist. He has just discovered and basks in a different kind of realism—an actual realism, a realism that decodes the perception of reality.

AN AESTHETIC REVOLUTION

Beyond Kiarostami's quiet aesthetic revolution is a claim to a great moral transformation, a Dionysian carnival of death-rejecting, life-affirming, and loving laughter. Kiarostami's cinema bothers his hostile critics so much because beneath its gentle touch lurks a deadly serious determination to take his (incurably) guilt-ridden Shi'i audience to a pre- and post-guilt encounter with the physical life. He has detected a festive Dionysian/Bacchanalian trait in life that is neither Greek nor Roman nor Persian nor the exclusive property of any historical culture. Culture, in fact, appears to

Kiarostami as the aestheticized institutionalization of an historical tyranny, a brutal denial of the Dionysian/Khayyamesque mode of being that comes naturally with life and which is more life-affirming than fatuous, death-rejecting than decadent, loving than libidinal. He wishes through the relentless, though gentle, intrusion of his camera, to de-aestheticize that brutal institutionalization of false guilt that quintessentially denatures the historical person. He is defiant, and thus the appearance of arrogance, to all scared moralizers who denounce him. In essence, they are envious of his Dionysian liberation from the deadening imperatives of a culture that more than metaphorically has sold the cash of this life for the promissory note of the one to come. In this, Kiarostami is true to the spirit of Khayyam, another, more distant of his poetic ancestors.

Kiarostami's cinema is a Dionysian/Khayyamesque celebration of life, made infinitely more poignant by the fact that he is a filmmaker caught in a guilt-ridden culture now having produced a theocracy. There is something festive, joyous, discreetly sensual about his subversive vision. His Rostamabad Trilogy ought to be seen precisely the same way historians of ideas today read Bakhtin's conceptualization of the carnivalesque under the Soviet system. Kiarostami's camera appears too lascivious, his vision too disquieting, for his hypermoralizing critics, those who represent a whole culture of death and denial, now the hegemonic instrument of an entire state apparatus. Kiarostami's cinema is mercilessly subversive to that for which his moralizing critics stand, proselytize, and fight. His "characters," who are real, not fictive, are called by their own names, not by fictitious ones. They get up in the morning and exercise, or go for a walk, or get the breakfast ready. Kiarostami has an uncanny eye for the stunning simplicity of the ordinary and catches its magical spell precisely at the moment when it begins to permeate and subvert the received metaphysics of meaning. The scene showing the camera crew waking up early one morning is Kiarostamiesque par excellence. The assistant director (acted splendidly well by Zarifeh Shiva), the only female member of the crew, and the most authoritative one, wakes up every male member of the crew to a breathtakingly beautiful early dawn. One man is fast asleep, another is bare-chested and exercising, another is getting the tea ready for breakfast, the fourth is getting ready to come out of his tent, while the director is out for his morning walk. That is a vastly different vision of reality—a woman awakening a multitude of men to get up and go to work—from one alternative conception of reality in which the first thing men and women do early in the morning is to do their ablutions, ritually to wash their hands, face, and feet, and then stand in obedient prayer. Kiarostami's cinematic genius is to work this supremely subversive sequence in a way that precisely because of its simplicity and uncodability marks and works its magic.

This uncodability is essential to Kiarostami's cinema. It would be not only futile but utterly inane to try to read Kiarostami's cinema metaphorically. He is in fact a master practitioner of subverting the metaphysics of interpretation by physical aesthetics. He is not trying to convey any hidden message. In fact, he destroys the very assumption of "hidden messages." His camera is naked. "It is only shallow people," he might say along with Oscar Wilde, "who do not judge by appearances. The mystery of the world is the visible, not the invisible."[46] He is against interpretation in a remarkably similar way as Susan Sontag has argued in her *Against Interpretation*:

> Today is such a time, when the project of interpretation is largely reactionary, stifling.... The effusion of interpretations of art today poisons our sensibilities. In a culture whose already classical dilemma is the hypertrophy of the intellect at the expense of energy and sensual capability, interpretation is the revenge of the intellect upon art. Even more. It is the revenge of the intellect upon the world. To interpret is to impoverish, to deplete the world—in order to set up a shadow world of "meaning." It is to turn the world into this world.[47]

It is perfectly natural that Kiarostami's hostile critics come up with rashes and experience anxiety attacks when confronted with the naked beauty of his well-shaped, full-bodied, and voluptuous camera work. Through that camera, the whole world could view Kiarostami's Iran. The 48th Locarno Film Festival, August 1995, gave Kiarostami until then the unprecedented honor of a complete retrospective of his films. It was first in Locarno, in 1989, that *Where Is the Friend's House?* received its international audience and won the Bronze Leopard. Since then, Kiarostami became a key feature at the Locarno Film Festival, either as a member of the jury or else introducing his Rostamabad Trilogy. The organizers of the 1995 Locarno Film Festival also arranged for the exhibition of a selection of Kiarostami's

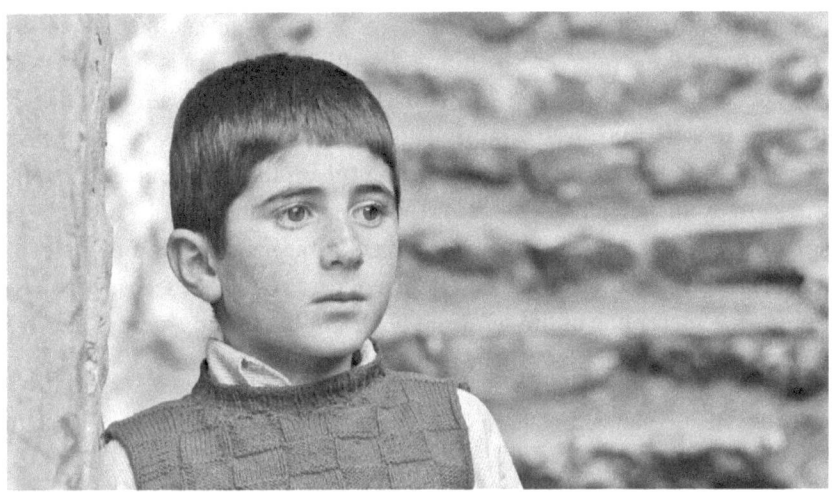

Figure 11. Babak Ahmadpoor as Mohamad Reza Nemat-zadeh in Abbas Kiarostami, *Where Is the Friend's House?* (1987). Courtesy of Abbas Kiarostami Foundation.

paintings and photographs at Locarno's museum of fine arts, the Museo Casa Rusca.[48] *Cahiers du Cinema* provided a full dossier of Kiarostami's work, while the chief editor of the journal, Thierry Jousse, called him "un des plus grand cineastes du monde." The cover of this issue featured a glorious shot from the last sequence of *Through the Olive Trees*, bracing a picture of Kiarostami by Carole Bellaiche, and the caption: "Kiarostami, Le magnifique!"[49]

Kiarostami had arrived, and with him the long list of a number of other Iranians—Hushang Golmakani, Zaven Qukasian, Ahmad Fouladvand, Ramin Jahanbagloo, Farrokh Gaffary, Jafar Panahi, Ebrahim Furuzesh, Farhad Kheradmand, Malekjahan Khazai, Mohammad Haghighat, Bahman Farmanara, Leyly Matin-Daftary . . . : All of them the magnificent decoders of a whole new reading of Iranian reality.

THE SELF-EFACING SUBJECT

The uncodability of Kiarostami's cinema, that it thrives on the surface of life, is elemental to the self-effacing thrust of his cinematic prose and poetry, and thus definitive to the nomadic (unknowing) subject he cross-references. Like a pilgrim, the nomadic subject wonders and wanders—does not interpret. Just like the Mehdi Akhavan-e Sales poem with which I began this chapter, Kiarostami's cinema, too, thrives on a self-effacing aesthetics—both crafting and yet effacing the unknowing subject it implicates. In Akhavan-e Sales's poem, the narrator continues to describe a snowy night when he and his fellow travelers are walking into the storm and stepping on fresh snow. The sojourn of these wandering nomads soon becomes a metaphor of life with the poet and his friends happy they are traversing on fresh paths. By the end, the narrator is solitary.

> Sadly, still the snow was falling
> Happy though I was
> To be far away from all the sheep and goats—
> I was both the shepherd and the flock
> All to myself—
> Under my feet fresh and virgin snow
> Had a delightful sound:
> My feet were planting their prints on snow.[50]

At the end he turns around and looks:
> My footsteps too were now covered by snow.[51]

Futile? Not really. The whole experience of self-effacing the pilgrim subject out on that snow-walk had left a glorious poem behind: A poetic premonition of the aesthetic of the foreign familiarity of the un/real that in about a decade after that poem was published would be definitive to Kiarostami's cinema.

5 Toward a Critique of Postcolonial Aesthetic Judgment

The Indians have a dominating taste of the grotesque, of the sort that falls into the adventurous. Their religion consists of grotesqueries. Idols of monstrous form.... What trifling grotesquerie do the verbose and studied compliments of the Chinese contain! Even their paintings are grotesque and portray strange and unnatural figures such as are encountered nowhere in the world.[1]

Immanuel Kant, *Observations on the Feeling of the Beautiful and Sublime* (1764)

I often say, although it is a dangerous thing to say publicly, that humanity consists of the Bible and the Greeks. All the rest can be translated: all the rest—all the exotic—is dance.[2]

Emmanuel Levinas, *French Philosophers in Conversation* (1991)

Let me start this chapter with two opposite reviews of Abbas Kiarostami's film *Dah/Ten* (2002)—one very positive and the other very negative. The positive review is by a British film critic and the negative review by an American film critic—both reviewers authoritative and highly respected.

In his review of *Ten* for the Guardian on 26 September 2002, Peter Bradshaw could not praise Kiarostami's film highly enough: "A very remarkable film from Abbas Kiarostami," he wrote, "one of the very best of the year, remarkable for its strenuous technical simplicity." He regrets that the world at large does not stand in queues to watch Kiarostami's films, for though it is a tough watch, he believes "it repays the investment of attention a thousandfold. With its imperceptible blend of actors, newcomers and non-professionals, and a happy mix of guided and unguided improvisations, it's a compelling realist document: challenging cinema conceived at the highest pitch of intelligence."[3]

Not so convinced was the late Roger Ebert (1942–2013), an exceptionally popular and perceptive American film critic. "I am unable to grasp the greatness of Abbas Kiarostami," he confessed at the outset of his review of Kiarostami's *Ten*, dated 11 April 2003, with disarming clarity. "His critical reputation is unmatched," Ebert went on to write, "His 'A Taste of Cherry' (1997) won the Palme d'Or at Cannes, and 'The Wind Will Carry Us' (1999) won the Golden Lion at Venice. And yet his films—for example his latest work, 'Ten'—are meant not so much to be watched as to be written about; his reviews make his points better than he does." Ebert proceeds to say praising Kiarostami's cinema is like "praising a child for coloring between the lines." He thinks other Iranian filmmakers like Tahmineh Milani or Jafar Panahi are far better filmmakers. He bluntly says Kiarostami stands in the way of other, better Iranian filmmakers being recognized for their superior filmmaking. "The shame is that more accessible Iranian directors are being neglected in the overpraise of Kiarostami." Finally, he goes for the kill: "If this approach [Kiarostami's] were used for a film shot in Europe or America, would it be accepted as an entry at Cannes? I argue that it would not. Part of Kiarostami's appeal is that he is Iranian, a country whose films it is somewhat daring to praise. Partly, too, he has a lot of critics invested in his cause, and they do the heavy lifting. The fatal flaw in his approach is that no ordinary moviegoer, whether Iranian or American, can be expected to relate to his films. They exist for film festivals, film critics and film classes."[4]

One can read other similar reviews, positive and negative, all by perceptive, insightful, persuasive, and authoritative American, British, French, German, and Italian film critics, some devoted to the cause of Kiarostami's cinema and others not so convinced he was a serious filmmaker.

Now let me insert a fictional Asian, African, or Latin American film critic in between these two renowned film critics from the US and the UK. They, too, can also write a review and publish it in one venue or another—as they often do. So, now we have three reviews: one negative by an American, one positive by a British, and a third, say, somewhere between

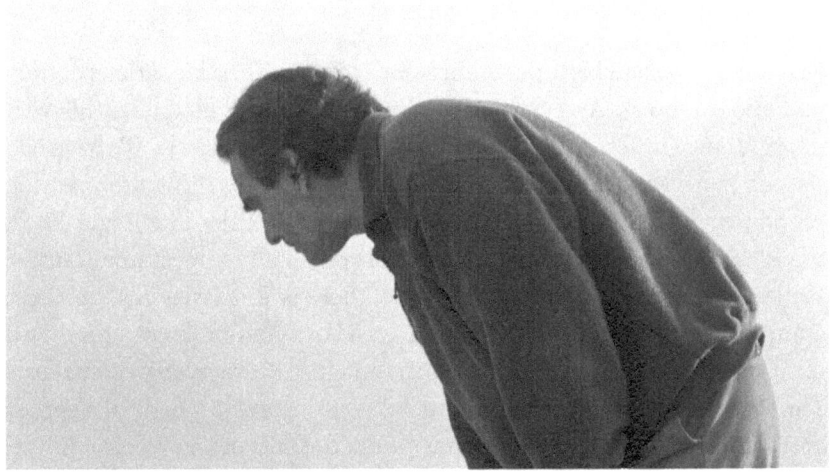

Figure 12. Homayoun Ershadi in Abbas Kiarostami, *Taste of Cherry* (1997). Courtesy of Abbas Kiarostami Foundation.

the two by an Indian, an Egyptian, a Chinese, a Congolese, or an Argentinian film critic. Which one of these three critics is more legitimate than the other two? Objectively, you might say they are all legitimate in their own way and there is no way one could say one judgment on Kiarostami's film is more legitimate than the other. But that objective position is not supported by a very basic and fundamental fact. The British and the American reviewers are entitled to their positions and aesthetic judgements not by the superiority of their critical intelligence (of which they have plenty) but by a long philosophical tradition that has stipulated, theorized, and authorized their authorial voices and their abilities to make an aesthetic judgment long before they sat at their keyboards, while an African, an Asian, or a Latin American reviewer lacks such a serious philosophical heritage foregrounding their voices—for they have been specifically and by name excluded from that system. That African or Asian or Latin American film critic is not even permitted to utter a judgment, for they are designated to dwell outside the selfsame philosophical system that has enabled and authorized Peter Bradshaw and the late Roger Ebert to make an aesthetic judgment. This was quite a mouthful thing to say— so allow me to explain in more detail.

CHAPTER FIVE

SAPERE AUDE

Kiarostami has had his ardent admirers and he has had his serious detractors and doubters. As I have argued in the previous chapters, this very interpretative differential forms a crucial hermeneutic circle. We have had serious European philosophers like Jean-Luc Nancy writing probingly on his oeuvre, and we have had equally serious film critics like Roger Ebert thinking this whole hoopla about Kiarostami is all tempest in a Cannes, Venice, or Locarno teacup. Meanwhile, there is a massive body of both appreciative and dismissive literature on Kiarostami in Persian produced in Iran that scarcely anyone reads outside Kiarostami's homeland. Through it all, however, what has remained constant is a body of rigorous and robust artwork that has demanded and continues to receive critical attention. The project of recasting Kiarostami's artworld onto a more leveled postcolonial scene is an urgent task so that his legacy will not waver with the fate of these extemporaneous considerations in one way or another. To do so, we need to address one serious issue of agential authority and the ability to pass critical aesthetic judgment head on before all else. I therefore wish to go way upstream from all these passing considerations and raise a very basic question.

I wonder if, as a person, as an Iranian who has spent much of his adult life outside Iran, as a cultural critic, a thinker, a human being, as someone whose homeland has been subject to the systematic assaults of European colonial and imperial powers (Russia, England, France, and above all, the US) and ruled by successive domestic tyrannies that has now resulted in a cruel Islamist theocracy on the heels of a forbidding monarchy: What do I see when I stand in front of a Kiarostami painting or photography, or sit to watch one of his films? What would or could or should an African, a Latin American, an Indian, a Chinese, a Japanese, an Arab, a Turk, a Muslim with histories similar to mine or even different from mine anywhere in the world see? If you can imagine all us "dark," non-European people inside that proverbial Platonic cave, what would anyone of us see when turning around to look at the source of the light cast upon us? How do we judge what we see, how do we make a decision, offer an argument, write in detail the contours of our encounter with a work of art or an entire artworld, whether our own, as it were, or from any other cultural context—including what has called itself "the Western art?" What do we see when we watch a Kiarostami film, and what, if anything, does our aesthetic judgment convey and imply or signify about what we see, or even more importantly, about us as a people, as postcolonial knowing or unknowing subjects facing what we hope is still a knowable world? The central nucleus of all these questions is the nature and disposition of a postcolonial aesthetic judgment, the subject of this chapter in my book on Abbas Kiarostami. But before I address the issue of aesthetic judgment in the works of Abbas Kiarostami, I will first have to make sure as a human being, as a postcolonial person, I am capable of that judgment. This may appear as a truism. But it is not, when it comes to the philosophical tradition hitherto applied to Kiarostami, empowering and authorizing a French, German, Italian, British, or American critic. So, the first question to raise is do I dare to think and know, or am I able to pass an aesthetic judgment?

To begin with: Is everything I see in Kiarostami reducible to my politics, to my political positions, and is his entire artworld also, as the eminent American literary critic Frederic Jameson thought about our literature, a product and a specimen of "third-World texts," and as such perforce and "necessarily project a political dimension in the form of national allegory?"[5] Does something remain irreducibly aesthetic about our works of art and about our thinking about our works of art—and if so, in what particular sense? Long before Jameson, other "Western philosophers," all the way back to Immanuel Kant, thought our sort of art was a picture of grotesqueries, while further down the line Emmanuel Levinas, an eminent Jewish, Lithuanian-French philosopher, thought all philosophy was either Biblical Hebrew or else classical Greek, and the rest, meaning us Asians, Africans, Latin Americans, could do nothing but "dance" (What is wrong with dancing, why opt for dancing as a metaphor of denigration?) to tickle his fancies and for his entertainment. But far beyond all these foundational thinkers, when a student of film-philosophy turns to Kiarostami, without a moment of hesitation they cannot think of any other kind of philosophy than the habitual "Western philosophy" that is applicable to the Iranian filmmaker and starts with Stanley Cavell and goes back to the later Ludwig Wittgenstein and from there to René Descartes, via detour to Walter Benjamin, and ultimately rests his case with the Paisley Livingston thesis on film and philosophy to make some very cogent observations about one or the other of Kiarostami's films.[6] This is not to say that all these European or Eurocentric philosophers do not or may not have something very serious to say just about anything, including about Kiarostami's cinema. But where would be the provenance of a philosophical imagination in which Iranian or Islamic or Chinese or Indian or African or Latin American philosophical thinking has no entrance—for as Levinas would say, all of these would be just "dancing."

In light of these facts, where would a postcolonial person, an Iranian, a Senegalese, a Mexican, or anyone from anywhere other than Europe or a European settler colony say anything about this "Film-Philosophy" without being beholden to this "Western philosophy," neither hostile to it nor obsessed with it, neither Eurocentric nor Europhobic? Then what, if anything, could this person have to say about Kiarostami and how valid might that be, when the leading European scholars of this "Film-Philosophy" could not read a word of Persian or Arabic or Chinese or Swahili if it hit them in the face? But again, the question is certainly not that what calls itself "Western Philosophy" and the sort of "Film-Philosophy" it has empowered and authorized is not insightful about Kiarostami's cinema, for it certainly could be and certainly is. But where would a non-European or Eurocentric thinker rooted as much in Kant and Descartes as in Avicenna and Suhrawardi, or any "other" philosophical tradition that is not "othered" by this very "Western Philosophy," stand and have a claim to agency, authorship, autonomous thinking, and moral, critical, and imaginative subjectivity?

The entire European provenance of this question is rooted in Kant's critique of aesthetic judgment, which has engaged much of the rest of European philosophy all the way down to Hans Georg Gadamer. The key question for people outside Europe or the philosophical Eurozone when reading these European sources is not whether aesthetic judgment is subjective or objective, which is an entirely luxurious and rather spurious question we cannot afford entertaining and find somewhat supercilious. The key question for us, in Asia, Africa, Latin America, Oeania, et cetera, when we read these European or Eurozone thinkers is how making a judgment about a work of art becomes the key operating philosophical apparatus about how we as human beings become or do not become a knowing subject, a caring, competent, confident, and qualified agent of our own history, not just the work of arts we and others might produce, but our agency as human beings with legitimate authority over our own minds, thoughts, lives, and yes, the works of art we produce. A French or Australian or English or German or Italian person might say whatever they damn well please about Kiarostami or anything else they wish—and they do so quite eloquently, and all power to them. My concern is if the rest of us—before we are "rested" and alienated from our own humanity, as we dwell in a different place (where our differentials are not yet fetishized)—have the moral and material agency to think on our own two feet. It is this philosophical proposition of the capacity to make an aesthetic judgment that is crucial for the rest of the world at the receiving end of the brutalities of European moral and material colonialism of our bodies and souls, our natural resources, and our critical and creative imagination. The question is even less whether we are capable of producing the sublime and the beautiful, but whether we are capable of recognizing, embracing, theorizing, philosophizing the sublime and the beautiful. Are we capable of producing something other than cinematic or artistic "objects of philosophical curiosity" for Europeans to explain to us what they mean? Kant thought making an aesthetic judgment was a matter of having a feeling, and the question then is are we non-Europeans capable of feelings? Yes, no, maybe, and if so, how would that feeling and that aesthetic judgment allow and afford us human (and perforce posthuman) agency and agential subjectivity, not just to be the master of our own destiny, or slaves of our desires, but far more importantly, the knower of the world where we live, where its frightful fragility no longer allows for European and non-European bifurcation?

Kant's three seminal critiques, definitive to his entire philosophy, constituted a knowing subject that was and remains exclusively European, a knowable colonial world this sovereign subject faces, which this European subject in turn went about conquering and knowing.[7] Kant's *Critique of Judgment* (1790) followed his *Critique of Pure Reason* (1781), in which he posited the sovereign knowing European subject, and *Critique of Practical Reason* (1788) where he placed a knowable world at his disposal. In *Critique of Judgment*, Kant decidedly turned to the domain of the aesthetic judgment by way of testing the most potent example of this interface between the European knowing subject and the ravaged world he placed at his disposal to conquer and to know—and where the four aesthetic judgments he outlines as the agreeable, the beautiful, the sublime, and the good all reflect the outline of his first Critique of Pure (European) Reason. The Kantian system is therefore decidedly closed and foreclosed, perforce closed circuited, and an exclusive philosophical project for the European knowing subject, which the eminent Argentinian philosopher Enrique Dussel has aptly called the *ego cogito* that comes after the *ego conquiro*.[8] This means within the Kantian system, or the Hegelian teleological trajectory in his philosophy of history, no non-European could ever be the sovereign subject of a knowable world, for we are part of that knowable world (like its minerals, animals, lakes, mountains, folklore, folkways, and enslaved labor) and if we were to ever dare follow Kant's own advice to sapere aude, and dare to know anything at all, any knowledge we might produce will collapse the Kantian philosophical system, while Levinas stands in a corner giggling, entertained by the sheer hilarity of our "dancing." Now you must imagine yourself a colonial subject, an Iranian or Indian or someone from Congo or Argentina, standing in front of a Kiarostami painting and daring to know what it means!

The closed circularity of the Kantian philosophical system is not a matter of critical contestation by a postcolonial person to be defended by a European philosopher. It is a matter of Kant's own pronounced and unabashed racism in (among other places) his seminal tract, *Beobachtungen über das Gefühl des Schönen und Erhabenen/Observations on the Feeling of the Beautiful and Sublime* (1764), where he categorically states:

> The Negroes of Africa have by nature no feeling that rises above the ridiculous. Mr. Hume challenges anyone to adduce a single example where a Negro has demonstrated talents, and asserts that among the hundreds of thousands of blacks who have been transported elsewhere from their countries, although very many of them have been set free, nevertheless not a single one has ever been found who has accomplished something great in art or science or shown any other praiseworthy quality, while among the whites there are always those who rise up from the lowest rabble and through extraordinary gifts earn respect in the world. So essential is the difference between these two human kinds, and it seems to be just as great with regard to the capacities of mind as it is with respect to color.... The

blacks are very vain, but in the Negro's way, and so talkative that they must be driven apart from each other by blows.[9]

African philosophers have been rightly horrified by such passages.[10] But the vulgar racism of Kant in this and similar passages should not detract from a far more serious issue, which is their systematic denial of agency to any human being to know anything worth knowing outside Europe. It is not that people in Asia, Africa, or Latin America are incapable of the sublime and the beautiful. The issue is that we are and we must remain part and parcel of the knowable world, like our minerals they analyze, our natural resources they steal, and our slave labor they profit from with total "moral" impunity, for we are not humans. We are like stones, mountains, the minerals under them, seas and the fish and the vegetal lives under the waters or over the hills and mountains. For which reasons, we lack taste and could not possibly have any sense of "the morally beautiful." This is how the father of European Enlightenment puts us in our place:

> The inhabitant of the Orient is of a very false taste in this point. Since he has no conception of the morally beautiful that can be combined with this drive, he also loses even the value of the sensuous gratification, and his harem is a constant source of unrest for him. He falls into all sorts of amorous grotesqueries, among which the imaginary jewel is one of the foremost, which he tries to secure above all others, whose entire value consists only in one's smashing it, and of which one in our part of the world generally raises much malicious doubt, and for the preservation of which he makes use of very improper and often disgusting means. Hence a woman there is always in prison, whether she be a maiden or have a barbaric, inept, and always suspicious husband.[11]

That women as women in the world at large are "always in prison" is not just a judgment on women and their predicament; it is also a statement of judgment as to where in the world we stand. Our "false taste" is not just because we produce and admire grotesque "art." (How could we have ever produced a Kiarostami worth Nancy's or Abbott's attention?) The grotesquery of our art and our inability to appreciate Kant's European art is a testament, the tip of the proverbial iceberg, that we are not human, that we lack human agency and are condemned to a slave mentality that can only risk the hazards of the Mediterranean Sea or the Mexico-US border concentration camps for the privilege of coming to clean their toilets, pick their strawberries, and wash their dishes in Europe and the US. Meanwhile, as the epitome of European humanism, Kant deeply cared for our womenfolk:

> In the lands of the blacks can one expect anything better than what is generally found there, namely the female sex in the deepest slavery? A pusillanimous person is always a strict master over the weaker, just as with us that man is always a tyrant in the kitchen who outside of his house hardly dares to walk up to anyone. Indeed, Father Labat reports that a Negro carpenter, whom he reproached for haughty treatment of his wives, replied: You whites are real fools, for first you concede so much to your wives, and then you complain when they drive you crazy. There might be something here worth considering, except for the fact that this scoundrel was completely black from head to foot, a distinct proof that what he said was stupid.[12]

Our stupidity is as natural to us as the color of our skin. Simple as that. The only way that we might be saved from this predicament is if we work hard, wear colorful contact lenses, dye our hair blonde, have a nose job perhaps, and then we might be admitted into the European versions of ourselves: Where Arabs become "the Spaniards of the Orient," Persians "the French of Asia," the Japanese the "Englishmen of this part of the world."[13] So, there is hope for humanity, if we were only to migrate onto the European side of their racist imagination.

There are of course earnest attempts by European scholars to whitewash, or "contextualize," such boldfaced racism of the father of "European Enlightenment."[14] It is perfectly understandable and even commendable that these European thinkers are trying to save Kant or Hegel or Levinas from themselves, and I in fact have total sympathy and even solidarity with them—as I do with those who try in vain to "contextualize" Heidegger's Nazism or Foucault's systematic sexual abuse of children in Tunisia. One should not, I always say, throw the proverbial baby and bathwater out together. These seminal European philosophers are signposts of a colonial history that at least in their temporal trajectory have much to teach us. Our task is to make particular what they made falsely universal, as we allow for a certain worldly universality what they exoticized and made particular.[15] But saving Kant or Levinas from their unabashed racism is not our primary concern, nor our paramount project. Kant in particular did nothing but with astounding philosophical ingenuity justify the colonial ravaging of the world by his fellow Europeans. I, for one, am not bothered by Kant's or Levinas's racism. We are the objects of those ravages, and we are now trying to figure out how in the world and where in the world we stand as we face a work of art like Kiarostami's. That is our project—not the verbal gesticulation that Kant did not mean what he said here, but that he meant everything else he said elsewhere. I in fact believe to be distracted by Kant's boldfaced racism that hides a more serious issue, which is how in his three consecutive critiques he privileges the European knowing subject to be capable of the sublime and the beautiful, and his theorization of racism is simply to make sure no non-European might be allowed anywhere near that systaltic philosophy of the European knowing subject. Kant's anthropologically based racism is not accidental to his philosophy. It is definitive to it. The project that remains for us after that fact is how we would dare to know—sapere aude, as Kant himself instructed us—understand, and face a work of art like those of Kiarostami's, as we work our way toward a critique of the postcolonial aesthetic judgment.

ANTHROPOCENTRISM AS EUROCENTRISM

You might say, as some contemporary scholars of Kant do, that Immanuel Kant (1724–1804) was the product of his time in the eighteenth and early nineteenth centuries—and therefore his racism should not offend anyone today! It is a bizarre argument. But on to the next atrocity. What about Emmanuel Levinas (1906–1995), who was our contemporary and who brings the selfsame philosophical racism down to our own time? He, too, thought anything we non-Europeans might say, such as writing a book on Abbas Kiarostami's film-philosophy, which might merit his philosophical attention, is in vain for they are merely dancing. How can I, then, or an Egyptian, a Japanese, a Malaysian, a Moroccan, any non-European thinker, say anything about Kiarostami or dare to write a book on his art-world with a reference to his "film-philosophy"—all with due modesty and in lower case? The issue is not one or two cases of inadvertent racism. The issue is much deeper. Robert Eaglestone has dug out other pieces of jewelry from this innately (not accidentally) racist European philosopher who, as a Jew and a Holocaust survivor at that, has himself been the victim of European racism and yet has evidently internalized that racism and believes: "When I speak of Europe, I think about the gathering of humanity. Only in the European sense can the world be gathered together. . . . In this sense Buddhism can be said just as well in Greek."[16] Let us please be clearheaded about all this. This is what Levinas believed and said in black and white, as it were. Eaglestone does an admirable work trying to rescue Levinas's philosophy from his racism by reminding the world of his own "postcolonial" traces.[17] I don't think that works. For Levinas would know better than anyone else the terror that very Europe had perpetrated on him and his "race." And still he believed the same Europe that had dispatched his entire "race" to concentration camps is the only place where humanity can gather. It is perfectly legitimate for Levinas to believe as he did: "I always say—but under my breath—that the Bible and the Greeks present the only serious issues in human life, everything else is dancing. . . . There is no racism intended."[18] If indeed "there is no racism intended," then why say it "under my breath?" I also have no idea what Levinas had against dancing, or why he thought we Asians and Africans do nothing but dance. To be sure, I see nothing wrong with dancing and doing some sort of philosophy at the same time. Yes, the so-called Whirling Dervishes, as Europeans call the followers of Maulana Jalal al-Din Rumi, do dance, and we in fact have a whole school of thinking about *Sama'/Dance*. But could a person presumably dance and think, or dance by way of thinking, or think as if dancing, at the same time, perhaps?

It is equally useless to try to save Levinas from his anthropocentrism, which disregards the fact that based on his barefaced racism, his anthropocentrism is really Eurocentrism.[19] For Levinas, the human is only European, and the non-European is not human—therefore an animal too busy dancing to be human. A persecuted European Jew, Levinas's entire philosophical preoccupation with "the face of the other" is really just a plea for the Christian Europe to accept the face of the Jewish Other as its own. His invitation of the European toward "Infinity" rather than dwelling in "Totality" is a pleading to allow for a space of the Jewish face of the Other. Otherwise, Levinas has no other conception of human being. Calarco tries to tease out a Levinasian space for overcoming anthropocentrism. But that is as impossible as overcoming Levinas's Eurocentric racism. What Calarco fails to understand is that when Levinas says "human," he means "European," and when Calarco insists that in Levinasian terms, "nonhuman animal is capable of genuine ethical response to the Other," or that "nonhuman animals are not the kinds of beings that elicit an ethical response in human beings," here animals and non-Europeans are one and the same for Levinas, as it was for Kant, as he firmly believed only Europeans are humans, and he could not imagine an African, or Asian, or Latin American to have any such response as would an animal. Levinas would sooner imagine a dog or a wolf or a horse or a bird to elicit such feeling in a European than an African or Indian or Latin American, or a Palestinian, and therefore Calarco says that, "although Levinas himself is for the most part unabashedly and dogmatically anthropocentric, the underlying logic of his thoughts permit no such anthropocentricism."[20] That anthropocentrism is actually Eurocentrism, as he has put it quite bluntly, that non-Europeans are outside the fold of humanity. His so-called ethical philosophy is therefore to plead with Europeans to accept him, a Jew, as a human being, as a legitimate Other.

Therefore: we could not possibly come anywhere near the assumption of Kiarostami's artworld as a site of philosophical reflection for a postcolonial person if we were not first and foremost to address the plausibility of that person to be a thinking, feeling, and able human being capable of aesthetic judgment, especially when we say so in the domain of English, French, Italian, or German languages, which as recent immigrant intellectuals we have confidently appropriated as the theater of our operation.

FABLING THE WORLD

The futile attempt to save Levinas from his incurable racism, or his Eurocentrism anthropocentrism, and the turn to tease a way out of his philosophical cul de sac through that very philosophy draws us back to a closer attention to animals in Kiarostami's cinema—for the simple proposition that the way out of the cul de sac of Kant, Hegel, Levinas, and the rest of European philosophical racism is first and foremost the work of arts we face themselves. In this task we are aided and equipped by serious philosophical discourses of thinkers like Y. V. Mudimbe from Congo, Enrique Dussel and Walter Mignolo from Argentina, Ashis Nandy from India, and Kojin Karatani from Japan. The common denominator of these and similar thinkers is that they are in significant conversation and contestation with European philosophical traditions but have radically different projects. The moral and intellectual agency they create is not nativist, reactionary, reactive, or localist. Quite to the contrary: they are impacted, integrated, with audacity and power over the philosophical legacy of "the West" but not part of the West. Like Edward Said, Ngũgĩ, and Frantz Fanon, they are critical of "the west," but unlike them they are not possessed by the West. Contrary to Said's lifetime project, the proof of the pudding is not in being possessed by the west or even possessing the West but in overcoming the west by placing it in its right historical place.

Back to the paramount question: In what way can I or any other non-European stand in front of any work of art, especially one of Kiarostami in this case, and claim to have a judgment of it? Whence and wherefore the authority and confidence of that voice? That question should not be traced immediately to its metaphysical foregrounding but kept limited to its epistemological character. There on the wall or the screen shimmers and reflects Kiarostami's artwork, and here stand I, like one of those thirty birds in Attar's allegory, staring at my own reflection in that mirror. What do I see and how do I articulate what I see, and based on what external means and inner justification can I at least convince myself that what I say makes sense, or even does not make sense, but still be in a position to make that aesthetic judgment standing decidedly outside Kant's three critiques?

If we were to start with Kiarostami's own work, it takes us in a different direction—for it is that piece of artwork that bestows authority, agency, and subjectivity. Take the issue of anthropocentrism, for example, which is a camouflage for Levinas's irredeemable Eurocentrism through which he denies the possibility of thinking to any non-European, busy as we are dancing for his entertainment. The issue of anthropocentrism takes us immediately to Kiarostami's very first and very last film, *The Bread and Alley* and *24 Frames*, beginning with a menacing dog and ending with all other kinds of wild animals, especially birds, which quite naturally takes us to metaphors of the bird in Avicenna and Suhrawardi. Let us consider this carefully. In *The Bread and Alley* (1970), we encounter a scary dog that frightens a boy who had gone to the bakery to fetch a fresh loaf of bread, and from there we cut to his very last work, *24 Frames* (2017), where he combines his two passions of film and photography and where we see still photographs of landscape with wildlife, especially birds, digitally animated. Animals therefore have a palpable presence in Kiarostami's cinema. This of course does not, ipso facto, absolve his cinema of androcentrism. But it does open a window into his visual imagination that allows us entrance into his artworld, restores and reconstitutes an authorial voice, and enables and resignifies a significant body of philosophical literature hitherto barred from his visual imagination.

Take Frame 10 of *24 Frames*, for example: Against the background of snow-covered mountains, gathered around a lonesome tree is a flock of sheep, guarded by a dog, as snow falls—pure ecstasy, and a lesson in ennobling patience. Eventually, the dog gets alerted by the sound of a wolf, and the dog starts barking. A similar setting defines Frame 11: the same background, a slightly slenderer tree, and a group of wolves—the wind blows, the wolves are devouring something. Soon one of the wolves leaves, then the second wolf leaves, done with their meal. They eventually all come back to the carcass meal. Fade out. Some have suggested this is all influenced by Japanese Haiku, perhaps. What is paramount is a symphonic gathering of animals and the vegetal: deer, wolves, horses, birds, cows, dogs. How are we to read these frames? Here is how one insightful commentator describes its origins, character, disposition, and meaning:

> The director would work for three years with collaborator, Ali Kamali, to produce a series of segments, comprising a still image—a painting or photograph—brought to life by the use of animation, stock footage and digital layering in an attempt to convey the moments before and after a photograph is captured. The result was around sixty or so "frames," from which thirty had already been selected by the time of Kiarostami's death, leaving his son, Ahmad Kiarostami, to complete the project. The resultant twenty-four sequences—the intended final number, its significance alluding to the sum of hours in a day as well as the shooting rate of film passing through a projector—are a haunting montage of "moving images," elegant and elegiac in nature and timeless and formless in essence, enabling us as audience to empathize and experience Kiarostami's innermost emotional and spiritual states.[21]

Others have been more impatient with the result:

> "24 Frames" can't help but be affecting because it is Kiarostami's final movie. But it's intellectually uninvolving, and its technical limitations prove frustrating. In a few shots, snow or rain falls, for instance, on the same left-to-right diagonal, creating a distracting pattern that suggests the software wasn't altered for each photograph.[22]

The body of work and the sheer weight of having seen something he wishes to share is the point here. The film as a result extends from his photography, becoming a moving apparition, and as such becomes a fable, not just an animal fable, but also a human fable, a transfusion of both, and thus we are suddenly transformed into a cinematic rendition of *Kelilah and Dimnah*—at which point we realize from beginning to end, Kiarostami was one master fabulist, visualizing what he and we had read from childhood. There are not just animal fables, but the entire humanity of the world becomes a fable.

Watching *The Bread and Alley* and *24 Frames* back-to-back is an exercise in patience, perseverance, and revelatory perceptions, meditative and pensive, finding a new rhythm to earth, to life, and reconnecting to our hermeneutic proclivities and disposition. We therefore must begin with the work of art itself and the way their artworld posits and implicates an aesthetic judgment and take it from there. Formation of an aesthetic judgment outside the Kantian system, but with no axiomatic fear of touching Kant, enables a postcolonial person to dare (Kant's own preferred term) to come close and dismantle Kant. This is to be done via a critical intimacy that reverses the colonial gaze that has stared the non-European world down. If we do so, and allow Kiarostami's fabular poetics to work itself through our aesthetic judgment, by the time we get to the first framing of a tree by a window in mesmerizing black and white and suddenly flies into the frame a bird, maybe a pigeon or a dove, and sits on the window sill, and then comes another bird, we might be excused if we are suddenly transformed into the most important philosophical tradition native to Kiarostami, which is the centrality of "*Resaleh al-Tayr*/Bird Treatises," in which humans are presumed to be incarcerated in "the Western" domain of their existence and through a divine emissary become aware of their "Eastern" abodes. The origin of these avian allegories is traced back to the mystical interpretations that the *Ikhwan al-Safa*/The Brethren of Purity, made of the chapter on "al-Hamamah al-Mutawwaqa/ The Ringdove" in *Kelilah and Dimnah*, from which eventually emerged Ibn Sina's famous *'Ayniyah Qasidah*, where the soul is also seen as a dove, which he also repeats in his treatise of *Hay ibn Yaghdhan*, where the protagonist bird is trapped with other birds. After Avicenna, Al-Ghazali writes his *Resaleh al-Tayr*, which his brother Ahmad Al-Ghazali translates into Persian, and after that comes Shahab al-Din Yahya al-Suhrawardi, who does the same in his *Aql-e Sorkh/The Red Intellect*.[23] The tradition continues until we come to Farid al-Din Attar and his *Mantiq al-Tayr/ Conference of the Birds*. Might we therefore consider Abbas Kiarostami's treatment of birds and other animals in his very first and his very last film in the context of an even richer tradition of animal fables we have received all the way from pre-Islamic periods?

If you were to bear with all these hidden and presumed allusions, we may then procced to add how this entire body of literature has been the premise of the idea of *al-Hikmah al-Mashriqiyah*, or "Oriental Philosophy," which has absolutely nothing to do with the current critical discourse around European Orientalism that began in 1978 with Edward Said's seminal text, and therefore the dignity and power of whose epithet transcends not just the disgraceful treatment of Orientalists but even the most cogent critic of it in Edward Said, both sides of which argument have remained blissfully ignorant of this philosophical tradition. The term *al-Hikmah al-Mashriqiyah* is the designation that Avicenna and his followers gave to a particular turn in this philosophy, and the French scholar Corbin was particularly excited about this turn, while other scholars like Dimitri Gutas have questioned the range and plausibility of this idea beyond the established Aristotelian proclivities of Avicenna.[24] Be that as it may, in Avicenna's own work the idea of "Oriental Philosophy" was valid. The question at this point is not the valid distinction Gutas rightly makes between "Oriental Philosophy" as an epistemological proposition and "Mysticism" as an entirely different proposition, in which distinction I completely agree with Gutas. But at the same time, the veracity of *Hikmah al-Mashriqiyah*, or Oriental Philosophy, remains factually evident as a bona fide domain in Avicenna's work, which was later expanded by al-Suhrawardi and their followers. Central to this idea of Oriental Philosophy are the allegories of birds that come to a crescendo in Avicenna and reaches its zenith in Suhrawardi and their subsequent commentators.

If we were to place Kiarostami's last work in the context of this robust tradition of animal fables as a predicate and frame of reference of Avicenna's Oriental Philosophy, then Kiarostami's entire oeuvre assumes a renewed significance that is integral to a universal philosophical imagination entirely outside the territorial authority of Kant or Levinas to disallow non-Europeans entry. On that domain, Kiarostami's cinema can begin to yield not just a different kind of film-philosophy but more importantly enable and empower a far richer and more diversified readership outside the limited philosophical imagination under the control of Kantian aesthetic, Hegelian philosophy of history, or Levinasian optical illusion to see the whole world outside Europe as just "dancing."

A MOBILE, ITINERANT, NOMADIC UN/KNOWING SUBJECT

Where would that relocation of the space of philosophical meditation that includes both the Kantian West and the Avicenna East, both in epistemological and not territorial (ideological) senses, and denies the former the false imperial hubris and teaches his philosophical descendent to learn humility and not to dismiss the whole world outside their provincial Europe take us? Here is where we would now be located: While at the heart of European Enlightenment (colonial) modernity, the experience of art is given an autonomous disposition to stage and offset the critique of the alienating effect of the selfsame modernity, aesthetic alienation on the colonial site is doubly removed from the material premises of life—where raw material and cheap labor leads directly to commodity fetishism minus the process of production that would lead to the formation of a bourgeois public sphere on one side and the organized revolt of the subaltern classes on the other. The precarity of that dynamic is both the condition and the consequence of a particular kind of the knowing, feeling, and sensing subject that still remains to be actively theorized on the models that Mudimbe has done in Africa, or Dussel and Mignolo for Latin America—and needs to be done elsewhere too. Blindness to this insight, I contend, is the central flaw of the transnational European public sphere that embraces the globalized artworld of filmmakers like Abbas Kiarostami while oblivious to their always already postcolonial disposition, to which a much richer moral, philosophical, and aesthetic field is now available. We should by all means resist the false temptation to call this state precolonial and must see its post-Western character more clearly. On that post-Western space, no knowing or unknowing subject can be except as mobile, itinerant, and nomadic.

How is that itinerant subject posited and enabled in Kiarostami's cinema? Let us look at three of his masterpieces and see what sort of an un/knowing subject they implicate. *Taste of Cherry* (1997) is about a man who presumably wants to commit suicide, as he drives through and around Tehran, and looks for someone to cover his grave when he is dead. *The Wind Will Carry Us* (1999) is about a truly obnoxious and intrusive documentary filmmaker who is in a Kurdish village harassing people and disrupting their peace. *Ten* (2002) is about a woman driving her car through the city and recording ten scenes of her encounter with various passengers. The point of entry into these films would be to see how the miasmatic disposition of the text of these films poses a hermeneutic resistance to such European readings that disregard the postcolonial aesthetic judgment at the heart of the artworld of artists like Kiarostami. These films are not about the subject of their stories, a possible suicide, an impending death and subsequent mourning ceremony, or women's predicaments in Iran. If they were about these prosaic matters, they would indeed be extremely boring and banal, and subject to all sorts of legitimate criticism about their anthropological gaze. We must look at these films not *about* something but *of* something, of the articulation of a certain kind of seeing and rendering reality. Reality here is rendered as suspenseful, contingent, *Mumkin al-Wujud*, as Avicennnan ontology would have it, and not *Wajib al-Wujud*/Necessary Being or *Mumtani' al-Wujud*/Impossible Being. In that ontology, only God is *Wajib al-Wujud*, for He is the Unmoved Mover—without whom nothing can be. Everything else is *Mumkin al-Wujud*, or Contingent Being. They may or may not exist, and they only become possible with the intermediary function of some other agent.[25] In these and most other of his mobile films, Kiarostami dwells on the passing and imperceptible moments of the *Mumkin al-Wujud* where things may or may not be, and they only are for an ephemeral and passing

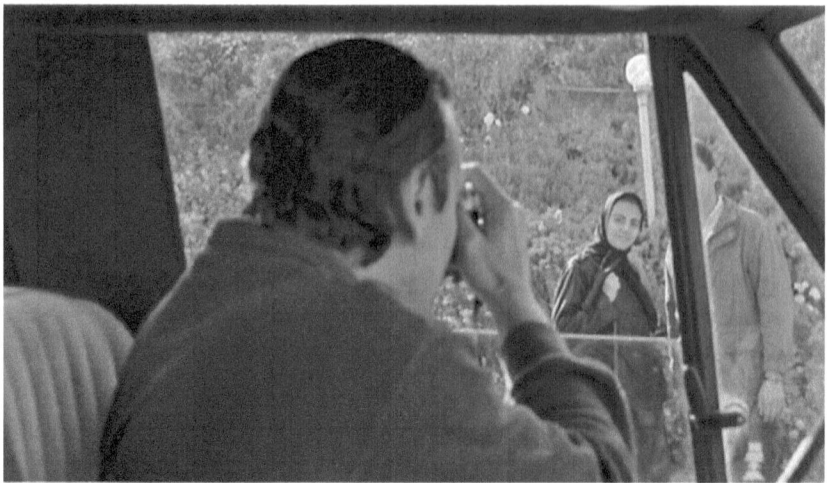

Figure 13. Homayoun Ershadi in Abbas Kiarostami, *Taste of Cherry* (1997). Courtesy of Abbas Kiarostami Foundation.

moment—and he makes an entire ontology of those passing moments. His aesthetics therefore is also his ontology.

Cars, winding roads, passing scenery, drivers, passengers, the passerby, and a mobile vision of reality have always been definitive to Kiarostami's cinema. In these three films they become ever more pronounced. At one and the same time both private and yet public, the space inside and around the moving car has always given Kiarostami a privileged position to see others while others do not see him—which is also the way we might understand his habitual dark glasses: He can see us but we cannot see "the instruments" of his seeing us. In his cinema, he shares that privileged position with his audience. Cinematic voyeurism here reaches a new height in Kiarostami's cinema. This proclivity toward roads and cars assumes an almost independent character in his photography of roads and rains. This aspect of his cinema places it in the larger frame of travel narratives, of participant observers, that extend all the way from classical cases of Ibn Battuta and Nasser Khosrow down to a vast constellation of world travelers in the eighteenth and nineteenth centuries. In a detailed book I wrote a few years ago on these travelogues, I have argued against the prevalent view that these travelers were going to Europe and have demonstrated, chapter and verse, they were in fact going around the world, that the writing they were producing in the process was a prose of discovering new worlds that from factual and actual travels eventually made it to the earliest works of fiction where travel narratives become the defining moments of these works of fiction.[26] As perhaps best evident in Zeyn al-Abedin Maragheh'i's *Safar-nameh Ibrahim Beik*, one of the earliest works of fiction delivered as a travel narrative, traveling became the modus operandi of the emerging vision of the changing world. In Kiarostami's cinema this proclivity for road travels assumes new aesthetic and epistemic significance, where reality itself becomes mobile, itinerant, transitory, and as a result the subject they implicate becomes equally nomadic—unknowing to itself, facing a renewed knowable world (entirely independent of Kant, Hegel, Levinas, and any other connoisseur of exotic dancing).

THE INTERSTITIAL SPACE AND POSTHUMAN AGENCY

Where is the moral and imaginative domain of this unknowing mobile subject as enabled and empowered in Kiarostami's artworld? If the Eurocentric or nativist public spheres that have received and celebrated or dismissed Kiarostami's cinema have both failed him, in one way or another, then where and how would be the space where he would now best be placed for a renewed reading? As I have argued in the past, it is the virtual interstitial space of art where that artworld and with it the postcolonial subjectivity it entails are both placed and posited.[27] In this case, I might be more specific to argue that the space where we actually watch Kiarostami's movies and look at his artwork is no longer Cannes, Tehran, Paris, New York, or Kalamazoo. It is actually the cyberspace, where it crafts its own modus operandi of subjectivity. I have been writing this book on Kiarostami while revisiting his films, studying his photography and painting and video installations and theatrical productions all in one space—this very MacBook Air laptop. Right here on this laptop I have downloaded and stored countless pdf copies of books and articles and photographs on Kiarostami. I access the Criterion collection of his films right here on this laptop, while having breakfast at the local Pret joint on the Columbia campus where I mostly do my work. Very rarely have I had to walk to Butler Library on our campus or send my research assistant to pick up a physical book on Kiarostami. Even when I physically travel across borders, I still think through and in this laptop. That is where all reality is located, that digitized space is Cannes, where I have been in person multiple times, Tehran where I went to college, or Paris, London, and the rest of Europe where I have traveled extensively, and in fact even New York, where I have lived with my family and taught at Columbia for decades. With all its irreality, the cyberspace has become the real space of aesthetic imagination. If the study of old European or non-European masters (what terribly false divisions we have inherited and must dismantle!) is not to degenerate into antiquarian exercises in academic futility, film-philosophy is perhaps one provocative space where that philosophy can become globally relevant. But that will not happen unless and until those who exercise and practice it are rescued from their embarrassing provincialism.

The most cogent case to be made against the Eurocentric gestation of anthropocentrism and post-anthropocentrism, which has now found a serious proponent in the unfolding work of Rosi Braidotti, is best at home in this cyberspace where there is no East for the West to colonize, Orientalize, alienate, humiliate, rob, abuse, and denigrate anymore. What Braidotti does not seem to recognize is the fact that the anthropocentrism at the heart of the European project she rightly wishes to dismantle was and has remained a fictional, blue-eyed and blonde Anthropos. As best evident in Kant, Hegel, and Levinas, and the entirety of the philosophical project over which they preside, that Anthropos and that human were and remain only Europeans. European anthropocentrism and humanism are both Eurocentrism in false universal disguises. Braidotti does not see this, with all the genuine nods she makes to postcoloniality. In her work, Braidotti has revived an interest in Spinoza's monism and the totality of reality working toward a critical posthumanism that speaks to our post-Western postcolonial world. On the premise of that posthumanism, she has outlined a liberating mode of critical subjectivity that now speaks to the world (of art) at large.[28] Interstitial spaces of the cyberspace, however, implicate the domain of mass surveillance that in turn leads to the field of digitized humanity and beyond that the evident presence of the digitized human. Recall when Kiarostami was denied entry into the US because his

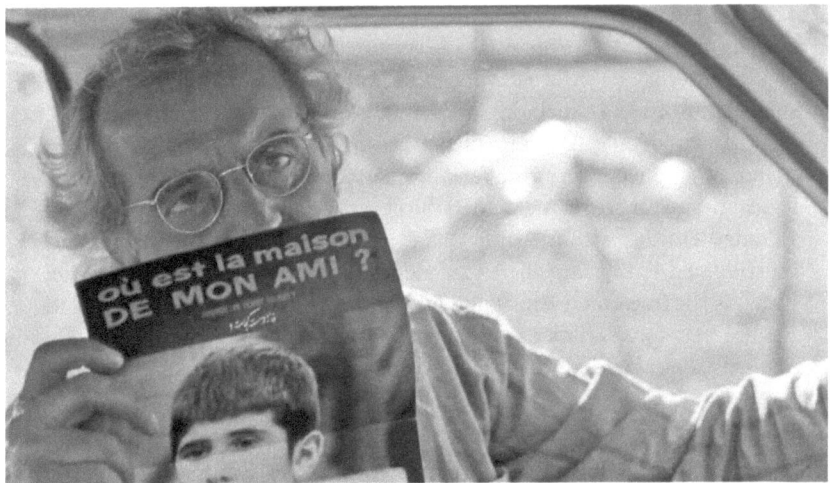

Figure 14. Farhad Kheradmand and Pouya Payvar in Abbas Kiarostami, *And Life Goes On* (1992). Courtesy of Abbas Kiarostami Foundation.

name is Abbas and he comes from Iran. From there, the rising critical discourse on posthumanism cannot but lead to the moral and philosophical prospects of post-anthropocentrism. The digital "second life" fully exposes the vulnerabilities of the posthuman body, as the ground under our sense of self is shifting.[29] As the field of humanism shifts toward the posthuman and the post-anthropocentric reading of reality, the context in which we are now watching the itinerant subject of Kiarostami's cinema, in all but especially in his Koker trilogy, and later in his signature films like *The Wind Will Carry Us*, *Ten*, and *Taste of Cherry*, becomes a potent interlocutor of any film-philosophy we might fancy. We therefore need to do precisely the opposite of what "Film-Philosophy" is doing now: Not to assimilate Kiarostami's legacy into what Eurocentric Film-Philosophy does but allow Kiarostami radically to recast a more humble and democratic claim on a more fully democratic and leveled playing field for film-philosophy.

The digital space on which we watch Kiarostami today and enter his artworld implicates an interstitial posthumanist agency that is the foregrounding of the post-anthropocentrism that for Rosi Braidotti begins with Spinoza as her philosophical point of departure. This is how she formulates it:

218   CHAPTER FIVE

Monism refers to Spinoza's central concept that matter, the world, and humans themselves are not dualistic entities structured according to principles of internal or external opposition, but rather materially embedded subjects-in-process circulating within webs of relations. The obvious target of criticism here is Descartes's famous mind-body distinction, but for Spinoza the concept goes even further: matter is one and driven by the ontological desire for self-expression. Subjects are constituted as bound or individuated entities within a differential process ontology. This makes each individuated entity into the expression of a common innermost essence, which is the freedom to affect and be affected by others (conatus). All entities are therefore variations on a common theme and they express the fundamental desire to endure in their existence and to go on becoming.[30]

This is all fine—if we were to remain limited to Rosi Braidotti's European philosophical genealogy. But, if we may, long before Spinoza (1632–1677) and deeply rooted in the doctrine of *Wahdat al-Wujud*/Unity of Being, crucial aspects of Islamic ontology have paid serious attention to this doctrine, which finds its most eloquent expression in books 3 and 4 of Rumi's *Masnavi* (circa 1258–1273) where "monism" has an evolutionary dimension from the most inanimate stony stage to the vegetal, to animal, to human, and posthuman (for Rumi angelic) stages. For Rumi, this cosmic conception of Being that includes our humanity but is not limited to it has a metaphysical dimension fully environmental in its contemporary resonances. Through a philosophical and gnostic genealogy much older and more rooted, Rumi in Book 4 of his *Masnavi* details this "posthumanism" (avant la lettre) as follows:

Amadeh Avval beh Iqlim-e Jamad . . .

Having first come to being in the domain of stony inanimity,
From the inanimate to the vegetal they went—
For years they lived in the vegetal,
And yet out of stubbornness could not remember the stony state—
And when from the vegetal to the animal they went,
They could not remember the vegetal,
Except for this attraction they have towards it,
Especially during the Spring and the season of fresh vegetation—
Just like the attraction of infants towards their mothers,
They don't know the secret of their desires in their lips—
Just like the attraction of a new novice,

CRITIQUE OF POSTCOLONIAL AESTHETIC JUDGMENT   219

Drawn towards their aging master. . . .
And from the animal towards humanity
Was pulling them that Creator whom you know—
Thus from one realm they went to another,
Until they became so rational, conscious, and intelligent—
They cannot now remember the previous stages of their reasoning, though
Even from this reasoning they will also change and evolve—
Until they will be liberated from this insatiable reasoning,
They will witness one hundred thousand strange reasonings—
Although they fall asleep and forgot their past,
They will not be left alone in their forgetfulness—
They will wake them up from their slumber,
So that they would laugh at their condition.[31]

On this case, Rumi has formulated the idea in terms of the third person plural. But on an earlier occasion, in Book 3, he puts the same idea in first-person pronoun:

Az Jamadi mordam o nami shodam . . .

I died to my stony inanimity and became vegetal,
Then I died to my vegetal and became animal—
I died to my animality and became human,
So why should I fear when did I become less by dying?
Next move and I shall die to my humanity,
So I can find wings and countenance among the angels—
Even from the angelic condition I must move forward,
For "Everything Perishes Except His Face."
On the next move I shall die to my angelic being
To become that which cannot even be fathomed—
Then I become nothing just like Organon—
Did he not tell me that "We are all of God and to Him shall we all return?"[32]

With Rumi the condition of the posthuman and post-androcentricity (entirely outside the European disguise) is collective, from the get-go, with an organic conception of human as both pre-and posthuman. It has always been there but unbeknownst to us. So, when today we think we are human or posthuman, we are already also the inanimate objects and we are the plants and the vegetations—for which reason we are drawn to them, especially when during the spring they renew themselves. We are the rivers, we are the mountains, we are the valleys, we are the tress, the shrubs, the woods, and we are all the animals we abuse and slaughter, and we are the posthuman we are about to become. This is a far superior kind of "monism" delivered in sublime poetic precision than what Braidotti has detected in Spinoza. We need not choose between Spinoza and Rumi. We can have them both (as I do and Braidotti does not)—with the added element that with Rumi we are liberated from the false universality of Eurocentrism as anthropocentrism. In Rumi's "monism" the whole world is included. With Spinoza's, Kant, Hegel, and Levinas have assured me I am denied entrance. It is a racist, exclusive club for its white members only.

With Rumi we can rest our case where a postcolonial aesthetic judgment must both face the detailed project of European philosophical legacy of denying human agency to non-Europeans to the point where Rumi's posthuman agency had been waiting for a very long time before Kiarostami picked up his digital camera and tried to see through a digitized humanity yet to be dreamed in Eurocentric Film-Philosophy.

Let us now invite all film critics and film-philosophers East and West, North and South, and gather around this glorious shot of Kiarostami's *24 Frames*, made possible in the interstitial space of the cyberspace, from which I just selected this shot. First and foremost, it makes us all identically itinerant un/knowing subjects of Kiarostami's work regardless of our place in the physical worlds. It has his signature finesse and it invites everyone passing by to stop and take a look. As we look at it and observe, it instantly fables the world by virtue of a compelling frame that brings two birds, an imposing tree, and a foreboding sky into a confident framing. You need not know either Avicenna or Suhrawardi or even Attar to feel its allegorical power. But if you did, so much the better. But if you know those allegories, please do not turn this picture into an anthropological object of curiosity. Those allusions empower this picture. This picture is not reducible to those allegories. As such, the shot also denies Eurocentrism to conceal itself as anthropocentrism, for it both informs and empowers a kind of post-anthropocentrism that is not Eurocentric. As our knowing subject becomes unknowing, and the world this picture reveals knowable, it also denies all identity politics and/or epistemic nativism. It is just a picture by a master photographer, filmmaker, poet, and painter. If we were to dare to know, sapere aude, that gesture relies on no philosophical legacy that has chapter and verse and specifically denied me, or someone else from Egypt, Pakistan, Congo, China, or Tajikistan, entry into this space. Its particularity becomes universal first and foremost by the embedded aesthetics it entails and second by the open-ended acts of successive signification it enables. It is beautiful and sublime and it makes anyone who comes near it beautiful and sublime. The late Jean-Luc Nancy could have looked at it, and so could Mathew Abbott, Mas'ud Farasati, or the late Roger Ebert. It harbors no philosophical and aesthetic prejudice as to who is capable and who is incapable of the sublime and the beautiful. It is at the forefront of a whole new platform of aesthetic judgment we might still call postcolonial simply because it has dismantled the coloniality of the condition that has privileged one criticism or another and disenfranchised the rest. Just look at it: It is the aesthete invitation to a future film-philosophy.

6 Surfacing of a Semblance of Subjectivity

I don't like storytelling in cinema. I don't like exciting the audience. I don't like preaching to the audience. I don't like belittling and insulting the audience. I don't like giving the audience a sense of guilt. . . . I think a good movie is a movie that endures and lasts, and in fact starts being made after you have left the theater. There are films that appear to be boring, but they are not bad films, and then there are films that affix you to your chair and you can't move, and forget about everything else. This is how much they impact you, and yet when you come out of the theater you realize it has been cheating you—it has in fact taken you hostage. Some filmmakers take their audience hostage. I don't like films in which their directors take their audience hostage and excite them. I in fact prefer films that sometimes make their audiences fall asleep, these are at least kind films. They at least give you time to take a nap. But they don't bother you when you leave the theater. I have seen films where I fell asleep in the theater and then later that night they kept me awake, and then the following day I woke up thinking about them, and then I have lived with them for weeks, these kinds of films I like better.[1]

Abbas Kiarostami, in an undated interview

Have you seen Kiarostami's *Five Dedicated to Ozu* (2003)? You should. It is something between a video installation suitable for a museum gallery and a documentary. But it is neither, and yet it is both, and then again it is a seventy-four-minute film, divided into five segments. It consists of five long takes on a nondescript location, presumably shot in Northern Iran near the Caspian Sea. What do we see? A piece of driftwood on the seashore, people walking on the same seashore, shapes on a winter beach, a pack of dogs, the waddling of loud ducks, a pond at night. People who have watched it do not know quite what to make of it. Here is one good example of how film critics have seen it:

> So what is the point of all this? Are we supposed to read some sort of meaning into these images, or just take them at face value and enjoy them? Kiarostami doesn't claim any sort of hidden agenda or subtext but each viewer will undoubtedly take something different from the film. I found it to be an intriguing piece of work. It's a calming experience which will only work if you completely surrender yourself to it, and there is also the genuine pleasure in seeing a filmmaker of Kiarostami's standing throwing all the conventions of cinema to the wind and trying to truly take the art form into new areas. Of course, the idea of watching a 74-minute film in which almost nothing happens would be anathema to many cinemagoers, but the curious viewer, approaching the film with patience and imagination, will find much here to treasure.[2]

Others have seen a close link between what Kiarostami does here and the legacy of Ozu: "The beauty of *Five Dedicated to Ozu* ultimately lies less in any grand philosophical or personal statements, and more in the way Kiarostami uses daringly distended long takes to attune us to a different kind of drama—the drama of everyday life, the kind of drama that only the cinema could make truly dramatic. In that sense, the film may not conform to Ozu in style, but it certainly aligns with Ozu in spirit."[3] Most critics are drawn to the film because of its radical take on long takes.

My take on *Five Dedicated to Ozu* is a bit more literal, all dwelling on the surface of what we see—for it has obviously pointed our way back to Ozu. We should start from there. When I saw Kiarostami's *Five Dedicated to Ozu*, I missed Ozu. So, I did what I usually do: I gave myself a one-person festival of Ozu on my iPad. When you sit close to your iPad, its screen is as big as that huge screen on Piazza Grande in Locarno. How would Ozu look if we were to watch him with Kiarostami's eyes? Yes, we can see *Five Dedicated to Ozu* as video installations in a museum gallery, or else stretch the idea of film and see it as a documentary. But we can also see it as a signature Kiarostami meditation on the digital camera and what it can do, altering our perception of reality around us—with patience, perseverance, a bit of irony, perhaps. Either way, this is a take on Ozu and we should take it as such. What would happen if we placed Ozu and Kiarostami next to each other? Two master practitioners of their craft who have shown us, each in his own way, there is more on the surface, not depth, of reality than meets the eye.

THE SEMBLANT SUBJECT AND THE SEMBLANCE OF SUBJECTIVITY

But why would we want to do so? What will we gain, what would be the point and purpose of spending some time looking at Ozu and Kiarostami together? I wish to draw your attention to similarities, semblances, and the way an aesthetics of the surface, rather than the illusion of the depth, would look like. My reasons to do so become clearer as this chapter unfolds apace. In this penultimate chapter, I plan to argue how the alienation effect of the interface between art and truth in the Europeanized world Kiarostami's cinema has entered paves the way for the formation of a semblant subject and the semblance of subjectivity in the experience of encountering his and similar kinds of cinemas. My intention is to break the violent binary between Asian (African, Latin American, etc.) art and European criticism in general and philosophical criticism in particular. My contention is that we need to craft a horizontal space that brings Ozu, Kiarostami, Satyajit Ray, Ousmane Sembène, and Alejandro González-Iñárritu, among countless others, together. This is not against Eurocentrism. This is to overcome the philosophical gaze of Europe as Europe over and above the world—a posture that is in and of itself self-alienating. Films like *ABC Africa* (2001), *Shirin* (2008), *Certified Copy* (2010), and *Like Someone in Love* (2012), filmed in Africa, Iran, Italy, and Japan, respectively, would give us ample space for this reflection—for here these films implicate a *semblant subject* far more congenital to the

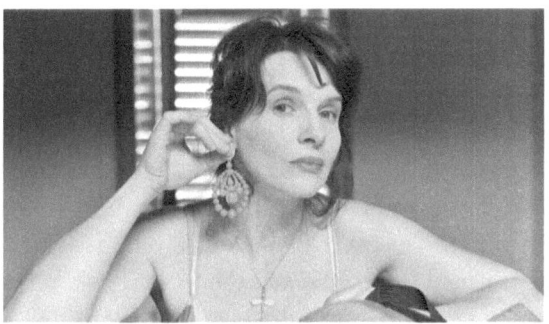

Figure 15. Juliette Binoche in Abbas Kiarostami's *Certified Copy* (2010). Courtesy of Abbas Kiarostami Foundation.

postcolonial aesthetic judgment I have hoped to develop in this book. In this context, my attention to Kiarostami's *Five Dedicated to Ozu* (2003) is by way of reading him in conjunction with a master Japanese filmmaker he deeply admired, and who had a lasting influence on his own cinema. When we place Kiarostami and Ozu next to each other, I contend, their close aesthetic affinity and subjective semblance comes to sharper contrast with the actively Europeanized reading of both their cinemas. I wish to dismantle the privileged position of that European gaze philosophically, not ideologically, though in tandem with a philosophical pedigree outside the archives of contemporary European philosophers, the French philosophers who are reading Kiarostami, in particular. The point of this argument is not directed toward a critique of the European reception of Kiarostami's cinema (which is what it is) but toward the articulation of the semblance of subjectivity (and thus the formation of a semblant subject) that his Asian habitat and European reception contrapuntally generate and sustain in the enduring legacy of his cinema.

I am first and foremost drawn to the idea of *semblance* through the Persian theatrical practice of Shabih-khani, or "Persian Passion Play" as it has been falsely equated to match Ta'ziyeh ritual performances—and about which Kiarostami had one of his most provocative theatrical stagings in Rome in July 2003. Most scholars of the subject believe the theatrical legacy today called Ta'ziyeh or Shabih-khani, and translated as "Persian Passion Play," is rooted in the ancient, pre-Islamic practice of

Sug-e Seyavash/Mourning for Seyavash—the commemoration of the martyrdom of a Shahnameh hero.[4] The term *Ta'ziyeh* is more common in both Persian and English. but the term *Shabih-khani* is a more accurate and technical term.[5] The key issue here is that as Ta'ziyeh moves toward Shabih-khani, a specific case of the ritual legacy standing for the larger event, the political uses and abuses of the former yields to the social effervescence of the genre. If we were to place Ta'ziyeh in the larger context of Shahnameh performances, or *Naqqali*, then its pre-Islamic roots in Sug-e Seyavash are connected to the post-Islamist transition of Ta'ziyeh to Shabih-Khani where a larger frame of reference is applicable to the genre. This dramaturgical transition is crucial if we are to take the key concept of Shabih to its fuller theoretical implications.

Once we do so, we see how Shabih forms a transition from *resemblance* to *semblance*, and from *simulation* to *mimesis*, when ordinary people (as opposed to professional actors) act as if the events of Karbala early in Islamic history were happening right now, and thereby mere resemblance gives the play a semblance of truth and reality. The term *Shabih-khani* is therefore more accurate than *Ta'ziyeh*, for many of the theatrical performances had very little to no relevance to the events of Karbala, and were fun and performed for the delight of the audiences. This fusion of tragedy and comedy remained true to Shabih-khani legacy. Between tragedy and comedy, and from resemblance to semblance, we can locate Kiarostami's cinema as a mode of performance where the apparition of truth gives it the evident semblance of truth. That semblance of truth in turn posits a semblance of subjectivity for its audiences—which is the philosophical predicate of my semblant (or unknowing) subject—a subject that has overcome the condition of their gendered coloniality not just against but through that coloniality.

Here we need to keep in mind that *Shabih* is also a cognate of *Tashbih*, which means "simile." A few other words are also crucial here; one is *Ta'biyeh*, which means "staging" or even "mise en scène"—which has also been used as a designation for the ritual performance.[6] We know, for example, of mobile Shabih-khani when a performance moves through the main streets and squares of a city with multiple actors playing the same role.[7] The mobility of Shabih-khani by nonprofessional actors is concomitant with its material mimesis when life and art are interwoven and an act of representation is not just representation—a feature that becomes the defining moment of Kiarostami's cinema.

What therefore I detect and purpose in the idea of Shabih is a Persianate theory of *Mimesis* entirely independent of the Aristotelian origins. From this premise we might then turn to the manner in which in Adorno's aesthetic theory he gives this idea of *semblance subjectivity* a more philosophical momentum. In a comprehensive collection of essays by some leading Adorno scholars, *The Semblance of Subjectivity: Essays in Adorno's Aesthetic Theory*, Tom Huhn and Lambert Zuidervaart have made a concerted effort to bring the two ideas of *semblance* and *subjectivity* in Adorno's *Aesthetic Theory* (written between 1956 and 1969, published posthumously in 1970) together. As the editors of the volume put it succinctly, "whereas the concept of semblance or illusion (Schein) points to Adorno's links with Marx, Nietzsche, and Freud, the so-called masters of suspicion, the concept of subjectivity (das Subjekt) recalls his struggle with a philosophy of consciousness stemming from Kant, Hegel, and Lukács." It is in this context that "arts, despite their being suspect of illusion, since Plato's Republic, turn out in Adorno's account of modernism to have an unusually sophisticated capacity to critique illusion, including their own."[8]

To be sure, Adorno's preoccupation was with the presumed epicenter of capitalist modernity in Europe and could never be bothered with its far more traumatized colonial edges. But nevertheless, we have much to learn from Adorno's project when it comes to this semblance of subjectivity because "Adorno's project amounts to a critique *of* the semblance of subjectivity," the editors tell us. "In each instance, the 'of' must be read as both subjective and objective. The critique takes aim at semblance, but it must occur within and by way of semblance. Subjectivity is a semblance, but one such that no semblance (and hence no critique) could occur in the absence of subjectivity."[9] This negative dialectic signature of Adorno wants to work through, not despite, the illusion of the knowing subject. What is paramount here is Adorno's position that "modern art is also a semblance of subjectivity, in both senses of that phrase: the production and reception of modern art requires the very subjectivity to whose pretensions and failures it attests."[10] The modernity of that art is a double take on the colonial sites of that modernity. If we therefore keep in mind that Adorno also believed "arts that resist the culture industry are . . . 'the social antithesis of society,'"[11] then the way colonial modernity works on the colonial site becomes the extension of the logic of European modernity—which proposition enables us to see a postcolonial semblant subject as the modus operandi of the unknowing subject.

Let us now take a look at Kiarostami's own version of Ta'ziyeh as he staged one in Rome in July 2003. Here is an eyewitness account of the performance:

> His open-air, hexagonal wooden theatre has a central stage surrounded by shallow tiers of seats. Above are six screens, on which we see the faces of Iranian spectators watching a previous performance of the same version of the Ta'ziyeh. The effect is a curious one: we watch the play, and a version of ourselves. This, says Kiarostami, is the idea: Ta'ziyeh is strictly linked to its audience—the event is actually created by the rapport between actors and spectators.[12]

This is Shabih-khani par excellence, when the Ta'ziyeh performance is doubly removed from its place of performance. We know from Persian sources that prior to this production in Europe, Kiarostami traveled to the surrounding villages of Isfahan with his colleagues Jafar Panahi and Niki Karimi and took shots of people watching Ta'ziyeh. By looking at those who are looking at Ta'ziyeh in Iran, and then in Rome looking at those who were looking at those who were looking at Ta'ziyeh in Iran, Kiarostami performs his signature dwelling on the mystic surface of things, abandoning all the illusions, false assurances, and goose chases after depth and hidden meanings. From that counter-metaphysics, he has staged a metaphysics of its own. By now, resemblance has become semblance, and the performance mimetic within the context of Shabih-khani.

Let us now link this production of Ta'ziyeh to another directorial adventure of Kiarostami—this one with European opera. He was invited to stage Mozart's *Cosi fan Tutte* in Aix-en-Provence in 2008, and the following year as part of the English National Opera's (ENO) summer season. On this latter occasion, again the British authorities denied him a visa to travel to London, for which reason he had to direct it in absentia. Caught between the censorial policies of the Islamic Republic and the banality of the European racist gaze on non-European artists, the uncanny prospect of "Kiarostami as potential terrorist" is in and of itself a crucial part of the exercise of reading and watching him as a postcolonial filmmaker. In this case, the prospect of "Kiarostami as potential terrorist " metamorphoses into Kiarostami as nonexistent director or director in absentia. This is how it works:

> Having encountered frustrating treatment at the hands of the British embassy in Iran while attempting to arrange a visa, the director took the decision not to travel to London. Instead, the reins were passed to the assistant director Elaine Tyler-Hall, and Kiarostami remained director in absentia, guiding the cast through e-mails and telephone calls. His involvement marks the film world's latest foray into the world of opera, but the idea of film directors taking on the genre of opera is nothing new.[13]

None of this of course means denial of European admiration for his work. "I've admired his work for a long time," the artistic director of ENO John Berry said on this occasion: "He has always said that with films, he will work with whatever constraints he has to, and he is aware of the limitations of opera."[14] But it means a cognitive dissonance, if not an altogether psychotic schizophrenia, between the European art scene and European politicians and policymakers.[15]

The two directorial ventures of Kiarostami into Shabih-Khani and opera are related in one key aspect: Kiarostami's own amateurish foray into two powerful theatrical traditions, one Iranian and the other European. That amateurish dilettantism (in the positive sense of the term, as an admirer of a fine art, literature, etc.) is precisely the point here. He suddenly finds himself in a strange place, where things look, but are not, familiar. He is as foreign on the set of Ta'ziyeh as he would be on the set of a Mozart opera. In the Iranian case, to be sure, all actors and directors are in fact not professional and come from all walks of life, while on the European scene the tradition has been highly professionalized, but so is inviting artists from other fields of art also quite common. I recall watching Franco Zeffirelli's production of Puccini's *Turandot* at the Metropolitan Opera in New York. But Zeffirelli of course has had a long history of involvement with opera. Be that as it may, Kiarostami's take on these two directorial occasions has placed him in a place out of his element, and it is precisely that state of being out of his element that gives him an uncanny access to the set. Add to this the fact that British and American authorities denying him a visa casts him as a "potential terrorist" that exacts a semblance of identity and authorship from the factual to figurative presence of Kiarostami as a filmmaker, so that as the European and American art scene loves and admires and celebrates him, the same nations first have to make sure he does not go to their countries to blow up buildings or commit a suicidal massacre. Right then and there, Kiarostami himself has become a semblant subject, performing, willy-nilly, a semblance of subjectivity, as he brings an ancient Iranian form of performing art to Europe or directs a venerable operatic piece in absentia.

OZU'S CAMERA IN KIAROSTAMI'S HANDS

Let us now go back to Kiarostami and Ozu and consider their respective visions as the content and the context of their worldly cinemas, the way that in retrospect they became the simulacrum of each other and posited a semblance of subjectivity for each other, a Shabih-khani in each other's respective stages. With and through Ozu, we see Kiarostami differently. With and through Kiarostami, we can go back to Ozu and see him differently. There is therefore more to *Five Dedicated to Ozu* than meets the eye. It is a historical allusion, not in temporal but in cinematic terms. How? Two master filmmakers have happened at the two ends of Asia like bookends, and at two ends of a century of cinema, Ozu at its Eastern beginning and Kiarostami at its Western end. These two masters, a Japanese and an Iranian, have become definitive to the global art of cinema. Cinema has had many masters; Ozu and Kiarostami are only two among many others. But these two masters have become interrelated in their cinematic forms, and by virtue of that structural link, they have framed for us a singularly significant vision of the world. As it happens, these two masters are both from Asia. This designation, "Asian filmmakers," would unduly nativize, domesticate, marginalize, and above all de-world these two filmmakers. To de-alienate and re-world Ozu and Kiarostami, we need to restore to them their towering presence in a renewed reading of "World cinema"—and in doing so we first need to recast the idea of "World Cinema," or more aptly what I propose to call "worldly cinema."

What is today called "World Cinema" is the phantasmagoria of a false consciousness—and yet the very source of overcoming it—as Adorno has proposed the idea of "semblance." But how exactly so? The formal fluidity of cinematic consciousness from around the world posits alternative worlds—worlds not imagined in Europe or Hollywood—three worlds to be exact: the world of the filmmakers that have created them, the world of the works of art they have created, and the world in which we receive them. These three interrelated worlds simultaneously posit, stage, and also overcome the idea of "World Cinema." What is today called "World Cinema" is a paradoxical site of colonial modernity—a modernity that self-consciously asserts itself on the Eurocentric topography of a world dominated by the myth of "the West." The idea of "World Cinema" emerged as a euphemism for "local cinema." The real world cinema was what Hollywood had hegemonically imposed on the world—and to disguise that conquest, it created the illusion of "World Cinema" to fool and disorient what it had robbed of its worldliness and forcefully localized, exoticized, alienated from itself. But at the same time, what is now falsely dubbed "World Cinema," once restored to its robust worldliness, carries within it the power of dismantling the hegemony of Hollywood by delivering its own worldliness.

How, then, are Ozu and Kiarostami worldly—in that sense? Why Ozu and Kiarostami in particular? Ozu gave Kiarostami the camera with which he shoots—not literally but figuratively. Without Ozu, we would not be able to read Kiarostami as we do today. Ozu was born and raised in Japan, and his cinematic career extended from the late 1920s through the 1950s. Kiarostami was born and raised in Iran, and his career extended from the 1970s to the late 2010s. Ozu had a towering presence over all subsequent filmmakers. There were three figures—Ozu, Mizuguchi, and Kurosawa—who have been dubbed the Bach, Mozart, and Beethoven of Japanese cinema. The single most important factor that connects Ozu and Kiarostami is their cinematic formalism—the specific forms of their cinemas. It is the primacy of their aesthetic formalism over their cinema that puts Ozu and Kiarostami like two bookends on two complimentary sides of a cinematic vision singularly unique to them. They in effect anticipate and complement each other—one literally and both figuratively. Ozu anticipates Kiarostami like no other filmmaker, and Kiarostami complements

Ozu like no other filmmaker. I am not here thinking of the influence of Ozu on Kiarostami at all—though that is quite obvious. Ozu has had an influence on many filmmakers, among them Kiarostami. But Kiarostami's cinema soon took over in his own unique direction, and it is that direction that I see and suppose to come back and correspond to Ozu's cinema in fruitful ways. What exactly is that way? Ozu and Kiarostami neither see nor show reality as it is. They are master craftsmen of putting a twist on reality. They see through and show a vision of the invisible in the visible. Showing the deceptively obvious but hidden, staging the mystic allure of the surface, they have become the mystic visionaries of the surface. For Ozu it is the metaphysics and aesthetics of presence; and for Kiarostami it is the metaphysics and aesthetics of motion. Ozu reveals the visions of the invisible in presence; Kiarostami does so with motion. Ozu's camera is earthly and grounded; Kiarostami's is introverted and intuitive. It is as if they were both busy telepathically making just one film: Ozu did the interior shots, Kiarostami the exterior shots. For Ozu, the interior shots have dexterity; for Kiarostami, the exterior shots are incandescent. For Ozu, reality is excavated. For Kiarostami, it is navigated. They both see through the surface and keep their respective gazes fixed on the surface—one interior and the other exterior. They have seen through the closed-circuited totality of the visible to get to the infinity of the invisible evident in the visible. As such, they are both prophetic visionaries of the invisible hidden in the plain sight of the visible.

Let us now ask a more specific question: What is it about Ozu's filmic prosody that is so unique to his cinema and so uniquely compelling? He combines two signature elements: his penchant for interior shots connected to each other with still exterior shots, and his legendary low-angle camera. His interior shots are deceptively simple and serene and decidedly set to contrast with the rumbunctious and crowded Hollywood shots. The skyline minimalism of Ozu echoes the simplicity of those interior shots. These shots are deceptive because they hide the real tensions that inform them. Ozu's camera was set less than three feet above the floor, decidedly lower than a person sitting on a tatami. There is no instrumental or functional point to this angle, and it is an epistemic violence to try to impose any such functionality on the angle: that it was the POV of a child or any other such purpose. This is his signature angle that makes his cinema conscious of its camera, and thus differentiates it from others that are always staged above the eye level of the audience. Ozu is not being theoretical or rhetorical in these shots. Quite to the contrary. He is being cinematic. By making his audience openly conscious of the bizarre location of the camera, and by not moving, the camera is in fact self-confident and self-conscious. The more his set lighting becomes incandescent and sedate, the more consciously cinematic becomes the camera. His timing is filmic, not natural timing. His camera is triangulated with two or more characters sitting next to each other, and not facing and confronting each other. This triangulation again gives the key role to his camera. His consistent violation of the 180-degree rule turns it inside out as it crosses the axis of the gaze—thus staging his camera, which is always already omniscient, omnipresent, and above all omnipotent. While the Hollywood camera informed by the Aristotelian mimesis moves for the complete disappearance of the camera and thus the complete identification with the characters, in effect the camera acting like the Fourth Wall, Ozu's camera has the full functioning of the Brechtian V-effect, of making sure we are watching a staged reality—opening that Fourth Wall to the real world, from which side Kiarostami would a generation later enter the stage of global cinema. Ozu's camera is fully conscious of its instrumentality and turns that instrumentality into the palette of its aesthetic formalism, which in turn formalizes Ozu's aesthetics. That palette and that aesthetics Ozu hands over to Kiarostami from one end of Asia to the other, from the early part of the twentieth century to the later.

 In the mirror of Ozu's cinema, Kiarostami thus becomes a semblant subject, predicated on the semblant reality Ozu had pictured and mapped out long before Kiarostami imagined himself behind a camera. Kiarostami's cinema is similar (*shabih*) but not identical with Ozu's. Kiarostami's cinema stages a *shabih-nama'i* (showing similarities)—not a *shabih-khani* (reciting similarities)—in conversation with Ozu's cinema. In *Five Dedicated to Ozu*, Kiarostami has left a solid document, a last will and testament, as it were, that his cinema was made possible by the camera Ozu had envisioned, enabled, empowered, and then sent as a gift to Kiarostami, from one end of Asia to another, turning that space into the epicenter of a new worldly cinema. Keep in mind: Ozu's formalism had reached its height by the time he made *An Autumn Afternoon* (1962), just a year before his passing, and it had reached its aesthetic sublimity by the time of *Tokyo Story* (1953), on which formalism he had been at work at least since *I was Born, But* ... (1932). By the time Kiarostami made *Five Dedicated to Ozu* (2003), it had taken him about half a century to acknowledge and register the aesthetic genealogy of his cinema.

DARKNESS, REVERSE ANGLE, COUNTERFEIT, AND MAKE-BELIEVE

Let us now put four of Kiarostami's mature masterpieces together and see what we see: *ABC Africa* (2001), *Shirin* (2008), *Certified Copy* (2010), and *Like Someone in Love* (2012). This is Kiarostami at his final best, the summation of all he did and all he meant. The final filmic fruition of a master at the peak of his creativity. He died, at the age of 76, about four years after *Like Someone in Love* premiered at Cannes, because of what his family and many of his friends believe was medical malpractice—or at least concealing from him and his family the nature and extent of his illness.[16] He was not ready to think his work was done. By all accounts he was still full of ideas and projects. He could have easily directed, painted, photographed, and written and published his poetry for another decade. But that was not meant to be, and we have what we have. These four films map the last decade of his life.

The entire film of *ABC Africa* (2001) hinges on a defining sequence of the film which is shot entirely in darkness where we can scarcely see anything. What sort of a film is that? At least since *Close-Up* (1990), Kiarostami has worked with the signature tactic of suspending a key factor in the making of a cinematic scene, which in that classical example comes toward the end when he deliberately cuts off the sound, denying his audience the chance of listening to the conversation between the real and the fake Makhmalbaf, pretending his equipment was faulty, making the two figures, as a result, almost indistinguishable. The result is uncanny. We wish we could eavesdrop on the conversation and yet we cannot, and yet we are compensated by the sheer impossibility of comprehending the joy of Sabzian spending a few private moments with Makhmalbaf. The result is spontaneous magic—when the two protagonists of the film, one real and the other fake, become identical, where fact and fantasy (or "factasy," as I have called it for decades now) form a tertiary space and enable a different kind of subjectivity. In *ABC Africa*, Kiarostami does the same, though this time with the visual. At the epicenter of *ABC Africa* halfway through the film is a prolonged, dark scene, where we hear things but can scarcely see anything. Think of John Cage's *4'33"* (1952), and now imagine staging it not just with the instruments playing absolutely nothing and remaining completely silent but doing so on a completely dark stage.

Spending a fortnight in Uganda at the request of the International Fund for Agricultural Development of the UN, for a project called Women's Effort to Save Orphans (UWESO), Kiarostami is given the impossible task of lending his intruding camera to a worthy cause without appearing condescending—as he did in another major film, *The Wind Will Carry Us* (1999), where his steadfast quest for his vision of the event trespasses into the abusive treatment of people who had welcomed him in their midst, especially in that terrible stable scene where the young woman milking the cow is framed and captured in an exceedingly violent sequence. Here, though, Kiarostami is in a gentler mood with orphaned children he faces and films. As all reviewers have noted, the dark sequence at the center of the film is the defining moment of the film, when the screen goes dark at midnight for the electricity has been turned off in Masaka, leaving Kiarostami and his crew and the rest of us in the dark, which is exactly where we should be from shame—though shame is not the central issue of the strategy here. The camera closes its eyes and thereby denies the rest of any vision of that surrounding misery. Just like in the very last sequence of *Through the Olive Trees* (1994), Kiarostami has taught his camera when to stay away from sanctified moments. In Uganda, he is there to film misery. Closing his camera's eyes, as it were, and with it ours, for a few minutes, is the best way of disciplining the rest of what he shows. He succeeds here where he had failed in *The Wind Will Carry Us* where that injudicious sequence in the stable mars the rest of the film. His judicious darkening of the scene here ennobles the rest of the film, and with it the fusion of revelation and concealment he brings together to sculpt and syncopate a far more balanced and precise perception of truth and the realities it reveals.

236   CHAPTER SIX

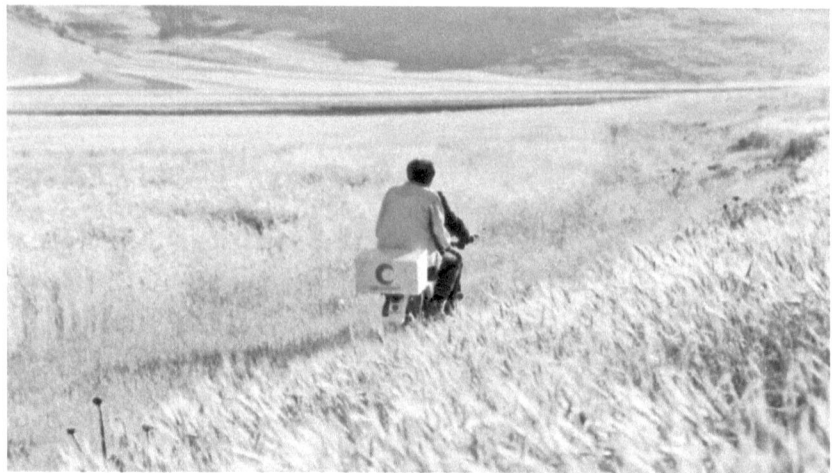

Figure 16. Abbas Kiarostami, *The Wind Will Carry Us* (1999). Courtesy of Abbas Kiarostami Foundation.

As for *Shirin* (2008), I have often found it quite useful to repeat the aesthetic rhetoric of the film when thinking about it—by watching those who have watched the film, meaning watching people who are watching a movie we never get to see. Let us "watch" Peter Bradshaw of *The Guardian*, an old Kiarostami enthusiast, watching *Shirin*! He is enthralled by the film, though a bit exacerbated too. He thinks *Shirin* is yet another "experimental" film, a word many European film critics regularly apply to Kiarostami's playing with "cinematic portraiture and fixed camera positions," while he finds the work "intriguing if somewhat exasperating." Bradshaw believes this film to be "an installation-type work that might work as well, or better, on a blank wall in an art gallery"—again a point that many of Kiarostami's film critics regularly share.[17] He then makes his own observations about how "our faces while watching a film in a cinema are a paradox. They are public and yet private. We are in the company of many others in the auditorium; this is partly, of course, what makes the experience so vivid. But once the film starts, we are utterly alone." Bradshaw's key insight is therefore clear: "Well, Kiarostami has created a stylized chamber piece in which the use of professional and well-known actors is arguably the point. They could have been cast in the film they are watching—though they are not, I think, supposed to be playing actors—and have instead been displaced out of the screen, and into the audience. This could be intended to create an eerie laboratory effect, a distilled, foregrounded emotion." His conclusion is, however, not very salutary: "Like much of his new work, Kiarostami's *Shirin* has been undertaken in something like a Godardian spirit of research: it is perhaps only for those prepared to approach it in a tolerant, indulgent spirit."[18] In short, as we read the distinguished *Guardian* film critic's review of *Shirin*, we are also "watching" his facial expressions, into which Kiarostami has tricked all his audiences. Years ago, I wrote an essay on contemporary Iranian art with the title "Quis custodiet ipsos custodes?/Who Will Watch the Watcher?"[19] This is also a case of that sort, where the spectators become the spectacle.

Now you can "watch" my face, as it were, as I watch Bradshaw watching *Shirin*. We can continue to read one review like this after another and they mostly concur this is an "experimental" film, better fit for a museum gallery, and that people need to exercise patience and perseverance to suffer through it for nearly two hours just staring at people's faces facing a movie they never get to see. I don't think it wise to suggest a master filmmaker at the peak of his career is still "experimenting" with his art, at a moment when he had perfected his techniques—nor do I think it would make much of a difference if we saw *Shirin* in a theater or in a gallery, unless we are sticking to a cliché and fetishized conception of "film," which Kiarostami spent a lifetime purposefully to dismantle. More than anything else, *Shirin* looks and feels like Kiarostami's take on Ta'ziyeh, where he invites his audience to watch other audiences watching something they are also watching. In this case, however, we are denied the reverse angle of seeing what exactly it is that these people are watching. The people we are watching are almost entirely women, made up, properly scarved so the Islamic Republic censorial policies are not offended. They are mostly known actors who might be acting as the lead character of *Shirin* if someone were to make a conventional film about Nezami's classic romance, *Khosrow and Shirin*. So, we are watching a whole gallery full of beautiful women watching themselves, imagining themselves as the lead character of a famous love story. The result is as close as we can get to seeing an erotic film that Kiarostami might be expected to make. This is Kiarostami's version of *Khosrow and Shirin*, a disjoined version we get to edit in our own mind.

So, we become implicated in the contorted erotic of the event. "*Taghazzol/ Lovemaking*," we call it in Persian poetic parlance. The camera is here making love to the faces of these women watching and imagining themselves in love with Khosrow. As such, they all become semblant subjects, as do we, all of us predicated on a widely staged semblant reality.

Perhaps things would become clearer if we were to watch *Shirin* along with Kiarostami's short film *Where Is My Romeo?* (2007)—which he made almost at the same time or perhaps even a bit earlier. This was his contribution to the anthology that Cannes had commissioned and called *Chacon son Cinema/To Each Their Own Cinema* (2007), where thirty-six directors from around the world were invited to contribute short films of less than three minutes. Here, too, we watch yet another group of beautiful women, this time watching the ending of Franco Zeffirelli's version of Shakespeare's *Romeo and Juliet* (1968). As *Shirin* celebrates a female lover, *Where Is My Romeo?* does the same with a male lover. The two come together to recast our conception of the lover and the beloved, and in doing so in both posit women as the subject of love and not its object, as it has been historically posited in Persian poetry. The short *Where Is My Romeo?* makes the feature *Shirin* more meaningful—both featuring close-up takes of females in love, reversing the historic gaze cast upon women to be loved, the irony of Kiarostami's own camera casting a male gaze at female faces in love notwithstanding. Now the choice of the character of Shirin from the story *Khosrow and Shirin* as the classic case of romance from Nezami's *Khamseh/Quintet* becomes more important. If we keep in mind that the renowned dissident intellectual Ali Akbar Saidi Sirjani (1931–1994), whose murder in the dungeons of the Islamic Republic became a global scandal, had written a book titled *Sima-ye Do Zan/ Portrait of Two Women* (1988), in which he had favorably compared Shirin against the character of Leili in the other famous romance, *Leili and Majnun*, in the same *Khamseh*, and celebrated the Persian princess as active and agential in her love for Khosrow and cast the Arab princess as passive and ineffable. If we were to consider that immediate background, then we have perhaps the most serious constitution of female subjectivity in Kiarostami's entire oeuvre. This would be the most radical staging of a semblant subject in the fuller context of Persian poetic imagination, where the figure of the beloved is actually degendered, and it can be male, female, or anything else in between. So, yes, "Film-Philosophy" is indeed a significant project. But these details are not to be dismissed as merely "cultural." Without them the film-philosophers are those proverbial blind men in a dark room touching various parts of an elephant and speculating what the creature might be, except an elephant.

When it comes to *Certified Copy* (2010), neither its French translation, *Copie conforme*, nor its English version, *Certified Copy*, resonate with the original *Copy Barabar-e Asl*, which is itself a neologism of a more recent coinage in Persian for the older version of "al-Musanna," which means the certified replica of an original official document like a birth certificate we would obtain from a public notary office to submit to schools or government agencies. This word eventually became "copy babarbar-e asl" when photocopy machines came to Iran in the 1960s, and thus did the word *copy*. Clerks no longer needed to handwrite these replicas and instead just made a photocopy of the original document and then certified it with various stamps and seals. As a teenager in the 1960s, I used to do those handwritten replicas as a summer job in the Ministry of Justice where my older brother worked. Photocopy machines took those exquisite summer jobs away from high schoolers. At any rate, the sense of the original Persian title, *Copy Barabar-e Asl*, makes an instant distinction between the original/*asl* and a copy/copy that has been obtained for an official purpose. With this explanation, the story of the film, or what passes for its story, would probably make more sense. The point of contention between the two protagonists, based on the recent book that he had evidently written on the subject of fake and original, is that there is no original of anything and anything is the copy of something else, even Leonardo da Vinci's *Mona Lisa* was the copy of the original woman he painted or imagined. Halfway through the encounter, the couple begin to act as if they were really a couple celebrating their fifteenth anniversary. So, which is which? Were they role-playing when they pretended they were strangers or were they role-playing when they acted as if they were husband and wife? Martin Scorsese's *Shutter Island* (2010) works the same way. Half of the film we think Leonardo DiCaprio's character, Teddy, is a US Marshal assigned to investigate a mental sanatorium, and the other half we see his entire investigation was in fact role-playing to cure him: he is not Teddy, but Andrew Laeddis, a man who had murdered his own wife after she drowned their three children. There are many other such examples, such as Gregory Hoblit's *Primal Fear* (1993) with the similar character of Aaron Stampler. In all these cases, the question is which version is the original and which one fake. Predicated on Shabih, as semblant truth, which I have offered as a Persianate theory of mimesis, the mimetic framing of the surface has now found a sustained staging in *Certified Copy*.

With *Like Someone in Love* (2012)—which we might consider his very last film, for *24 Frames* (2017) was incomplete when he died and was released posthumously, and there are a couple of other shorts here and there—we see Kiarostami moving into Ozu's territory in more than one sense: physically, emotively, and cinematically. A young female student freelances as an escort. She has an encounter with an older man, which causes rage in the young woman's boyfriend. Signs of violence are evident on her face, and violence is brought to the older man's doorsteps. Again, the key issue would start with the title of the film, *Like Someone in Love*, which signals Ella Fitzgerald's 1957 version of the beloved song of the same title, originally composed by Jimmy Van Heusen with lyrics by Johnny Burke for William Seiter's film *Belle of the Yukon* (1944). In his essay for the Criterion Collection on *Like Someone in Love*, Nico Baumbach, a professor of film-philosophy at Columbia, comes closest to seeing the significance of simulation and semblance in this and a few other Kiarostami films.[20] He goes off the mark, however, when he opts for a moral reading of this aesthetic issue: "Kiarostami generates, as perhaps no other filmmaker has before him, a moral relationship with what we are seeing." That may indeed be the issue that concerns Baumbach, and indeed an important issue. But this is not the paramount matter for an artist who comes from the Shabih-khani tradition (of which Baumbach is of course entirely unaware), when pretending to be in the Karbala of almost a millennium-and-a-half earlier and acting accordingly is definitive of not just a vast dramatic tradition but a veritable article of faith.

In interjecting strategic darkness, reversing the angle for the entire duration of a film, staging counterfeit to conflate and confuse the real, and speculating on simulation, Kiarostami might be seen not just engaged in a cinematic version of the Persianate mimetic tradition of artworks long before the advent of cinema, the Shabih-khani or Shabih-nama'i, but also practicing the Shi'i precept of Dissimulation, or *Taqiyya*, also known as

Kitman, both meaning prudent fear or dissimulation—a doctrinal precept usually interpreted as concealing one's political or religious identity for one's own safety. But here in cinematic terms, Kiarostami has extended its aesthetic and philosophical dimensions into vastly uncharted territories. This mimetic framing of the surface—where what we see is what we get—will remain the grandest aesthetic gesture of Kiarostami's artworld and his singular signature in a worldly cinema we need to recover.

REMEMBERING THE FORGOTTEN METAPHORS

Throughout this book I have sought to read Kiarostami in three simultaneous frames of reference: national, postnational, and world cinemas. There are many insightful works done already on Kiarostami in all three of these frameworks—and yet there is always something lacking in each. Consider a typical example of Mathew Abbott's method in his pioneering work *Abbas Kiarostami and Film-Philosophy* (2016). Abbott takes a film such as *Someone in Love* and first offers a detailed description of its "plot" and then plunges into a "philosophical" discussion of the plot with a certain degree of plausibility, which is fine except the film and perforce its creator are plucked out of their immediate and distant moral and imaginative, creative and critical, habitat, which is dismissed as "political and cultural,"[21] to which he is perfectly entitled, except when he is done and we are done reading him, Kiarostami's artworld looks like a few barrels of oil or volumes of natural gas, or a shipload of copper or any other natural resource excavated from Iran, sold on the international white or black market, taken to Cannes, Paris, or Australia and subjected to some sort of manufacturing process. The product that is produced is not entirely without merit but is attained at the terrible price of cannibalizing the soul of its creator. Abbott specifically tells us "these domains [political and cultural] are not the domains in which the medium specific philosophical propensity of film does its work."[22] This is where he is just plain wrong. As I have detailed chapter and verse in this book, what he calls "political and cultural" has deep-rooted philosophical resonances that are indeed medium-specific to Kiarostami's films and of which Abbott is just ignorant. That does not mar or compromise or discredit his own philosophical reflections on Kiarostami, limited and confined as he is to European and Eurocentric philosophical traditions, which are perfectly fine and plausible. But when he goes out of his way to dismiss what he does know as irrelevant, he is shooting himself in the foot for he looks like a settler colonial Alice in Kiarostami's Wonderland.

Kiarostami once said love is a misunderstanding. The same perhaps might be said about Europeans and Eurocentric critics' love affair with Kiarostami—that they love him because they don't quite understand him.[23] This is a productive misunderstanding and does not mean that non-Europeans, Iranians in particular, or especially those who dislike his cinema understand him better but that his cinema has that enigmatic power of inviting productive misunderstanding—of various sorts. My take on Kiarostami has been consistently to place him onto three interlaced worlds of national, postnational, and world cinemas. In the productive interstice of that crossroads, and in between those who like his cinema and those who do not, there is a crucial and productive margin I have sought to explore to understand his artworld better. We can therefore begin with some basics: Is the prospect of film-philosophy something serious, genuine, and for real? For sure. But both film and philosophy will have to be liberated from their endemic incarceration in their European provincialism. It is as unwise to disregard what European and Eurocentric scholarship says about Kiarostami as it is to disregard what people in Iran or in Persian reflect on his legacy, positive or negative. The question is not a golden mean of wisdom and insight. The purpose is to find and dwell on the interstitial space where Kiarostami is ultimately located, and in those locations come to terms with the artworld he has now left for posterity. Sitting or standing in front of that legacy entails a mode of subjectivity that is the defining momentum of how a major artist left his indelible mark for that posterity.

When approaching his artworld, if we begin with the crucial but undertheorized word, the concept of Shabih in the dramaturgical tradition of Shabih-khani, it will direct us toward the ideas of simile, semblance, simulacrum, and simulation where truth is evident but still hiding in illusions it provokes. At least since Nietzsche this relation between truth and illusion has been evident: "What, then, is truth? A mobile army of metaphors, metonyms, and anthropomorphisms. . . : truths are illusions about which one has forgotten that this is what they are; metaphors which are worn out and without sensuous power."[24] More recently, Jean Baudrillard in his seminal work *Simulacra and Simulation* goes to the postmodern extremity of arguing that today simulacrum has supplanted truth through the force of its the hyperreality.[25] But we also have a much older instance in Farid al-Din Attar's (circa 1142–1220) classic account of the encounter with truth as mirroring effect—at the point in his *Conference of the Birds* when the surviving thirty birds in search of truth reach their final destination. Here is how it goes:

> Their souls rose free of all they'd been before;
> The past and all its actions were no more.
> Their life came from that close, insistent sun
> And in its vivid rays they shone as one.
> There in the Simorgh's radiant face they saw
> Themselves, the Simorgh of the world—with awe
> They gazed, and dared at last to comprehend
> They were the Simorgh and the journey's end.
> They see the Simorgh—at themselves they stare,
> And see a second Simorgh standing there;
> They look at both and see the two are one,
> That this is that, that this, the goal is won.
> They ask (but inwardly; they make no sound)
> The meaning of these mysteries that confound
> Their puzzled ignorance—how is it true
> That "we" is not distinguished here from "you"?
> And silently their shining Lord replies:
> "I am a mirror set before your eyes,
> And all who come before my splendor see
> Themselves, their own unique reality;
> You came as thirty birds and therefore saw
> These selfsame thirty birds, not less nor more;
> If you had come as forty, fifty—here
> An answering forty, fifty, would appear;
> Though you have struggled, wandered, travelled far,
> It is yourselves you see and what you are."
> (Who sees the Lord? It is himself each sees;
> What ant's sight could discern the Pleiades?
> What anvil could be lifted by an ant?
> Or could a fly subdue an elephant?)

"How much you thought you knew and saw; but you
Now know that all you trusted was untrue.
Though you traversed the Valleys' depths and fought."[26]

We are, when watching Kiarostami's screen, facing that mirror. Put together, Kiarostami's filmic legacy, his signature artworld, and thus his aesthetic project in general are all geared toward the constitution of a semblance of subjectivity predicated on a semblance aesthetics of re/presenting reality via a reversal of the angle of vision to which we are habitually accustomed and in which we are located. Everything is in reverse angle, as if we are watching ourselves watching. This mirroring effect places us both as the subject and the object of our own perceptions, back to the Simorgh metaphor in Attar's *Conference of the Birds*. This mirroring effect designs the semblance of subjectivity, posits oneself as another, which is also what is happening in Ta'ziyeh or Shabih-khani, when we enact truth as if knowingly deceiving ourselves. Here is also where art as both truth and illusion come together. In his artworld, Kiarostami both deceives and reveals at one and the same time, because for him truth is embedded in untruth, as I am embedded in the other, as subject is in the object, as if mirroring the truth. All of this semblance surfaces from the deeper layers of reality that has forever preoccupied the world. Kiarostami is not in the least interested in that depth or its layers of representations. His fascination has always been with the mystery of the surface.

7 The Aesthetic Formation of a Nomadic Pilgrim Subject

Cho ziadeh mast gashtim, cheh kelisa cheh Ka'beh . . .

When intoxicated the Ka'beh and the Cathedral are the same—
Once I abandoned myself, union and separation are the same—

I went to a gambling house—
I found everyone honest and true—
Once I reached a convent—
They were all hypocrites . . .

I went for a pilgrimage to the Ka'beh—
They would not let me into the inner sanctum—
Asking: What did you do behind this door
To deserve coming into this house?

I knocked at the door of a faraway temple—
Someone came to the door and said:
Come in Iraqi come in—you are one of us![1]

Fakhr al-Din Iraqi (1213–1289)

What is specific to Abbas Kiarostami's artworld in general and his cinema in particular? As I said at the very outset, any number of other Iranian filmmakers of his generation could have received identical attention the world has happily offered Kiarostami. We should therefore neither fetishize Kiarostami (as some have tended to do) nor look at his work suspiciously (as others have done) because the world did justly offer him that deserved attention. It is neither accidental nor a conspiracy that first the

French and subsequently others paid Kiarostami the attention he deserved. Bahram Beiza'i is perhaps even richer in his cinematic oeuvre and visual diction than Kiarostami, as is Amir Naderi or before them all Forough Farrokhzad if she had not died so tragically young, or after them the still unfolding work of Jafar Panahi. This is not mere speculation but marks the fact that Kiarostami did not fall from the sky or grow like a mushroom out of nowhere. He richly deserved and widely received the recognition that he did, which occasioned a global pedestal that enabled even more serious attention to his legacy.

One could easily sit down and do the same with Beiza'i's, Naderi's, Mehrjui's, or Panahi's respective cinemas, as I have done with Makhmalbaf's.[2] If Kiarostami's artworld has received wider global attention, all the more reason to add a particularly philosophical twist to his work that is beyond the reach of his foreign admirers. Beiza'i's cinema is no less philosophical, or Naderi's, or Panahi's—each in their own terms. But now that Kiarostami has been placed on the forefront of global attention, we need to ask, again: What is particular about his cinema? In the making of that particularity, the global attention given to him is of course a key factor, but so is the home and habitat of his aesthetic imagination— where he was born and raised, and where he came to full artistic fruition, with Persian as his only confident language to his dying day. Even a nasty Islamist regime with its draconian censorial policies could not drive Kiarostami out of his homeland, as it did many other filmmakers, poets, and artists. He was born, raised, and remained an Iranian filmmaker and artist through and through, and yet when the world embraced that particularity it also gave it a universal cast. But in what particular terms and to what effect?

THE PILGRIM SUBJECT

Today the literature that has gathered around the artistic legacy of Kiarostami is still growing, overwhelming, and deeply contradictory. Some love and admire and write panegyrics and poetry about him. Others remain thoroughly suspicious of his work and think him a French misunderstanding. Some Iranians are very proud, others entirely unsure of his work. Many American critics do not know quite what to do with him—while others like Richard Peña, Dave Kehr, and Godfrey Cheshire have been admiring his work for a very long time. Cineastes around the world are quite appreciative of his work and write learned essays and books about his oeuvre, while the French fancy themselves having cornered the market on appreciating him. In the midst of this, film-philosophy as a probing and promising field has had much to say about his work. Constant in this cacophonous chamber, however, remains the fact that somewhere in the middle of all this global attention something in the heart of Kiarostami's work demands and exacts attention. Paramount in my thinking about his legacy has been the totality of this picture—for and against, appreciative or critical—and the kind of knowing, unknowing, and above all, nomadic subject it crafts and implicates.

The idea of "the nomadic subject" that has been central in my reading of Kiarostami—and in this final chapter, I wish to expand it to his poetry and photography—is a key concept in the unfolding work of the contemporary feminist philosopher Rosi Braidotti, who has usefully transformed her own lived experiences as a migratory critical thinker into the cornerstone of this idea.[3] I have unfolded this idea in specific postcolonial directions far beyond Braidotti's own concerns. In this chapter, I wish further to explore it into the domain of the metaphor of "the pilgrim" as a nomadic subject. Here is how Braidotti has thought through the idea of the nomadic subject:

> My lifelong engagement in the project of nomadic subjectivity has been partly motivated by the conviction that, in these globalized times of accelerating technologically mediated changes, many traditional points of reference and age-old habits of thought are being re-composed, albeit in contradictory ways. Paradoxically, old power relations are not only confirmed but in many ways exacerbated in the new geo-political context. At such a time more conceptual creativity is necessary, and more theoretical courage is needed in order to bring about the leap across inertia, nostalgia, aporia and the other forms of critical stasis induced by our historical condition.[4]

This project of "conceptual creativity" and "theoretical courage" spells out differently in different fields. But certainly "inertia and nostalgia" are very much evident in much of what we read about Kiarostami. For me the idea of the nomadic subject is not just in terms of its timeliness and urgency but also something deeply rooted and evident in Kiarostami's own work and the postcolonial context of its emergence. Once the global gaze was cast upon him, a particular assemblage of significance gathered around Kiarostami. In that assemblage, and in light of that global attention, we now realize how Kiarostami was the chronicler and convener of a parabolic prose his camera had discovered, envisioned, and enabled in a way that no one before him had seen it shown. People entirely alien to Iranian and Islamic visual and performing arts, and moral and intellectual and aesthetic imagination, could relate to his works, as did others who were familiar with those roots. The secret of that common attraction was no secret. Kiarostami began simple and he remained simple and he made of simplicity a cinematic virtue no one other than him had ever sensed or seen in quite the same way. That simplicity he had learned from Ozu and Sepehri alike. If there is a philosophy to his cinematic prose, and there is, it is rooted, and it has come to full fruition in a soil that is rich with a poetic mystique best captured and detailed by Sohrab Sepehri.

Sadeh bashim...

Let us be simple—
Let us be simple:
Whether at a bank teller or under a tree.
It is not our business to discover "the secret" of the red rose.
Our business is perhaps
To swim in "the mystique" of the red rose—
And camp behind where knowledge is—
Wash our hands in the gravitation of a tree leaf—
Before we sit at a tablecloth to eat—
[Our business is perhaps to]
Come back to life in the morning every time the sun rises.

Let us fly our excitements—
Sprinkle a little water on the surface of sensing the air,
The color, the sound, and the window—
Let us place the sky in between the two syllabi of "Being"—
Let us inhale and exhale our lungs with Eternity—
Let us unload the weight of knowledge
From the wings of a sparrow—and put it down on the ground—
Let us take the name away from the cloud—

Away from the poplar tree, from the fly, from the summer—
On the wet footsteps of rain,
Let us climb to the height of kindness—
Let us open the door to the human, the light, the plant, the insect—
Our business is perhaps
To listen for the song of truth—
Somewhere in between the lilies and the century.[5]

Yes, indeed the thinking of Stanley Cavell, Jean-Luc Nancy, Gilles Deleuze, Martin Heidegger, Ludwig Wittgenstein, or any other European or Eurocentric philosopher will do wonders teasing out aspects of Kiarostami's cinematic philosophy. Let us continue to do so. But I would also like to plant a Sepehri, or a Nezami, a Hafez, a Fakhr al-Din Iraqi, an Avicenna, a Suhrawardi, a Mulla Sadra, or a Shafi'i-Kadkani, or any number of other such citations—all outside the archive of the exceedingly limited and provincial Eurocentric imagination—at the front door of Kiarostami's cinema, his poetry, his photography, and his painting.[6] This is neither a rhetorical or ideological proposition nor does it fathom a zero-sum totality. Nothing is at the expense of the other. Kiarostami's legacy has room for all. What I propose here will enrich our reading and watching and sensing of Kiarostami even better. We must overcome the European philosophical provincialism and liberate the word, the practice, and the proposition of "film-philosophy" to include a more enabling and enriching prairie of thoughts that has plenty of room for Europe but is not limited to or defined by it. Otherwise, there is something truly obscene in what we see today—an exclusively European philosophical parlance applied to an Asian filmmaker rooted in an entirely different cultural, civilizational, philosophical, and aesthetic provenance.

When in a ghazal composed more than seven hundred years ago, a towering Persian poet like Fakhr al-Din Iraqi equates a mosque, a church, and a synagogue with a gambling house and finds the latter more true and honest, and when he says as a Muslim he was not even permitted into the sacrosanct site of Muslim pilgrimage to the Ka'beh because first he had to account for what he had done in the world outside, then we have a solid premise upon which the generation of Kiarostami's poetic disposition would find, cast, articulate, and refine a form of subjectivity beyond the reach of the sedentary fixations of all cultures and of every clime. It is that

250   CHAPTER SEVEN

rising universalism whose nomadic mode of subjectivity—evident in the figure of the pilgrim—needs a closer understanding.

THE TEMPORAL TENOR OF THE SACRED

Kiarostami's artworld captures the temporal tenor of the sacred in his time, the moral universe that was no longer reducible or assimilable backward to Islam or any other institutional religion—and as such, his aesthetic imagination emanates from the moral universe at the heart of the lived experiences of his time, perhaps best evident in Persian poetic imagination, particularly by Hafez and his key idea of "Rendi"—an impossible word to translate, which must be thought as somewhere between defiant chivalry and moral sublimation of the orderly and the ordinary. By virtue of the global attention Kiarostami richly deserved and widely received, he made it possible for not just Iranians but the world at large to experience the aesthetic of the moment that an entire history of sacred certitude had enabled in Persian and Islamic mysticism—with Irfan and Tasawwof as the key operative concepts at work here. This idea of the aesthetic temporality of the sacred—the sacred evident in the material evidence of life—became definitive to his artworld.

This ennobling virtue of Kiarostami's artworld, however, has had a fatal flaw when he indulged in his own poetry. He was no poet but he dabbled in poetry. He was no poet and should have remained content with the poetic cast of his cinematic imagination. But he did not. He knew he was no poet and was trespassing on some sacred ground himself. In his interviews, he would sarcastically use the verb *mortakeb shodan*, meaning "to commit a criminal act," and say "sometime I have committed poetry," as in committing a crime.[7] But still the fact that in the Iranian context and in Persian he dared to not just "commit poetry" but actually publish it is a critical factor in the hazards of the zigzag passageways he traversed. Kiarostami's fatal attraction to poetry was at best the evidence of his amateurish (in the best sense of the word) affection for the venerable Persian poetic tradition. One can neither completely disregard his attraction to poetry nor exaggerate his limited poetic gift—but seek judiciously to place them in the larger context of his artworld. He was a pious and pensive pilgrim, we might say, into the revered realm of Persian poetic legacy, as perhaps best evident in the three volumes of poetry he prepared of the three pillars of Persian poetry—Rumi, Sa'di, and Hafez: *Hafez beh Revayat Abbas Kiarostami/Hafez as Told by Abbas Kiarostami* (2006), *Sa'di az dast Khishtan Faryad/Sa'di, Woe Unto Thee* (2007), and *Atash dar Bad/ Fire in the Wind: A Selection of Rumi's Ghazals* (2011). The key feature of these three selections, beginning with his volume on Hafez, is when he deliberately violates the poetic prosody of the complete *bayts*/lines and *mesra'*/hemistich and plays with broken-down passages of various hemistiches. This very much irritated some classicists and yet others were bashfully appreciative of what he was doing, in effect bringing closer attention, as his admirers would say, to the visual and acoustic sound effects of these broken-down passages. The act was also a clumsy nod toward the New Persian Poetry or the Nimaic poetry that had consistently and purposefully dismantled the classical Persian prosody, much to the chagrin of the classicists.

Consider Kiarostami's take on Hafez: *Hafez beh Revayat Abbas Kiarostami/Hafez as Told by Abbas Kiarostami* (2006).[8] It begins with quoting the French poet Arthur Rimbaud (1854–1891): "Il faut être absolument modern"—to instruct us all, French or not, that we must be "absolutely modern"—and therefore take liberty with Hafez and "modernize" him! Why? Why should we listen to Rimbaud or any other European poet, glorious in their own terms, butcher Hafez? Compare that with when Goethe wrote his *West-östlicher Divan* (1814–1819)! An entire European class of literati were doing exactly the opposite of what Kiarostami orders his Iranian readers to do. It does not bode well for Kiarostami to publish such truly unfortunate things. From there, Kiarostami proceeds to divide the book into eighteen chapters, each dealing with a particular topic—such as "*Eshq va Shabab*/Love and Youth," "*Dar Madhat-e Ma'shuq*/Praising the Beloved," "*Shab-e Feraq*/The Night of Separation," "*Asrar-e Eshq va Masti*/Secrets of Love and Ecstasy," et cetera. All these titles are taken from Hafez's own poetry though plucked out of their poetic context and thus cast as rather banal and cliché designations. On each mostly blank page, he then cites a phrase or a part of a hemistich of a revered ghazal of Hafez, such as "I am famous throughout the city for loving," or "My heart chooses nothing but loving the beautiful!," or "God made a covenant between me and those with sweet lips." Hafez has never sounded so banal as in Kiarostami's rendition. For learned Persian-speaking people, these phrases are iconic and memorial. They read them and they are triggered to remember the full line or the hemistich. The volume is thus entirely frivolous and playful, if not perky and flippant.

One thumbs through the volume page after mostly blank page perhaps a bit amused and entertained by the frivolous exercise, but at the same time somewhat perturbed by the sheer audacity of the idea. It is like taking a snapshot of a Behzad or a Reza Abbasi painting, or a painting by Titian or Tintoretto, and then digitally blowing up a small inch or two of them and asking people to see how marvelous they are, or else like taking a Beethoven symphony and cutting it into five-second snippets and blasting them out loud and asking people to listen and enjoy the indulgence. As he is reported to have said when serious people got offended by the spectacle, he was perfectly entitled to break down Hafez's poems, as he did, say, over a lighthearted dinner party at his house with his friends, but to then proceed and publish it and call it *Hafez as Told by Abbas Kiarostami* exuded a certain wanton arrogance that he could only get away with by branding it with his name. Every single word, syllable, phrase, hemistich, and line of these ghazals has been the subject of generations of meticulous scholarship by ingenious scholars of textual criticism to prepare critical editions from piles of manuscripts. From Mohammad Ghazvini to Parviz Natel Khanlari, a succession of deeply learned scholars had parsed letters, words, and even diacritical notes of these ghazals. When the revered contemporary Persian poet Ahamd Shamlou did a similar but far more respectful rendition of Hafez, serious scholars of the text mopped the floor with his disrespectful attitude. But Kiarostami had learned no such lesson from Shamlou's dilettantism. The same branding is evident in his supercilious encounter with Sa'di and Rumi. It is more than anything else sad and regretful he so abused his own name, banking on sycophantic receptions of whatever he sold with his branded name on it. Disregarding or just bracketing this unfortunate aspect of his work (akin to the idea of a fashion brand for sunglasses he had once been asked to market with his name), one still must see these mostly harmless and innocent (however unfortunate) sojourns into the revered realm of Persian poetic legacy as acts of piety and pilgrimage by an artist indulging his injudicious impulses.

In his own ventures into poetry, in volumes like *Bad-o Barg/The Wind and the Leaf* (2011), *Hamrah ba bad/Walking with the Wind* (2006), or *Gorgi dar Kamin/A Wolf in Hiding* (2005), he opts for a very simple and easily accessible take on the Nimaic tradition that had already seen its masters in the previous generation of Ahmad Shamlou, Mehdi Akhavan-e Sales, Forough Farrokhzad, and Sohrab Sepehri—masters who were far beyond the capacities of Abbas Kiarostami.[9] One has to approach his own poetry with a similar kind of hesitation. He was trespassing into the revered domain of the Persian poetry china shop like a Cannes-crowned bull. As inaugurated, theorized, and practiced by the master of the domain Nima Yushij (1895–1960), New Persian poetry (*She'r-e No*) had a rhyme and a reason precisely at the moment when, from Nima to his followers, the history of Persian prosody was being revolutionized.[10] Kiarostami was entirely oblivious to this logic and rhetoric of She'r-e No. He was for sure a beneficiary of it. But he had no evident grasp of its inner logic.

The Wind and the Leaf begins with something he calls "In Lieu of an Introduction":

> From the tyranny of time
> I seek refuge in poetry
> From the cruelty of the Beloved
> I seek refuge in poetry
> From the wanton injustice
> I seek refuge in poetry.[11]

The rest of the Haiku-like poems are almost the same:

> Tonight I have a date with Moon—
> With the Full Moon—
> At Seven Minutes to Seven.[12]

> I shared my secret with the Moon—
> When the sun rose my secret was revealed.[13]
> Under the Moonlight

My cup was empty
My heart sunken.[14]

In my life—
Not too short not too long—
It snowed for ten years.[15]

For some the summit is to be conquered
For the summit it is a place for snow.[16]

When one reads this collection of poems cover to cover and places them next to Kiarostami's other detours into the august halls of Persian poetry, there is a sense of being in the presence of a sensitive, at times perceptive, and gentle soul. Excited to go public with his love for Persian poetry, he knew full well he would be severely criticized for his daring dilettantism by those who take both Persian poetry and his own cinema and other artworks seriously, and yet praised vacuously by those who loved him anyway—and were beholden to his global celebration. In the final analysis, it is good that he collected these little poetic phrases and published them for, poor and mediocre as they are, they add a significant dimension to his artworld—if in nothing else, in exposing an aspect of his cavalier dilettantism that risked exposing him. Be that as it may, the fact is that outside his artworld, if we were to take his films and photography out of the picture, then these poems will not amount to much. The problem with Kiarostami daring the elements to lay a claim on Persian poetry was that by the time of Ahamd Shamlou's death in 2000, the monumental episteme of Nimaic New Poetry had completely exhausted itself. There were of course still significant poets like Esmail Khoi or Shafi'i-Kadkani around and who continued to be productive. But no significant vision, even by more serious poets who surfaced after the Islamist regime took over, like Qeysar Aminpour and Ali Moallem Damghani, was added to what was already there. Kiarostami's poetry was nowhere near that universe that Nima had envisioned and enabled and after a glorious spectrum that extended from Forough Farrokhzad and Ahmad Shamlou to Mehdi Akhavan-e Sales and Sohrab Sepehri had come to a closure. What these innocent sojourns into the sanctity of Persian poetry do is to register Kiarostami's partaking in the temporal tenor of the poetic sacred paramount in his age—a precinct where Abbas Kiarostami's more serious artistic work, his cinema and photography, had a far more pronounced and enduring presence. Like a pious pilgrim visiting a distant and unreachable mausoleum, Kiarostami wanted to touch the talisman of Persian poetic legacy and be blessed by it. He would not be admitted into the pantheon. But still his act of piety would be gently acknowledged. The temporal tenor of the sacred defining the provenance of his time and space had already embraced and claimed him, right and wrong moves alike.

If not in and of itself, then by virtue of the enduring consequences of his encounter with Persian poetry there remains something significant for the rest of Kiarostami's artistic projects. Perhaps the most important dimension of seeing Kiarostami so seriously engaged with Persian poetry despite his own limited wherewithal is that this poetic preoccupation is very much present in him when he stands behind his camera and shows the world what he sees. With all their frivolities and playfulness, his encounter with Rumi, Sa'di, and Hafez point to the philosophical poeticity these landmarks of Persian poetry entail. The relationship between Persian poetry and Iranian philosophical heritage is deep rooted and widespread. Some philosophers like Nasser Khosrow (1004–1088) were masters of philosophical prose who have left us multiple philosophical treatises, and their poetry reflects that philosophical nature.[17] Iconic poets like Ferdowsi, Nezami, Rumi, Sa'di, and Hafez are not devoid of their own respective philosophical dispositions. More recent philosophers like Muhammad Iqbal (1877–1938) composed their philosophical treatises, such as *Asrar-e Khodi* and *Romuz-e Bikhodi*, entirely in exquisite Persian poetry. These iconic examples point to the fact that there are significant philosophical dimensions to the poets with whom Kiarostami was keeping fruitful and active company. Based on this evidence, reaching for the philosophical aspects of his cinematic legacy would be impossible without serious attention to a Persian philosophical heritage with which he was conversant. This is not to suggest that any and all such philosophical aspects of his or any other filmmaker's must be assimilated backward to one philosophical tradition or another. There is something specifically philosophical about Kiarostami's cinema itself. But that very specificity has a poetic-philosophical provenance that cannot be entirely disregarded. If we are rightly exploring the interface between film and philosophy to tease out the philosophical disposition of cinema and in doing so we freely rush to leading European philosophers like Wittgenstein and Heidegger, there is no reason for the philosophical pedigrees of poetry or the poetic disposition of philosophy to have any less presence in these philosophical dimensions, as perhaps best evident in Heidegger's later turn to poetry, especially that of Rilke and Hölderlin.[18] Kiarostami may not have been a good poet himself, but the poetic cast of his mind has given a decidedly Persian poetic disposition to his cinema and photography. At least two of his major films, *Where Is the Friend's House?* and *The Wind Will Carry Us*, specifically allude to the poetry of Sohrab Sepehri and Forough Farrokhzad.[19] The point here is not a mere archeological excavation of poetry influencing cinema but far more importantly the fact that something about the temporal tenor of the time was breathing in and out the contemporaneity of the sense of the sacred—and Abbas Kiarostami's poetic disposition (if not his own poetry) was right at the heart of it.

THE PILGRIM AS THE UNKNOWING SUBJECT[20]

Zigzagging his pious passage through the landscape of the aesthetic imagination and the poetic texture of the sacred in his time had remained constant in Kiarostami's visionary filmmaking and sublime photography—scripting and enabling a semblant subject that was the pure product of his artworld. At the epicenter of that semblance of subjectivity, with a semblant subject as its principal interlocutor formed in Kiarostami's artworld when it entered the feast of his global celebration, is a nomadic subject—or put in other words, an unknowing semblant subject knowable only through its varied nomadic gestations as the epitome of a liberation from the alienating consequences of a partition of truth and art imposed from the center of always already "European" colonial modernity and yet epistemically subverted on its colonial edges. All the hitherto earnest attempts to reflect on Kiarostami's work philosophically have in fact paradoxically helped alienate him further from his artwork and artworld by assimilating them backward into the generic and cliché conception of "Western philosophy." Kiarostami's poetry, limited as it is, his occasional paintings, and his sublime photography, particularly his series on roads featured in his *Roads of*

Kiarostami (2005), would offer a fruitful space for these reflections. The unknowing nomadic subject thriving on the semblance of proximity to the renewable world is where these works bring Kiarostami's artworld to a peaceful, confident, and still defiant conclusion. There is no more joyous and fruitful occasion to reflect on this space than his landscape photography in *Roads and Rain*: perhaps the most aesthetically robust, potent, and joyous legacy he has left behind on par with the best of his cinema.

What a sublime joy to leave his unfortunate indulgence in poetry behind and salute him on the premise of his awe-inspiring photography! The landscape photography of Abbas Kiarostami has a significant place in his visual imagination and expansive oeuvre as a major landmark of his artworld. It has an almost identical place in both his photography and in his films—both punctuating his spatial serenity and giving them room to breathe and meditate. He is not the only Iranian filmmaker with a serious interest in photography. Amir Naderi and Nasser Taghva'i are also serious photographers. But Kiarostami's photography is now seen from the vantage point of his global celebration with a much wider and richer spectatorship. Today we inevitably look at his photography recalling his films and watch his films through the photographic memories of his fascination with landscapes—as in his famous *Roads and Rain*. The key question for coming to terms with the significance of this photographic landscape of his legacy is what to do with them—what they mean and how they figure in his artworld. Is it sufficient to say, well, "they are beautiful." Yes, they are beautiful. No, that is not sufficient. We need to know they are beautiful in what particular terms. First and foremost, we must begin with Kiarostami's home and habitat, where he was born and raised, where his mind's eye was first nourished, and where he came to artistic fruition. Kiarostami was born in 1940 and came to artistic consciousness in the 1960s and 1970s (for convenience, I just stick to the Gregorian calendar), the two exceedingly crucial decades in Iranian artistic production and aesthetic consciousness. The traumatic military coup of August 1953, through which the US and the UK conspired to abort the prospects of a nascent democracy and bring the runaway monarch Mohammad Reza Pahlavi (1919–1980) back to power, had an enduring effect on subsequent generations in both political and cultural domains. Despite crucial political unrest in the aftermath of the coup of 1953, which in a crescendo of public protests ultimately culminated in the Iranian revolution of 1977–1979, the most significant events of these iconic decades were in fact cultural, artistic, literary, poetic, and cinematic rather than political. One could arguably propose these two decades, particularly the 1970s that came to a crushing closure with the 1979 revolution and the establishment of an Islamist theocracy, were the most significant years of contemporary Iranian history. Kiarostami was a product of this environment. There was a restless, searching, probing, and overwhelming disquietude about this post-coup period.

Despite the fact that much of the world knows Kiarostami primarily as a filmmaker, he has a place no less significant in contemporary Iranian art. But how do we distinguish between "contemporary" and "modern" art in an Iranian context—or more crucially, do we even need such a distinction, and what precisely is the place and significance of the "modern" in this domain? In his most recent book, *The Art of Iran in the Twentieth and Twenty-First Centuries: Tracing the Modern and the Contemporary* (2023), the eminent art historian and critic Hamid Keshmirshekan re-examines the two adjacent concepts of *modern* and *contemporary* art in both a local and a global context, with a particular reference to the Saqqa-khaneh movement, a widespread aesthetic preoccupation with specifically Shi'i sacred objects, which he places within the context of "modern art" but judiciously calls "neo-traditionalist."[21] As Keshmirshekan points out: "Crucial debates over the creation of a balance between the two polarities of modernism and cultural authenticity that had started in the earlier decades reached to a peak in the 1960s and resulted in the creation of the most acclaimed neo-traditionalist movement, the Saqqā-khāneh tendency."[22] Describing major figures in this movement, Keshmirshekan writes: "In their view, these sources had to be linked to modern styles to create a markedly national artistic expression. The neo-traditional Saqqā-khāneh movement in the 1960s was in particular a response to this desire."[23] But why would, or should, a "national artistic expression" necessarily assume a "modern" or even a "traditional" style? Could a national artistic expression eventually find its own aesthetic idiomaticity without either a modern or traditional (a.k.a. "authentic") claim on it? Kiarostami's place at the very heart of this artistic movement would offer a crucial answer.

For the purpose of reading Kiarostami's artwork in the context of his contemporary art scene in Iran, I wish to suspend and question the validity of the term "modern" and look at his art in the general framework of perhaps the most potent and original artistic movement of the time known as "Saqqa-khaneh" as a reality sui generis, as an event, rooted in the aesthetic consciousness of the time with only tangential and entirely dubious connection to the idea of "modernity." This exercise requires an epistemic rupture with the way Saqqa-khaneh art has been hitherto understood, though must by necessity start with that point of departure—seeking to revise, expand, and perhaps even recast and update its significance. The word *Saqqa-khaneh* means a water station visible in urban or rural or even nomadic landscapes, where thirsty people can have a sip of water. The location has profound religious significance, for the third Shi'i Imam Hossein is believed to have been murdered in the year 680 in Karbala, thirsty. Saqqa-khanehs are therefore usually decorated with iconic, talismanic, and religious objects and paintings—and the site therefore looks like a mausoleum honoring the memory of Imam Hossein. The term "Saqqa-khaneh," coined by art critique Karim Emami (1930–2005) in 1962, referred to an art movement that was particularly drawn to these locations and objects and recast them in contemporary art forms. The term "modern art" in this same Iranian context is a misnomer and a false conflation of three Persian words identified with contemporary art: *Mo'aser*, *No*, and *Jadid*, none of which exactly correspond to "Modern." We in fact do not have a word for "Modern" in Persian or Arabic or any other neighboring languages, as we do not have a word for "Secular," and we just use these words in either their European pronunciations or neologisms coined to mark them in an altogether critically unexamined way. When we wish to say "Contemporary Art," we use two Persian words: *Honar-e Mo'aser*. But when we refer to "Modern Art," we have no choice but to use an English or French pronunciation of the word *Modern* and the Persian word *Honar*. *Mo'aser* means "contemporary," *No* means "new," and *Jadid* means "most recent." The problem with extending the English or French or German or Italian words marking "modernity" into Persian is the confusion and conflation of two distinct aspects of a word—its etymological roots and its idiomatic weight. Etymologically, you can even place *Tajaddod*, for example, as an equivalent of "Modernity"—but that etymological equation leaves the idiomatic weight and the historical disposition of the term "Modernity" and its capitalist and colonial connotations behind. That idiomatic legacy of the word translates into the ideological banner of the global capitalism that has robbed the world blind and on whose map Iran, as indeed the rest of the world, is at the receiving end of a categorical desubjection where it cannot be the author and agent of any aesthetics or epistemology of its own. The response to that sense of "Modernity" is of course not "Tradition" or any sense of the "Authentic Self" or any other such equally ideological proposition in the opposite direction. The response is to take the original Persian or Arabic words people have used intuitively—such as *Jadid* or *Mo'aser* or *No*—and theorize them from the ground up—the ground zero of peoples' lived, aesthetic experiences. Kiarostami's expansive "Roads" series mapping a profoundly consecrated landscape offers a robust space for reflecting on the contemporaneity of this sacred precinct and the nomadic subject, a wandering soul, that it implicates as a pilgrim.

ASCETIC LENSWORK AGAINST MODERNITY AS A POLITICAL PROJECT

With this move, we are critically placing Kiarostami's artworld right at the heart of the artistic provenance of his time. The misbegotten rush to call all these deeply rich and empowering possibilities "Modern" was not an analytical, theoretical, epistemic, or aesthetic choice but a mostly political project in tune with the Pahlavi court-affiliated modernization ideology. The Shah and his father were "modernizing" Iran and that modernization needed an art—and thus the political provenance of the term "Honar-e Modern," which is otherwise an entirely outlandish proposition when uttered in Persian. In his new book, *The Art of Iran in the Twentieth and Twenty-First Centuries*, Keshmirshekan has carefully studied all these terms. I am, however, taking one step further and going upstream from the Pahlavi-court modernization project and completely dispensing with the term "modern" when it comes to Saqqa-khaneh art, which was not modern, but a contemporary, or new, or recent gestation of the sacred iconography of Shi'ism with which it was inspired and to which it both materially and allegorically alluded. More than half a century after its coinage, and with actively thinking through Kiarostami's artwork, the term "Saqqa-khaneh" needs revisiting with a more critical, informed, and embracing frame of reference that in fact revalidates and prolongs its enduring significance.

By now the sustained legacy of Saqqa-khaneh has a solid repertoire and major representative figures, and a bona fide historiography, which are perfectly persuasively argued and articulated. But there is something in Kiarostami's landscape photography, and through that a different archive of aesthetic sensibilities, that allows us to reconsider the boundaries of the Saqqa-khaneh legacy, with a deliberate pivot toward the formation of what Keshmirshekan correctly calls "national artistic expression." That "national expression" could not be compromised either by the Pahlavi state-sponsored modernism that falsely claimed it or the Islamism of the Islamic Republic that followed it. We need to restore to the artistic movement its own inner logic. Following my previous book on the idea of the *nation*, I make a clear distinction between the *national* as a mode of collective consciousness and *nationalism* as a political ideology of state-building.[24] The idea of "modern art" was squarely rooted in Pahlavi dynasty bourgeois nationalism as a state ideology, whereas Saqqa-khaneh as a movement of national art expressed the exact opposite of that state-sponsored nationalism—a conception of national aesthetic consciousness that the Pahlavi court could not have appropriated for its own ideological purposes. Whereas the state-sponsored modernism and its cultural accoutrement sought to twist and turn the Saqqa-khaneh movement as a modus operandi of secular nationalism as state ideology, the Shi'i roots and overwhelming allegorical iconography of the art movement itself had tapped into a sacred repertoire above and beyond that state appropriation, but still short of enabling any Islamic Republic that would come after it and violently claim it. With the global gaze now cast on Kiarostami's artworld, and given the limited and ill-informed critical apparatus at the disposal of Eurocentric provincialism, this crucial art movement in Iran needs a reconsideration.

The Saqqa-khaneh art movement was neither modern nor traditional—bracketing both these ideological propositions in the interest of something internal to the logic and rhetoric of the movement itself. It was and it remains an "event," as Alain Badiou would call and philosophize it. The ground zero of the post-coup Iranian political scene forms the "inconsistent multiplicities" that the Pahlavi modernism project sought in vain to cover and camouflage. The Saqqa-khaneh was the site of the aesthetic event that exposed that political lie, and the revolutionary lie that would come after it in the form of the Islamist ideology faking a modern republic. Here is how Badiou defines the event:

> Situations are nothing more, in their being, than pure indifferent multiplicities. Consequently it is pointless to search amongst differences for anything that might play a normative role. If truths exist, they are certainly indifferent to differences.... Structure of situations does not, in itself, deliver any truths. By consequence, nothing normative can be drawn from the simple realist examination of the becoming of things.... A truth is solely constituted by rupturing with the order which supports it, never as an effect of that order. I have named this type of rupture which opens up truths "the event."[25]

That truth asserted itself first and foremost in aesthetic and not in political terms—though Pahlavi monarchic modernism sought to appropriate, twist and turn, and claim it as its own state ideology, and first some court-affiliated art critics articulated that appropriation and then other critics (unthinkingly) followed suit. The Saqqa-khaneh event has played an outsized normative role and sustained its aesthetic potency despite the epistemic violence perpetrated on it by force-feeding it into a modernist narrative, as a variation, perhaps, on the theme of European and Eurocentric schemata of contemporary art histories, thus paradoxically in fact corroborating, authenticating, and universalizing that self-raising and other-lowering modernity. With the project of Pahlavi monarchy now collapsed and the Islamist theocracy that followed it in deep legitimacy crisis, and with the towering figure of Abbas Kiarostami on the global scene, a far more robust reading of the event of the Saqqa-khaneh art movement is now possible.

I am of course fully aware that my proposal here goes against the grain of the normative way Saqqa-khaneh art has been historically understood over the last half century and more by the leading scholars and practitioners of the field. This discomfort is basically in two terms: first my decoupling of Saqqa-khaneh art from its dubious attachment to "modern art," and second for pushing its aesthetic boundaries to include aspects of the artwork of artists like Abbas Kiarostami, Amir Naderi, Bahman Jalali, Shirin Neshat, and Azadeh Akhlaghi, who have historically not been seen in such terms. These two conflated perspectives are integral to my purpose of articulating the formation of the unknowing postcolonial subject as both rooted and nomadic, which of course was not part of the initial analytic encounter with Saqqa-khaneh art. But that purpose is now crucial in my project for two reasons: the event of Saqqa-khaneh has had more theoretical potentials than it initially or hitherto realized, and pushing it in specifically philosophical terms that form the epistemic foregrounding of the postcolonial unknowing subject. A key issue is of course the fact that Saqqa-khaneh artists themselves used the terms "modern" interchangeably with "*No-gara'i*"—which is precisely the etymological root of the confusion, for the word *No*/New in Persian does not carry the same historical, political, idiomatic, or epistemic resonances as do the words *modern* or *modernity* in any European languages. The same is true for the Arabic word *Jadid*/Most Recent, that does not have the same resonances as does "modern" or "modernity."

That etymological conflation, though, points to something more important. In their potent discovery of a new art form, Saqqa-khaneh artists were formally and aesthetically caught between those artists who thought of themselves as militant secular modernists, on one side, and such critics as Jalal Al-e Ahmad (1923–1969) who would accuse them of Westoxication, obsessed with "the West," and therefore inauthentic and abusive of their own artistic traditions, on the other.[26] But they were neither—if we were to look at their artworks from the distance of more than half a century and the collapse of the Pahlavi dynasty followed by the deeply troubled Islamist theocracy that followed it. Judged by their artworks, these artists were neither reactionaries seeking solace in a distant sacred past nor modernists aware of the colonial space of the reception of European modernism around the globe. They had intuited, staged, recast, and performed something rooted in the relics of Shi'i iconographies that served their aesthetic purposes—for which of course some were also criticized for being sacrilegious. Against the combined force of the reactionaries, the modernists, the traditionalists, or even their own assessments of what they were doing, the intentions of the texts they were producing (*intentio operis*, as Umberto Eco would say)[27] were the artworks themselves overcoming even the modernist anxieties of their own creators.

    The extraordinary gift of Karim Emami was to coin this poignant term in 1962, referring to artworks that were created in the late 1950s and early 1960s, while the movement had peaked and plateaued when the Pahlavis were still in power. Calling these artists modern, traditional, reactionary, sacrilegious, or Westoxicated was all wrong and symptomatic of a societal reaction that could not quite grasp what they were witnessing. Some of these artists themselves may have even intended sacrilegious abuses of these items to be intentionally provocative, and they were thus hoping to dismantle their original sacred certitude, but still they were crafting a new iconography of their own age (elements of a post-Islamist aesthetics) from the relics of the ages they wished to discredit and overcome. There was a powerful post-Islamist liberation theology evident in the aesthetics they were practicing. Influenced by their Eurocentric aesthetic education, they may have indeed been drawn only to the formal aspects of these icons, either ignorant of or indifferent to their symbolic significance in a Shi'i iconography. But those forms were like the proverbial Trojan horse—the artists may have had no clue what they were carrying in their bellies. The artists may have used them for their "purely formal" dimensions, but those very forms carried forward the active memories and the sacred resonances of what they have always meant. Of course, as always, Eurocentric art historians would very much welcome these artworks as "modern" for they would add an exotic and Oriental twist to their consistently Eurocentric conceptions of the so-called multiple or alternative modernities. But today, something far more precious would be lost if we failed to transcend those limitations and think of Kiarostami's landscape photography in the light of those crucial decades in which he came to artistic fruition.

    The idea of the aesthetic pilgrimage I propose here, therefore, or the canvas as a sacred site, and the deserted roads and landscapes we see in Kiarostami's photography as the hallowed grounds and pilgrim routes place the idea of the unknowing subject of this emancipatory aesthetics thematically and theoretically outside the purview of both the state-sponsored modernism the Pahlavi court had sponsored and the

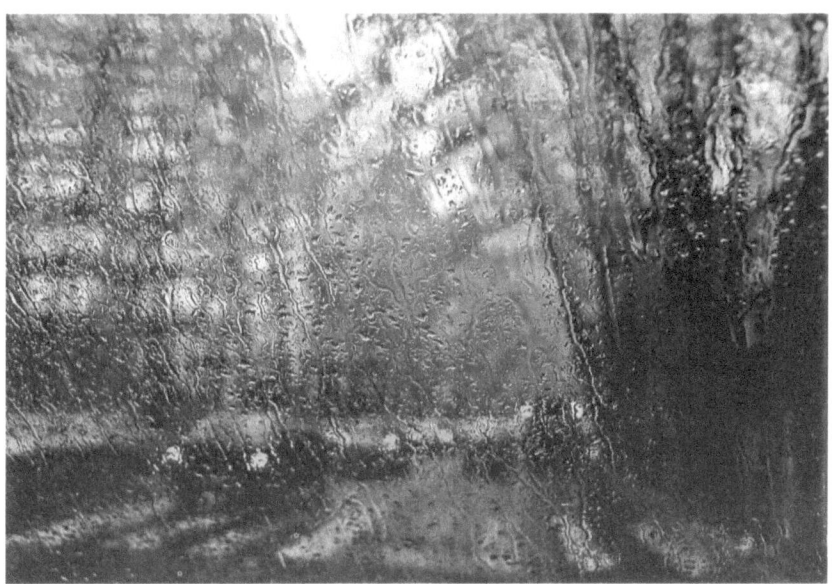

Figure 17. Abbas Kiarostami, *Roads and Rain* (2007). Courtesy of Abbas Kiarostami Foundation.

subsequent militant Islamism that would have an equally dubious and discredited claim on it. My contention here is that the idea of Saqqa-khaneh art was articulated and identified correctly at a particularly potent moment in contemporary Iranian art history without a full awareness of the sacred aesthetics provenance or the wider theoretical implications of that designation. It was done mechanically and site-specifically, without any expansive theorization into its aesthetic and iconic implications. I also contend the movement was assimilated forward and backward, with palpable epistemic violence, into a state-sponsored modernism that in turn aborted its theoretical potency. The *Roads and Rain* photography of Abbas Kiarostami coming to the surface a generation or two later in the 1990s and 2000s recasts the Saqqa-khaneh tradition in a new light and places the movement on the plain where the unknowing nomadic subject has been waiting for a full moral, imaginative, and philosophical recognition.

What gives particular power and presence to Kiarostami's landscape photography in light of the Saqqa-khaneh art phenomenon is the cinematic asceticism at the heart of his lenswork—both in his films and his photography. This asceticism shows itself in the sparse settings of his films, the simplicity of his filmic culture, the vast universe of his landscapes, and the economy of their productions, where his entire cast and crew would fit inside a small truck, as we see throughout his Koker Trilogy. That sublime asceticism becomes particularly evident in the context of such obscenely rich cinematic events as the summer 2023 blockbusters like Christopher Noland's *Oppenheimer* (which I went to see when I was writing this chapter). Only the obscenity of the wealth and power evident in that kind of filmic culture can reveal to us the moral authority and the sacred provenance of the simplicity behind an Ozu, a Ray, or a Kiarostami film. In the case of Kiarostami in particular, that ascetism is not accidental or just material in his productions but deeply evident in the moral and imaginative minimalism we see in his lenswork.

KIAROSTAMI AND HIS FELLOW TRAVELERS: IN *SAFAR* AND *HAZAR*/HOME AND ABROAD

Let us continue this argument by looking closer at one of Kiarostami's "Roads": this shot is identical or reminiscent of the iconic zigzag road of *Where Is the Friend's House?* The idea is revisited repeatedly in Kiarostami's work with *Roads and Rain* and *24 Frames*. The central motif of these pictures, reiterated in his cinema, is travel, which is echoed and mirrored in his famous car shots throughout his cinema, particularly in the Koker Trilogy. The point of view of all these shots is always from here and now, from the eye of the beholder, either from the vantage point of the omniscient narrator or one of the protagonists. These roads all fade into an eternity, a posterity, an unknown futurity. Even when we are inside the car where Kiarostami's protagonists sit, still the sound design is the omniscient narrator through which we remain aware of the outside world. *Safar/*Travel, therefore, or its sacred rendition as *Ziarat* has here become cinematic, staged, photographic, visible, and iconic. This cinematic sublimation of the sacred journeys, of Ziarat, has a long trajectory in Persian poetry and Islamic philosophy, from the poetry of Hakim Sanai in his *Seyr al-Ibad ila al-Ma'ad/The Journey of Man to Eternity* in the twelfth century to the philosophy of Mulla Sadra in his *Al-Asfar al-Arba'ah/The Four Journeys*

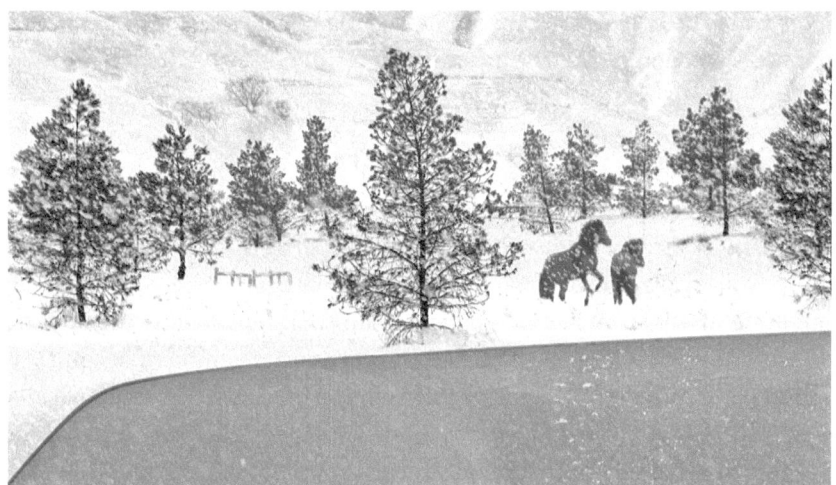

Figure 18. Abbas Kiarostami, *24 Frames* (2017). Courtesy of Abbas Kiarostami Foundation.

in the sixteenth. But in Kiarostami's artworld these allegorical journeys assume a minimalist prose in his films (looking for a friend's house, etc.) and sublimate into complete abstractions in his photography.

The same deserted landscape leitmotif shows itself in the desert paintings and photography of Kiarostami's contemporaries—Parviz Kalantari and Bahman Jalali. All these desert and deserted landscapes point to their opposites, urbanity and humanity, and especially in the Shi'i iconography to the site and institution of Saqqa-khaneh, or water stations, which has lent its name to the whole artistic movement in Iran. Historically, scattered sites of the Saqqa-khanehs in and out of major and smaller cities and on highways and byways of the country, plus the sanctified sites of famous or obscure Imam-zadeh and Sufi saint mausoleums, were there to map the urban and the distant spaces—as perhaps best evident in Parviz Kalantari's paintings and Bahman Jalali's photography. Kiarostami's landscape photography is entirely in the same visual register.

While in Parviz Kalantari the desert architecture becomes iconic and allegorical, in Bahman Jalali's photography it reaches for the exterior abstractions of the absented interiors—where we know there is life inside but we see none, where we know there is commotion inside but we suspect none from the outside. We are on the abstracted surface side of truth, the quieted suspicion of facts, the strange apparition of reality looking suspiciously familiar, where we know we are in the presence of life but we are not sure how. These roofs are the negative spaces of an otherwise positively blinded vision. We look at them and we feel suspended from somewhere in the heavens looking at a strange apparition of Earth. Parviz Kalantari's abstractions are decidedly nostalgic but in perfectly realistic gestations and gestures. We know we have seen or must have seen these pictures but not quite so—for here fact and fiction, reality and mirage, fuse together to create a sense of factasy at once true and yet strange—unheimlich and yet not so disconcerting. We love to believe in the objects we see but are saddened to see them unreal. All the items and the entire canvas look like Sepehri's poetry—deceptively simple, simply deceptive, and yet still reassuring. They are all parabolic works and they work through visual and poetic parables. The vista of the parabolic here works exactly like Tamsil, or metonymic allusions to truth. Parable as Tamsil etymologically means to tell a story in which something is expressed in terms of something else, from Latin *parabola*, "comparison," from Greek *parabole*, "a comparison," which is exactly what Tamsil also does—it uses something for something else in order to understand it better. We understand an object not because but despite itself. We the beholders of these parables, the wandering pilgrims on these strangely inviting lands, have by now become the unknowing subjects of the world they have vicariously crafted, placed as they are somewhere between *safar* and *hazar*, neither at home nor abroad, feeling fine with the sense of the unheimlich. Parviz Kalantari as a painter and Bahman Jalali as a photographer are the aesthetic sojourners of the same truth Kiarostami has seen in his photography. As a pilgrim artist, he is in Safar and Hazar, Home and Abroad, in their company.

THE INTERIORITY OF THE SACRED

The works of two other artists are crucial here in a more expansive and enabling reading of the Saqqa-khaneh tradition as the aesthetic location of a sense of the unknowing subject beyond the reach of European modernity into which it has been wrongly force-fed either by Pahlavi ideological modernism or else by the colonial Islamism to which it has also fallen prey.[28] Nasser Oveissi and Sadegh Tabrizi are seminal figures in this movement. But how do they expand upon the spectrum of the idea of Saqqa-khaneh? What is missing in the vast exteriority of the landscape in Kalantari, Jalali, and later Kiarostami is overcompensated by the intimate interiority in Oveissi and Tabrizi. The two come together to complement the abstracted infinity of the exterior with the rich intimacy of the interior. The formal citations of the actual Saqqa-khaneh items are here extrapolated into dreamlike textures that give normative substance to that powerful formalism. If the exterior "shots" of Kiarostami, Kalantari, and Jalali open up the vista into infinity, the interior "shots" of Oveissi and Tabrizi detail its totalities. The dialectic that ensues between the infinity of the exterior shots and the totality of the interior shots, to borrow and extrapolate form Levinas's stipulations,[29] completes and authorizes the aesthetic intuition of transcendence in the Saqqa-khaneh movement.

The key issue in both Saqqa-khaneh as a spatial institution and the art movement to which it gives its name is to touch and thus to partake in the sacred—which is exactly the opposite of the aesthetic alienation caused by the condition of modernity, as persuasively detailed and argued by J. M. Bernstein in his seminal work, *The Fate of Art: Aesthetic Alienation from Kant to Derrida and Adorno* (1992)—which I introduced back in chapter 2. In Saqqa-khaneh, we touch the sacred objects, kiss them, and rub our hands on our face to bless it. That is the memory that is invoked in the sacred objects we see in Saqqa-khaneh art. This is exactly the opposite of modern art, where we are not allowed to touch, even in the moment of creativity. As Bernstein puts it, "modern, autonomous art—the art whose forms have become autonomous from the dominion of the metaphysical assumption and orientations of Christian faith—has been expelled from modern societies, from the constitutive, cognitive, and practical mechanisms producing and reproducing societal modernity."[30] Astonishingly aloof and blindsided by such insights, the proposition of Saqqa-khaneh as modern art was a terribly flawed assumption that the Pahlavi court, court-affiliated art critics, and critical observers like Karim Emami entirely innocent of such philosophical discussions had proposed. What has therefore finally come to full fruition in Saqqa-khaneh art is in fact the exact opposite of modern art. In its normative understanding, as

Keshmirshekan puts it, "it was initially applied to the works of artists, both in painting and sculpture, which used already existing elements from votive Shi'i art in their own modern work. It gradually came to be applied more widely to various forms of modern Persian painting and sculpture that used traditional-decorative elements."[31] The word *modern* in this accurate description is entirely misplaced and superfluous and the sentence would make much better sense without it—as is the adjective "decorative." Those "votive" relics were anything but decorative. They are richly invested with meaning and significance, rooted in the historical consciousness and doctrinal history of the faith and now branched out and flowering into a potent contemporary art movement.

We need to be fully cognizant of the source of aesthetic alienation in modern art at the very presumed epicenter of it in order to see the significance of why Saqqa-khaneh is not a modern (or antimodern, for that matter) aesthetic movement. Bernstein traces this alienating effect of aesthetic modernity back to the three *Critiques* of Kant:

> The significance of Kant's work is twofold. On the one hand, it is Kant's third Critique that attempts to generate, to carve out and constitute, the domain of the aesthetic in its wholly modern signification. In securing an autonomous domain of aesthetic judgement, a domain with its own norms, language and set of practices, Kant was simultaneously securing the independence of the domain of cognition and moral worth from aesthetic interference. Following Habermas, I shall argue that the categorical divisions of reason represented by the three Critiques inscribes a theory of modernity through its provision of a categorical understanding of the differences between what have come to be called the language games of knowing, right action and moral worth, and art and aesthetics. Modernity is the separation of spheres, the becoming autonomous of truth, beauty and goodness from one another, and their developing into self-sufficient forms of practice: modern science and technology, private morality modern legal forms, and modern art.[32]

Please note: These are European critical thinkers from Max Weber over Jürgen Habermas to J. M. Bernstein who are offering this cogent critique of aesthetic modernity. These are not reactionary Muslim thinkers (as, for example, Jalal Al-e Ahamd has been abusively read by his political nemeses) who are against modernity and on a goose chase of "their own tradition." Please also note: We have not even thought through this cogent critique of Kant and Habermass and Bernstein from a postcolonial perspective that will doubly question the global predicament of European modernity and the critics of its subject being parroted by ill-informed Iranian art critics to their own colonial conditions. For if we were to pay closer attention to those "language games of knowing" of which Bernstein writes, there is a seismic sea of difference between the colonizers and the colonized as to how these language games are played out. At the receiving end of European colonial modernity, we in the colonial backyards of the European empires were not even agents of any Kantian knowing subjectivities, for as the objects of the European knowing subjects we were only knowable things—just like the minerals under our feet, or the artworks we produced which were being staged as oddities of "European modernity." It was a distinct feature of European colonial modernity to enable and disable at one and the same time—to enable the discursive power of the European subject to gaze and own and rob the world, measure its topography, map its geographies of domination, and "appreciate" the art it looted from around the world, while at the same time to disable the subjects of these colonial possessions from any such claim to agency. It is therefore doubly ironic for an art from anywhere outside Europe to be called "modern" when the very creators of that art were denied any such agential authority to be modern. To be modern was to be white, male, and above all a European whose Christianity was affirmed and concealed as "secular." No Muslim, no Jew, no Hindu, no one could be modern and secular without having willy-nilly converted to Christianity and concealed it as "secularism." But in Iran, all such considerations alas went under the generic rubric of the flawed, muted, and half-baked concept of Al-e Ahmad's "Westoxication" and therefore "antimodernity" and "nativism," which blinded all other insights.[33]

At this point, one cannot have anything but utmost respect and admiration for the pioneering insights of Karim Emami (1930–2005) for having correctly identified an art movement in his time. But time has passed and new works of art are produced and more probing and critical ways of thinking are available to us that may occasion a reconsideration of his insights. Insecure in the theoretical and philosophical disposition of his own time, Emami thought of Saqqa-Khaneh art as a kind of curiosity shop cannibalism, where artists went to pick and choose and salvage some iconic relics without knowing what exactly those relics meant. But this is not what was happening. These artists were not cannibals, walking on the dead bodies and remaining relics of other people's pieties. They were also Muslims, Shi'is more specifically, and of course above all else artists and as such recasting those relics as the allegorical disposition of a whole different register of the sacred certitude of a thriving culture. They may have considered themselves "secular" or "modern" or even "progressive"—all of which are in fact the signature anxieties underlining what they were doing in their artworks.

When Emami coined the expression "Saqqa-khaneh art" in 1962, the actual artworks were about a decade old on the Iranian art scene, which places it between the CIA-MI6 coup of 1953 that had brought the Pahlavis back to power and the first attempt of Ayatollah Khomeini to topple the Pahlavi regime in 1963, which means the historical roots of the Saqqa-khaneh tendency (as Keshmirshekan prefers to call it) was right at a moment when the court-affiliated secular modernism of the Pahlavis and the militant Islamism of Ayatollah Khomeini were at each other's throats. Assimilating the Saqqa-khaneh art either to Pahlavi modernism or militant Shi'ism would be identically flawed. As the faux Pahlavi modernism faced its most serious challenge in the nationalization of the oil industry in the 1950s, militant Shi'ism was categorically repressing its own aesthetic reasons to stage its revolutionary asceticism. In my book *Shi'ism: A Religion of Protest*, I call this "radical and self-alienating split between the politics and aesthetics of the Shi'i critical and creative imagination."[34] The idea of Saqqa-khaneh art therefore emerges right at the moment when the creative force of Shi'ism had parted ways with its militant politics. This is when artists like Zenderoudi and others turned to Shi'i iconographies. Emami was not just innocent of the philosophical roots of modernism and modernity, he was equally unaware of the historical moment of Shi'ism in his own homeland. An entire generation of subsequent art critics followed both his blindness and his insight.

The centrality of the "votive" Shi'i practices as elements of this art must be put back at the epicenter of our reading of this art, collapsing the false distinction between modern and contemporary as we seek a larger aesthetic frame of reference for it. As Keshmirshekan notes, not all the artists usually grouped in this category were happy with the designation, which is a clear indication the creative tension between the ideas of modernity and tradition were already pulling away in both creative and contradictory ways. Citing the late Karim Emami, who had coined the term, Keshmirshekan writes: "These colors, accompanied by black, had made up the collection of Shi'ite mourning colors. As for the choice of the term 'Saqqā-ḵāna,' Emami suggested that a viewer of Zenderoudi's canvases would be reminded of Shi'ite shrines and religious gatherings. Although the spiritual atmosphere conveyed by the paintings was not as religiously sublime, or on such a grand scale as that of some of the finest decorations in Persian mosques, it did convey the air of familiarity and intimacy associated with traditional Saqqā-ḵānas."[35] The Saqqa-khaneh art being short of that religious sublimity, however, could only point to the allegorical allusions of the contemporary to the classical. In hindsight, through the coinage of the term "Saqqa-khaneh art" we can see how that religious sublimity was being recast, re-aestheticized, and updated for a different temporal gestation. Kiarostami's "Roads" a generation later, and as I read them here, would seal that fate.

Three seminal figures in the Saqqa-khaneh tradition came together to give the movement its formal link to Shi'i iconography in calligraphic allusions, figurative archetypes, and talismanic memories. What we see in Hossein Zenderoudi, Faramarz Pilaram, and Parviz Tanavoli is the most potent evidence of formal rootedness in Shi'i iconography being given a contemporary (*Mo'aser*, not Modern) gestation. What is by now quite clear is the effective way in which Shi'i doctrines and traumatic history that had given rise to their political, scholastic, and philosophic dimensions had now found their pronouncedly aesthetic terms—in direct juxtaposition to its naked politicization by militant Shi'ism.[36] Although in the public and institutional domains for at least since the Safavids, these terms were now decidedly bringing to formal consciousness the aesthetic memories of the sacred they had formally sublated. This sublimation was happening on a moral and aesthetic domain somewhere in between the political modernism of the Pahlavi court and the militant Islamism of the opposition to it. In between these two dominant and defiant battlefields pitting the secular modernism of the royal court and the militant Islamism of the opposition, the Saqqa-khaneh artworld was breathing in an entirely different universe. We may even venture to say the trauma of the coup of 1953 had in the Saqqa-khaneh art movement triggered the defining trauma of Shi'ism not in boldly political but in decidedly potent and mediative aesthetic terms—rooted in the artistic sublimity of much earlier Shi'i artifacts from mosque and mausoleum architectures to manuscript illustrations. The centrality of the figure of the pilgrim as the unknowing subject of this art, at home both in safar and hazar, homebound or outbound, detailed how the interiority of the sacred had by now become the site of not a "modern" or "traditional" subjectivity but of a potently nomadic disposition—the unknowing subject as a pilgrim to realms of knowing without staying anywhere in particular, giving a new twist to the famous prophetic hadith: "Seek knowledge even in China!" Kiarostami's "Roads" maps the topography of that pilgrimage.

THE REDEMPTIVE POLITICS OF A POST-ISLAMIST LIBERATION AESTHETIC

The accuracy of the term "Saqqa-khaneh art" is as much apt as its forced designation with "modern" is dubious and distorting. As Keshmirshekan writes: "One of the main founders of the School, the sculptor Tanavoli, describes how he and Zenderoudi became fascinated in the late 1950s by printed posters depicting religious scenes, talismanic seals, and pictorial forms in the south of Tehran, while they searched for local Iranian raw material to be used and developed in their works."[37] These relics may have appeared as "raw material" to a generation of artists in search of their own idiomaticities. But that "raw material" was the remnants and relics of an overwhelming sacred aesthetics in which they breathed. Keshmirshekan's judicious and insightful reading is at its best when he writes: "Saqqā-ḵāna artists looked to cults, rituals, and visual elements of folk and local vernacular culture for inspiration. . . . Viewed from this perspective, Saqqā-ḵāna artists could be in fact considered successors to Iranian craftsmen of earlier centuries—miniaturist, illuminators, calligraphers, and goldsmiths." He is, however, on shakier grounds when he writes: "In the view of the above-mentioned modern artists however, these roots had to be linked to modern styles and fused to create a distinctly national artistic expression."[38] The first part of this description is by far the most potent understanding of the genre that places it within the larger frame of reference going back to the Qajar and Safavid periods. The rush to wed this movement to "Iranian modernism," however, or alternative modernities or else the interplay between tradition and modernity is symptomatic of a Pahlavi-period obsession with European modernity that many art historians of the period, some affiliated with the Pahlavi court, exacerbated. Some art historians were too much in a rush to compare it with, for example, the "Pop Art movement in the West," which is of course entirely flawed but obviously indicative of the Pahlavi court-affiliated art critics and their proclivities to assimilate the Saqqa-khaneh art movement to the "West" of their colonized imagination.

The key issue is how the Pahlavi court had sought to appropriate this movement into the ideological apparatus of its monarchy, as Keshmirshekan points out, "as the major sponsors of artistic activities at that time, the governmental cultural departments tried to establish, through patronage of individual artists and movements, a 'formal art' that would form the basis of a sort of national school of art." This priceless insight has paved the way for my critical observations here. Keshmirshekan further elaborates:

> The state's sponsorship, support from other institutions such as the Iran-America and the Iran-Italy Cultural Association . . . making links with international associations, employing some foreign instructors, and transformation of the old educational curriculum to a modern one, all had combined to help modern Iranian visual arts to become, like modern Persian poetry, a significant entity in the cultural life of the country. Like modern poetry, it was basically an urban art and limited to the middle classes. But in contrast to modern poetry, visual arts benefited from extensive state support. Gradually, many government institutions and private companies became patrons of modern art; in particular one can name the Farah Pahlavi Foundation. Others, including Ministries, National Iranian Radio Television, banks, corporations led by the Behshahr Industrial group, the Lajevardi Foundation, and the Prime Minister, Amir Abbas Hoveyda, were all effectively patronizing visual arts.[39]

If we were to subtract that ideological force which had through its critical apparatus been represented by court-affiliated art critics and consider the fact that the movement had already peaked and plateaued before the Islamic Republic could twist it to its own uses, we are left with a body of evidence that neither Pahlavi modernism nor Islamic Republic traditionalism could abuse. We will then be facing a body of aesthetic force that demands a renewed reading on the global stage where Kiarostami is already located.

Freed and liberated from that faux modernism, the Saqqa-khaneh art movement has now more breathing ground beyond the overthrown Pahlavi regime and the discredited Islamic Republic—appearing as a national art event. With the complementary works of Azadeh Akhlaghi and Siah Armajani, the redemptive power of the Karbala Complex comes back to recast the idea of Saqqa-khaneh into a larger sacred memory. As one of the earliest members of the Saqqa-khaneh movement, Siah Armajani eventually left Iran and became a key figure in American public art. In the early 2000s, soon after the US invasion and occupation of first Afghanistan and then Iraq, Armajani's sculptural work became increasingly and openly political. *Fallujah* (2004–2005), for example, was a major antiwar monument. While allusions to Picasso's *Guernica* (1937) are suggested in this work, the piece is more accurately read as a reference back to his own earliest involvement with the Saqqa-khaneh tradition. Equally important is his series *Seven Rooms of Hospitality* (2015) where he addresses issues of refugees and migrants. What we are witnessing here is the Shi'i ritual of redemptive suffering and battle for justice making an appearance in a faraway land, where the iconic phrase "*Kull Yawm Ashura wa Kull Ard Karbala*/Every day is Ashura and every land is Karbala" has assumed a renewed significance.

Meanwhile, Azadeh Akhlaghi's work is almost obsessively fixated on the traumatic moments of contemporary Iranian history with martyrdom and sacrifice as its major leitmotif. In a series of staged photography, she has recreated the most traumatic deaths of our history—from Mirzadeh Eshqi to Gholamreza Takhti over revolutionary guerrillas fighting against the Pahlavi dynasty and heroic soldiers defending Iran against Saddam Hussein to Sohrab Shahid Sales—with herself always appearing somewhere in the corner of the picture as the mourning simulacrum of Zeinab, the sister of Imam Hossein. This is Saqqa-khaneh art galore if we were to allow the genre to breathe in fresher and more robust air.

At the same time, Amir Naderi has carried the moral imaginary of the genre to New York City and given it an urban twist with his city photography. In this series of photographs we curated and exhibited at La Maison Française on the Columbia campus in 2003, Naderi turns to the traumatic moments of urban life in New York City with a series of photographs he made as collages and staged from the street fliers in downtown Manhattan. The profound sense of urban anomie and anxiety carries the implications of the moral imaginary of the Saqqa-khaneh art into fresher domains.

The same traces of Saqqa-khaneh art formed entirely outside Iran are of course the early work of Shirin Neshat—with its powerful invocation of Shi'i iconography. Putting women at the epicenter of her consistently iconic artwork, she invoked themes of Shi'i pieties mirroring the earliest stages of the movement in the works of Tanavoli and Pilaram. Her black-and-white photography formally went back upstream from the specifics of the Saqqa-khaneh artists and crafted a whole new register for the genre. With Nikzad Nodjoumi the genre received its most potent ironic twist where the clerical figures of power and authority are staged in obscene and subversive versions. Nodjoumi's canvases could have only assumed this bold and powerful sharpness far away from Iran. But the degeneration of Shi'i political powers into political chicaneries could have only come out from under his ruthless brushes. On these canvases, what we are seeing is the sharper edge of the aesthetic of emancipation always embedded in the Saqqa-khaneh art going against the morally depleted clerical order.

With Shoja Azari, Karbala themes and Saqqa-khaneh tradition assumed decidedly subversive tones in New York City. In a series of drawings and video intellections he did at Leila Heller Gallery in New York City in 2010, he becomes purposefully provocative, subversive, and iconoclastic. Here he takes the iconic representations of the Karbala event and gives them homoerotic twists while keeping the allegorical formations of the icons intact.

The nomadic subject—evident in Kiarostami's roads; Bahman Jalali's and Parviz Kalantari's deserts; Oveissi's, Pilaram's, and Tanavoli's idyllic oases; and travels abroad in Amir Naderi's tactile urban nomadism in his New York photography—comes home to Azadeh Akhlaghi's traumatized memories; goes public in Siah Armajani's redemptive recollections, and in

Shirin Neshat, Nikzad Nodjoumi, and Shoja Azari's extraterritorial meditations to aesthetic and ironic twists; and then reaches a crescendo in the most recent work of Farshid Mesqali where a cosmic order as marked by Omar Khayyam has embraced the entirety of the artistic event. By now we can confidently think of Saqqa-khaneh as a national art movement so epistemically rich and fruitful that it has never been limited to a Pahlavi court modernism, the depleted Shi'i clericalism of the ruling Islamist regime, or the vagaries of diasporic art scenes.

Put together, the trajectory of *ziarat*/pilgrimage, as the implicit site of Saqqa-khaneh art, begins with the deserted roads that take the pilgrim to the site of the resurrected mausolea and forms the subconscious domain of our sublated sacred imagination into a nomadic subjectivity. The stage of Ta'ziyeh, to which Kiarostami and many other contemporary filmmakers like Bahram Beiza'i were drawn as beholders and performers, is where this road comes to a nomadic station. At the site of the Saqqa-khaneh, the nomadic subject pauses for a drink in the memory of the thirsty lips of Imam Hossein and there and then is witness to a mimetic semiosis of the Karbala Complex where our misplaced pieties announce the semblance of a subjectivity we did not know we had. That mimetic semiosis enables a secondary mimesis as witness in the Saqqa-khaneh art where repressed and resurrected aesthetics stand in lieu of the repressed and yet-to-be-revealed theologies. That purgatorial pilgrimage passage announces the post-Islamist and postmodernist theologies to which this iconography has already announced and declared the ends of both the political Islamism and the colonial modernism that had sought to take political advantage of it. The pilgrim as the unknowing subject has now overcome both safar and hazar, being equally at home and away from home, where the interiority of the sacred has been internalized, and where the redemptive politics of a post-Islamist and postmodernist liberation aesthetic has defiantly declared itself.

PLEASE TOUCH: THE BEAUTY OF THE RELEVANT

Let us now bring an even richer aesthetic theory to the Saqqa-khaneh art as a self-transcendentalized national art consciousness—to which Kiarostami's landscape photography added a definitive twist.

A major contribution of Hans Georg Gadamer's hermeneutic engagement with art is his key and perhaps even counterintuitive contention that the task of the aesthetics is not to distance us from the work of art but quite to the contrary to bring us back into the work of art and through that entanglement help us understand the nature of truth. We do not understand the work of art if we put it on a pedestal and do not just physically but even mentally touch it. We understand it by allowing it to touch and thus to transform our understanding of truth. Only by allowing a work of art to touch us do we understand how it reveals truth. Gadamer's hermeneutical aesthetics therefore is rooted in an active involvement with the work of art rather than a distant appreciation of it. Gadamer's major essay, "The Relevance of the Beautiful" (1977), is an extensive examination of this proposition.[40] One of the key points he makes in this essay is the following:

> The essence of the beautiful does not lie in some realm simply opposed to reality. On the contrary, we learn that however unexpected our encounter with beauty may be, it gives us an assurance that the truth does not lie far off and inaccessible to us, but can be encountered in the disorder of reality with all its imperfections, evils, errors, extremes, and fateful confusions. The ontological function of the beautiful is to bridge the chasm between the ideal and the real.[41]

This is the quintessence of the work of art being rooted in the lived historical experiences of its creators and its audiences without the ideological interference of people in position of power to claim, appropriate, and abuse it. Central to Gadamer's argument is the metaphoric significance of "touching" the work of art, for it is by touching it, and allowing it therefore to touch us in return, that we get to understand the work of art. This is something of a contradictory metaphor, for in current museums and galleries we are not allowed to touch the work of art, and in fact a physical barrier like a rope or a line supervised by a guard in semi-military uniform guarantees that we go nowhere near the work of art and appreciate and admire it from a physical distance. This is in marked contrast to places like mosques and mausolea in the Muslim world (particularly in Iran and other Shi'i countries) where we are in fact required and encouraged to touch the icons that are believed to have a certain talismanic power only when they are touched by humans.[42] Saqqa-khaneh art is the sublime art of touching. Saqqa-khanehs themselves, the water stations ritually decorated with various talismanic objects, are one such site where touching of the iconic objects takes place and in fact the entire artistic movement in contemporary Iranian art is named after this Saqqa-khaneh premise. Here we are required not just to touch but in fact to kiss the talismanic object, for touching and kissing it seemingly awakens their talismanic power of blessing the pilgrim who has traveled from afar precisely for this physical encounter. Drinking the blessed water on that premise—thus the name "water station"—is further indication of ingesting the sacred in a totemic gesture.

If we were to take Gadamer's insight in his seminal essay but reverse his hermeneutic point of departure about the relevance of the beautiful in revealing truth by seeing how what is relevant to a people, a culture, a community, becomes beautiful. We must begin this reflection by first and foremost locating the works of art outside the European aesthetic and hermeneutic imagination on the periphery of their vision, as indeed we do Gadamer's insights themselves, and then take this peripheral vision as the theoretic thrust into the distorting imbalance of the presumed European center and the global periphery it engenders and seek to correct it by peripheralizing the self-centering "Europe"—itself the most talismanic object of desire we are not allowed to touch or travel into but only admire and revere from a distance. By critically distancing ourselves from the troubled domain of European modernity, and taking the inaugural moments of the Saqqa-khaneh art movement seriously, actively severing its false implications into a colonial modernity it could never claim, we would be in a position to cast a wider net when thinking of the larger implications of the return of the sacred, which art critics like Karim Emami were too enamored by the Pahlavi era project of modernity and too much in the light of their own secularity to see.

To see that liberating prospect, we must dwell on moments when the photography of an artist like Abbas Kiarostami begins with prosaic details and then eventually dissolves itself into pure abstraction, as both the substance and the summation of Saqqa-khaneh aesthetics of space and object, just like Bahman Jalali and Parviz Kalantari in the exteriorities of that pilgrimage route, as interior meditations are the simulacrum of the rich interiorities of

Nasser Oveissi or Sadegh Tabrizi. Opening up the frame of that interiority, we reach out to a different exteriority that is evident in the triangulation of the sacred as the simulacrum of truth. By the time we see Kiarostami's roads as those pilgrim routes and byways, the pilgrim as the unknowing subject has brought the condition of safar and hazar together, being at home in the world, where the interiority of the sacred has mapped out the redemptive politics of both a post-Islamist and a postmodernist liberation aesthetic that has invited the world to join this pilgrimage and encourages us to please touch the objects where once again we see the relevance of the beautiful but far more importantly attend to the beauty of the relevant.

The Saqqa-khaneh movement was the most potent artistic event of mid-twentieth-century Iran when artists and filmmakers like Abbas Kiarostami were entering the scene and coming to fruition. The movement was rooted in Iranian and Islamic (Shi'a) sensibilities and yet in collective communion with the temporal tenor of its postcolonial time. The turn to the iconographic elements in Shi'i aesthetic heritage was not "decorative," as sometimes it was falsely called, or nostalgic as it may appear. It was iconic, talismanic, and richly allegorical. Karim Emami, who first noticed the talismanic forces of that art and wisely identified it as rooted in the Saqqa-khaneh, was not fully aware of what appeared to him as a secular moment and therefore "decorative," for he was entirely innocent of the rising iconic, archaic, and therefore allegorical rootedness of the practice. What appeared in the collective works of Saqqa-khaneh artists were remnants and relics, as Walter Benjamin would say, of once-edifices of a people's faith, and as such had assumed full allegorical power to redefine a postcolonial world. Before they were categorized as such by Emami, the artists themselves knew intuitively what they were doing when they turned to these iconic elements, for as Shi'i children they had deep affections and enduring affinity with and for these items. They were not theorizing an art movement—they were playing with those relics, touching them, as it were, for they could see the beauty of their relevance, in which they had now detected the relevance of their beauty. Kiarostami's landscape photography maps the pilgrimage routes and the fulfilled promises of their collective sacred memories—as the aesthetic formation of a nomadic subject finally discovers the newly knowable world from which no one and nothing can alienate it.

Conclusion

WHEN THE EARTH IS SHAKEN AND PEOPLE
WONDER WHY

Dar Nazar bazi-ye ma bi-khabaran heyranand ...

The way we playfully see things
Bewilders those who are unaware—
This is the way I am, they can
Do as they wish—
Philosophers are the focal point of the compass of existence
But only love knows how lost they are in this circle.[1]

Hafez

As I make clear from the outset of this book, any articulation of a postcolonial film-philosophy specific to the site of Abbas Kiarostami's artworld has to begin with the clear understanding of an interface between two complementary forces: (1) the transnational public sphere upon which his artworld and now his legacy have been staged, received, and interpreted; and (2) the postcolonial persona that stands in front of that stage trying to make head from tail of Kiarostami's artworks, very much like those proverbial migrant birds facing themselves in Attar's allegorical mirror. The idea of Kiarostami's cinema and artworld as a simulacrum of Attar's iconic mirror and we humans watching ourselves in the mirror of that otherwise invisible world is not just to introduce a potent alternative to the Platonic cave as a metaphor for cinema. The idea of the postcolonial un/knowing subject as an itinerant, mobile, and nomadic pilgrim is definitive to the way I have sought to read and see and show Kiarostami's camera as the unseen seer of the world otherwise too close to us for us to see. Now I wish to bring the idea of Kiarostami's camera as the unseen seer to a final conclusion.

KIAROSTAMI'S CAMERA AS THE UNSEEN SEER

You recall in chapter 3 I cited the moment when in his conversation with the French philosopher Jean-Luc Nancy, Abbas Kiarostami suddenly recites the original Arabic of the Surah Al-Zalzalah/The Earthquake from the Qur'an.[2] He further adds he has always been fascinated by this chapter. Let us revisit that chapter, for what neither of them address in the published record of that interview is the fact that at the end of this iconic chapter of the Qur'an, the word *seeing* appears twice—here is the full English translation of the chapter (Surah 99: Az-Zalzalah/The Earthquake):

> In the name of Allah, Most Gracious, Most Merciful.
>
> 1. When the earth will be shaken with utmost force.
> 2. And the earth will throw up her burden,
> 3. And man will say: "What has happened to her,"
> 4. On that Day she will relate her chronicles
> 5. Because your Lord will have given her the command.
> 6. On that Day people will proceed in different groups to be shown the deeds that they had done.
> 7. Then whosoever has done an atom's weight of good will see it,
> 8. And whosoever has done an atom's weight of evil, will see it.

As attested by the twelfth-century Qur'anic commentator Shaykh Abu al-Futuh al-Razi (circa 1077–1161), among many other commentators, this chapter is a description of the Day of Judgment according to Muslim belief—when the earth will be turned upside down and we the mortals will have to face our Creator and see the result of our deeds on this earth.[3] But what exactly is it that we will see—whether we have done good or ill in this world? The Qur'an specifically cites the moment of physically seeing, when we see the consequences of what we have done—seeing good things if we have done good and seeing bad things if we have done badly. So, "seeing" here implies rewards and punishment too—meaning there is a moral and ethical dimension to seeing. The text of the Qur'an therefore cites visions of the yet invisible. This visuality is predicated on what Razi cites previous commentators having said on this day the earth will speak of what has happened to it ("On that Day she will relate her chronicles"), meaning what we humans have done to it. In other words, our humanity is placed in a post-anthropocentric frame of reference—where the earth independent of us and under Divine command relates her stories. We will have witness to our deeds—which is the earth. The chapter of the Qur'an that Kiarostami cites, and says is his most favorite, is where the vision of yet invisible things has assumed moral, ethical, and metaphysical presence.

What was Kiarostami doing citing the Qur'an to the French philosopher, who in turn asks him if he knows the whole Qur'an by heart (quite a cliché question), to which Kiarostami says no? Kiarostami's generation of artists, poets, dramatists, and filmmakers had a concealed and convoluted encounter with their ancestral faith, and it had equally sublimated the Qur'an in the poetic prose of their own temporal idiomaticity. What does that mean and how does it work? The whole Saqqa-khaneh movement in contemporary art, as I argued in the previous chapter, was a subterfuge for coming close to the sacred sanctity of their faith through a multifaceted aesthetic gesture. By this time, Islam as a world religion had become too familiar, not just too political in a vulgar sense. The inner sanctum of Islam as a vast civilizational spectrum was now renewing itself in echoes and shimmers. There were a number of significant signposts that marked Kiarostami's generational encounter with the sublimated sacred. Forough Farrokhzad's iconic "Kasi key Mesl-e Hich Kas Nist/Someone Who Is Like No One" had cast in a delightful poem with a teenage girl as its narrator the expectation of the coming of the Mahdi. Ahamd Shamlou in his equally important poem "Ebrahim dar Atash/Abraham in Fire" opted for the biblical/Qur'anic figure of Abraham as a prototype of revolutionary heroes. The centrality of the figure of Zarathustra in Mehdi Akhavan-e Sales's poetry had given it a particularly potent prophetic dimension. Sohrab Sepehri's sublime stanza, "I am a Muslim," in his iconic poem "The Sound of the Footstep of Water," which I have cited earlier, was chief among some of the major signposts of this renewed encounter with the sacred—Islam, Judaism, Christianity, Zoroastrianism, et cetera.

On multiple occasions in the past, I have discussed in detail the centrality of the visual and performing arts in the moral imagination of Shi'ism. In my essay on Surah Yousef, I have discussed in detail the repressed visuality as a potent hermeneutic mechanism in reading the Qur'an.[4] In my extensive writing on the early work of Shirin Neshat, I have demonstrated the way her work reveals that repressed visuality.[5] I have also cited earlier my discussion of the split between Shi'i revolutionary politics and its repressed aesthetic imagination, for which Kiarostami's artworld becomes a key factor. Central to all these discussions is to see how in Islamic aesthetics seeing entails the in/visibility of God, as I have had occasions to refer to Attar's allegory of *Conference of the Birds* and the specific sections in Nezami's poetry where he discusses Mi'raj—the prophet's nocturnal journey to the heavens. The point being: Kiarostami remembering a verse of the Qur'an that perhaps best corresponded to his Koker Trilogy which is also about an earthquake is part and parcel of a larger frame of reference in the contemporary Iranian art scene of which both he and the French philosopher may not have been fully aware.

This preoccupation with vision, visuality, and a potent ocularcentrism in Persianate, Iranian, and Islamic contexts remains steady.[6] From the time of its Qur'anic references through its poetic gestations in a wide spectrum of poets from Nezami to Omar Khayyam, we finally get to Hafez. The central concept of vision, visuality, and perception transmutes into a cornerstone of his poetry, which he calls *Nazar-bazi*—as in the hemistich "*Dar nazar-bazi-ye ma bi-khabaran heyranand.*" Here I have opted for the phrase "playfully seeing things" for "nazar-bazi" precisely because of the impossibility of translating this crucial word—which begins with having flirtatious looks at an object of desire, such as a beautiful face, which is here reminiscent of the Divine Beauty, but from there extends to moral, aesthetic, and philosophical speculation as to how to see, imagine, and envision things. All these connotations are embedded in the realm of Nazar-bazi—a mystical vision of truth in the material evidence of a beautiful face. From Nezami to Hafez, constant remains this preoccupation with the in/visibility of the transcendental signifier. To meditate on this in/visibility becomes the condition of the formation of the semblant subject. We become a semblant subject by virtue of seeing something that stands for something else, something sublime, and yet that sublimity is present in this material evidence we behold.

As I had an earlier occasion to detail this in chapter 1, here I wish to take the argument in a different direction. In Islamic theology this Transcendental Signifier becomes the quintessential attribute of God as the Unmoved Mover and the Unseen Seer or, as Avicenna termed it, "*Wajib al-Wujud*/Necessary Being"—which in subsequent theological rationalism amounts to the logical necessity of the Divine Being. Avicenna had divided beings into *Wajib*/Necessary, *Mumkin*/Possible, and *Mumtani'*/Impossible Beings. The possible is everything that can be but needs a necessary being to make it possible, like a carpenter to a desk. Impossible things are logical impossibilities. If we put a succession of possible and necessary beings together, we finally get to the Transcendental Necessary Being.[7] The transcendental necessary being therefore becomes the unseen seer—the invisible whose absence is for Avicenna logically impossible. This position is further verified by the Qur'anic passage that "vision perceives Him not, but He perceives [all] vision; and He is the All-Subtle, the All-Aware" (Qur'an 6:103).

In a potent streak of Islamic philosophy, the Avicennan or Peripatetic, as we technically call it, and from there to the best of Persian poetry, the dialectic between seeing and not seeing becomes definitive to the metaphysical ocularcentrism of the aesthetic culture from which knowingly or unknowingly contemporary artists like Kiarostami have been nourished. If we were to take a quick detour to Derrida and read his *Grammatology* with an Avicennan eye, we see his conception of logocentrism as the metaphysics of presence that is animated by the necessity of a center (that would be Avicenna's Wajib al-Wujud) which is presumed permanent and which sustains the structure of all other significations.[8] Derrida considered this center the "transcendental signified" (or *primum signatum*) for all other signifiers emanate from it, which is itself beyond signification—which in Avicennan terms we call the transcendental signifier, or Wajib al-Wujud, or the Unseen Seer, in a Derridean semiotic twist to Avicenna's metaphysics—which brings the semiotics of the proposition more vividly forward.

Put together, we might consider this Unseen Seer, or the Transcendental Signified, dwelling at the center of Kiarostami's artworld as an aesthetic transfiguration of the Divine In/Visibility, which in Islamic theological terms becomes the transcendental signifier. In his artworld in general and his cinema in particular, Kiarostami always points to that transcendental signifier without naming, showing, or even consciously knowing it. The irreducible mobility of the itinerant knowing subject it thereby implicates is a hidden desire for a "reassuring certitude" in the face of a certain dissolution of all other worldly signifiers. This transcendental signifier is the aesthetic sublimation of the internalized Other that is the subterfuge for that In/Visible Divinity that cannot be named or shown or seen. Beginning with *Where Is the Friend's House?*, the Koker trilogy becomes a search for that Unseen Seer, that Transcendental Signified, which in *Taste of Cherry* assumes the guise of a search for death. Thereafter, *Where Is the Friend's House?* becomes the abode of semblance and the missing friend the sublime allusion to God as Friend—a common allusion in Persian Sufi literature. Kiarostami's cinema itself becomes an aesthetic theology in a post-Islamist world, or a subdued theodicy in search of an always already absented, transcendental signifier. Is this what Jean-Luc Nancy and other French admirers of Kiarostami have intuited in his cinema but been unable to articulate—caught in the postmetaphysical conundrum of their own "crisis of the subject?" Perhaps.

We have no way of knowing the extent to which Kiarostami knew or cared to know about the Qur'an. Even closer to his profession in the same interview, he also confesses to Nancy he does not know much about Persian Negargari or the so-called miniature painting. But we know for a fact of his fascination and close proximities to the three towering Persian poets—Rumi, Sa'di, and Hafez. No artist is ever fully conscious of their aesthetic and metaphysical frames of conscious or unconscious references (which is the way it should be), and always the intentions of their texts supersede their own authorial intentions. The dialectic of seeing and unseeing, what to show and what to hide, most evident in Kiarostami, is the replication of the In/Visibility of the transcendental signifier. Mr. Badii (Homayoun Ershadi) in *Taste of Cherry* is not looking for someone to cover his grave when he commits suicide—but for someone to tell him what his life is all about. The entire winding search of Badii through *Taste of Cherry*, as indeed Kiarostami's more general fascination with winding roads, is a desperate but still graceful search for meaning, for this dizzying succession of days and nights seemingly with no ends to have a purpose.

REFRAMING THE SUBJECT

These metaphysical, theological, and epistemic foregroundings of Kiarostami's camera as the unseen seer and the dialectics between seeing and not seeing it implies has provided an extraordinary visual evidence that long precedes him and that has happily reached us. There is a painting by the exquisite Qajar-era figurative artist Abu al-Hasan Sani' al-Molk (1814–1866) that stages a bold and provocative crosscurrent of gazing that deeply complicates our viewing of it. The subject of this painting is not clear.[9] There are suggestions that perhaps a state edict is being read by a member of the court chancellery to members of the clergy. Prominent in the picture is the name of the artist and the date of the work: Abol-Hassan Naqqashbashi Ghaffari 1261/1845. Whatever the subject or the occasion of the painting might be, the visual mise-en-scène and structure of the painting is important for my argument for here we see a group of spectators watching a seated man, perhaps a storyteller, perhaps an official reciting a proclamation—watching and listening to him. Even behind the central figure, whose back is to us, there are seated men whose gaze is downcast and who are not looking at him for they are facing his back anyway. But our own perspective that the artist has enabled is to see this whole spectacle from a point of view that transcends the event in the picture. The whole event is framed by a green curtain—as if in a playhouse or an opera house or a movie theater. This could very well be a coffee house, a state reception—or else an entirely fictive space. But what makes it exceptionally bold and brilliant is the POV that the artist has given to his spectator—to us: to see both the storyteller and his audiences together—from a vantage point that the central figure could and also could not see. This is an astoundingly complicated perspective for its age or any other age. But we must not rush to call it "modern"—despite the fact that the artist did spend some time in Europe. It is what it is and it complicates our perception of the periodization of Iranian art for it effectively places us—the spectator—inside the picture by vicariously identifying with the central seated figure whose back is to us (his spectators) and thus mimics our own encounter with the work. In this context, the face of that central figure with his back to us becomes the primogeniture and the simulacrum of Kiarostami's camera, the unseen seer.

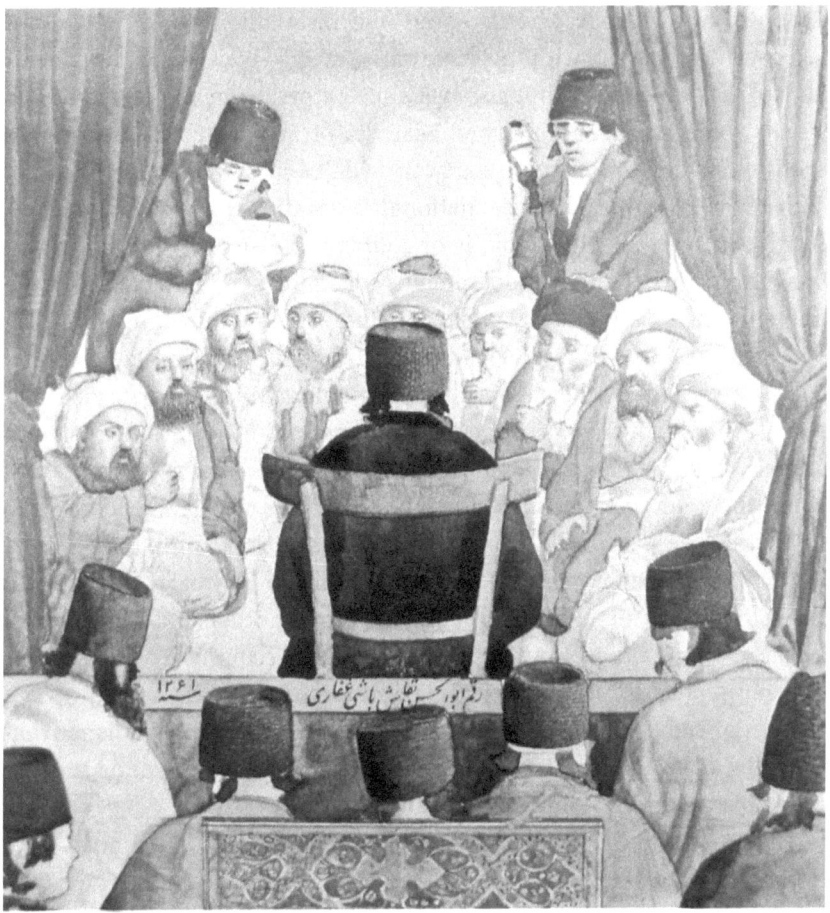

Figure 19. Abol-Hassan Naqqashbashi Ghaffari, "Untitled" (1845). Watercolor and ink on paper, 12.5 × 13.5 cm. Private collection, Italy. Public domain.

Now a jump-cut from Sani' al-Molk to Kiarostami: In May–June 2005, the Victoria and Albert Museum exhibited a work by Kiarostami he called "Forests without Leaves." It consisted of turning one of the galleries of the museum into a "forest" made up of hollow tubes covered by life-size photographs of bark. By way of an explanation, Kiarostami was quoted as having said "we have lost the ability to look at nature in natural surroundings and that it is only when an item is 'framed' and then placed in an artificial or museum environment, that we observe it in detail."[10]

Throughout his filmic, photographic, and installation work, Kiarostami has been preoccupied with this issue of "framing"—which is applicable not just to his own lenswork but also to his spectators. In how many frames do we see, understand, and interpret Kiarostami? Among all the varieties of framing in which Kiarostami's artworld can be located, within the metaphor of the Borromean rings of national, postnational, and world cinemas I proposed early in this book, is of course the history of Persian visual imagination, where his camera remains constant as the simulacrum of the unseen seer. This Iranian context should not be the only frame of reference, for the world at large, including Europe, has a legitimate claim on Kiarostami. But neither should this Iranian frame be disregarded and repressed. Without his Iranian context, his artworld becomes vacuous and generic. Without his global context, it becomes local and provincial. If we stage him where he actually was in the world, we will have extended the aesthetic imagination at the heart of his cinema deeply into a poetic, literary, and visual heritage that is beyond the reach of any particular ring on that Borromean metaphor, European, Iranian, or otherwise. That agonistic disposition of those contexts and that history requires a different kind of seeing—both deeply theoretical and yet beyond the bounds of European, or even multiple and alternative, "modernities." The global audience that has been offered Kiarostami has enabled us to excavate a different aesthetic historiography for his artworld.

Predicated on the premise of that Borromean rings metaphor I have suggested in this book, I have put forward the idea that Iranian cinema has always been at home in the world—while the condition of coloniality has been the defining moment of this location. The point of the argument here is to make sure we fully understand that the world, too, was at home in Iranian cinema, and therefore when Abbas Kiarostami entered the global stage, the close-ups, the long shots, and the cuts he staged were all on familiar grounds. These first steps were preparatory to thinking through the prospects of a postcolonial film-philosophy that was tailormade for Abbas Kiarostami as a floating signifier, predicated on the fact that he was always somewhere else—both in his artworld and in the ways he was received on multiple platforms. My review of the state of the art in Kiarostami scholarship paved the way toward a reading of where we might locate his legacy, for which I introduced the idea of the mirror of the invisible world if we were to turn to the wide spectrum of imaginative imageries in Persian poetic legacies. All this I proposed by way of revisioning the world anew as the sign, signature, and significance of an intuition of transcendence that would be the philosophical foregrounding of Kiarostami's cinema.

Central to Kiarostami's cinema, I have argued throughout this book, is his collapsing of form and fact, through which he has managed to alter the nature of reality as we perceive it, which he has perhaps best put to the test in his *Taste of Cherry* where the Verfremdungseffekt at the end of the film works as Being-toward-Death. This meditation on Being-toward-Death then underlies his overriding poetic ontology of Being Un/Real, which I have proposed as a mode of repressed aesthetics of a decidedly post-Islamist disposition—a poetics that is rooted in the vast body of the literature on Divine in/visibility. If we therefore approach the prospects of aesthetic alienation as the self-centering blind spot of his artworld, we witness the political duress under which the proposition of "comparative modernities" reveals and discredits itself. The case I have consistently made against colonial modernity, or its reflections in the ideas of alternative modernities, leads us to positing a mode of aesthetic contemporaneity that is an alternative to colonially mediated self-alienation, which I have proposed in Kiarostami is evident in his creative substitution of allegories over categories. The fusion of Reason/Unreason or Fact/Fiction that results perforce leads to the moment of the poetic "Now," or the palimpsest and pentimento of the "Now" where his artworld overcomes that alienation. Located somewhere between aesthetic and nonaesthetic reasons, Kiarostami emerges as a catalyst of aesthetic subjectivity, to which his Iranian critics have been blindsided by an animated animosity, which is not compensated by many of his French admirers but must be traced as I have proposed to the poetry of Sohrab Sepehri to overcome that sense of alienation.

DECOLONIZING THE UNKNOWING SUBJECT

My pivot toward the discovery and articulation of the unknowing (nomadic) subject in this book is predicated on an agonistic philosophical heritage that allows me to map the aesthetic sovereignty of this subject which drives the foreign familiarity of the world toward a rereading of reality. This proposition was made possible by seeing how Kiarostami's cinema was complicating his foreign admirers' view of Iran, while he had also remained a stranger at home. The foreign familiarities at the heart of the sense of "Ostranenie," definitive to Kiarostami's cinema "Itself," works through the fictive transparency of the real that had paved the way toward the crafting of a new Adam and Eve in his *Through the Olive Trees* and the aesthetic revolution it had occasioned. By now I was prepared to work my way through a thorough critique of the postcolonial aesthetic judgment, where we can dare to know, sapere aude, in our own terms, for by now anthropocentrism as Eurocentrism is fully exposed. By fabling the world, Kiarostami had made it possible for a mobile, itinerant, and nomadic (or what I called "pilgrim") un/knowing subject to emerge in the interstitial space where a posthuman agency allowed for the surfacing of a semblance of subjectivity undetected before. The semblant subject had made it possible for me to place Ozu's camera in Kiarostami's hands, as it were, and see how through elements of darkness, reverse angle, counterfeit, and make-believe in his final films he had allowed for the aesthetic formation of a nomadic pilgrim subject. By now the temporal tenor of the sacred was the premise of the pilgrim as the un/knowing subject to rise and work itself through the ascetic lenswork against a whole widespread political project of state-sponsored modernity. Kiarostami and his fellow travelers, artists of multiple adjacent generations, in Safar and Hazar/Home and Abroad, were the architects of the exteriorities and interiorities of the sacred forming a redemptive politics of a post-Islamist liberation aesthetics.

My articulation of the ipso facto decolonized postcolonial subject I have designated as "un/knowing" positions the critical thinker as theorist on the borderline of a fictive frontier colonially manufactured between the East and the West I have long since happily trespassed. The pilgrim subject by definition cannot sport a "double consciousness" for they have always already crossed both stationary loci of any critical consciousness. The prose, prosody, and politics of writing this book on Kiarostami's film-philosophy has been an evident exercise in the ease with which the nomadic subject moves from the Persianate to the Europeanized world of theory, aesthetics, and philosophy. The very idea of "philosophy" is today up for grabs, film-philosophy in particular, and Kiarostami's artworld is precisely where this claim comes to rest its case. Neither Eurocentric nor nativist, this decolonized postcolonial subject has been happily roaming through its unknowing subjectivities. There was a time I thought of this stage through the lenses of "colonial modernity," which we had unknowingly and uncritically received entirely unbeknownst to ourselves. But now through Kiarostami's artworld, critically retrieved, I believe we have crossed that border between coloniality and modernity. A decolonized mind trespasses the alienating forces of such boundaries where the idea of pointing out the dark side of European modernity (Mignolo) or provincializing it (Chakrabarty) through a liberation philosophy (Dussel) have done their respective services and propelled us to move forward.

Thus anchored, Kiarostami's cinema and artworld have created a dialectically contentious transnational public sphere—for and against itself—from which a postcolonial unknowing subject would emerge facing a knowable world by virtue of its rootedness in that public sphere. Much of the existing bodies of literature on Kiarostami are by and large unaware of one another—creating a cacophonous dissonance, sometimes antagonistic but mostly agonistic. When the two sides are brought together, a mobile, nomadic subject is enabled and envisioned that now resides in Kiarostami's artworld: neither domestic nor foreign but ipso facto a transnational public sphere. That postcolonial nomadic subject would now become the author of Kiarostami's film-philosophy—which proposition goes against the very grain of the way students of this field have hitherto conducted their thinking, while the self-consciously un/knowing subject, the authors of Kiarostami's film-philosophy, are unaware of their own authorial subjection—either assimilating Kiarostami backward into what they already know of mostly Eurocentric (film) philosophy or else nativizing and domesticating his artworld to an alienated and estranged provincialism. The aesthetic constitution of the nomadic subject at peace with a knowable postcolonial world, thus decolonized, would be the final stage of this project. Through thick and thin, through happy and hostile encounters, at home and abroad, Kiarostami joined the world and became a worldly filmmaker and with it we all became capable and conscious of our knowing subjectivity—unknowingly facing now the fragile but knowable world. He gave internal coherence and global recognition to an Iranian aesthetic imagination—the site of a film-philosophy that has transcended the limited philosophical imagination of Eurocentric discourses productively or clumsily applied to him. By masterfully reframing the knowing subject, from the heart of his Iranian aesthetic imagination to the widest screens at major film festivals around the world, Kiarostami's cinema is now ready not just to think in its own aesthetic terms but to invite, enable, and empower a nomadic knowing subject who has learned how to watch, how to read, and how to write his film-philosophy.

My concerns in this project have never been as much the prospects of a "non-European" film-philosophy but of a post-European film-philosophy—where we do not dispense with what has termed itself "Western philosophy" but in fact gently embrace and firmly liberate it from its prolonged and outdated provincialism. In what Robert O'Meally in his magnificent new study of jazz calls "antagonistic cooperation" or Chantal Mouffe in her political philosophy terms "agonistic pluralism" are the ideas I have in mind with a post-Western critical theory and film-philosophy. In doing so, my meditations on a prospect of a postcolonial film-philosophy are of course rooted in a larger decolonizing project on the entire field of philosophy, a veritable task that is now global and transcontinental in its prospects. In doing so, we need to take Persian philosophical prose, poetry, and film criticism much more seriously than it has been—and do so beyond the limited imagination of area studies scholars who have effectively run the Iranian Studies field aground. My discussions of Kadkani's *Suvar-e Khayal* or Avicenna's *Hikmah al-Mashriqiyah*, or Suhrawardi's concept of *Na-Koja-abad*, or the idea of *Shabih* throughout this book are the clear indices of this purpose. The result, I imagine, is a philosophical alchemy site-specific to Persian literary and philosophical heritage and yet equally conversant with the world around Kiarostami's cinema. I have done my best to make these materials accessible to a wide spectrum of critical thinking that is alas categorically alien to it. My point here has been to allow Kiarostami to breathe as happily in his immediate Iranian habitat as he has in his global reception. We do not have a zero-sum proposition here. He richly deserves both and more. An exclusive attention to European philosophical traditions blindly applied to Kiarostami is as much vacuous and disorientating as an exclusive attention to Iranian philosophical traditions would be nativist and claustrophobic.

There are of course serious epistemic issues at stake here—of which I have been fully aware. The impossibility of total equivalency trafficking between cultures and concepts is the modus operandi of any and all decolonial projects. My theoretical prose inevitably operates as it oscillates between the Persian and non-Persian, Arabic and non-Arabic, European and non-European imbalances that frame and form any and all philosophical meditations in a postcolonial and decolonial mood. When I say Suhrawardi is similar to Plato in one concept or another but not entirely so, I am marking the enduring differential register that is not totally happy with the logic and rhetoric of untranslatability. I am not convinced that things are entirely untranslatable—nor am I too sanguine about translatability. On the porous borderline of that either/or and neither/nor, I have always seen a wide and widening highway where I drive my point and where I find Kiarostami's cinema particularly poignant, for his work has attracted divergent vocabularies almost in identical terms but different prosodies—and yet unaware of one another they have driven toward Kiarostami with ease and confidence. In doing so, I am ultimately more after performing decoloniality than preaching it or preaching by performing it. This is what I mean by the location of my thinking being on a tertiary space that is more a double-edged sword than a case of "hybridity." I in fact intensely oppose the idea of "hybridity" of the sort Homi Bhabha preaches. It is a liberal cop-out. The idea of a tertiary space is strategically syncretic, organic, living, always crafting agency. If I bring Avicenna and Suhrawardi into a conversation with Walter Benjamin or Paul De Man, it is not out of any theoretical urgency or biographical happenstance. It just comes natural to me as a liberated and confident postcolonial thinker deeply committed to a post-Western and post-Islamist decolonial project.

As evident in this and most of my other books, the idea of "colonial modernity" for me has always been a critical paradox on both sides of its reality, and I have been theoretically committed to that paradox until overcoming it. The critical prose that results is not something that might be easily assimilated backward into European or non-European, Islamic or non-Islamic, Iranian or non-Iranian. Overcoming both sides of the illusion, it is a reality sui generis and has happily crafted its own space rooted in the altered reality in which we live, where alterity is far more definitive to our hermeneutics than identity. We are beyond the provincialization of

Europe, which is now a fait accompli. I do realize full well much more serious theoretical issues are at stake in that space, but this book remains committed and thus limited to Kiarostami and I have only ventured in theoretical issues so far as they help me and my readers watch and see him better. The study of cinema in its national, postnational, and worldly contexts requires this agonistic pluralism of locations and spaces his cinema has occupied. The judicious introduction of Persian sources from a variety of historical periods and artistic genres is one way of practicing what decolonial criticism should look like. More than anything else it expands our archive of hermeneutic wherewithals. The same is with my reflections on European colonial modernity, and critique of its comparative conceptions, and thus my contention that Kiarostami's cinema cannot be severed from the poetry, art, and philosophy that comprises its worldly whereabouts.

As I was near finishing this book on Kiarostami, I realized the idea of it had come to me entirely from left field, as it were, though I had been writing on him for decades. Even I could not suspect such a (mostly) calm and quiet book surfacing from the deepest hopes and fears of my soul in the rugged edges of our presence in a deeply troubled world—emerging as a soothing fresh air whispering over our bruised bodies. The evidence of this serenity and solitude of our unsuspecting souls I believe to be the most lasting legacy of Kiarostami's artworld. In the midst of all the terrors that have come our way—all the troubled world around us, all manmade and cruel—this is one peaceful prose of salvation that kept me purposeful in one streak of melodious meditations, where I discovered a soulful serenity surfacing in my diction from the steady stream of Kiarostami's sights and sounds. After watching Kiarostami's work for so many years and thinking and writing and lecturing on him around the globe, it is now clear to me that throughout these troubled years I have been searching to unpack his quiet certitude of which I was convinced and yet I could not quite fathom how in the world he had detected and mastered and shared it. The writing of this book is where I finally found Kiarostami and where I leave a record of my looking for that serene certitude, and as I conclude my thinking on him for one last time, I have finally sorted out my unending joy at looking at him being what he was best: the chronicler of our despair in hope. Happiest I have been when I began gently to expand and complicate the

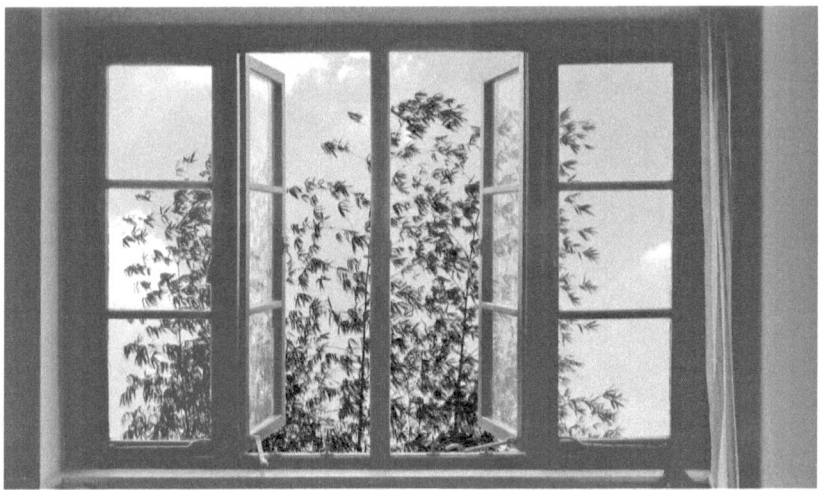

Figure 20. Abbas Kiarostami, *24 Frames* (2017). Courtesy of Abbas Kiarostami Foundation.

critical archive of film-philosophy in terms and texts and contexts mostly unknown to the existing literature in the field. If Kiarostami was an Iranian gift to the world, and he was, I have done my best to make that gift more meaningful, his vision brighter, and his swing more joyous. Let me then conclude with the joy of that swing, with the Ralph Ellison quote with which Robert O'Meally begins his magnificent new study of jazz:

> The world is ever unexplored, and ... while the complete mastery of life is mere illusion, the real secret of the game is to make life swing.[11]

Kiarostami made life swing. Of his last film and first posthumous work, *24 Frames*, James Slaymaker once said: "It is one of the most ravishingly beautiful and aesthetically radical swansongs in cinema history. At the center of 24 Frames is a serious enquiry into the ontological basis of the digital image, its place in the larger genealogy of the visual arts, and the nature of cinema in the era of the post-filmic."[12] Listening to that swansong and watching that final masterstroke is where Kiarostami's film-philosophy and the next generation of film-philosophers he has enabled will have a historic rendezvous. When on 4 July 2016 I received the news of Kiarostami's passing while I was in Ocho Rios, Jamaica, with my children, the distant echoes and the shimmering vistas of those priceless shots had declared the commencement of that rendezvous. I was happy to have been there when it happened—and happier to have arrived here where I made it swing.

Notes

INTRODUCTION

1. For more details on E. M. Cioran's fascism, see Marta Petreu, *An Infamous Past: E. M. Cioran and the Rise of Fascism in Romania* (Chicago: Ivan R. See, 2005).

2. See Stuart Hall, "Encoding, Decoding," in *Culture, Media, Language: Working Papers in Cultural Studies, 1972–79*, ed. Stuart Hall, Dorothy Hobson, Andrew Lowe, and Paul Tillis (London: Hutchinson, 1980), 128–38.

3. See Hamid Dabashi, "Interstitial Space of the Art of Protest," in *The Emperor Is Naked: On the Inevitable Demise of the Nation-State* (London: Zed Books, 2020), 118–51.

4. See "The 100 Greatest Foreign-Language Films," *BBC*, 29 October 2018, Culture, https://www.bbc.com/culture/article/20181029-the-100-greatest-foreign-language-films.

5. On this occasion, BBC Culture invited me to write a short essay on Iranian cinema; some of the ideas in this section I shared in that essay. "Why Iran Creates Some of the World's Best Films," *BBC*, 16 November 2018, Culture, https://www.bbc.com/culture/article/20181115-the-great-films-that-define-iran.

6. For an excellent example of the growing body of literature on "World Cinema," see Shekhar Deshpande and Meta Mazaj, *World Cinema: A Critical Introduction* (London: Routledge, 2018).

7. For a comprehensive study of the social history of Iranian cinema, see Hamid Naficy, *A Social History of Iranian Cinema*, 4 vols. (Durham, NC: Duke University Press, 2011–2012).

8. I have addressed some of these issues in my book *Close-Up: Iranian Cinema: Past, Present, Future* (London: Verso, 2001), 12–32.

9. I have made this point in extensive detail in my book *Iran without Borders: Towards a Critique of the Postcolonial Nation* (New York: Verso, 2016).

10. For more on *Cow*, see my book *Masters and Masterpieces of Iranian Cinema* (Washington, DC: Mage, 2007), 107–34.

11. For a preliminary sketch of Kiarostami's cinema in the context of Iranian history, see my book *Close-Up*, 33–75. For a more detailed account, see Mehrnaz Saeed-Vafa and Jonathan Rosenbaum, *Abbas Kiarostami*, 2nd ed., Contemporary Film Directors (Champaign: University of Illinois Press, 2018).

12. Some of the ideas expressed in this section I first shared in an essay entitled "Is This the End of Iranian Cinema?," *Aljazeera*, 18 February 2015, https://www.aljazeera.com/opinions/2015/2/18/is-this-the-end-of-iranian-cinema.

13. I have developed this idea of national cinema as a sign of national trauma in my edited volume on Palestinian cinema. See Hamid Dabashi, ed., *Dreams of a Nation: On Palestinian Cinema* (London: Verso, 2006).

14. See Nancy Tartaglione, "Berlin: Banned Iranian Helmer Jafar Panahi's 'Taxi' Takes Golden Bear," *Deadline*, 14 February 2015, https://deadline.com/2015/02/berlin-film-festival-winners-2015-awards-ceremony-winner-list-1201373679/.

15. See Kevin B. Lee, "Berlin Review: Jafar Panahi's 'Taxi' Is a Unique Cinematic Masterpiece," *IndieWire*, 6 February 2015, https://www.indiewire.com/2015/02/berlin-review-jafar-panahis-taxi-is-a-unique-cinematic-masterpiece-65369/.

16. See Mohammad Abdi, *"Taxi-ye Panahi: Sargardan Mian-e Vaghe'iyyat va Tasnnao'*/Panahi's "Taxi": Lost between Reality and Make-Believe," *IranWire*, 6 February 2015, https://iranwire.com/fa/culture-and-arts/1870/.

17. For the text and context of these exchanges, see this 25 April 2005 *The Guardian* interview with Kiarostami: https://www.theguardian.com/film/2005/apr/28/hayfilmfestival2005.guardianhayfestival.

18. I first developed this idea in a short essay for *Aljazeera*. See "Cinema and the Condition of Coloniality," *Aljazeera*, 11 June 2013, https://www.aljazeera.com/opinions/2013/6/11/cinema-and-the-condition-of-coloniality.

19. There is an extensive body of critical literature on the relationship between cinema and colonialism. For a pioneering study, see David H. Slavin, *Colonial Cinema and Imperial France, 1919–1939: White Blind Spots, Male Fantasies, Settler Myths* (Baltimore, MD: Johns Hopkins University Press, 2001).

20. Some initial thoughts of this section I first published as "How Did Iranian Cinema Go Global?," *Aljazeera*, 21 March 2018, https://www.aljazeera.com/opinions/2018/3/21/how-did-iranian-cinema-go-global.

21. See Hamid Dabashi, *The Shahnameh: Persian Epic as World Literature* (New York: Columbia University Press, 2019).

22. See Deshpande and Mazaj, *World Cinema*, 1–14.

23. Some of the thoughts in this section were first published as an obituary on the occasion of his passing. "Abbas Kiarostami: Close Up, Long Shot, and Cut!," *Aljazeera*, 5 July 2016, https://www.aljazeera.com/opinions/2016/7/5/abbas-kiarostami-close-up-long-shot-and-cut.

24. See Nathan Andersen, *Shadow Philosophy: Plato's Cave and Cinema* (London: Routledge, 2014).

25. The bona fide field of film-philosophy now has a veritable journal of its own published by Edinburgh University Press since 1997, where the journal is "dedicated to the engagement between film studies and philosophy," exploring the ways in which films develop and contribute to philosophical discussion. The journal also provides a forum for the thoughtful re-evaluation of key aspects of both film studies and philosophy as academic disciplines. The journal is open access and can be reached here: https://www.euppublishing.com/loi/film?expanded = vfilm-1.

26. See David Sorfa, "What Is Film-Philosophy?," *Film-Philosophy* 20 (2016): 1–5.

27. Sorfa, 1–5.

28. See my *Can Non-Europeans Think?* (London: Zed, 2015); and *Europe and Its Shadows: Coloniality after the Empire* (London: Pluto, 2019), especially chapter 6, "Europe: The Indefinite Jest," 132–58.

29. See Edward W. Said, *After the Last Sky: Palestinian Lives*, photographs by Jean Mohr (New York: Columbia University Press, 1988), 6.

30. See Enrique Dussel, *Philosophy of Liberation*, trans. Aquilina Martinez and Christine Morkovsky (New York: Orbis Books, 1980); and Boaventura de Sousa Santos, *Epistemologies of the South: Justice against Epistemicide* (London: Routledge, 2014).

31. See Sandra Ponzanesi and Marguerite Waller, eds., *Postcolonial Cinema Studies* (London: Routledge, 2011), 18.

32. See Jonardon Ganeri, *Attention, Not Self* (Oxford: Oxford University Press, 2018).

33. I have studied these aspects of European and, by extension, global interests in Persian art and culture in my *Persophilia: Iranian Culture on the Global Stage* (Cambridge, MA: Harvard University Press, 2015).

34. Abbas Kiarostami, *Dad az Gham-e Tanha'i: Dar She'r-e Sha'eran-e Kohan va Mo'aser/Alas the Sorrow of Loneliness: In the Poetry of Classical and Contemporary Poets* (Tehran: Nazar Publishers, 1392/2013), 10.

35. For the initial articulation of "contrapuntal reading," see Edward W. Said, *Culture and Imperialism* (London: Vintage, 1993), 55, 66.

36. See Dudley Andrew, "An Atlas of World Cinema," *Framework* 45, no. 2 (Fall 2004): 9–23.

37. See Bryan van Norden's *Taking Back Philosophy: A Multicultural Manifesto* (New York: Columbia University Press, 2017), 128. A key critical intervention that is inspirational in this very respect is Robbie Shilliam's crucial essay, "Social Death and Rastafari Reason," *Du Bois Review* (2023): 1–9, https://doi.org/10.1017/S1742058X23000115. The project of decolonizing that calls itself "Western philosophy" has varied and complimentary sites.

38. For a detailed account of this "aesthetic negativity," see Christoph Menke, *The Sovereignty of Art: Aesthetic Negativity in Adorno and Derrida*, trans. Neil Solomon (Cambridge, MA: MIT Press, 1998).

39. Menke, 3.

40. See Mathew Abbott, *Abbas Kiarostami and Film-Philosophy* (Edinburgh: Edinburgh University Press, 2016). The Persian translation of this seminal book by Saleh Najafi (Tehran: Lega Publishers, 1399/2020) has generated widespread excitement among Iranian cineastes. Before Mathew Abbott, Farhang Erfani had published a similarly insightful study of Iranian cinema in relationship to European philosophy. See his excellent study, *Iranian Cinema and Philosophy: Shooting Truth* (New York: Palgrave, 2012). In this study, Erfani matches a few Iranian filmmakers with a few European philosophers—Majid Majidi, for example, once with Deleuze and once with Merleau-Ponty, Kiarostami once with Heidegger and once with Lacan—and the study continues in the same vein with Marziyeh Meshkini and Bahman Qobadi. More recently, Sareh Javed wrote an excellent doctoral dissertation at SOAS, "The Traveler: A Philosophical Journey through Kiarostami's Cinema" (2017). In her case, too, Kiarostami is seen almost exclusively from the vantage point of European philosophers—as she puts it: "I analyzed Kiarostami's cinema through Gilles Deleuze's philosophy of the cinema, Jean-Paul Sartre's notion of nothingness and the specific role that Martin Heidegger grants to poets in the destitution time." The result is an exceptionally detailed and informed perspective on Kiarostami's cinema, though not an attempt to see the world philosophically from within Kiarostami's own cinema, without the scaffoldings these European philosophers offer the Iranian filmmaker, especially as he was located in the interstitial space of multiple hermeneutic grids—at once national, postnational, and worldly.

41. See Andrew O'Hehir, "Iran's Leading Filmmaker Denied U.S. Visa," *Salon*, 27 September 2002, https://www.salon.com/2002/09/27/kiarostami/.

42. In protest to Kiarostami being denied a visa, the Finnish filmmaker Aki Kaurismäki refused to attend the same festival. See Celestine Bohlen, "One Visa

Problem Costs a Festival Two Filmmakers," *New York Times*, 1 October 2002, https://www.nytimes.com/2002/10/01/movies/one-visa-problem-costs-a-festival-two-filmmakers.html.

CHAPTER 1

1. See Mohammad Reza Shafi'i-Kadkani, *Suvar-e Khayal dar She'r-e Farsi/ Imaginative Imageries in Persian Poetry* (Tehran: Agha Publications, 1350/1971).
2. Shafi'i-Kadkani, 10. My translation of the original Persian.
3. Shafi'i-Kadkani, 10–14.
4. Shafi'i-Kadkani, 416–18.
5. Shafi'i-Kadkani, 421.
6. Shafi'i-Kadkani, 422.
7. Abbas Kiarostami, *Nima Yushij: Ab/Nima Yushij: Water* (Tehran: Nazar Publisher, 1389/2011).
8. Kiarostami, 130.
9. Kiarostami, 196.
10. Martin Heidegger, *Being and Time*, trans. Joan Stambaugh (New York: State University of New York Press, 1927/1996), 3.
11. Heidegger, 4.
12. Heidegger, 4.
13. For one among many gestations of this theory of Eco, see Umberto Eco, *Interpretation and Overinterpretation* (Cambridge: Cambridge University Press, 1992).
14. For the details of this earlier articulation of the varieties of realism in Iranian cinema, including Kiarostami's, see Hamid Dabashi, *Masters and Masterpieces of Iranian Cinema* (Washington, DC: Mage, 2009).
15. For a sample of my writing on Neshat in which I have sought to detect and connect her artworld to the larger reservoir of Iranian aesthetic and philosophical traditions, see Hamid Keshmirshekan, ed., *Contemporary Art, World Cinema, and Visual Culture: Essays by Hamid Dabashi* (London: Anthem Press, 2019). The power of the art gallery promoting and radically commercializing and Orientalizing her work was of course far more effective than my limited ability to argue the contrary.
16. For years I did my best to rescue Neshat's work from these Orientalist tropes and link it to the deeper visual proclivities of Iranian metaphysics and aesthetics. But the overwhelming power of her European and American art market was far more in tune with those Orientalist tropes I actively dismantled. Her lucrative marketability was commercially invested in promoting those

Orientalist readings of her work. For some of my earliest writings on her work, see Keshmirshekan, *Contemporary Art, World Cinema*.

17. See Hamid Dabashi, *Iran without Borders: Towards a Critique of the Postcolonial Nation* (New York: Verso, 2016).

18. I have detailed the historic roots of this alternative humanism in Hamid Dabashi, *The World of Persian Literary Humanism* (Cambridge, MA: Harvard University Press, 2012).

19. See Theodore W. Adorno, *Kierkegaard: Construction of the Aesthetics*, translated, edited, and with a foreword by Robert Hullot-Kentor (Minneapolis: University of Minnesota Press, 1989), 131.

20. Adorno, 128.

21. These photographs were first exhibited at "Kiarostami: Beyond the Frame," 15 October 2022–9 April 2023, at the Oklahoma City Museum of Art, https://www.okcmoa.com/visit/events/beyond-the-frame/.

22. For more details about the circumstances of Kiarostami's death, see Saeed Kamali Dehghan, "Abbas Kiarostami Death Sparks Debate on Patient's Right to Be Informed in Iran," *The Guardian*, 14 July 2016, https://www.theguardian.com/film/2016/jul/14/abbas-kiarostami-film-maker-death-sparks-debate-patient-right-be-informed-iran.

23. I have done so in my *Shi'ism: A Religion of Protest* (Cambridge, MA: Harvard University Press, 2012).

24. I have dealt extensively with the body of work present in Persian travelogues of the nineteenth century when this renewed understanding of being-in-the world (both literally and figuratively) was actively articulated. See my *Reversing the Colonial Gaze: Persian Travelers Abroad* (Cambridge: Cambridge University Press, 2019).

25. See *Shi'ism: A Religion of Protest*, 208–20.

26. For more on Al-e Ahmad, see Hamid Dabashi, *The Last Muslim Intellectual: The Life and Legacy of Jalal Al-e Ahmad* (Edinburgh: Edinburgh University Press, 2020).

27. Hakim Nezami, *Makhzan al-Israr/Treasure House of Secrets*, ed. Vahid Dastgerdi (Tehran: Ali Akbar Elmi Publishers, 1313/1934), 1:19.

CHAPTER 2

1. Sohrab Sepehri, "Lahzeh-ye Gomshodeh/The Lost Moment," in *Hasht Ketab/Eight Books* (Tehran: Tahuri, 1977), 105.

2. Walter Benjamin, *Illuminations*, translated by Harry Zohn, introduction by Hannah Arendt, and preface by Leon Wieseltier (New York: Schocken Books, 1968). (Translator's note on the word *Now*: "Benjamin says 'Jetztzeit' and indicates by the quotation marks that he does not simply mean an

equivalent to Gegenwart, that is, the present. He clearly is thinking of the mystical nunc stans.)

3. See J. M. Bernstein, *The Fate of Art: Aesthetic Alienation from Kant to Derrida to Adorno* (University Park: Pennsylvania State University Press, 1992), 1.

4. Jürgen Habermas, *The Philosophical Discourse of Modernity: Twelve Lectures*, trans. Frederick G. Lawrence (Cambridge, MA: MIT Press, 1990), 1.

5. I have explored these aspects of the dialectic in my *Persophilia: Persian Culture on the Global Scene* (Cambridge, MA: Harvard University Press, 2015).

6. See Fredric Jameson, *Postmodernism, or, The Cultural Logic of Late Capitalism* (Durham, NC: Duke University Press, 1992).

7. See Jonathan Rosenbaum, "Abbas Kiarostami," in Mehrnaz Saeed-Vafa and Jonathan Rosenbaum, *Abbas Kiarostami* (Champaign: University of Illinois Press, 2003), 1–3.

8. For more details on the mission of this Institute, visit https://icm.as.cornell.edu. Accessed on 10 March 2023.

9. See here: https://as.cornell.edu/department_program/institute-comparative-modernities. Accessed on 10 March 2023.

10. *Exterminate All the Brutes* (2021) is an HBO series directed by Raoul Peck based on Sven Lindqvist's *Exterminate All the Brutes*, Roxanne Dunbar-Ortiz's *An Indigenous Peoples' History of the United States*, and Michel-Rolph Trouillot's *Silencing the Past*.

11. For more details and a sustained argument of this point, see Walter D. Mignolo, *The Darker Side of Western Modernity: Global Futures, Decolonial Options* (Durham, NC: Duke University Press, 2011).

12. This is my free and verbatim translation of the original quatrain. In the famous Fitzgerald translation, this quatrain becomes "On rising Moon that looks for us again / How oft hereafter will she wax and wane / low oft hereafter rising look for us / Through this same Garden and for one in vain!" See Omar Khayyam, *Rubaiyat of Omar Khayyam*, trans. Edward Fitzgerald (1859), https://www.gutenberg.org/cache/epub/246/pg246-images.html.

13. The first person to have detected this traction toward Walter Benjamin in my work and traced it back to the link between Benjamin and a larger constellation of contemporary Muslim thinkers was my graduate student Ajay Singh Chaudhary when writing his doctoral dissertation with me at Columbia in the 2010s. His unpublished dissertation, "Religions of Doubt: Religion, Critique, and Modernity in Jalal Al-e Ahmad and Walter Benjamin" (2013), was based on close reading of my work and extensive research on other contemporary Shi'i thinkers from Ali Shariati to Abdolkarim Soroush. As for Levinas, he was a conscious presence on my mind when I was writing my *Islamic Liberation Theology: Resisting the Empire* (London: Routledge, 2008).

14. See Robert Koehler, "Abbas Kiarostami Remembered: Why He Was Iran's Essential Filmmaker—Critic's Notebook," *IndieWire*, 4 July 2016,

https://www.indiewire.com/2016/07/abbas-kiarostami-dead-tribute-iran-close-up-1201702436/.

15. Koehler, "Abbas Kiarostami Remembered."

16. At a conference organized by Iran Heritage Foundation in 2005, a number of the participants, including Michael Beard, Sima Daad, Narguess Farzad, Ahmad Karimi-Hakkak, and Riccardo Zipoli, addressed aspects of Kiarostami's films and poetry and their link to modern Persian poetry. For an abstract of their presentations, see https://web.archive.org/web/20070927221105/http:/www.iranheritage.com/kiarostamiconference/abstracts_full.htm.

17. See Shahrokh Meskub, *Dar Ku-ye Dust/In the Friend's Neighborhood* (Tehran: Khwarizmi Publications, 1357/1978).

18. Meskub, 5–6. My translation from the Persian original.

19. Although I read Avicenna and Suhrawardi's works differently, I remain deeply indebted to previous scholars like Henry Corbin and Taqi Pournamdarian (among others) for their pioneering works in this field. See Henry Corbin, *Avicenna and the Visionary Recital* (Princeton, NJ: Princeton University Press, 1960/2018); and Taqi Pournamdarian, *Ramz va Dastanha-ye Ramzi dar Adab Farsi: Tahlili az Dastan-ha Ye Erfani–Falsafi Ibn Sina va Suhrawardi/Symbolism and Symbolic Stories in Persian Literature: An Interpretation of Mystical-Philosophical Stories of Avicenna and Suhrawardi* (Tehran: Sherkat-e Entesharat-e Elmi va Farhangi, 1364/1985).

20. Mehdi Akhavan-e Sales, "*Khwan Hashtom*/The Eighth Task," in *Collected Works* (Tehran: Zemestan Publishers, 1397/2018), 1:857.

21. Michell Foucault, *Madness and Civilization: A History of Insanity in the Age of Reason* (New York: Vintage Books, 1965/1988), x–xi.

22. Foucault, 107–8.

23. I have detailed this process in my *Europe and Its Shadows: Coloniality after Empire* (London: Pluto Press, 2019).

24. See Susan Shariati, "Ba man beh zaban-e Ishareh Sokhan Begu/Speak to Me Allegorically," in *Bad Ou ra Nakhahad Bord: Yadnameh Zendeh yad Abbas Kiarostami/The Wind Will Not Carry Us: A Memorial Volume for Abbas Kiarostami*, ed. Mohammad Valizadh (Tehran: Bamdad, 1398/2019), 201–4.

25. Benjamin, *Illuminations*.

26. See Werner Hamacher, "'NOW': Walter Benjamin on Historical Time," in *The Moment: Time and Rupture in Modern Thought*, ed. Heidrun Friese (Liverpool: Liverpool University Press, 2001), 164.

27. Nezami's *Makhzan al-Asrar* is usually translated as "Treasury of Secrets," which may be fine as a literal translation but is rather meaningless in English and farthest removed from what the original implicates. Yes, "Makhzan" means "Treasury" in an etymological sense, but here it means a "Source," meaning the poem itself as a Source, as a Treasure House. Yes, "Asrar" is the plural of "Ser," and "Ser" means "Secret," but in plural here, "Asrar" means the truths that

Nezami intends to reveal in his poem. Thus my preference of "Source of Wisdom" as a better translation for "Makhzan al-Asrar."

28. Mathew Abbott, *Abbas Kiarostami and Film-Philosophy* (Edinburgh: Edinburgh University Press, 2016), 4.

29. Abbott, 4.

30. Abbott, 13.

31. Henry Corbin, *Spiritual Body and Celestial Earth: From Mazdean Iran to Shi'ite Iran* (Princeton, NJ: Princeton University Press, 1977). See Hamid Dabashi, "Bordercrossings: Shirin Neshat's Body of Evidence," in *Contemporary Art, World Cinema, and Visual Culture: Essays by Hamid Dabashi*, ed. Hamid Keshmirshekan (London: Anthem Press, 2019): 145–66.

32. See Sohrab Sepehri, "Neshani/Address," in *Hasht Ketab* (Tehran: Tahuri, 1977), 358–59. My translation.

33. The Persian press is flooded with the details of this news. For a summary, see *"Vaqti Kiarostami Mottaham Mishavad*/When Kiarostami Is Accused," *Khabar Online*, 10 Azar 1399/30 November 2020, https://www.khabaronline.ir/news/1461180/وقتی-کیارستمی-متهم-می-شود.

34. *"Vaqti Kiarostami Mottaham Mishavad*/When Kiarostami Is Accused," 1399/2020. My translation and interpretation of the poem.

CHAPTER 3

1. Sohrab Sepehri, "Seda-ye Pa-ye Ab/The Sound of the Footsteps of Water," in *Hasht Ketab/Eight Books* (Tehran: Tahuri, 1977). My translation from the Persian original.

2. Jean-Luc Nancy, *L'Évidence du film: Abbas Kiarostami* (Brussels: Yves Gevaert Editeur, 2001), 56–57.

3. See Maziyar Eslami and Morad Farhadpour, *Paris-Tehran: Sinema-ye Abbas Kiarostami—Dialog/Paris-Tehran: The Cinema of Abbas Kiarostami, A Conversation* (Tehran: Farhang Saba, 1387/2008).

4. Eslami and Farhadpour, 8.

5. Eslami and Farhadpour, 145–68.

6. Eslami and Farhadpour, 183.

7. For the original poem, see Mohammad Reza Shafi'i-Kadkani, "My Pigeons," in *Bad Ou ra Nakhahad Bord: Yadnameh Zendeh yad Abbas Kiarostami/The Wind Will Not Carry Us: A Memorial Volume for Abbas Kiarostami*, ed. Mohammad Vali-zadeh (Tehran: Bamdad, 1398/2019), 300–304. All translations are mine.

8. Shafi'i-Kadkani, 300–304.

9. Available online here: http://azmaonline.com/2019/06/23/شفیعی-کدکنی-تو-خواندC8%80%2Eرا-به-طبیعت-می/.

10. See Nancy's *L'Évidence du film*, 2001.

11. See Laurent Kretzschmar, "Is Cinema Renewing Itself?," *Film-Philosophy* 6, no. 1 (February 2002), https://www.euppublishing.com/doi/full/10.3366/film.2002.0015.

12. Kretzschmar, "Is Cinema Renewing Itself?"

13. Kretzschmar, "Is Cinema Renewing Itself?"

14. Theodore Adorno, "Cultural Criticism and Society," in *Prisms*, trans. Shierry Weber Nicholsen and Samuel Weber (Cambridge, MA: MIT Press, 1983), 34.

15. "But it so happens that when the native hears a speech about Western culture, he pulls out his knife—or at least he makes sure it is within reach." Frantz Fanon, *The Wretched of the Earth*, preface by Jean-Paul Sartre, trans. Constance Farrington (New York: Grove Press, 1963). 43.

16. Kretzschmar, "Is Cinema Renewing Itself?"

17. Kretzschmar, "Is Cinema Renewing Itself?"

18. Kretzschmar, "Is Cinema Renewing Itself?"

19. Kretzschmar, "Is Cinema Renewing Itself?"

20. I have discussed these examples in more detail in my book *Persophilia: Persian Culture on the Global Scene* (Cambridge, MA: Harvard University Press, 2015).

21. Kretzschmar, "Is Cinema Renewing Itself?"

22. Kretzschmar, "Is Cinema Renewing Itself?"

23. Kretzschmar, "Is Cinema Renewing Itself?"

24. Kretzschmar, "Is Cinema Renewing Itself?"

25. Kretzschmar, "Is Cinema Renewing Itself?"

26. Kretzschmar, "Is Cinema Renewing Itself?"

27. See Hamid Dabashi, *Close-Up: Iranian Cinema: Past, Present and Future* (New York: Verso, 2001), 52.

28. See Hamid Dabashi, "Re-reading Reality: Kiarostami's *Through the Olive Trees* and the Cultural Politics of a Postrevolutionary Aesthetics," *Critique: Journal for Critical Studies of the Middle East* 4, no. 7 (1995): 63–89. A much revised version of that essay is now chapter 4 of this book.

29. See Moinak Biswas, "The Many Absences of Abbas Kiarostami," *The Wire*, 7 July 2016, https://thewire.in/film/many-absences-abbas-kiarostami.

30. See Douglas Morrey, "Introduction : Claire Denis and Jean-Luc Nancy," *Film-Philosophy* 12, no. 1 (February 2008), i–vi, https://www.euppublishing.com/doi/abs/10.3366/film.2008.0001.

31. Kristin Lené Hole, *Towards a Feminist Cinematic Ethics: Claire Denis, Emmanuel Levinas, and Jean-Luc Nancy* (Edinburgh: Edinburgh University Press, 2015), 2–3.

32. Nancy, *L'Évidence du film*, 78, as cited in Hole, 15.

33. Hole, 12–13.

34. See Josef Früchtl, "The Evidence of Film and the Presence of the World: Jean-Luc Nancy's Cinematic Ontology," the short English version of the longer

German version, "Die Evidenz des Films und die Präsenz der Welt." Jean-Luc Nancy's Cineastische Ontologie will subsequently be published in Ludger Schwarte, ed., *Bild-Performanz: Die Kraft des Visuellen* (München: Fink, 2010). The English version is available online here: https://www.academia.edu/58751264/The_Evidence_of_Film_and_the_Presence_of_the_World_Jean_Luc_Nancy_s_Cinematic_Ontology.

35. Nancy, *L'Évidence du film*, 42–43.

36. Nancy, 56–57.

37. For an English translation, see Jean-Luc Nancy, *The Sense of the World*, translated and with a foreword by Jeffrey S. Libretto (Minneapolis: Minnesota University Press, 1997).

38. For an English translation, see Jean-Luc Nancy, *The Creation of the World or Globalization*, translated and with an introduction by François Raffoul and David Pettigrew (Stony Brook, NY: SUNY Press, 2007).

39. For an English translation, see Jean-Luc Nancy, *The Muses* (Palo Alto: Stanford University Press, 1996).

40. Nancy, *L'Évidence du film*, 80–81. Kiarostami does not name this graduate student. I have searched for this doctoral dissertation to which Kiarostami refers but have not been able to locate it.

41. Nancy, 80–81.

42. See A. O. Scott, "How Abbas Kiarostami Had Me Thinking in Persian," *New York Times*, 5 July 2016, https://www.nytimes.com/2016/07/07/movies/how-abbas-kiarostami-had-me-thinking-in-persian.html.

43. Scott, "How Abbas Kiarostami Had Me Thinking in Persian."

44. Nancy, *L'Évidence du film*, 80–95.

45. Nancy, 96–97.

46. Nancy, 88–89.

47. See Umberto Eco, *The Open Work*, translated by Anna Cancogni and with an introduction by David Robey (Cambridge, MA: Harvard University Press, 1989), 84–104.

48. Sohrab Sepehri, "Seda-ye Pa-ye Ab/The Sound of the Footsteps of Water," *Hasht Ketab/Eight Books*. All translations from the original Persian are mine.

49. Sepehri, "Seda-ye Pa-ye Ab/The Sound of the Footsteps of Water."

50. Sepehri, "Seda-ye Pa-ye Ab/The Sound of the Footsteps of Water."

51. Sepehri, "Seda-ye Pa-ye Ab/The Sound of the Footsteps of Water."

52. Sepehri, "Seda-ye Pa-ye Ab/The Sound of the Footsteps of Water."

53. See Hamid Dabashi, *Persian Literary Humanism* (Cambridge, MA: Harvard University Press, 2012).

54. See Mohammad Reza Shafi'i-Kadkani, *An-su-ye Harf-o-Sut: Gozideh Asrar al-Tawhid/Beyond Words and Sound: A Selection of Attar's Asrar al-Tawhid* (Tehran: Sokhan, 1372/1993), 8.

55. Shafi'i-Kadkani, *An-su-ye Harf-o-Sut*, 9.

56. I borrow the term "agonistic" here from the seminal work of Chantal Mouffe and the idea of agonistic pluralism in her political thinking, but I extend it into the varied and conflictual philosophical traditions. See Chantal Mouffe, *Agonistics: Thinking the World Politically* (New York: Verso, 2013).

57. See Christoph Menke, *The Sovereignty of Art: Aesthetic Negativity in Adorno and Derrida*, trans. Neil Solomon (Cambridge, MA: MIT Press, 1998), 3.

58. Menke, 3.

59. Menke, vii.

60. Menke, viii.

61. Menke, xiii.

62. Menke, xiii.

63. I have detailed this idea of "parapublic sphere," extending it from Habermas's incurably Eurocentric take on public sphere in my book *Persophilia*.

64. See Stephen Holden, "'Close-Up': The Pathos of Deceit by a Victim of Longing," *New York Times*, 31 December 1991, https://archive.nytimes.com/www.nytimes.com/library/film/123199closeup-film-review.html.

CHAPTER 4

1. Mehdi Akhavan-e Sales, "Barf/Snow," in *Collected Works*, 2 vols. (Tehran: Zemestan Publishers, 2018), 1:538–45.

2. The first version of this chapter was published as an essay in Hamid Dabashi, "Re-reading Reality: Kiarostami's *Through the Olive Trees* and the Cultural Politics of a Postrevolutionary Aesthetics," *Critique: Journal for Critical Studies of the Middle East* 4, no. 7 (1995): 63–89. In this chapter I have thoroughly revised that essay, but its main arguments remain the same.

3. *Premiere* (March 1995): 50–51.

4. *The New Republic*, 20 March 1995, 28.

5. *Premiere* (March 1995): 50.

6. *Sureh* 48 (June-August 1992): 4–5.

7. *Sureh*, 49–50.

8. *Sureh*, 51.

9. *Sureh*, 52.

10. *Sureh*, 53. All translations of these passages from the original Persian are mine.

11. *Film*, no. 128 (August 1992): 16.

12. *Film*, 16.

13. *Film*, no. 143 (June 1993): 87.

14. *Film*, 90.

15. *Film*, 91–92, 94–95.

16. See Gholam Heydari, *Zaviyeh did dar cinema-ye Iran/Point of View in Iranian Cinema* (Tehran: Daftar-e Pazhuhesh ha-ye Farhangi, 1369/1990), 72–73.
17. *Film*, no. 143 (June 1993): 93–94.
18. *Film*, 94.
19. *Film*, 94.
20. *Film*, no. 156 (December 1993): 21.
21. *Film*, no. 167 (November 1994): 59–60.
22. *Film*, 60–61.
23. *Film*, 61.
24. *Film*, no. 168 (December 1994): 104.
25. *Naqd-e Cinema*, no. 1 (Spring 1994): 86.
26. *Naqd-e Cinema*, 88.
27. *Naqd-e Cinema*, 89.
28. *Naqd-e Cinema*, 90–91.
29. *Naqd-e Cinema*, 82–83.
30. *Naqd-e Cinema*, 83.
31. For further details, see *Film*, no. 143 (June 1993): 99.
32. See Reza Allamehzadeh, *Sarab-e Cinema-ye Islami-ye Iran/The Illusion of Iranian Islamic Cinema* (Saarbrucken: Nawid Verlag, 1991).
33. Allamehzadeh, 199–200.
34. Allamehzadeh, 202.
35. *Film*, no. 158 (February 1994): 17.
36. *Positif: Revue mensuelle de cinema*, no. 380 (October 1992): 28.
37. *Positif*, 31.
38. *Village Voice*, 21 February 1995, p. 54.
39. For further details, see *Film*, no. 143 (June 1993): 11.
40. *Film*, no. 144 (July 1993): 18.
41. For a discussion of Vattimo's conception of *il pensiero debole*, see his *The End of Modernity* (Baltimore: Johns Hopkins University Press, 1988). Vattimo's discussion of "Ornament/Monument" in chapter 5 is particularly pertinent here.
42. My translation of Sohrab Sepehri, "Seda-ye Pa-ye Ab/The Sound of the Footsteps of Water," in *Hasht Ketab/Eight Books* (Tehran: Tahuri, 1977), 271–72.
43. Sepehri, 272.
44. Sepehri, 281–82.
45. See Gayatri Chakravorty Spivak, *Outside in the Teaching Machine* (New York: Routledge, 1993), 1–23.
46. Quoted in Susan Sontag, *Against Interpretation* (New York: Farrar, Straus and Giroux, 1986), 3.
47. Sontag, 7.

48. See the official catalogue of 48th Festival internazionale del film Locarno, 3–13 August 1995, 201–13. The film festival also had a special section on Iranian women filmmakers featuring the cinema of Rakhshan Bani-Etemad, Puran Derakhshandeh, Forough Farrokhzad, and Tahmineh Milani. This festival undoubtedly will go down in history as one of the most significant international exposures of Iranian cinema. The competition section of the festival showed Bani-Etemad's *The Blue-Veiled* (Rusari-ye Abi, 1994), while in Piazza Grande was shown Jafar Panahi's *The White Balloon* (Badkonak-e Sefid, 1995), and in the Cinema/cinemas section, devoted to films made about cinema, was shown Mohsen Makhmalbaf's *Salam Cinema* (1994). Altogether, thirty Iranian films were shown in the course of this festival, the highest number presented after Italian (85) and Swiss (37) films. Bani-Etemad's *The Blue-Veiled* won the Bronze Leopard.

49. See *Cahiers du Cinema*, no. 493 (July/August 1995): 5, 68–114.

50. Akhavan-e Sales, "Barf/Snow," 1:544.

51. Akhavan-e Sales, 1:545.

CHAPTER 5

1. See Immanuel Kant, *Observations on the Feeling of the Beautiful and Sublime*, trans. John T. Goldthwait (Berkeley: University of California Press, 1960), 110.

2. Emmanuel Levinas, in Raoul Mortley, *French Philosophers in Conversation* (London: Rutledge 1991), 18, cited in Robert Eaglestone, "Postcolonial Thought and Levinas's Double Vision," in *Radicalizing Levinas*, ed. Peter Atterton and Matthew Calarco (Albany, NY: SUNY Press, 2010), 58.

3. See Peter Bradshaw, "*Ten* Review—Extraordinary Film Giving Access to the Thoughts of Iranian Women," *The Guardian*, 26 September 2002, https://www.theguardian.com/culture/2002/sep/27/artsfeatures.

4. See Roger Ebert's 11 April 2003 review of *Ten* on his website: https://www.rogerebert.com/reviews/ten-2003.

5. See Frederic Jameson, "Third-World Literature in an Era of Multinational Capitalism," *Social Text*, no. 15 (Autumn 1986): 69.

6. See Mathew Abbott, *Abbas Kiarostami and Film-Philosophy* (Edinburgh: Edinburgh University Press, 2016), 4–8.

7. I have had multiple occasions to articulate the European provenance of this philosophical articulation for the European subject, which has been falsely thought to be universal. For the most recent, see Hamid Dabashi, *Islam after the West: The Future of Two Illusions* (Oakland: University of California Press, 2022), 86–97, where I also include a discussion on a similar project in Hegel's philosophy of history.

8. See Enrique Dussel, *Philosophy of Liberation*, trans. Aquilina Martinez and Christine Morkovsky (New York: Orbis Books, 2003).

9. Kant, *Observations on the Feeling of the Beautiful and Sublime*, 110–11.

10. See, for example, Emmanuel Chukwudi Eze, "The Color of Reason: The Idea of 'Race' in Kant's Anthropology," in *Postcolonial African Philosophy: A Critical Reader*, ed. Emmanuel Chukwudi Eze (Oxford: Blackwell, 1997), 103–31.

11. Kant, *Observations on the Feeling of the Beautiful and Sublime*, 112–13.

12. Kant, 113.

13. Kant, 109–10.

14. Kant's racism and philosophical preoccupation with race was not limited to these boldface statements in just one of his books. Some scholars even believe he single-handedly invented the idea of race. See Robert Bernasconi, "Who Invented the Concept of Race? Kant's Role in the Enlightenment Construction of Race," in *Race*, ed. Robert Bernasconi (Oxford: Blackwell, 2001). Others have sought to locate it in the context of Kant's "philosophical position on the systematic unity of nature and of knowledge in the first and third Critiques, and his account and defense of teleological judgment, [which] are developed out of problems first articulated in his solution to the problem of the unity in diversity of the human species—that is, in his theory of race" (Stella Sandford, "Kant, Race, and Natural History," *Philosophy and Social Criticism* 44 [2018]: 950–77).

15. As an excellent example of how European particular, personal even, feigns to be universal, see Maurice Blanchot, *Friendship*, trans. Elizabeth Rotternberg (Palo Alto: Stanford University Press, 1971), which is almost entirely devoted to Blanchot's private meditations on contemporary thinkers, many of them his own personal friends. Once plucked out of that context, translated into English, and published by a university press, we then read it with the air of expectation that these personal meditations have profound universal significance.

16. Levinas, as cited in Eaglestone, "Postcolonial Thought," 58.

17. Levinas, as cited in Eaglestone, 65.

18. Levinas, as cited in Eaglestone, 58.

19. See Matthew Calarco, "Faced by Animals," in *Radicalizing Levinas*, ed. Peter Atterton and Matthew Calarco, 113–36 (Albany, NY: SUNY Press, 2010).

20. Calarco, 113.

21. See Paula Marvelly, "Abbas Kiarostami: *24 Frames*; Stillness in Motion, Motion in Stillness," *Culturium*, 13 October 2019, https://www.theculturium.com/abbas-kiarostami-24-frames/.

22. See Manohla Dargis, "Review: The Persistence of Abbas Kiarostami's Vision in '24 Frames,'" *New York Times*, 1 February 2018, https://www.nytimes.com/2018/02/01/movies/24-frames-review-abbas-kiarostami.html.

23. One of the best studies of this body of allegorical literature is Taqi Pournamdarian, *Ramz va Dastan-ha-ye Ramzi dar Adab-e Farsi/Symbolism and

Symbolic Stories in Persian Literature (Tehran: Sherkat Entesharat-e Elmi va Farhangi, 1364/1985).

24. See Dimitri Gutas's take here in *Encyclopedia Iranica*, s.v. "Avicenna v. Mysticism," updated 17 August 2022, https://iranicaonline.org/articles/avicenna-v.

25. I am simplifying a much more detailed theory of existent beings in Avicenna's ontology. For more details, see the excellent essay by Peter Adamson, "From the Necessary Existent to God," in *Interpreting Avicenna: Critical Essays*, ed. Peter Adamson, 170–89 (Cambridge: Cambridge University Press, 2013).

26. See Hamid Dabashi, *Reversing the Colonial Gaze: Persian Travelers Abroad* (Cambridge: Cambridge University Press, 2020).

27. I first developed this idea of "the interstitial space of art" in "Interstitial Space of the Art of Protest," chapter 5 in my book *The Emperor Is Naked: On the Inevitable Demise of the Nation-State*, 118–51 (London: Zed, 2020).

28. See Rosi Braidotti, *The Posthuman* (Cambridge: Polity, 2013), especially chapter 2, "Post-Anthropocentrism: Life beyond the Species," 55–104.

29. I have addressed this extensively in my book *Corpus Anarchicum: Political Protest, Suicidal Violence, and the Making of the Posthuman Body* (New York: Palgrave, 2012).

30. See Rosi Braidotti, "Anthropos Redux: A Defense of Monism in the Anthropocene Epoch," *Frame* 29, no. 2 (November 2016): 29–46, https://www.frameliteraryjournal.com/29-2-perspectives-on-the-anthropocene/1450/.

31. Mawlana Jalal al-Din Rumi, *Masnavi Ma'navi*, ed. Reynold A. Nicholson (Tehran: Amir Kabir, 1924): Book 5, lines 3637–50. My translation from the original Persian.

32. Rumi, *Masnavi*, Book 3, lines 3901–6. My translation from the original Persian. The expressions "Everything perishes except His face" and "We are all of God and to Him shall we all return" are Qur'anic phrases, Verse 28:88 and Verse 2:156, respectively.

CHAPTER 6

1. See "Abbas Kiarostami Talks about His Movies: Abbas Kiarostami Interview," accessed 15 June 2024, https://www.youtube.com/watch?v=_HvTCbN-Scjc. My transcription and translation from the original Persian.

2. See Philip Concannon, "Review—*Five Dedicated to Ozu*," Phil on Film, 22 May 2005, http://www.philonfilm.net/2005/05/review-five.html.

3. See Kenji Fujishima, "*Five Dedicated to Ozu*: Abbas Kiarostami," *In Review Online*, 25 September 2011, https://inreviewonline.com/2011/09/25/five-dedicated-to-ozu/. Part of *The Self-Reflexive Cinema of Abbas Kiarostami*, https://inreviewonline.com/2011/08/21/kiarostami-retro/.

4. For a detailed account of the origins and dramaturgy of Ta'ziyeh, see *Encyclopedia Iranica*, s.v. "Ta'zia," accessed 15 June 2024, https://iranicaonline.org/articles/tazia.

5. There is an extensive body of literature in Persian on this transition from ritual to play and from the religious to the more mundane dimensions of the play, embedded in the transition from Ta'ziyeh to Shabih-khani. See, for example, Mariam Ne'mat Tavusi, *"Shabih-khani: Az A'in ta Namayesh*/Shabih-Khani: From Ritual to Drama," *Fasl-nameh Mardom va Farhang* 1, no. 1 (Winter 1393/2014): 173–87. As always, those who write in English or French about this theatrical tradition scarcely refer to Persian sources—which is of course irresponsible if not preposterous. A classical study of Ta'zieh is Sadegh Homayun, *Ta'ziyeh va Ta'zieh-khani* (Tehran: Entesharat-e Jashn-e Honar, 1971). More detailed studies have followed since.

6. For more details, see the excellent work of Davood Fath and Ali Beigi, *Shabih Khani* (Tehran: Sureh Mehr, 1396/2017).

7. Fath and Beigi, 27. As a child in my hometown I used to join these mobile performances, or *Dasteh*, as they were called.

8. Tom Huhn and Lambert Zuidervaart, eds., *The Semblance of Subjectivity: Essays in Adorno's Aesthetic Theory* (Cambridge, MA: MIT Press, 2997), 7.

9. Huhn and Zuidervaart, 8.

10. Huhn and Zuidervaart, 9.

11. Huhn and Zuidervaart, 4.

12. See Lee Marshall, "People Watching," *The Guardian*, 14 July 2003, https://www.theguardian.com/film/2003/jul/14/theatre.artsfeatures.

13. See Bianca Bonomi, "Cosi fan Kiarostami," *The National*, 6 June 2009, https://www.thenationalnews.com/arts/cosi-fan-kiarostami-1.512286.

14. See Charlotte Higgins, "Cinema's Poet of Silence Switches to Opera with Mozart Debut at ENO," *The Guardian*, 6 June 2009, https://www.thenationalnews.com/arts/cosi-fan-kiarostami-1.512286. For a more detailed and fruitful study, see Jenny Chamarette, "Transitional Borders and Intermedial Spectacle: Kiarostami and Opera, between France and Iran," *Studies in French Cinema* 13, no. 3 (2013): 257–71, https://doi.org/10.1386/sfc.13.3.257_1. In this useful study, Jenny Chamarette works through the two key concepts of intermediality and spectacle—which are useful but limited in her attempt to overcome the aesthetic politics of the French philosophical gaze.

15. This schizophrenia corroborates and complicates the superb work of critical thinkers like Sarah Ahmed in her pioneering work *The Cultural Politics of Emotion* (Edinburgh: Edinburgh University Press, 2014) in understanding the political embodiment of national sentiments, emotions, and affects being overcompensated by the overwhelming European celebration of Kiarostami's cinema.

16. For more details about the circumstances of his illness and passing, see Saeed Kamali Dehghan, "Abbas Kiarostami Death Sparks Debate on Patient's

Right to Be Informed in Iran," *The Guardian*, 14 July 2016, https://www.theguardian.com/film/2016/jul/14/abbas-kiarostami-film-maker-death-sparks-debate-patient-right-be-informed-iran.

17. See Peter Bradshaw, "*Shirin*," *The Guardian*, 25 June 2009, https://www.theguardian.com/film/2009/jun/26/shirin-film-review.

18. Bradshaw, "*Shirin*."

19. See Hamid Dabashi, "Quis Custodiet Ipsos Custodes: Who Watches the Watchers?," *Middle East Journal of Culture and Communication* 1, no. 1 (2008): 24–29, https://doi.org/10.1163/187398608X317397.

20. See Nico Baumbach, "Like Someone in Love: On Likeness," *Criterion Collection*, 19 May 2014, https://www.criterion.com/current/posts/3170-like-someone-in-love-on-likeness.

21. See Mathew Abbott, *Abbas Kiarostami and Film-Philosophy* (Edinburgh: Edinburgh University Press, 2016), 13.

22. Abbott, 13.

23. See "Abbas Kiarostami: 'Someone once said that love is the result of misunderstanding,'" undated interview, https://www.facebook.com/100077507670666/videos/abbas-kiarostami-someone-once-said-that-love-is-the-result-of-misunderstanding-w/296840532408062/.

24. Friedrich Nietzsche, *On Truth and Lie in an Extra-Moral Sense*, in *The Portable Nietzsche*, ed. Walter Kaufmann (New York: Penguin, 1954), 46–47. For an excellent recent doctoral dissertation that explores this aspect of Nietzsche's work in detail, see Timothy A. Stoll, "Semblance and Authenticity: Nietzsche on the Use and Misuse of Illusion" (PhD diss., Princeton University, 2018), https://dataspace.princeton.edu/handle/88435/dsp01w9505316m.

25. See Jean Baudrillard, *Simulacra and Simulations*, trans. Sheila Faria Glaser (Ann Arbor: University of Michigan Press, 1994).

26. Farid al-Din Attar, *The Conference of the Birds*, translated and with an introduction by Afkham Sarbandi and Dick Davis (London: Penguin, 1984), lines 4232–54.

CHAPTER 7

1. Fakhr al-Din Iraqi, *Koliyyat*, ed. Sa'id Nafisi (Tehran: Sana'i Publications, 1959), 296. My translation from the Persian original.

2. See Hamid Dabashi, *Makhmalbaf at Large: The Making of a Rebel Filmmaker* (London: I. B. Tauris, 2008).

3. For a detailed account of her thoughts on this matter, see Rosi Braidotti, *Nomadic Subjects: Embodiment and Sexual Difference in Contemporary Feminist Theory* (New York: Columbia University Press, 2011).

4. Rosi Braidotti, "Writing as a Nomadic Subject," *Comparative Critical Studies* 11, no. 2–3 (2014): 163.

5. Sohrab Sepehri, "Seda-ye Pa-ye Ab/The Sound of the Footsteps of Water," in *Hasht Ketab/Eight Books* (Tehran: Tahuri, 1977), 297–99.

6. In his *Provincializing Europe: Postcolonial Thought and Historical Difference* (Princeton, NJ: Princeton University Press, 2008), Dipesh Chakrabarty outlined some specific contours of a project of provincializing Europe. But his project remained very much limited in its historical and civilizational imagination—and as a result sometime going against the grain of his own thought and in fact re-centering Europe. For my more radical project, see Hamid Dabashi, *Europe and Its Shadows: Coloniality after Empire* (London: Pluto Press, 2019)—especially chapter 6: "Europe: The Indefinite Jest," 32–158.

7. Here is an interview, accessed 15 June 2024, where at 3:36 he sarcastically says *"man gahi mortakeb goftan she'r ham misham*/sometime I also commit poetry": https://www.youtube.com/watch?v=neYgsuUC8pw.

8. See Abbas Kiarostami, *Hafez beh Revayat Abbas Kiarostami/Hafez as Told by Abbas Kiarostami* (Tehran: Farzan Ruz, 2006).

9. There is an English translation of his poetry by two veteran students of Persian poetry, who alas head over heels fall into the uncontrolled and injudicious sycophantic prose of lavishly praising Kiarostami on entirely unfounded grounds, which is a truly sad thing to behold. See Abbas Kiarostami, *Walking with the Wind*, translated with an introduction by Ahmad Karimi-Hakkak and Michael C. Beard (Cambridge, MA: Harvard University Film Archive, 2002).

10. See Abbas Kiarostami, *Bad-o Barg/The Wind and the Leaf* (Tehran: Kiarostami Foundation, 1390/2011).

11. Kiarostami, 1. Translation from the original Persian is all mine.

12. Kiarostami, 2.

13. Kiarostami, 11.

14. Kiarostami, 16.

15. Kiarostami, 29.

16. Kiarostami, 63.

17. For a pioneering study of Nasser Khosrow's poetry and philosophy, see Alice C. Hunsberger, *Nasir Khusraw, the Ruby of Badakhshan: A Portrait of the Persian Poet, Traveler and Philosopher* (London: I. B. Tauris, 2002). In a subsequent volume, she paid particular attention to the poetic aspects of Nasser Khosrow's philosophy. See *Pearls of Persia: The Philosophical Poetry of Nasir-i Khusraw*, ed. Alice C. Hunsberger (London: I. B. Tauris, 2013).

18. This philosophical disposition of poetry has of course a larger field of conversation. See, for example, Lars Iyer, "The Birth of Philosophy in Poetry: Blanchot, Char, Heraclitus," *Janus Head* 4, no. 2 (2001): 358–83. But in the case of

Martin Heidegger specifically, see his iconic text *Poetry, Language, Thought* (New York: Harper Perennial Modern Classics, 2013).

19. For a study of the influence of Persian poetry on Iranian cinema, see Khatereh Sheibani, *The Poetics of Iranian Cinema: Aesthetics, Modernity and Film after the Revolution* (London: I. B. Tauris, 2011).

20. An earlier, shorter version of this section of this chapter was published as "Rethinking the Saqqa-khaneh Art: The Pilgrim as Unknowing Subject," in *Rethinking the Contemporary Art of Iran*, ed. Hamid Keshmirshekan (Milan: Skira Editore, 2024): 29–44. I am grateful to Hamid Keshmirshekan for his helpful comments on the earlier draft of this section.

21. See Hamid Keshmirshekan, *The Art of Iran in the Twentieth and Twenty-First Centuries Tracing the Modern and the Contemporary* (Edinburgh: Edinburgh University Press, 2023).

22. Keshmirshekan, *Art of Iran*, 4.

23. Keshmirshekan, 31.

24. See Hamid Dabashi, *Iran without Borders: Towards a Critique of the Postcolonial Nation* (New York: Verso, 2016).

25. Alain Badiou, *Being and Event*, trans. Oliver Feltham (New York: Continuum, 1988/2005), xii.

26. For a detailed account of Al-e Ahmad's thoughts, see my recent book, Hamid Dabashi, *The Last Muslim Intellectuals: The Life and Legacy of Jalal Al-e Ahmad* (Edinburgh: Edinburgh University Press, 2021).

27. In his hermeneutics and semiotics, Umberto Eco makes a distinction among three intentions: intention of the author (*intentio auctoris*), intention of the reader (*intentio lectoris*), and intention of the text (*intentio operis*). Here I make a deliberate distinction based on his triangulation to underline the intentions of the works of Saqqa-khaneh art themselves, or what they intend and insinuate in their fields of meanings beyond the intention of their creators or how they were initially received by their contemporaries. See Umberto Eco, *The Open Work*, translated by Anna Cancogni with an introduction by David Robey (Cambridge, MA: Harvard University Press, 1962/1989). See especially chapter 4, "The Open Work in Visual Arts," 84–104. For a more concise account of his theory, see Umberto Eco, "Intentio Lectoris," *Differentia: Review of Italian Thought* 2 (1988): Article 12, https://commons.library.stonybrook.edu/differentia/vol2/iss1/12.

28. For an authoritative short introduction to the Saqqa-khaneh art movement, see also the earlier essay of Hamid Keshmirshekan in *Encyclopedia Iranica*, s.v. "Saqqa-Kana School of Art," updated 15 August 2009, https://www.iranicaonline.org/articles/saqqa-kana-ii-school-of-art.

29. See Emmanuel Levinas, *Totality and Infinity: An Essay on Exteriority*, trans. Alphonso Lingis (Pittsburgh, PA: Duquesne Universities, 1969).

30. J. M. Bernstein, *The Fate of Art: Aesthetic Alienation from Kant to Derrida and Adorno* (University Park: Pennsylvania State University Press, 1992), 1.

31. Bernstein, 1.

32. Bernstein, 5–6.

33. For a critical reading of Al-e Ahmad's notion of "Gharbzadegi," see my most recent book on him, *The Last Muslim Intellectual: The Life and Legacy of Jalal Al-e Ahmad* (Edinburgh: Edinburgh University Press, 2020), 140–77.

34. See Hamid Dabashi, *Shi'ism: A Religion of Protest* (Cambridge, MA: Harvard University Press, 2012), 212.

35. Dabashi, 212.

36. Dabashi, 207–27, where I have made a more elaborate argument in reference to the artworlds of Abbas Kiarostami, early Shirin Neshat, and other contemporary artists.

37. Keshmirshekan, "Saqqa-Kana School of Art."

38. Keshmirshekan, "Saqqa-Kana School of Art."

39. Keshmirshekan, "Saqqa-Kana School of Art."

40. See Hans-Georg Gadamer, "The Relevance of the Beautiful," in his *The Relevance of the Beautiful and Other Essays* (Cambridge: Cambridge University Press, 1977/1986), 3–53.

41. Gadamer, 15.

42. In Saint Peter's Basilica in Rome, pilgrims who come to pay their respects to the bronze statue of Saint Peter touch and even kiss his feet—so much so that the bronze foot is now deformed. When I saw this for the first time in person it reminded me of similar gestures we Shi'i Muslims make when visiting the mausolea of our saints.

CONCLUSION

1. Hafez, *Divan*, edited with an introduction by Mohammad Ghazvini and Qassem Ghani (Tehran: Zavvar Publications, 1320/1941), 130. My translation from the Persian original.

2. Jean-Luc Nancy, *L'Évidence du film: Abbas Kiarostami* (Brussels: Yves Gevaert Editeur, 2001), 80–95.

3. See Shaykh Abu al-Futuh al-Razi, *Rawzat al-Jinan wa Ruh al-Janan* (Qom: 1404/1983), 5:567–73.

4. See Hamid Dabashi, "In the Absence of the Face," *Social Research* 67, no. 1 (Spring 2000): 127–85, https://www.jstor.org/stable/40971381.

5. See Hamid Keshmirshekan, ed., *Contemporary Art, World Cinema, and Visual Culture: Essays by Hamid Dabashi* (London: Anthem Press, 2019), chapters 2–7.

6. Film theorists such as Vivian Sobchack and Laura Marks have brought our attention to haptic visuality—Marks in particular has done so via an exciting inroad into Islamic philosophical traditions. My working through the visuality

complements these theorists in a decidedly different way. My preference at this stage is to bring attention to the ocularcentric proclivities in Persian and Persianate poetic imagination. See in particular Laura U. Marks, *The Skin of the Film: Intercultural Cinema, Embodiment, and the Senses* (Durham, NC: Duke University Press, 2000).

7. For an introductory but reliable volume on Avicenna's theology, see Arthur J. Arberry, *Avicenna's Theology* (London: Hyperion Press, 1951).

8. See Jacques Derrida, *Of Grammatology*, corrected edition, trans. Gayatri Chakravorty Spivak (Baltimore, MD: Johns Hopkins University Press, 1974). See Spivak's introductory remarks on this point on page xxxiv-xxxv and Derrida's own identification of "transcendental signified" as "primum signatum" on page 21.

9. For more on Abu al-Hasan Sani al-Mulk, see *Encyclopedia Iranica*, s.v. "Abu'l-Hasan Khan Gaffari," updated 21 July 2011, https://www.iranicaonline.org/articles/abul-hasan-khan-gaffari-sani-al-molk-1814–66-painter-in-oils-and-miniature-lacquer-artist-and-book-illustrator. For a more detailed study in Persian, see Yahya Zoka, *Zendegi va Asar-e Ostad Sani' al-Molk Abu al-Hasan Ghaffari/Life and Works of Master Sani' al-Molk Abu al-Hasan Ghaffari*, comp. and ed. Sirus Parham (Tehran: Markaz-e Nashr-e Daneshgah: Sazeman-e Miras-e Farhangi-e Keshvar, 2003). More details about this particular painting appear on page 147.

10. For more details on the *Forest without Leaves* exhibition, see its official website: https://www.exhibitiondesign.com/projects/forest-without-leaves.php.

11. Robert G. O'Meally, *Antagonistic Cooperation: Jazz, Collage, Fiction, and the Shaping of African American Culture* (New York: Columbia University Press, 2023), 1.

12. See James Slaymaker, "Cinema Never Dies: Abbas Kiarostami's *24 Frames* and the Ontology of the Digital Image," *Sense of Cinema*, no. 92 (October 2019), https://www.sensesofcinema.com/2019/feature-articles/cinema-never-dies-abbas-kiarostamis-24-frames-and-the-ontology-of-the-digital-image/.

A Filmography and Selected Works

Note: It is almost impossible to trace the proliferation of material on Abbas Kiarostami's cinema, photography, gallery works, poetry, stage productions, painting, and video installations. What follows is fairly representative of these materials but by no means exhaustive, which is both impossible and pointless. I am grateful to my research assistant Hoda Mohamed Elsharkawy for her help preparing this selected filmography and bibliography.

ABBAS KIAROSTAMI'S FEATURE FILMS

Kiarostami, Abbas, director. *Tajrobeh/Experience*. Iran: Janus Films, 1973.
——, director. *Mosafer/The Traveler*. Iran: Criterion Collection, 1974.
——, director. *Lebasi bara-ye Arusi/A Wedding Suit*. Iran: Kanun, 1976.
——, director. *Gozaresh/The Report*. Iran: Janus Films, 1977.
——, director. *Qaziyeh Shekl-e Avval, Shekl-e Dovvom/Case #1, Case #2*. Iran: Janus Films, 1979.
——, director. *Hamshahri/Fellow Citizen*. Iran: Janus Films, 1983.
——, director. *Avvali-ha/First Graders*. Iran: Janus Films, 1984.
——, writer. *Kelid/The Key*. Iran: Kanun, 1987.
——, director. *Khaneh-ye Dust Kojast/Where Is the Friend's House?* Iran: Criterion Collection, 1987.

———, director. *Mashq-e Shab/Homework*. Iran: Kanun, 1988.
———, director. *Kloz-Ap/Close-Up*. Iran: Kanun, 1989.
———, director. *Zendegi va Digar Hich/Life, and Nothing More* or *And Life Goes On*. Iran: Kanun, 1992.
———, script writer. *Safari beh Diar-e Mosafer/A Journey to the Land of the Traveler*. Directed by Bahman Kiarostami. Iran: Abbas Kiarostami Productions, 1993.
———, writer. *Badkonak-e Sefid/The White Balloon*. Directed by Jafar Panahi. Iran: Farabi Cinema Foundation, 1994.
———, writer. *Safar/The Journey*. Directed by Alireza Raissian. Iran: Hamrah Filmmaking Group, 1994.
———, director. *Zir-e Derakhtan-e Zeytun/Through the Olive Trees*. Iran: Miramax, 1994.
Kiarostami, Abbas, et al., directors. *Dar Bareh Nis/À propos de Nice, la Suite*. Italy: Margo Films, 1995.
Kiarostami, Abbas, et al., directors. *Lumier va Shoraka/Lumière and Company*. France: Cinétévé, 1995.
Kiarostami, Abbas, director. *Ta'm-e Gilas/Taste of Cherry*. Iran: Artificial Eye, 1997.
———, writer. *Bid-o-Bad/Willow and Wind*. Iran: Cima Media International, 1998.
———, director. *Bad Ma ra Khahad Bord/The Wind Will Carry Us*. Iran: New Yorker Films, 1999.
———, director. *ABC Afriqa/ABC Africa*. Iran: Abbas Kiarostami Productions, 2000.
———, director. *Dah/Ten*. Iran: Abbas Kiarostami Productions, 2001.
———, writer. *Istgah-e Matruk/Deserted Station*. Iran: Farabi Cinema Foundation, 2001.
———, director. *Dah Daghigheh Pirtar/Ten Minutes Older*. Iran, 2003.
———, director. *Panj/Five Dedicated to Ozu*. Iran: Janus Films, 2003.
———, writer. *Tala-ye Sorkh/Crimson Gold*. Directed by Jafar Panahi. Iran: Jafar Panahi Film Productions, 2003.
———, director. *10 Ro-ye 10/10 on Ten*. Iran: Abbas Kiarostami Productions, 2004.
———, director. *Belit-ha/Tickets*. Iran: Artificial Eye, 2005.
———, writer. *Kargaran Mashqul-e Karand/Men at Work*. Iran: Aftab Negaran Institute, 2006.
———, director. *Víctor Erice–Abbas Kiarostami: Correspondences*. Spain: Centre de Cultura Contemporània de Barcelona, 2006.
———, director. *Farsh-e Iran/Persian Carpet*. Iran: Farabi Cinema Foundation, 2007.
Kiarostami, Abbas, et al., directors. *Harkas Sinema-ye Khodash/To Each Their Own Cinema*. France: Cannes Film Festival, 2007.

———, director. *Shirin/Shirin*. Iran: Abbas Kiarostami Productions, 2008.
———, director. *Kopy Barabar-e Asl/Certified Copy*. Iran: Mk2 Films, 2010.
———, writer. *Ashna'i ba Leila/Meeting Leila*. Iran, 2012.
———, director. *Mesl-e Yek Asheq/Like Someone in Love*. France: Mk2 Films, 2012.
———, writer. *Emtehan Nahaee/Final Exam*. Iran: Motion Picture Marketing, 2016.
———, director. *24 Feraim/24 Frames*. Iran: Kiarostami Foundation, 2017.

ABBAS KIAROSTAMI'S SHORT FILMS

Kiarostami, Abbas, director. *Nan va Kucheh/The Bread and Alley*. Iran: Kanun, 1970.
———, director. *Behdasht-e Dandan/Dental Hygiene*. Iran: Kanun, 1971.
———, director. *Zang-e Tafrih/Recess*. Iran: Kanun, 1972.
———, director. *Do Rah-e Hal bara-ye Yek Mas'aleh/Two Solutions for One Problem*. Iran: Janus Films, 1975.
———, director. *Man Ham Mitavanam/So Can I*. Iran: Janus Films, 1975.
———, director. *Rangha/The Colors*. Iran: Kanun, 1975.
———, director. *Az Oqat-e Feraqat-e Khod Cheguneh Estefadeh Konim/How to Make Use of Our Leisure Time*. Iran: Kanun, 1976.
———, director. *Bozorgdasht-e Mo'alem-ha/Tributes to the Teachers*. Iran: Kanun, 1977.
———, director. *Jahan-nama Palace*. Iran: Kanun, 1977.
———, director. *Rah-e Hal/Solution*. Iran: Kanun, 1977.
———, director. *Beh Tartib, Bedun-e Tartib/Orderly or Disorderly*. Iran: Kanun, 1980.
———, director. *Hamsarayan/The Chorus*. Iran: Kanun, 1982.
———, director. *Tavallod-e Nur/The Birth of Light*. Iran: Waka Films, 1997.
———, writer. *Volte sempre, Abbas/Come Back Soon, Abbas!* Brazil: Filmes da Mostra, 1999.
———, director. *Jaddeh-ha-ye Kiarostami/Roads of Kiarostami*. Iran: Abbas Kiarostami Productions, 2005.
———, director. *Kojast Jay-e Residan/Is There a Place to Approach?* Iran, 2007.
———, director. *Ayandeh do bareh por shodeh/The Future Is Again Filled*. Venice, 2013.
———, writer. *La chica de la fábrica de limones/The Girl in the Lemon Factory*. Spain, 2013.
———, director. *Tokhm-e Morgh-ha-ye Darya'i/Seagull Eggs*. Iran: Abbas Kiarostami Productions, 2014.

ABBAS KIAROSTAMI'S BOOKS

Abbas Kiarostami. *Abbas Kiarostami: Photo Collection*. Translated by Claude Karbassi. Tehran: Iranian Art Publishing, 2000.

———. *Abbas Kiarostami: Photographies, Photographs, Fotografie*. Paris: Fernand Hazan, 2000.

———. *Walking with the Wind*. Translated by Ahmad Karimi-Hakkak and Michael Beard. Cambridge, MA: Harvard Film Archive, 2000.

———. *Des Milliers d'Arbres Solitaires*. Translated by Tayebeh Hashemi. Jean-Restom Nasser, Niloufar Sadighi, and Franck Merger. Illustrated by Mehdi Moutashar. France: Érès, 2004.

———. *A Wolf Lying in Wait*. Translated by Ahmad Karimi-Hakkak and Michael Beard. Iran: Sokhan, 2004.

———. *Hafiz beh Revayat Abbas Kiarostami*. Iran: Farzan, 2006.

———. *Una Poética de lo Real*. Italy: Malba, 2006.

———. *Sa'di az dast Khishtan faryad*. Iran: Niloofar, 2007.

———. *Pluie et Vent*. France: Gallimard, 2008.

———. *Un Loup Aux Aguets*. Translated by Jean-Claude Carrière and Nahal Tajadod. France: Table Ronde, 2008.

———. *Trees and Crows*. Edited by Arsalan Mohammad, Mehrnoush Fatholahi, and Charles Pocock. London: Art Advisory Associates Limited, 2009.

———, ed. *Ab—Nima Yushij*. By Nima Yushij. Tehran: Nazar Art Publications, 2010.

———. *Snow White*. Tehran: Nazar Publishing, 2010.

———. *Atish dar bad*. Tehran: Nazar Art Publications, 2011.

———. *Bad va Barg*. Tehran: Nazar Art Publications, 2011.

———. *The Wall*. Translated by Sohrab Mahdavi. Tehran: Nazar Art Publications, 2011.

———. *A Window into Life*. Preface by Catherine Millet. Tehran: Nazar Art Publications, 2011.

———. *Havres*. France: Érès. 2012.

———. *Abbas Kiarostami: Images, Still and Moving*. Edited by Silke von Berswordt-Wallrabe, Alexander Klar, and Ingrid Mössinger. Berlin: Hajte Cantz, 2013.

———. *Dad az Gham Tanha'i*. Tehran: Nazar Art Publications, 2013.

———. *Il Vento e La Foglia. Testo persiano a fronte*. Florence: Le Lettere, 2014.

———. *Doors and Memories*. New York: Nazar Publishing, 2015.

———. *Shab 'Asheqan Bi-del: Shab dar Ash'ar-i Sha'eran-i Kohan-i Parsi*. Tehran: Nazar Art Publications, 2015.

———. *Shab nadarad sar-e Khab: Shab dar Ash'ar-e Sha'eran-e Mo'aser*. Tehran: Nazar Art Publications, 2015.

———, ed. *Tears: Poetry by Saadi*. Vol. 1. By Saadi Shirazi. Translated by Iman Tavassoly and Paul Cronin. New York: Sticking Place Books, 2015.
———, ed. *Tears: Poetry by Saadi*. Vol. 2. By Saadi Shirazi. Translated by Iman Tavassoly and Paul Cronin. New York: Sticking Place Books, 2015.
———, ed. *Water: Poetry by Nima*. By Nima Yushij. Translated by Iman Tavassoly and Paul Cronin. New York: Sticking Place Books, 2015.
———. *Wind and Leaf*. Translated by Iman Tavassoly and Paul Cronin. New York: Sticking Place Books, 2015.
———, ed. *Wine: Poetry by Hafez*. By Khwajeh Shams-od-Din Mohammad Hafez-e Shirazi. Translated by Iman Tavassoly and Paul Cronin. New York: Sticking Place Books, 2015.
———. *With the Wind*. Translated by Iman Tavassoly and Paul Cronin. New York: Sticking Place Books, 2015.
———. *A Wolf on Watch*. Translated by Iman Tavassoly and Paul Cronin. New York: Sticking Place Books, 2015.
———, ed. *Fire: Poetry by Rumi*. Vol. 1. By Jalal al-Din Rumi. Translated by Iman Tavassoly and Paul Cronin. New York: Sticking Place Books, 2016.
———, ed. *Fire: Poetry by Rumi*. Vol. 2. By Jalal al-Din Rumi. Translated by Iman Tavassoly and Paul Cronin. New York: Sticking Place Books, 2016.
———, ed. *Fire: Poetry by Rumi*. Vol. 3. By Jalal al-Din Rumi. Translated by Iman Tavassoly and Paul Cronin. New York: Sticking Place Books, 2016.
———, ed. *Fire: Poetry by Rumi*. Vol. 4. By Jalal al-Din Rumi. Translated by Iman Tavassoly and Paul Cronin. New York: Sticking Place Books, 2016.
———. *In the Shadow of Trees: The Collected Poetry of Abbas Kiarostami*. Translated by Iman Tavassoly and Paul Cronin. New York: Sticking Place Books, 2016.
———, ed. *Night: Poetry from the Classical Persian Canon*. Vol. 1. Translated by Iman Tavassoly and Paul Cronin. New York: Sticking Place Books, 2016.
———, ed. *Night: Poetry from the Classical Persian Canon*. Vol. 2. Translated by Iman Tavassoly and Paul Cronin. New York: Sticking Place Books, 2016.
———. *Nuvens de Algodão*. Brazil: Ayine, 2018.
———. *Lessons with Kiarostami*. Edited by Paul Cronin. New York: Sticking Place Books, 2020.

SELECTED WORKS ON ABBAS KIAROSTAMI

Abbott, Mathew. *Abbas Kiarostami and Film-Philosophy*. Edinburgh: Edinburgh University Press, 2017.
Abedini, Husam. *In Safheh Sefid ast: Honar-e Ghayb Samu'el Beket va Abbas Kiarostami*. Tehran: Mo'asseseh-ye Farhangi-ye Pazhuheshi-ye Chap va Nashr-e Nazar, 2018.

Afarin, Farideh. *Khaneshi pasa-sakhtgara az Asar-i Abbas Kiarostami.* Tehran: Ilm, 2010.

Elena, Alberto. *The Cinema of Abbas Kiarostami.* London: Saqi Books, 2005.

El Khachab, Walid. "Sufi Cinema and Filmic Poetry in Abbas Kiarostami's Work." *Alif: Journal of Comparative Poetics,* no. 35 (2015): 204–26. https://www.jstor.org/stable/24772831.

Frodon, Jean-Michel, and Agnès Devictor. *Abbas Kiarostami: L'œuvre ouverte.* France: Gallimard, 2021.

Grønstad, Asbjørn. "Abbas Kiarostami's Shirin and the Aesthetics of Ethical Intimacy." *Film Criticism* 37, no. 2 (2012): 22–37. https://www.jstor.org/stable/24777860.

Holl, Ute. "Different Time, Different Space: Filmic Forms of Counter-Memory in Abbas Kiarostami's Koker Trilogy." In *Counter-Memories in Iranian Cinema,* edited by Ute Holl and Matthias Wittmann, 99–118. Edinburgh: Edinburgh University Press, 2021. https://www.jstor.org/stable/10.3366/j.ctv27zdj7w.12.

Hosseini, Emad, et al. *Sinema digar.* Tehran: Iranian Artists Forum, 2021.

Howell, Peter. "A Man of Depth and Surprises: Iran's Abbas Kiarostami Has a Penchant for Secrets." *Toronto Star,* 12 April 2013. https://www.thestar.com/entertainment/movies/abbas-kiarostami-a-man-of-depth-and-surprises-howell/article_de206058-ed4c-55c6-aba8-38939644322f.html.

Khosrowjah, Hossein. "Unthinking the National Imaginary: The Singular Cinema of Abbas Kiarostami." PhD diss., University of Rochester, 2011. ProQuest (UMI 3442770). https://www.proquest.com/dissertations-theses/unthinking-national-imaginary-singular-cinema/docview/853642294/se-2.

Langford, Michelle. "Seeking Love in the Interstices: Acousmatic Listening as Counter-Memory in Abbas Kiarostami's Shirin." In *Counter-Memories in Iranian Cinema,* edited by Matthias Wittmann and Ute Holl, 146–66. Edinburgh: Edinburgh University Press, 2021.

Mehdi Kimiagari, Mohammad. "The Frames That Unframe: Abbas Kiarostami's Method of Decreation in 24 Frames." *Film Criticism* 46, no. 1 (2022). https://doi.org/10.3998/fc.2713.

Mosavat, Mohamad, and Faezeh Mohajeri. "The Rhetoric of Imagism in the Cinepoetry of Jean Cocteau and Abbas Kiarostami: A Comparative Study." *Primerjalna Knjizevnost* 45, no. 2 (2022): 167–85. https://doi.org/10.3986/pkn.v45.i2.10.

Najafi, Saleh. *Ishq dar Sinema: Mesl-e yak Asheq.* Tehran: Laqa, 2019.

Pourahmad, Kayumars. *Khaneh-ye Dust kojast: Vaqaye'-negari-e Posht-e Sahneh, Film-nameh, Nazar-e Montaqedan va Tamashagaran.* Tehran: Kanun-i Parvaresh-i Fekri-i Kudakan va Nojavanan, 2016.

Rahbaran, Shiva. *Iranian Cinema Uncensored: Contemporary Filmmakers since the Islamic Revolution.* London: I. B. Tauris, 2016.

Sabouraud, Frédéric. *Abbas Kiarostami: Le cinéma revisité*. France: Presses Universitaires De Rennes, 2010.
Sa'ebi, Marjan. *Khaneh'i ba Shirvani-e Qermez: Goftugu ba Abbas Kiarostami va Aydin Aghdashloo*. Tehran: Sales, 2016.
Saeed-Vafa, Mehrnaz, and Jonathan Rosenbaum. *Abbas Kiarostami*. 2nd ed. Contemporary Film Directors. Champaign: University of Illinois Press, 2018.
Safarian, Robert. *Sinema-yi Abbas Kiarostami*. Tehran: Entesharat-e Rozaneh, 2016.
Saljoughi, Sara. "Seeing, Iranian Style: Women and Collective Vision in Abbas Kiarostami's 'Shirin.'" *Iranian Studies* 45, no. 4 (2012): 519–35. https://www.jstor.org/stable/23266445.
Sani, Mahmud Riza. *Abbas Kiarostami va Dars-ha-'i az Sinema*. Tehran: Entesharat-e Mo'in, 2014.
Sanjabi, Arash. *Menqar-e Baz-e Parandeh: Sinema-ye Abbas Kiarostami*. Tehran: Kitab-e Ameh, 2013.
Sheibani, Khatereh. "Kiarostami and the Aesthetics of Modern Persian Poetry." *Iranian Studies* 39, no. 4 (2006): 509–37. http://www.jstor.org/stable/4311855.
Sterritt, David. "With Borrowed Eyes." *Film Comment* 36, no. 4 (2000): 20–26. https://www.filmcomment.com/article/with-borrowed-eyes-an-interview-with-abbas-kiarostami/.
Vatulescu, Cristina. "'The Face to Face Encounter of Art and Law': Abbas Kiarostami's *Close-Up*." *Law and Literature* 23, no. 2 (2011): 173–94. https://doi.org/10.1525/lal.2011.23.2.173.

Index

NOTE: Page numbers in *italics* denote photographs.

Abbott, Mathew, *Abbas Kiarostami and Film-Philosophy*, 43-44, 102, 116-119, 241-242, 302n40
ABC Africa, 22, 34, 224-225, 234-235
Abdi, Mohammad, 12-13
Ab/Water (Kiarostami's anthology of poems of Nima Yushij), 55-56, 57
Academy Awards: Farhadi's *A Separation*, 10; *Through the Olive Trees* nominated, 166
actual realism of Kiarostami: central normativity of form in, 46; as decoding the perception of reality, 189-190; definition of, 45; and global triangulation, 61-62; the Koker Trilogy and, 23, 164, 171-172, 177; mobile vision of reality, 214-215; nonaesthetic reason (condition of coloniality) as suspended and overcome in, 45-46; ontology of *Mumkin al-Wujud* (Contingent Being) as aesthetics of, 213-214; as political act, 45, 46. *See also* factasy; fictive transparency of the real; nomadic un/knowing subject; poetic ontology of the un/real; realism; revisioning the world anew
Adorno, Theodor W.: aesthetic formalism and existential angst, 69-70, 71; aesthetic negativity, 42-43, 158; impossibility of representation after the Holocaust, 135, 136; modernity and the Holocaust, 96, 97, 99, 135, 136; partition between truth and the beautiful, 88; as questioning modernity's tyranny of Reason, 97, 99, 101; and the semblance of subjectivity, 227-228, 231. Works: *Aesthetic Theory*, 227; *Dialectic of the Enlightenment* (with Horkheimer), 96, 99
aesthetic alienation: anthropological gaze as exacerbating, 116-117, 118-119; autonomy of artworks and, 88, 89, 121, 160, 269; colonial modernity and, 90, 92, 96, 115, 212, 271; commodification of Kiarostami's artworks and, 125; definition of, 88; European (capitalist) modernity as defined by, 88-90, 92, 115, 212, 269; European and Eurocentric film-philosophy as exacerbating, 95, 116-119, 256; European philosophical partition between truth and the beautiful as, 88-89, 92, 224, 256; the global audience and generation of, 86-87, 90; and political duress, 90-92, 291; postcolonial audiences and, 87; Ta'ziyeh and lack of need for, 3

329

330   INDEX

—overcoming: overview, 164–165; alternative theories *to* modernity and, 95; collapse of false binary between East and West and, 109–110; embrace of repressed universalities as, 95, 97; European film-philosophy noticing, in Kiarostami's work, 116; factasy and, 106, 107; hyperreality as, 105; the Koker Trilogy and, 87, 115–118, 164–165; the nomadic un/knowing subject as, 163, 165; "the Now" and, 111, 115, 119–122, 125, 291; postcolonial liberation from (tertiary space), 109–110, 165; the sovereignty model as safeguard, 160, 163
aesthetic formalism: and existential angst, 69–71; framing the framer, 71–72; of Ozu and Kiarostami, compared, 231–234. *See also* form and fact, collapse of
aesthetic judgment. *See* European and Eurocentric philosophy—aesthetic judgment; postcolonial aesthetic judgment
aesthetic negativity, 42–43, 159
aesthetic pluralism. *See* agonistic philosophical heritage
aesthetic positivity, 42
aesthetic sovereignty of the unknowing subject: overview, 125; as contingent on an agonistic epistemology, 158–159; as enabled by the sovereignty of the work of art, 160–161
aesthetic sovereignty of the work of art: the agonistic disposition and, 159; autonomy and, 159–160; as exceeding the bounds of reason, 159–160; as safeguard against aesthetic alienation, 160, 163; the sovereign nomadic un/knowing subject enabled by, 160–161
aesthetic subjectivity, Kiarostami as catalyst for, 133, 291
African philosophers: as horrified by the racism of European philosophers, 203. *See also* Mudimbe, V. Y.
Africa, racist dismissal as site of critical and creative intelligence: Farhadpour and Islami, 129, 131; Kant, 199, 202–205, 313n14. *See also* European and Eurocentric philosophy—racism
Agamben, Giorgio, 43, 131
agency. *See* knowing European subject; nomadic un/knowing subject
Age of Discovery as age of colonial conquest, 109
Aghdashloo, Aydin, 79

agonistic cohabitation. *See* agonistic philosophical heritage
agonistic philosophical heritage: abandonment of fictive/idyllic reconciliation of East and West, 158; abandonment of "Western philosophy" as not the issue, 156, 294; as aesthetic pluralism/agonistic cohabitation, 157, 158, 294; as alchemy of Persian sources, 50–51, 294–296; as allowing cinema to breathe first in its own immediate natural habitat, 156–157, 158, 290, 294; and bodies of literature on Kiarostami, bringing together, 293; and contingent sovereignty of the nomadic un/knowing subject, 158–159, 291–292; contrapuntal reading of "Western philosophy" allowed by, 158; defined as wider philosophical imagination embracing both and irreducible to neither, 157, 158, 290, 294–295; definition of "agonistic," 157, 310n56; Eurocentrism of "Western philosophy" and need for, 155–156; inclusivity of, 158; negative dialectic resulting from, 158; as post-European film-philosophy, 294–295; provincialization of Eurocentric philosophy, need for, 28–29, 41, 89, 134–136, 212, 216, 242, 249, 294, 295–296, 317n6; Shafi'i-Kadkani on the aesthetic interpretation of Sufi texts, 157–158. *See also* interstitial space; postcolonial film-philosophy; Saqqakhaneh art movement; tertiary space
Ahmad, Aijaz, 128
Ahmed, Sarah, *The Culture Politics of Emotion*, 315n15
Ai Weiwei, 22
Akhavan-e Sales, Mehdi: "Barf/Snow," 164, 194; and the foreign familiarity of the un/real, 194; fragmentation revealing infinity, 106; in Kiarostami's collection of lines from Persian poets, 35; in New Persian Poetry/Nimaic tradition, 253, 254; and Nima's poetics, 65; self-effacing aesthetics of, 194; Zarathustra as central figure in, 284
Akhlaghi, Azadeh, 263, 276, 277
Akrami, Jamshid, 163
Al-e Ahmad, Jalal, 78–79, 80, 263, 270–271
Alexander Lighthouse, 32–33
alienation. *See* aesthetic alienation; *Ostranenie* (Viktor Shklovsky); Verfremdungseffekt (Bertolt Brecht's alienation effect)

Alizadeh, Ghazaleh, 77
Allamehzadeh, Reza, 175
the allegorical vs. the categorical: overview, 291; dialectic of Avicenna and Suhrawardi, 104; dialectic of Benjamin and De Man, 104; factasy and, 106, 107; Kiarostami on censorship in Iran and need for, 110; "Nowhereville" and, 102; and Ozu, 104; reading Kiarostami as (*Tamsil*), as liberating from colonial modernity, 104–105; and *Roads and Rain* landscape photography, 104–105, 266; and the worldly context of Kiarostami, 104–105. *See also* aesthetic alienation—overcoming; "Now, the"
allegory: national, Jameson reducing non-European artworks to, 199; the Saqqakhaneh art movement and allegorical iconography, 261, 273–274, 277, 281. *See also* avian allegories
alterities, repression of: alternative theories *to* modernity and embrace of the repressed, 95, 97, 98; as colonial project, 94, 95; by Eurocentric philosophy, 58
alterity, vs. totalizing identity: overview, 5; and cinematic identity, 18; heteroglossia and expression of, 106; and national identity, 7; and postcolonial film-philosophy, 30–31, 295
alternative theories *to* modernity: caution on dwelling overmuch on colonial modernity and postcolonial reason, 98; civilizational sites capable of, 99; European philosophers puncturing the preoccupation with "Modernity," 99–101; nativism and other traps preempting, 97; Persian literary humanism, 93; repressed alterities embraced in, 95, 97, 98; *Take Me Home* and need for, 94–95; as tertiary space of "both/and," 98–99, 105. *See also* allegorical vs. the categorical, the; intuition of transcendence; postcolonial film-philosophy
American Film Institute, 166
American Transcendentalism, 90
Aminpour, Qeysar, 254
Andersen, Nathan, 25, 26
Andrew, Dudley, 40–41
animals: in Kiarostami's cinema, as fabling the world, 208–212, 220, 292; non-Europeans considered to be, 207
anthropocentrism is Eurocentrism, 205–207, 208, 216, 220, 292

anthropology: as aiding colonialism, 97–98, 99; gaze of, as exacerbating aesthetic alienation, 116–117, 118–119; Kant's racism based in, 205; postnational cinema as, 13
anticolonial struggle, 109
Arab Spring, 16
area studies, 99, 294
Arendt, Hannah, 69
Argo (dir. Ben Affleck), 45
Aristotelian origins: European and Eurocentric philosophy claiming exclusivity to, 51, 155, 157; the Hollywood camera and mimesis of, 233; non-European philosophies and use of, 102, 156, 211; Shabih theory of mimesis as independent of, 227
Armajani, Siah, 276, 277; *Fallujah*, 276; *Seven Rooms of Hospitality*, 276
Arnold, Matthew, *Sohrab and Rustum: An Episode*, 89, 137
arrogance, Kiarostami charged with, 190
asceticism: of Ayatollah Khomeini/militant Shi'ism, 75, 272; of Kiarostami's camera, 265–266, 292; of Nima, 55
Ashtiani, Seyyed Jalal, 103
Ashuri, Daryush, 76
assimilation into Eurocentric philosophy. *See* European and Eurocentric philosophy—assimilation of non-Europeans backward into
Atash dar Bad/Fire in the Wind: A Selection of Rumi's Ghazals, 251, 252–253, 255
Attar, Farid al-Din, *Mantiq al-Tayr/Conference of the Birds*, 25–26, 33, *162*, 163, 208, 211, 243–244, 282, 285
Atwood, Blake, 40
avian allegories: Attar's metaphor of the birds, 25–26, 33, *162*, 163, 208, 211, 243–244, 282, 285; Avicenna's *al-Hikmah al-Mashriqiyah* (Oriental Philosophy), 210–212, 294; and cinema of Kiarostami, 208, 210–212, 220; *Resaleh al-Tayr/Bird Treatises*, 210–211. *See also* Persian poetic imageries (*Suvar-e Khayal*)
Avicenna: Aristotelian proclivities of, 211; and European philosophy cast as Philosophy, 200, 249; fusion of fiction and philosophy, 106–107, 122; as philosopher, 156; and reading of Kiarostami as allegory, 103–104; and the tertiary space, 109–110; visionary recitals of, 106–107, 122; the vision of God as metaphoric, 81.

Avicenna (continued)
   Works: *Ayniyyah Qasidah*, 211; *Hay ibn Yaghdhan*, 211; *al-Hikmah al-Mashriqiyah* (Oriental Philosophy), 210-212, 294. See also Islamic theology
Azari, Shoja, 277-278

Badiou, Alain, 131, 261-262
Bafghi, Vahshi, 35
Behbahani, Simin, 35
Bahrani, Ramin: author's friendship with, 24, 47; *Chop Shop*, 10, 24; as postnational filmmaker, 22
Bakhtin, Mikhail, 191
Bani-Etamad, Rakhshan, 10, 76-77, 312n48; *The Blue-Veiled*, 312n48
Baqi, Emad al-Din, 75
Bashar ibn Burd, 53, 54
Baudrillard, Jean, *Simulacra and Simulation*, 243
Baumbach, Nico, 240
BBC Culture's top 100 greatest foreign-language films, 6
BBC Persian, 11-12
Behzad, Kamal al-Din, 94
Beiza'i, Bahram: as active in the 1980s, 127; as altering how reality is perceived, 67; censorship/banning of, 76; Farhadpour and Islami assigning nativism to, 129; and the Iranian New Wave, 35; mythic realism of, 57, 61-62, 67; and postcolonial film-philosophy, 249; reception of, 24, 61, 62, 246; and Ta'ziyeh, 278; theater of, 79
Bejo, Berenice, 15
Bellaiche, Carole, 193
Benjamin, Walter: and allegory, 104; author's resonance with, 100, 305n13; Copernican turn in historiography, 18; and European philosophy's claim to Philosophy, 199-200; Jewish heritage of, 100; and Kiarostami, 117-118; and the "Now," 111-112, 119, 304-305n2; as questioning modernity's tyranny of Reason, 99, 100-101; on relics, 281; and the tertiary space, 109-110; "Thesis on the Philosophy of History," 86; translations by Farhadpour and Islami, 131
Bergman, Ingmar, 34, 62, 121; *The Blessed Ones*, 127
Berlin Film Festival: Mehrjui's *Gav/The Cow*, 8; Panahi's *Taxi* (Golden Bear), 11-12. See also European film festivals

Bernstein, J. M., 88-89, 92, 160, 269, 270-271
Berry, John, 229
Bhabha, Homi, 295
Bible, Levinas on all Philosophy as based in, 195, 199, 206
Binoche, Juliette, *225*
Bishara, Marwan, 46
Biswas, Moinak, 143, 144
Blanchot, Maurice, 99-100, 313n15
Blumenberg, Hans, 24
"Borromean rings" of national, postnational, and world cinemas: condition of coloniality and, 18; definition of, 4-5, 11; European film festivals and theoretical momentum of, 6-7; and Kiarostami as floating signifier, 41-42, 47, 290; and liberating reading of existential materialism and aesthetic formalism, 70; and reception theory, 5; as "trilectic," 11, 18, 63. See also agonistic philosophical heritage; alterity, vs. totalizing identity; interstitial space; national cinemas; postcolonial film-philosophy; postnational cinema; world cinema; worldly cinema
Bradbury, Ray, *Fahrenheit 451*, 24
Bradshaw, Peter: review of *Shirin*, 236-237; review of *Ten*, 195-196, 197
Braidotti, Rosi, 216, 217-218, 220, 247
The Bread and Alley/Nan va Kucheh, 56, 208-209, 210
Brecht, Bertolt. See Verfremdungseffekt (Bertolt Brecht's alienation effect)
Breivik, Anders Behring, 44
Brethren of Purity, 211
Burke, Johnny, 240
Bush, George W. administration, 44

Cage, John, *4'33"*, 235
Cahiers du Cinema, 146; dossier of Kiarostami's work, 193
Calarco, Matthew, 206-207
Calvin, John, 108
camera of Kiarostami: asceticism of, 265-266, 292; contingency of the real as location of, 85; as de-aestheticizing the institutionalization of false guilt, 191; *Five Dedicated to Ozu* as meditation on the digital, 224; and the foreign familiarity of the un/real, 24, 47, 292; Ozu as figuratively giving to Kiarostami, 231, 233, 292; parabolic prose of, 248; and the poetic ontology of the un/real, 77; private

moments, staying out of, 172, 186–187, 235; shaking/shaky, 178, 180–181; as strategically counter-essentializing, 190; as the Unseen Seer (Transcendental Signified), 84–85, 282–288, 290. *See also* long shots/long takes

Campion, Jane, 127

Cannes Film Festival: Bahrani's *Chop Shop*, 24; Farhadi's *The Past*, 15; Kechiche's *Blue Is the Warmest Color*, 15; *Like Someone in Love*, 234; Makhmalbaf's *Sib/Apple*, 9; Roberto Rossellini award given to Kiarostami (1992), 174; *Taste of Cherry* (1997 Palme d'Or), 23, 27, 31, 34, 37, 196; as vacation destination, 70. *See also* European film festivals

Caravaggio, 147

Carroll, Noël, 43

Cassirer, Ernst, *Myth of the State*, 96

Cavell, Stanley, 43, 199, 249; *The World Viewed*, 28

censorship. *See* Iran (Islamic Republic)—censorship

Certified Copy/Copy Barabar-e Asl, 34, 224–225, *225*, 234, 239–240

Césaire, Aimé, 78, 96; *Discourse on Colonialism*, 135

Ceylan, Nuri Bilge, 158

Chacon son Cinema/To Each Their Own Cinema, 238

Chahine, Youssef, 127

Chakrabarty, Dipesh, *Provincializing Europe*, 293

Chamarette, Jenny, 315n14

Chelkowski, Peter, 49

Cheshire, Godfrey, 247

Chomsky, Noam, 78

Christianity and Christian philosophy: Aristotelian domain and, 51, 155, 157; art as autonomous from, 88, 89, 269; Avicenna and Suhrawardi's visionary recitals and, 106; constructed as "Western philosophy," 58; the knowing European subject as Christian, 271; the secular as concealment of, 271

Cioran, E. M., 1–2

Cissè, Souleymane, 127

Cixous, Hélène, *ecriture feminine*, 42

class, 183

Close-Up/Nama-ye Nazdik, *141*; in BBC Culture's top 100 greatest foreign-language films, 6; factasy and, 67, 140–141, 177–178, 234–235; and the fictive transparency of the real, 144, 161; and global recognition of Kiarostami, 34; intuition of transcendence and, 66–67; long shot in penultimate sequence, 186; as masterpiece, 23; mimetic mis/representation between truth and fiction, 125, 163, 234–235; mysteries of, 151–152; reception of, 6, 163; rumors of unacknowledged sources used in, 120; and the sovereign nomadic un/knowing subject, 125, 161, 163; spectators as mirror image of themselves, 163; tongue-in-cheekness and, 67, 161

coloniality, condition of: actual realism and suspension/overcoming of, 45–46; aesthetic alienation exacerbated by dispossession of the product of colonized labor, 125, 212; colonized persons as knowable objects, 96–97, 100–101, 202; definition of, 221; denial of visas to Kiarostami as assertion of, 44–46, 216–217, 228–229, 230, 302–303n42, 315n15; enslavement justified by racism, 202–204; as epistemically severed from non-European philosophies, 58–59; as epistemic contingency, 63; the European partition between truth and the beautiful as alienation, 88–89, 256; historicization of, 40; national cinemas/Iranian cinema and, 15–18, 45, 290; postcolonial film-philosophy and overcoming of, 29–30, 119; as premise, 59; self-hatred and (Farhadpour and Islami), 126–131; the semblant subject and overcoming of, 226

colonial mentality, sanctioned ignorance of material published in non-European languages, 134

colonial modernity: and aesthetic alienation, 90, 92, 96, 112, 115, 291; as critical paradox, 295–296; as global capitalist project of terror, 96–97, 135–136, 308n15; as making non-Europeans alien to their own history, 109, 115, 231; and postcolonial aesthetics, 94–95, 98–99; and provincialization of Eurocentric philosophy, need for, 28–29, 41, 89, 134–136, 212, 216, 242, 249, 294, 295–296, 317n6; as stage the nomadic un/knowing subject leaves behind, 293. *See also* nomadic un/knowing subject

"comparative" or "alternative" modernities, argument against, 92–95, 96, 97, 98, 291, 296

contemporaneity of Kiarostami's artworld, 59–60, 256, 260, 291
contemporary art (*Honor-e Mo'aser*): Persian words identified with (*Mo'aser, No, Jadid*), 259, 260, 263; the Saqqa-khaneh movement as, 259, 260–261, 270, 273–274
contextual embeddedness, 73
contingency of the real, location of Kiarostami's camera as, 85
Copy Barabar-e Asl/Certified Copy, 34, 224–225, *225*, 234, 239–240
Corbin, Henry, 103, 104, 106, 211, 306n19
cosmopolitanism: of Kiarostami's cinema, 68; of pre-Islamic Republic Iran, 65, 74–75
counter-essentialism, 190
COVID-19 pandemic, 12
Crary, Alice, 43
critical theory: postcolonial, 135; postmodernist debate in, 135–136, 308n15
cyberspace, as interstitial space of art: and mass surveillance, 216–217; and the nomadic un/knowing subject, 220–221; and post-anthropocentricism that is not Eurocentric, 218–220; and posthuman agency, 217–220; as real space of aesthetic imagination, 215–216. See also digital technologies

Dabashi, Hamid: *Close-Up: Iranian Cinema, Past, Present, Future*, 13, 31, 141; *Iran without Borders: Towards a Critique of the Postcolonial Nation*, 94; *Islamic Liberation Theology: Resisting the Empire*, 305n13; *Masters and Masterpieces of Iranian Cinema*, 31, 45, 101; *Persophilia: Persian Culture on the Global Scene*, 93, 310n63; "Quis custodiet ipsos custodes?/ Who Will Watch the Watcher?," 237; *Shi'ism: A Religion of Protest*, 78, 93–94, 272; *The World of Persian Literary Humanism*, 93, 97, 157
Dad az Gham-e Tanha'i/Alas the Sorrow of Loneliness, 35–36
Damghani, Ali Moallem, 254
Daneshvar, Simin, *Savushun*, 17
Dauphin, Gary, 186
Deadline (website), 12
decolonial projects: of entire field of philosophy, 294; and the impossibility of total equivalency trafficking between cultures and concepts, 295; postcolonial film-philosophy as, 39–40, 224–225, 291–295
deferred aesthetic difference, 42

Dehkhoda, Ali Akbar, 69
Deleuze, Giles: backward assimilation of Kiarostami's cinematic thinking to, 302n40; *Cinéma I: L'image-mouvement*, 39; *Cinéma II: L'image-temps*, 39; and European film-philosophy, 134, 249; and periodization, 135–136, 146
De Man, Paul, 104, 109–110
Denis, Claire: and ethics, 143–144; interest of Jean-Luc Nancy in, 143, 144; *Vers Nancy*, 143
Derakhshandeh, Puran, 312n48
Derrida, Jacques: aesthetic negativity, 42–43; colonial condition of, 101; *différance*, 42, 164; and European claim on Philosophy, 57; and Kiarostami, 117–118; *Of Grammatology*, 286; partition between truth and the beautiful, 88; as questioning modernity's tyranny of Reason, 99, 100; Transcendental Signified (*primum signatum*), 81, 83, 286
Descartes, René, 199, 218
Deshpande, Shekhar, 18
De Sica, Vittorio, 62; *Bicycle Thieves*, 9
despair, politics of, 46, 78, 138
DiCaprio, Leonardo, 239–240
digital technologies: as allowing films to be made while incarcerated, 14; *Five Dedicated to Ozu* as meditation on the digital camera, 224; screening of films, 12, 14, 223; *24 Frames* as inquiry into the digital image, 297. See also cyberspace, as interstitial space of art
Dionysian celebration of life: Kiarostami and, 138, 165, 190–192; Sohrab Sepehri and, 188–189
Dissimulation (*Taqiyya, Kitman*), 240–241
Dolatabadi, Mahmoud, 76; *Colonel*, 76
Dorostkar, Reza, 170
Dostoyevsky, Fyodor Mikhailovich, 99, 100
Dulku, Shahrokh, 170–171
Dussel, Enrique, 30, 202, 208, 212, 293
Dustdar, Aramesh, 76

Eaglestone, Robert, 205–206
Ebert, Roger, review of *Ten*, 196, 197, 198
Eco, Umberto, triangulation of intention, 61, 152, 264, 318n27
Elkhas, Hannibal, 79
Ellison, Ralph, 297
Emami, Karim, and the Saqqa-khaneh art movement, 259, 264, 269, 271–272, 273, 280, 281

INDEX 335

Emerson, Ralph Waldo, "Saadi," 137
Enlightenment, as ideology of global conquest, 96, 99, 107–109
enslavement justified by racism, 202–204
epistemic violence: assimilation and approximation of non-Europeans backward into Eurocentric philosophy as, 44, 71–72; Eurocentric theories of modern art as, 262; Eurocentric theories of modernity as, 99; Pahlavi state-sponsored modernism as, 265; as perpetrated by non-Europeans reading "Western philosophy," 118
Erfan, 250
Erfani, Farhang, *Iranian Cinema and Philosophy: Shooting Truth*, 302n40
Ershadi, Homayoun, *197*, *214*, 287
Eshqi, Mirzadeh, 69, 276
E'tesami, Parvin, 64, 69
Europe: the Enlightenment as ideology of global conquest, 96, 99, 107–109; and secularist/modernist cadre opposed to Islamic Republic, 75–76; Spring of Nations (1848), 108. *See also* coloniality, condition of; European (capitalist) modernity; European and Eurocentric film-philosophy; European and Eurocentric philosophy; European film festivals
European (capitalist) modernity: aesthetic alienation as definitive to, 88–90, 92, 115, 212, 269; anthropology and other academic fields at the service of, 97–98, 99; assimilation of non-Europeans backwards into, 95, 101; autonomy of art works, 88, 89, 159, 160, 269; binary of realism and modernism, 101, 102; center and periphery rhetoric of, 94, 96, 115, 119, 280; as colonial project, 88, 90, 92, 93–94, 96–99, 135–136; as commodity fetishism (Marx), 125, 212; "comparative" or "alternative" modernities, argument against, 92–95, 96, 97, 98, 291, 296; defined as term, 88; disenchantment with the world (Weber), 89, 125; the Enlightenment as ideology of global conquest, 96, 99, 107–109; as epistemic tyranny of Reason, 97–98, 99–101; epistemic violence produced by, 99; falsely cast as global Modernity, 88; false universal claims made by, 89, 95; as global capitalist project of terror, 96–97, 135–136, 260, 308n15; the Holocaust as end of, 96, 97, 99, 135, 136; partition between truth and the beautiful, 88–89, 92, 224, 256; Persophilia, 90; philosophers puncturing the European preoccupation with, 99–101; postmodernist debate, 135–136, 308n15; post-postmodernism, 147; provincial Eurocentricity of, 89; "tradition" invented to justify colonial conquests, 95, 98–99, 100, 104; the transnational public sphere and, 93–94. *See also* alternative theories *to* modernity; colonial modernity; knowing European subject; modern art; Pahlavi dynasty—state-sponsored modernism

European and Eurocentric film-philosophy: overview, 28–29, 302n40; absence of awareness of Eurocentricity, 134, 156; aesthetic alienation exacerbated by, 95, 116–119, 256; the anthropological gaze and, 116–117, 118–119; colonialization by, 95; commodification of Kiarostami's artworks and, 241; "comparative" and "alternative" modernities, argument against, 92–95, 96, 97, 98, 291, 296; definition of, 28; double vision (Said), 28, 29; ethics, 143–144; as excluding non-European philosophies, 199–200; humanist readings of Kiarostami, 68–70; Islamic philosophy unrecognized by, 117–118; moral reading of Kiarostami, 240; periodization of cinema, 135–137, 138; Persian poetic allusions unrecognized by, 49, 50–51, 54, 117; Plato's allegory of the cave, 25–26, 33, 102, 198, 239, 282; and the poetic disposition of philosophy, 256; as productive misunderstanding, 43, 241–242; provincialization of, need for, 28–29, 41, 89, 134–136, 212, 216, 242, 249, 294, 295–296, 317n6; the real as unrepresentable, 144; as retaining the security blanket of "Western philosophy," 156; rightful pride of place of, 134; sanctioned ignorance of material published in non-European languages and archive, 134, 200; temporal (and spatial) lagging of engagement with, 133–134. *See also* agonistic philosophical heritage; film-philosophy; postcolonial film-philosophy

European and Eurocentric philosophy: absence of awareness of Eurocentricity, 156; agonistic philosophical heritage, the need to expand to, 155–156; alterities repressed by, 58; anthropocentrism is Eurocentrism, 205–207, 208, 216, 220, 292; canon of, as no longer sufficient, 41;

European and Eurocentric philosophy *(continued)*
  falsely cast as all and only Philosophy, 57-60, 102, 116-117, 155-156, 199-200, 224; partition between truth and the beautiful, 88-89, 92, 224, 256; postcolonial thinkers as unintended readership of, 118; poststructuralism, 100; provincialization of, need for, 28-29, 41, 89, 134-136, 212, 216, 242, 249, 294, 295-296, 317n6; as "Western philosophy," 58. *See also* agonistic philosophical heritage; European (capitalist) modernity; European and Eurocentric film-philosophy; humanism—and European philosophy; universalizing claims by Eurocentric philosophy, as false
  —aesthetic judgment: feelings as basis of, 201; Kant's critique of, 200, 201-202, 270-271; the morally beautiful, 203; postcolonial aesthetic judgment as engaged with but not possessed by, 207-208, 210, 212-213, 215, 216, 217-218, 220, 220-221; as subjective or objective, as question, 200; the sublime and the beautiful, capacity to appreciate, 201, 202, 205. *See also* knowing European subject
  —assimilation of non-Europeans backward into: overview, 43-44, 50, 302n40; as colonialization, 95, 97, 98; as epistemic violence, 44, 71-72; as exacerbating aesthetic alienation, 256; postcolonial film-philosophy vs., 217, 293; recent work on Kiarostami's cinema, 64
  —racism: anthropocentrism is Eurocentrism, 205-207, 208, 216, 220, 292; enslavement justified by, 202-204; internalized, 206, 207; of Kant, 199, 202-205, 313n14; Kant as inventing race, 313n14; of Levinas (non-Europeans are just "dancing"), 195, 199, 200, 202, 204-206, 207, 212; non-Europeans as animals, 207; Spinoza's monism and, 220; "whitening" processes and, 204; whitewashing or "contextualization" as attempts to save European racists from themselves, 204-205, 206-207
European film festivals: and aesthetic alienation, 87, 115; commodification of Kiarostami's artworks at, 125; and construction of "world cinema," 6-7, 18-19; Eurocentric detractors of Kiarostami dismissing success at, 196, 198; festival curators from around the world as taking their cues from, 7; global reception of Kiarostami as indebted to, 23, 27, 31, 34, 37, 86, 196; Iranian detractors of Kiarostami denouncing, 168-169, 175; postnational cinema as catering to, 11, 21; as reprieve from late capitalist boredom, 70; "the West and the Rest" narrative of, 115. *See also* Berlin Film Festival; Cannes Film Festival; Locarno Film Festival; Venice Film Festival
European Romanticism, 96
exile, 62, 63, 66

fabling the world, 208-212, 220, 292
factasy: and aesthetic alienation, liberation from, 106, 107; and allegories transmuted into categories, 106, 107; as alternating between expected factual familiarity and fantasy, 185; *Close-Up* and, 67, 140-141, 177-178, 234-235; compared to fusion of fiction and philosophy of Avicenna and Suhrawardi, 106-107; definition of, 13, 23, 67, 107; Farrokhzad and, 8, 23; irony and, 177, 181, 183; Koker Trilogy and, 23; Latin American magical realism and, 185; as the opposite of Nancy's notion of film giving back its own real, 140-141; Panahi and, 13; in the Saqqa-khaneh art movement, 268; self-parody and, 179; as signature of Kiarostami, 185; as studied unstudiedness, 177; Suhrawardi's Mundus Imaginalis and, 185; as tertiary space, 97, 107, 235; *Through the Olive Trees* and, 177, 178-179, 181, 185. *See also* fictive transparency of the real
Fakhr, Mostafa Jalai, 172
Fanon, Frantz, 78, 136, 208, 308n15; *Black Skin, White Masks*, 17
Farasati, Mas'ud: review of *And Life Goes On*, 168-169; review of *Through the Olive Trees*, 172-174
Farhadi, Asghar, 15-16, 17, 18; *Joda'i Nader az Simin/A Separation*, 6, 10; *The Past*, 15
Farhadpour, Morad, and Maziyar Islami, *Paris-Tehran: The Cinema of Abbas Kiarostami*, 119, 126-131, 133, 148
Farid, Samir, 87
Farmanara, Bahman, 10, 76, 193
Farrokhzad, Forough: and the 1995 Locarno Film Festival, 312n48; death of, 73, 76,

246; factasy and, 8, 23; as founding mother of Iranian cinema, 8, 23, 65; in Kiarostami's collection of lines from Persian poets, 35; in New Persian Poetry/Nimaic tradition, 65, 253, 254; and the Persian poetic disposition of Kiarostami, 256; reception of, 61. Works: "Kasi key Mesl-e Hich Kas Nist/Someone Who Is Like No One," 284; *Khaneh Siah Ast/The House Is Black*, 8, 23, 91

fascism, Cioran and, 2

Fassbinder, Rainer Werner, 127

Fellini, Federico, *La Dolce Vita* as influence, 176

Ferdowsi Tusi, Abul-Qasem, 89, 90, 137, 255

fictive transparency of the real: *Close-Up* and, 144, 161; definition of, 142–143; intrusion and interruption as operative modes of, 185–187; Kurosawa and, 142–143; Nancy and, 144; as the pre-interpretive moment of the world, 142; Sepehri and, 142, 143, 154–155; subversive reading of a culture of inhibition, 182–184; *Through the Olive Trees* and, 182–187, 292; as verisimilitude, 144. *See also* factasy

Film (journal), 169, 175–176

film-philosophy: Alexander Lighthouse metaphor, 32–33; Attar's metaphor of the birds, 25–26, 33, *162*, 163, 208, 211, 243–244, 282, 285; definition of, 28; and movies as inventing a new way of thinking, 150; multiple periodizations in, 135; multiple provenances in, 134; Plato's allegory of the cave, 25–26, 33, 102, 198, 239, 282. *See also* European and Eurocentric film-philosophy; postcolonial film-philosophy

Film-Philosophy (journal): overview, 301n25; and Nancy-Denis encounter, 143. *See also* Nancy, Jean-Luc, *L'Evidence du film: Abbas Kiarostami*—Laurent Kretzschmar review of

Film Studies, 28

Fitzgerald, Edward, translation of *Rubaiyat of Omar Khayyam*, 33–34, 89, 137, 305n12

Fitzgerald, Ella, 240

Five Dedicated to Ozu, 104, 223–224, 225, 230, 233–234

floating signifier, Kiarostami as: and global recognition, 63; and location within the adjacent spaces of national, postnational, and world cinemas, 41–42, 47, 290; and placement within various theoretical narratives, 39. *See also* nomadic un/knowing subject

foreign familiarity of the un/real: overview, 105–106; Akhavan-e Sales and, 106, 194; the camera of Kiarostami and, 24, 47, 292

"Forests with Leaves" (installation at Victoria and Albert Museum), 289–290

form and fact, collapse of: overview, 291; framing the framers, 71–72; and the poetic ontology of the un/real, 77, 291; postcolonial humanism and, 71–72; as tertiary space, 77; and Verfremdungseffekt as being-toward-death, 72–74, 291

Forster, E. M., *Howards End*, 109

Foucault, Michel: on the language of psychiatry, 107; *Madness and Civilization*, 107; modernity and technologies of repression, 97; and sexual abuse, 204; on the unreason, 107

Fouladvand, Ahmad, 193

framing, and Ghaffari's "Untitled" (painting), 288, *289*

—Kiarostami and: framing the framers, 71–72, 290; as necessity, 5, 289

France: claim on Kiarostami due to global emergence at Cannes, 148, 247; and colonial condition of Tunisia, 15–17; French Revolution (1789), 108; inclusion of Kiarostami in "leading directors" article naming their influences, 175–176; opera, Kiarostami as director of Mozart's *Così fan Tutte*, 35, 228, 229–230, 315nn14–15. *See also* Cannes Film Festival

François Truffaut Prize, 174

Freud, Sigmund: Adorno and, 227; "Mourning and Melancholia," 128; the Uncanny, 164

Furuzesh, Ebrahim, 193

Gadamer, Hans Georg, 200; "The Relevance of the Beautiful," 279–280

Gaffary, Farrokh, 193

Ganeri, Jonardon: *Attention, Not Self*, 30–31; "Blueprint for a Cosmopolitan Philosophy in a Polycentric World," 41

Ganji, Akbar, 75

German Romanticism, 90

Ghaffari, Abol-Hassan Naqqashbashi ("Sani' al-Molk"), "Untitled" (painting), 288, *289*

Ghaffari, Farrokh, 10, 65

338 INDEX

Al-Ghazali, *Resaleh al-Tayr*, 211
Al-Ghazali, Ahmad, 211
Ghazvini, Mohammad, 252
global context, Al-a Ahmad and preparation of Persian culture for, 78–79
global recognition of Kiarostami as visionary filmmaker: overview, 22–23, 26–27, 34–35, 245–246; aesthetic alienation as generated by, 86–87, 90; assemblage of significance in, 248; death of Kiarostami and, 73–74; and hermeneutic triangulation, 61–62; Iranian social context and, 65; Kiarostami as most significant cultural event of Iran in the twentieth century, 89–90; as mitigating Islamic Republic censorship, 76, 77; the Palme d'Or award (1997 Cannes) and emergence of, 23, 27, 31, 34, 37, 196; and the photographic landscape, 257; as reprieve from late capitalist boredom, 70; and reticence to criticize Kiarostami trespassing Persian poets' works, 55–56; and rootedness of cultural heritage, 62–63, 66; and vacuous praise for poetry of Kiarostami, 254, 317n9; visa denials to Kiarostami as schizophrenic divide between European art scene and politicians, 228–229, 230, 315nn14–15. *See also* European film festivals; literature on Kiarostami; transnational public sphere
Godard, Jean-Luc, 14–15, 237
Goethe, Johann Wolfgang von, *West-östlicher Divan*, 33–34, 89–90, 137, 251
Golestan, Ebrahim, 10, 61, 65, 76
Golmakani, Houshang, 169, 187, 193
Golshiri, Houshang, 76
Golzar, Farhad, 168
González-Iñárritu, Alejandro, 224
Gören, Şerif, 14
Greek philosophy, classical: Levinas on Philosophy as based on, 195, 199, 206. *See also* Aristotelian origins; Plato
Griffith, DW, 14
The Guardian, 195, 236–237
Güney, Yilmaz, *Yol*, 14, 127
Gutas, Dimitri, 211

Habermas, Jürgen, 89, 92, 101, 270, 271, 310n63
Hafez: *Divan*, 282; Goethe's *West-östlicher Divan* as inspired by, 33–34, 89–90, 137, 251; as influence, 94; in Kiarostami's collection of lines from Persian poets, 35–36; Kiarostami's volume on (*Hafez beh Revayat Abbas Kiarostami/Hafez as Told by Abbas Kiarostami*), 251–253, 255, 287; Meskub on, 103; *Nazar-bazi* (playfully seeing things), 285; ocularcentrism of, 285–286; philosophical disposition of, 255; and postcolonial film-philosophy, 249; Rendi, 250; Shamlou's rendition of, 252
Haghighat, Mohammad, 193
Haiku, 209
Hajjarian, Saeed, 75
Hall, Stuart, 5
Hamacher, Werner, 111–112
"al-Hamamah al-Mutawwaqa/The Ringdove," 211
Hatami, Ali, and the Iranian New Wave, 35
Hatoum, Mona, 22
Hedayat, Sadegh, 64, 66, 73, 77, 79
Hegel, Georg Wilhelm Friedrich: Adorno and, 227; anthropocentrism and humanism as Eurocentrism, 216; and moments of divergence in European philosophy, 100–101; postcolonial film-philosophy as outside the system of, 212, 215; racist exclusion of non-Europeans from system of, 202, 204, 207, 216, 220
Heidegger, Martin: backward assimilation of Kiarostami's cinematic thinking to, 43, 302n40; and European claim on Philosophy, 57, 58–59, 249; on humanism, 68–69, 97; and Kiarostami, 117–118; Nazism of, 204; the ontic thingness of things, 138, 147, 153; phenomenology, 138, 147, 153; as questioning modernity's tyranny of Reason, 99, 100, 101; turn to existentialism, 70; turn to poetry, 256. Works: *Being and Time*, 58–59; "Question Concerning Technology," 97–98
Hekmat, Manizheh, 10
heteroglossia: alterities denoted and connoted in, 106; and assemblages of language in the postcolonial mind, 106; and contrapuntal reading of the literature, 38–39; nomos, logos, and mythos, 106
Heydari, Gholam, 170
Hilli, Allamah, 52
Hiroshima, 96
Hoberman, J., 166–167
Hoblit, Gregory, *Primal Fear*, 240
Holden, Stephen, 163
Hölderlin, Friedrich, 256
Hole, Kristin Lené, 143–144

Hollywood: camera of, informed by Aristotelian mimesis, 233; the sublime asceticism of Kiarostami in contrast with, 266; "world cinema" as disguise for hegemony of, 231
Holocaust: as end of European capitalist modernity, 96, 97, 99, 135, 136; Levinas as survivor of, 100, 206
Homework/Mashq-e Shab, 70–71, 84–85
homocentric (*Tasawwuf*) proclivities, 157, 250
homoeroticism, 277
Horkheimer, Max, *Dialectic of the Enlightenment* (with Adorno), 96, 99
Hossein, Imam, 259, 276, 278
Hou Hsiao-Hsien, 41, 127, 139
Huhn, Tom, ed., *The Semblance of Subjectivity: Essays in Adorno's Aesthetic Theory*, 227–228
humanism: Islamic philosophy and (*Adab*), 157; Persian literary, "secularism" and "modernism" as terms not found in, 93
—and European philosophy: aesthetic formalism and existential angst, distinction between, 70; as Eurocentrism in false universal disguise, 216; "Existentialism is Humanism," 68; Iranian cinema and dimensions of, 91–92; and modernity as tyranny of Reason, 97; and post-anthropocentrism, 217–218, 220; readings of Kiarostami as humanist, 68–70, 163, 166; as robbing authorial agency and visual idiomaticity, 68–69
—and postcolonial Iranian cinema: aesthetic formalism in tune with existential angst, 69–71; collapse of form and fact onto each other, 71–72; and condition of coloniality, 69; and Rumi's condition of the posthuman and post-androcentricity, 218–221; the transnational public sphere and, 69
Hume, David, 202
Hussein, Saddam, 276
hybridity, 295

Ibn Battuta, travel narratives, 214
Ibn Sina. *See* Avicenna
identity politics, the nomadic un/knowing subject and denial of, 220–221
Ikhwan al-Safa/The Brethren of Purity, 210–211
Illuminationist Philosophy (*Falsafah Ishraq*), 102–103, 156
Imamura, Shôhei, 127, 128
Imam-zadeh mausoleums, 267

India, Iranian cinema first produced in, 7–8
Indian philosophy, 30–31
Institute for Comparative Modernities, 92–93
interpretation, subversion of, 192
interstitial space: overview, 5, 6, 7, 34; and backward assimilation of Kiarostami's cinematic thinking into Eurocentric philosophy, 302n40; and collapse of the false binary of aesthetics vs. politics, 31–32; and formation of the semblant subject, 292; Lefebvre's "social space" and, 6; postnational cinema distinguished from, 11; Soja's "third space" and, 6; as surpassing both nativist and globalized readings, 42, 242. *See also* cyberspace, as interstitial space of art; nomadic un/knowing subject; tertiary space
In the Shadow of Trees: The Collected Poetry of Abbas Kiarostami, 35
intuition of transcendence: overview, 291; affinity with Suhrawardi's "Nowhereville" ("*Na-koja-abad*"), 101–103, 294; alienation of artists from Persian philosophy and need for theorization of, 157; and *Close-Up*, 66–67; and collapse of the false binary of aesthetics vs. politics, 32; and the collective unconscious of Iranian literary and artistic scene, 102–104; the condition of coloniality as context of, 66, 69; vs. European binary of modernity and realism, 101, 102; framing the framers and, 71–72; global recognition of Kiarostami and, 65–66, 77; harbingers of, 69; phantom liberties and, 69; and poetic of Divine in/visibility, 85; and the Saqqakhaneh art movement, 269
Iqbal, Muhammad: *Asrar-e Khodi*, 255; as philosopher, 156; *Romuz-e Bekhodi*, 255
Iran: artists as "philosophers" in, 66; Constitutional period (1906–1911), 51, 65, 69, 74–75; cosmopolitanism and, 65, 74–75; coup of 1953 (staged by CIA-MI6), 45, 64, 257–258, 272, 274; in the geopolitics of coloniality, 16, 45, 64–66; Iranian revolution (1977–1979), 8, 65–66, 75, 257–258; military coup by Reza Khan (1921) and establishment of Pahlavi dynasty, 64; "al-Musanna" (certified copy of official document), 239; occupations during the First and Second World Wars, 16, 64, 198; and rise of modern Persian fiction, 65; Tudeh Party, 64. *See also* Iranian cinema; Pahlavi dynasty; Shi'ism

Iran (Islamic Republic): Ayatollah Khomeini dictatorship, 9, 65, 75–76, 272; corruption, brutality, and violence in, 75–76; culture of inhibition, 182–184; demonization of Iranian people and state in the US, 91–92; global attention as protecting Iranian cultural workers, 76, 77; Green Movement (2008–2010), 9; Iranian revolution (1977–1979), 8, 65–66, 75, 257–258; Iran-Iraq War (1980–1988), 8–9, 65, 75; "Islamic dress," 180, 237; reactionary asceticism of, 75, 272; reformist movement, 65; "religious intellectuals" as ideological officers of, 75–76; the Saqqakhaneh art movement as exceeding attempts to claim, 261, 264–265, 268–269, 272, 273, 276, 278; secularist/modernist cadre, as opposition in Europe, 75–76; US hostage crisis (1979–1981), 45, 91–92; US hostilities with, 166
—censorship: overview, 75, 76–77; cultural workers silenced and censored, 75, 76–77; global attention on cultural workers as mitigating, 76, 77; Kiarostami as caught between, and treatment as "prospective terrorist" in the West, 228–229; Kiarostami on symbolic language demanded by context of, 110; Kiarostami remaining in Iran despite, 246; Naderi's response to, 20–21; *Naqd-e Cinema*, review of *Through the Olive Trees*, 172–174; of Panahi, 9, 12, 13–14; and postnational cinema, rise of, 13–14; propaganda policies vis-a-vis European film festivals, 175; of Sirjani, 115; women in Kiarostami's works wearing Islamic dress to avoid offending, 237
—cinema officials: overview, 11; denouncing the Berlin Film Festival for Panahi's *Taxi* prize, 11–12; Kiarostami's cinema, value to, 166, 174–175, 176
Iranian cinema: "*Ab-e-ru-ye Sinema-ye Iran/The Honor of Iranian Cinema*" (honorary title of Kiarostami), 130; and BBC Culture's 100 greatest foreign-language films, 6–7; and coloniality, conditions of, 15–18, 45, 290; the defining national trauma of, 17, 45; ethical and humanist dimensions of, 91–92; Farrokhzad as founding mother of, 8, 23, 65; filmmakers assumed to be representatives of the Islamic Republic, 166–167; global audience as possibility for, 79; rise and flowering of, 65–66, 76–77; the transnational public sphere in formation and history of, 7–10; and world cinema, 6–7, 9, 10, 19, 290. *See also* interstitial space; Iran (Islamic Republic)—censorship; Iranian literature on Kiarostami; Iranian New Wave; national cinemas; realism; *specific filmmakers*

Iranian literature on Kiarostami: appreciative critics, 167, 169–170, 172, 174–175, 198; cultural issues and, 167–168; Eurocentric critics: Farhadpour, Morad, and Maziyar Islami, *Paris-Tehran: The Cinema of Abbas Kiarostami*, 119, 126–131, 133, 148; and the false binary of politics vs. aesthetics, 31–32; hostile critics, 167–169, 170–171, 172–174, 175, 189–191, 192, 198; as ignoring and as ignored by studies in other languages, 31, 32, 38, 198, 293; and the interstitial space of Kiarostami's location, 242; Kiarostami's responses to criticisms, 171–172; Koker Trilogy reception, 165–166, 167–174, 175; by political opponents of the Islamic Republic, 174–175; and the politics of ressentiment, 32. *See also* literature on Kiarostami

Iranian New Wave: overview, 22–23, 35; Farhadpour and Islami attack on, 126, 128–130; Kiarostami and, 23, 35; as many potential movements, 91; Naderi and, 19, 35

Iranian Studies, 294

Irani, Ardeshir, *Dokhtar-e Lor/Lor Girl*, 8

Iraqi, Fakhr Al-Din, *Koliyyat*, 245, 249–250

Islamic mysticism. *See* Sufism

Islamic philosophy: *Alam al-Mithal*/Mundus Imaginalis, 101–102, 185; backward assimilation of filmmakers into, 64; the beautiful is the true ("Inna Allah Jamilun wa Yuhibbu al-Jamal/God is Beautiful and He loves Beauty!"), 88–89, 157–158; and claim of European philosophy to Philosophy, 58–60, 102; Day of Judgment, and moral/ethical dimension to seeing, 283–284; death and bodily resurrection (*Ma'ad-e Jismani*), 116; "Die before your death," 72; the earth as witness to our deeds, 284; European film-philosophy as not recognizing, 117–118; homocentric (*Tasawwuf*) proclivities, 157, 250; *Ikhwan al-Safa*/The Brethren of Purity, 211; Illuminationist Philosophy (*Falsa-

fah Ishraq), 102–103, 156; and literary humanism (*Adab*), 157; logocentric (*Falsafah*) proclivities, 157; Neoplatonic Philosophy, 156; nomocentric (*Shari'ah*) proclivities, 157; Orientalists' version of, 156; Peripatetic Philosophy, 156; physical resurrection on Day of Judgment/ *Yawm al-Qiyamah*, 117; Platonic and Aristotelian traditions in, 102, 156, 157; and sacred journeys (*Ziarat*), 266–267; "Seek knowledge even in China!" (hadith), 274; Transcendental Philosophy (*al-Hikmah al-Muta'aliyah*), 117–118, 156. *See also* avian allegories; Shi'ism; Sufism

Islamic theology: Divine in/visibility, 80–85, 285–287, 291; *Mumkin al-Wujud*/Contingent (Possible) Being, 83, 213–214, 286; *Mumtani' al-Wujud*/Impossible Being, 213, 286; *Wahdat al-Wujud*/ Unity of Being, 218; *Wajib al-Wujud*/ Necessary Being/Transcendental Signified, 83, 213, 285–287

Islami, Majid, 170

Islami, Maziyar. *See* Farhadpour, Morad, and Maziyar Islami, *Paris-Tehran*

Islamism, as invention of the "West," 75

Jacir, Emily, 22
Ja'farian, Hossein, 187
Jahanbagloo, Ramin, 193
Jaikumar, Priya, 30
Jalali, Bahman, 79; and Saqqa-khaneh art, 263, 267–268, 269, 277, 280–281
Jameson, Fredric, 90, 136, 199
Japan, 231; Haiku, 209. *See also* Kurosawa, Akira; Mizuguchi, Kenji; Ozu, Yasujirō
Jarmusch, Jim, 127
Javed, Sareh, 302n40
Jewish philosophy, 58, 157
Jousse, Thierry, 193
Jung, Carl, 102–103

Kadivar, Mohsen, 75
Kaige, Chen, 34, 127, 158
Kalantari, Parviz, and Saqqa-khaneh art, 267–268, 269, 277, 280–281
Kalari, Mahmoud, 10
Kamali, Ali, 209
Kant, Immanuel: Adorno and, 227; the colonized person as knowable object, 97, 100–101, 202; critique of aesthetic judgment, 200, 201–202, 270–271; and European philosophy cast as Philosophy, 200; on feelings as basis of aesthetic judgment, 201; on the "grotesqueries" of non-Europeans, 195, 199, 203; partition between truth and the beautiful, 88; postcolonial aesthetic judgment as standing outside of system of, 208, 210, 212, 215, 216, 220–221; race as invented by, 313n14; racism of, 199, 202–205, 207, 220, 313n14; sovereign subject, 99. Works: *Critique of Judgment*, 201–202, 270; *Critique of Practical Reason*, 201; *Critique of Pure Reason*, 201, 202; *Observations on the Feeling of the Beautiful and Sublime*, 195, 202–204

Karatani, Kojin, 208
Karbala Complex, 226, 240, 259, 276, 277, 278
Karimi, Niki, 120, 228
Kauffmann, Stanley, 166
Kaurismaki, Aki, 44, 302–303n42
Kechiche, Abdellatif, 15–16, 17, 18; *Blue Is the Warmest Color*, 15
Kehr, Dave, 19, 247
Kelilah and Dimnah, 210–211, 294
Keshavarz, Mohammad Ali, 178–179, 186
Keshmirskekan, Hamid, 258, 260, 261, 269–270, 272–273, 274–275
Khanlari, Parviz Natel, 252
Kharaqani, Abu al-Hasan, 158
Khayyam, Omar: cinema of Kiarostami as Dionysian/Khayyamesque celebration of life, 138, 165, 190–192; on death, 49, 72–73, 98; European reception of, 90; Fitzgerald's translation of *Rubaiyat of Omar Khayyam*, 33–34, 137, 305n12; Kiarostami as liberated in the spirit of, 191; ocularcentrism of, 285; repetition (*tekrar*) in, 98; the Saqqa-khaneh movement and, 278; the unseen seer, 1, 26
Khazai, Malekjahan, 193
Kheradmand, Farhad, 189, 193, *217*
Khoi, Esmail, 254
Khomeini, Ayatollah, 9, 65, 75, 272
Kiarostami, Abbas, *3*; alienation from Persian artistic traditions, 149, 157; author's relationship with, 1–2, 3, 22, 24–25, 46–48; background of, 22–23, 64, 246, 257; birth of, 64; death of, 24, 25, 33, 34, 35, 46–48, 73–74, 234, 297–298; and Dionysian/Khayyamesque celebration of life, 138, 165, 190–192; on Fellini's *La Dolce Vita*, 176; and Niki Karimi (intimate companion), 120; language

Kiarostami, Abbas *(continued)*
 translation as issue at international events, 150; political scripts written for Panahi films, 23, 45, 46; and politics, relationship with, 23, 32, 188 (*see also* actual reality); as prophetic visionary, 24; quiet and peace on sets of, 187; quiet certitude of, 24, 150, 296–297; as scarcely watching films, 175–176; script written by Naderi for, 56–57; as semblant subject, 229–230, 233; Shafi'i-Kadkani's poem in honor of ("My Pigeons"), 131–133; social and intellectual context of, 64–66, 74–77, 176–177, 257–258; on storytelling in cinema, 222; suspending a key factor in the making of a scene, as signature tactic of, 234–235; and the temporal tenor of the sacred, 250, 254–256, 292; visas denied to, as "prospective terrorist," 44–46, 216–217, 228–229, 230, 302–303n42, 315nn14–15. *See also* camera of Kiarostami; global recognition of Kiarostami as visionary filmmaker; literature on Kiarostami; opera; paintings by Kiarostami; poetry by Kiarostami; poetry collected by Kiarostami; postcolonial film-philosophy; post-Islamist liberation theology; Shabih-khani ("Persian Passion Play")
Kiarostami, Ahmad, ix, 209
Kierkegaard, Søren, 57, 69, 70, 71, 99, 100–101
Kieslowski, Krzysztof, 127
Kimia'i, Masoud: and the Iranian New Wave, 35; *Qeysar*, 56
Kimiavi, Parviz, and the Iranian New Wave, 35
Kitano, Takeshi, 139
knowing European subject: as Christian, 271; definition of, 200–201; and the *ego conquiro*, 202; as enabling and disabling at the same time, 271; as exclusively European, 201–202, 271, 312n7. *See also* European and Eurocentric philosophy—aesthetic judgment
—exclusion of non-Europeans from: overview, 196–197, 260, 271, 312n7; anthropocentrism is Eurocentrism, 205–207, 208, 216, 220, 292; colonialist exploitation justified by, 205; "false taste" as excuse for, 203; racism as enforcement of, 199, 202–206, 207, 215, 220, 313n14

Koehler, Robert, 101
Koker Trilogy (Earthquake Trilogy): overview, 115–116, 167–168; and actual realism, 23, 164, 171–172, 177; and aesthetic alienation, liberation from, 87, 115–118, 164–165; and asceticism of Kiarostami, 266; centrality of death and bodily resurrection (*Ma'ad-e Jismani*), 116, 117–118; as Dionysian/Khayyamesque celebration of life, 138, 190–192; and factasy, 80, 140, 177, 178–179, 181; and the nomadic un/knowing subject, 217; and "the Now," 115–116, 119–122; and Persian poetic imageries of Sepehri, 119–120, 121–122, 187–189; and Qur'an verse quoted by Kiarostami during Nancy interview, 285; reception of, global, 34, 165–167, 174–175, 176, 186; reception of, Iranian, 165–166, 167–174, 175; repetition as element (*tekrar*), 98; as "Rostamabad Trilogy," 167, 187, 189; as search for the Unseen Seer, 287; and soteriology (metaphysics of salvation, *Rastegari*), 79–80, 87, 115–116, 118, 171; *Taste of Cherry* as thematically grouped with, 115; tongue-in-cheekness of, 80. *See also Life Goes On, And (Zendegi va digar hich)* (aka *Life, and Nothing More...*); *Through the Olive Trees*; *Where Is the Friend's House?/Khaneh-ye Dust Kojast*
Kretzschmar, Laurent. *See under* Nancy, Jean-Luc—*L'Evidence du film: Abbas Kiarostami*
Kubrick, Stanley: *A Clockwork Orange*, 25, 26; *Eyes Wide Shut*, 127; *Full Metal Jacket*, 127; *The Shining*, 127
Kurosawa, Akira: overview, 127, 231; and the agonistic philosophical heritage, 158; film-philosophy ignoring immediate provenance of, 134; and global cinema, 62; as influence, 34; and postcolonial cinema, 30, 41. Works: *Dreams*, 127; *Kagemusha*, 127; *Ran*, 127; *Rashomon*, 142–143
Kusturica, Emir, 127

Labasi bara-ye Arusi/A Wedding Suit, 60–61
Lacan, Jacques, 302n40
Ladanian, Tahereh, 180, *180*, 184
Lahuti, Abolqasem, 69
language, assemblages of, 106
Latin America: magical realism, 185. *See also* Dussel, Enrique; Mignolo, Walter

Lee, Ang, 127
Lee, Kevin B., 12, 13
Lefebvre, Henri, 6
Leila Heller Gallery (NYC), 277
Leonardo da Vinci, *Mona Lisa*, 239
Levinas, Emmanuel: as a Holocaust survivor, 100, 206, 207; anthropocentrism of, as Eurocentrism, 205-207, 208, 216, 220, 292; author's resonance with, 100, 305n13; on the dialectic of the exterior and the interior, 269; *French Philosophers in Conversation*, 195; and Kiarostami, 117-118; non-Europeans as animals, 207; racism of (non-Europeans are just "dancing"), 195, 199, 200, 202, 204-206, 207, 212, 215, 220; rearticulating the tension between same and other, 106-107
Life, and Nothing More.... See *Life Goes On, And (Zendegi va digar hich)*
And Life Goes On/Zendegi va digar hich (aka *Life, and Nothing More...*), 80, *217*; overview, 80, 115-116, 167; aesthetic alienation, liberation from, 115-116; and factasy, 177; as film within the film *Through the Olive Trees*, 178, 181; François Truffaut Prize awarded to, 174; reception of, global, 174-175, 176; reception of, Iranian, 168-171, 172. *See also* Koker Trilogy (Earthquake Trilogy)
Like Someone in Love, 34, 224-225, 234, 240-241
literature on Kiarostami: overview, 36-41; agonistic bringing together of bodies of, 293; as cacophony, 38-39, 246-247; the Cannes Palme d'Or (1997) and, 37; contrapuntal reading of innate heteroglossia in, 38-39; existing bodies of, as largely unaware of each other, 31, 32, 38, 198, 293; and the false binary of aesthetics vs. politics, 31-32; non-cinema projects largely ignored in, 36, 38; tertiary interstitial space and, 32. *See also* European and Eurocentric film-philosophy; global recognition of Kiarostami as visionary filmmaker; Iranian literature on Kiarostami; Nancy, Jean-Luc; *other reviewers and scholars*
Livingston, Paisley, 199-200
Locarno Film Festival: 1995 program of Iranian cinema, 312n48; Kiarostami as key feature of, 192-193; retrospective of Kiarostami (1995), and concurrent exhibition of paintings and photographs, 192-193; as vacation destination, 70; *Where Is the Friend's House?* (Bronze Leopard), 9, 175, 192. *See also* European film festivals
logocentrism (*Falsafah*), 106, 157, 286
long shots/long takes of Kiarostami: overview, 23-24; and being-toward-death in *Taste of Cherry*, 72; concluding scene of *Through the Olive Trees*, 172, 185-187, 235; *Five Dedicated to Ozu*, 104, 223-224, 225, 230, 233-234; as hated by critics, 190; and paintings illustrating Nezami's poetic Now, *113*, 114; penultimate sequence of *Close-Up*, 186; as strategic distancing representation, 190; in *The Wind Will Carry Us*, 24. *See also* camera of Kiarostami
Louis XIV, 108
Lukács, John, 227
Luther, Martin, 108

McDowell, John, 43
magical realism, 185
Majidi, Majid, 13; backward assimilation of cinematic thinking to Eurocentric philosophy, 302n40
Makhmalbaf, Mohsen: and the 1995 Locarno Film Festival, 312n48; as character in Kiarostami's *Close-Up*, 67, 140, 151, 161, 163, 178; as Muslim, 175; politics of, 32; reception of, 77; virtual realism of, 61-62. Works: *The Cyclist*, 151; *Peddler/Dastforush*, 175; *Salam Cinema*, 312n48
Makhmalbaf, Samira: *Sib/Apple*, 9; and world cinema, 22
Malcolm X, 136
Maragheh'i, Zeyn al-Abedin, *Safar-nameh Ibrahim Beik*, 215
Marks, Laura, 319-320n6
Maroufi, Abbas, 77
Marx, Karl: Adorno and, 227; alienation effect, 125; *Capital*, 125; commodity fetishism, 125, 212
Matin-Daftary, Leyly, 193
Mazaj, Meta, 18
Mechkat, Farhad, 2
Mehrjui, Dariush, 35, 61, 87, 246; *Gav/The Cow*, 8, 56; *Pari*, 25
Memmi, Albert, 78; *The Colonizer and the Colonized*, 17
Menke, Christoph, *The Sovereignty of Art*, 42-43, 159-161

Merleau-Ponty, Maurice, 302n40
Meshkini, Marziyeh, 10, 302n40
Meskub, Shahrokh, *Dar Ku-ye Dust/In the Friend's Neighborhood*, 103
Mesqali, Farshid, 278
Mignolo, Walter, 208, 212, 293
Milani, Tahmineh, 196, 312n48
mimesis: Aristotelian, the Hollywood camera and, 233; mis/representation between truth and fiction, 125, 163, 234–235. *See also* Shabih (semblant truth) as Persianate theory of mimesis
mimetic semiosis, 278
Miramax, 166
Miro, Joan, 21
mirroring, 33, 163, 208, 243–244, 282, 290–291
Mirsepassi, Ali, 40
Mirza, Iraj, 69
Mizuguchi, Kenji, 231
modern art: English or French pronunciation of "modern" used for, 259; Eurocentric narratives of, the Saqqa-khaneh art movement as exceeding, 262, 264, 275, 278; lack of Persian or Arabic words for, 259, 263; as misnomer for the Saqqa-khaneh art movement, 259–260, 262–263, 264, 269–272, 274–275, 280; Saqqa-khaneh art as formally and aesthetically caught between modernists and reactionaries, 263–264, 271; translation of "modern" to Persian (*Tajaddod*) as idiomatically insufficient, 259–260, 263; votive Shi'aite art used in, 270. *See also* European (capitalist) modernity
Mohammad Reza Shah, 64
Mohassess, Bahman, 67
Mohr, Jean, 29
monism: of Rumi, 218–220; of Spinoza, 216, 217–218, 220
Montesquieu, *Persian Letters*, 137
Mosaddegh, Mohammad, 64
Mosafer/Traveler, 56, 77
Motahhari, Morteza, 75
Mottahedeh, Negar, 40
Mouffe, Chantal, 294, 310n56
Mozart, Amadeus: *Così fan Tutte*, Kiarostami's productions of, 35, 228–230, 315nn14–15; and Zarathustra, 89, 90
Mudimbe, V. Y., 208, 212; *Invention of Africa*, 129
Mulla Sadra Shirazi, 59, 249; *al-Asfar al-Arba'ah/The Four Journeys*, 266–267; Transcendental Philosophy (*al-Hikmah al-Muta'aliyah*), 117–118
Museo Casa Rusca, exhibition of paintings and photographs, 192–193
Museum of Modern Art (MoMA), Amir Naderi retrospective, 19
Mysticism, distinguished from Oriental Philosophy, 211
mythos, 106

Naderi, Amir: overview, 19–20, 24, 127; and allegory, 20–21; friendship with author and Kiarostami, 25, 47; and the Iranian New Wave, 19, 35; and national cinema, transcendence of, 19, 20, 21; as photographer, 257; reception of, 61, 62, 246; and Saqqa-khaneh art, 263, 277; and trauma, 21; visual realism of, 20, 61–62; and world cinema, 19, 22; as worldly filmmaker, 19–20, 21. Works: *Davandeh/The Runner*, 8–9, 19, 20, 21; *Khodahafez Rafiq/Goodbye Friend*, 19–20; MoMA retrospective, 19; *Mountain*, 20; *Saz-Dahani/Harmonica*, 20; script for Kiarostami's *Tajrobeh/The Experience*, 56–57; *Tangsir*, 20; *Water, Wind, Dust*, 21
Naderpour, Nader, 35
Naficy, Hamid, 39–40
Nagasaki, 96
Nair, Mira, 127
Na-Koja-abad ("Nowhereville") (Suhrawardi), 101–103, 294
Namjoo, Mohsen, 65
Nancy, Jean-Luc: and Claire Denis, 143–144; and Kiarostami, 27, 117–118, 287; mondialisation (world-forming process), 147; and provincialization of European film-philosophy, need for, 249. Works: *La creation due monde ou la mondialisation/The Creation of the World or Globalization*, 147; *Le sens du monde/The Sense of the World*, 147; *Les Muses/The Muses*, 147
—*L'Evidence du film: Abbas Kiarostami*: overview, 133; agonistic philosophical heritage needed to produce serious interchange, 157, 158, 161; antecedents to this encounter, 137; Moinak Biswas on, 143, 144; the blind spot within evidence, 146; cinema as an art of looking at the world, 137–139, 141–142, 145, 146–147, 153–155; film as giving back its own real (self-referential), 138–139,

140–141, 161; focus on the surface of many-faceted aspects of reality, 116; the gaze, seeking of, 143, 144; Kristin Lené Hole on, 143–144; and Kiarostami as Iranian artist and filmmaker, 147–148; Kiarostami breaks into reciting the Surah Al-Zalzalah/The Earthquake of the Qur'an, 150, 283–284, 285, 287; on *Life and Nothing Else*, 136–137; mysteries of their own artwork, filmmakers unable to unravel, 151–152; mystery in film, preservation of, 151; provenance of the essay and structure of, 145, 146; question to Kiarostami on influence of Persian manuscript illustrations (*Negar-gari*, mistranslated as "miniatures"), 148–150, 287; relation between discourse and image, 150–151; and Sepehri's poetry, 152–155; translation of English as troubled, 149; translation of Persian as troubled, 145–146, 149; as trilingual text, 145
—Laurent Kretzschmar review of: on cinema as an art of looking at the world, 137–139, 141–142, 153; as curbing his enthusiasm, 139–140; on film giving back its own real (self-referential), 138–139; on Kiarostami as new form of cinema, 136–137; on periodization of cinema, 135–137, 138; on the temporal lagging of engagement with film-philosophy, 133–134; on verisimilitudes in fictive transparencies of the real, 144

Nandy, Ashis, 208; *The Intimate Enemies*, 17
Nan va Kucheh/The Bread and Alley, 56, 208–209, 210
Naqd-e Cinema (journal published by Islamic Propaganda Organization), 172–174
Naqqali, 226. *See also* Shabih-khani ("Persian Passion Play")
Naraqi, Arash, 75
Nasr, Seyyed Hossein, 103
Nasser Khosrow, 156, 214, 255
national allegory, Jameson as reducing non-European artworks to, 199
the national, as mode of collective consciousness, 261
national cinemas: and coloniality, condition of, 15–18, 45, 290; global recognition and return of works to, 62; postnational cinema and coloniality, condition of, 18; as predicated on national traumas, 11, 15, 16–18, 21; transcendence of, 21–22; the world of cinema as deeply influencing, 17–18; as yielding to postnational and world cinemas, 12, 13–14, 21–22. *See also* "Borromean rings" of national, postnational, and world cinemas
nationalism, 261
nativism: Al-e Ahmad's "Westoxication" and, 271; assimilation of Kiarostami into, 293; postcolonial aesthetic judgment not a project of, 208, 220; as preempting development of alternative theory *to* modernity, 97; readings of Kiarostami as foreclosing cosmopolitanism, 68; and the Self-Orientalizing art market, 66
nature, 188–189, 219–220, 289
Neshat, Shirin: in the commercialized "Oriental" art industry, 22, 62–63, 66, 303–304nn15–16; repressed visuality revealed in, 285; and Saqqa-khaneh art, 263, 277–278; *Women without Men*, 10
New Persian Poetry (*She'r-e No*): classical Persian prosody dismantled by, 251, 253; fading of, 254; Kiarostami's own poetry as take on, 253–255; Kiarostami's volumes on Persian poetic legacy and nod to, 251; masters of, 64–65, 253, 254; Nima Yushij as inaugurating, 64–65, 78, 253, 254; Sepehri and, 188, 253, 254. *See also* Persian poetry
The New Republic, 166
New York Film Festival: *Ten*, 44; *Through the Olive Trees*, 166
New York Times, 150, 163, 166
Nezami Ganjavi, Hakim: and the Mi'raj, 285; philosophical disposition of, 255; the poetic Now, 112, 114–115, 119; poetic of Divine Visibility, 81, 84–85, 285–286; and postcolonial film-philosophy, 249; as site-specific poetic context, 117. Works: *Khamseh/Quintet*, 81, *82*, 114, 238; *Khosrow and Shirin*, 114–115, 237–238; *Leili and Majnun*, 114–115, 238; *Makhzan al-Asrar/Source of Wisdom*, 112, *113*, 114, 119, 306–307n27
Ngũgĩ wa Thiong'o, 208
Nietzsche, Friedrich: Adorno and, 227; as ally to postcolonial thinkers, 100; *Beyond Good and Evil*, 80; and discordance of art and truth, 88; and European claim on Philosophy, 57; as questioning modernity's tyranny of Reason, 99, 100; on relation of truth and illusion, 242–243; *Thus Spoke Zarathustra*, 89, 90, 137
Nigeria, 109

Nikfar, Mohammad Reza, 76
Nimaic poetry. *See* New Persian Poetry (*She'r-e No*)
Nima Yushij: *Ab/Water* (Kiarostami's anthology of poems of), 55–56, 57; Al-e Ahmad as writing on, 79; as altering how reality is perceived, 67; death of, 76; filmmakers and works of, 77; and Kiarostami's storytelling, 66; New Persian poetry inaugurated by, 64–65, 78, 253, 254. *See also* New Persian Poetry (*She'r-e No*)
Nodjoumi, Nikzad, 277–278
Noland, Christopher, *Oppenheimer*, 266
nomadic un/knowing subject: overview, 212–213, 291–294; aesthetic alienation counteracted by, 163, 165; agonistic philosophical heritage and sovereignty of, 158–159; becoming the knowing subject, 293–294; Braidotti on, 247; and the camera of Kiarostami as Unseen Seer, 282; in *Close-Up*, 125, 161, 163; contingent sovereignty of, 33, 125, 158–159, 160–161, 291–292; definition of, 256; at home in Safar/Travel and Hazar/Home, 268, 274, 278, 281, 292; and the interstitial space of cyberspace, 220–221; in the Koker Trilogy, 217; mobile vision of reality and, 215; as not interpreting, 194; as postcolonial subject, 161, 163, 292–294; and posthuman agency, 217–220; as rooted in the transnational public sphere, 293–294; as self-effacing, 165, 193–194; the semblant subject and formation of, 256, 292; as sovereign agency, 161; in *Taste of Cherry*, 213, 217; temporal tenor of the sacred, 250, 254–256, 281, 292; in *Ten*, 213, 217; in *The Wind Will Carry Us*, 213, 217. *See also* postcolonial aesthetic judgment; postcolonial film-philosophy; semblant subject
—as pilgrim: and the camera of Kiarostami as Unseen Seer, 282; double consciousness by definition not possible for, 292–293; exteriority of the pilgrimage route, 267–268, 269, 280–281; Fakhr al-Din Iraqi's *Koliyyat* and, 245, 249–250; as rising universalism, 249–250; and *Roads and Rain* landscape photo series, 256–257, 260, 264, 265; the Saqqa-khaneh art movement and, 263, 264, 265, 268, 274, 277–278, 280–281
nomocentric (*Shari'ah*) proclivities, 106, 157

Norden, Bryan van, *Taking Back Philosophy: A Multicultural Manifesto*, 41
"the Now": overview, 110–111; aesthetic alienation liberated via, 111, 115, 119–122, 125, 291; Benjamin and, 111–112, 119, 304–305n2; composite disposition of, 121, 122; Kiarostami and, 112, 114, 115, 119–122; Nezami and, 112, 114–115, 119; in Persian paintings illustrating Nezami's *Makhzan al-Asrar*, 113, 114; post-Islamist liberation theology and, 112, 291; Rumi on, 111; Sepehri and, 121–122
"Nowhereville" (*Na-Koja-abad*) (Suhrawardi), 101–103, 294

ocularcentrism in the Persian and Persianate poetic imagination: overview, 53–54, 285–286, 319–320n6; and Kiarostami's cinema, 51, 53–54, 80–81, 102; and the poetics of Divine in/visibility, 80–85, 285–287, 291
O'Meally, Robert, 294, 297
opera: Kiarostami's productions of (Mozart's *Così fan Tutte*), 35, 228–230, 315nn14–15; Zeffirelli's production of Puccini's *Turandot*, 229
Orientalism: distinguished from "Oriental Philosophy," 211; "Islamic philosophy" dubbed by, 156; Shirin Neshat and the art market, 22, 62–63, 66, 303–304nn15–16; Persian manuscript illustrations (*Negar-gari*, mistranslated as "miniatures"), 148–149, 287; postnational filmmakers degenerating into, 22, 62–63; as trap preempting development of alternative theories *to* modernity, 97
"Oriental Philosophy" (*al-Hikmah al-Mashriqiyah*), 210–212, 294
Ostranenie (Viktor Shklovsky), 3, 164, 292
Oveissi, Nasser, 269, 277, 280–281
Ozu, Yasujirō: aesthetic formalism of, 231, 233–234; and aesthetics of the surface: presence/interior, 232; and the agonistic philosophical heritage, 158; as allegory, 104; background of, 230, 231; Brechtian V-effect of camera of, 233; as influence, 17, 34, 39, 68, 225, 231, 232, 248, 292; interior shots connected by still exteriors, 232; and Kiarostami, as interrelated in their cinematic forms, 225, 230, 231–234, 240, 292; Kiarostami's *Five Dedicated to Ozu*, 104, 223–224, 225, 230,

233–234; low-angle camera, 232–233; and postcolonial cinema, 30; and simplicity, 232, 248, 266; triangulation of camera in, 233; worldly cinema of, 230–231, 233. Works: *An Autumn Afternoon*, 233–234; *I was Born, But...*, 234; *Tokyo Story*, 9, 234

Pahlavi dynasty: establishment by Reza Khan, 64; height of, 19; reinstatement of Mohammad Reza Shah by US-UK military coup (1953), 45, 64, 257–258, 272, 274
—state-sponsored modernism: as cover for the post-coup political scene, 262; and desire for "national school of art," 261, 275; and the historical moment of the Saqqa-khaneh art movement, 272; and nationalism as state ideology, 261; patronage of artists and movements, 275; the Saqqa-khaneh art movement as exceeding attempts to appropriate, 260, 261, 264–265, 268–269, 272, 273, 275–276, 278
paintings by Kiarostami: retrospective exhibition in Locarno (1995, Museo Casa Rusca), 192–193; as shared interest with Sepehri, 189. *See also* Persian paintings
Pakbaz, Ruyin, *Da'erat al-Ma'aref-e Honar/ Encyclopedia of Art*, 149
Pak-Shirazi, Nacim, 40
Palestine, 29, 136
Panahi, Jafar: and the 1995 Locarno Film Festival, 193, 312n48; censorship of, 9, 12, 13–14; and factasy, 13; films based on Kiarostami's scripts, 23, 45, 46; and Kiarostami's Ta'ziyeh footage, 228; in new generation of filmmakers, 76–77; politics of, 9, 32; as protégé of Kiarostami, 9; reception of, 12–14, 61, 77, 196, 246. Works: *Crimson Gold*, 13, 45; *Dayereh/ Circle*, 9; *Taxi*, 11–13; *The White Balloon*, 45, 312n48
parables (as *Tamsil*), 268
parapublic sphere, 161, 310n63
Parham, Baqer (translator of Nancy's *L'Évidence du film*), 145–146
Partovi, Kambuzia, 120
Payvar, Pouya, 217
Peña, Richard, 1, 247
Persian classical music, 170
Persian dramatists and the theater: global audience not attainable for, 79; the Islamic Republic and silencing of, 76–77. *See also* Shabih-khani
Persian fiction: the Islamic Republic and silencing of, 75, 76–77; travelogues and, 214–215; as untranslatable for a global audience, 79
Persian paintings: alienation of artists of Kiarostami's generation from traditions of, 149, 157; of Parviz Kalantari, 267–268; Nancy's question to Kiarostami on influence of Persian manuscript illustrations (*Negar-gari*, mistranslated as "miniatures"), 148–150, 287; "the Now" illustrated in, 113, 114; *Shamayel* and *Temsal* (portraits), 149, 157; *Tasvir* as term, 149–150
"Persian Passion Play." *See* Shabih-khani
Persian philosophy, relationship with Persian poetry, 255–256
Persian poetic imageries (*Suvar-e Khayal*): overview, 49–51; abstraction as overcome with evident materiality, 53; allegorical reading (*Tamsil*), 104, 268; allusions as making the invisible world visible, 49; as common aesthetic repertoire, 49, 53–54; definition of "imaginative imageries"/ *Suvar-e Khayal*, 51–52, 54–55; Divine in/visibility, 80–85, 285–287, 291; European film-philosophy as not recognizing, 49, 50–51, 54, 117; Greek philosophy and, 51; inaugural moments, 54; as metonymic deferral to the invisible world made cinematically visible, 49, 50; repetition as element (*tekrar*), 98; sacred journeys (*Ziarat*), 266–267; as seeing the world anew, 53–55; *Taghazzol*/Lovemaking, 237–239; and "the Now," 112–115, 119, 121–122; as tropes of imagination, 63. *See also* ocularcentrism in the Persian and Persianate poetic imagination; *specific poets*
Persian poetry: classical prosody, violations of, 251; Emerson's "Saadi" (inspired by Sa'di), 137; European imperial hegemony and, 34, 90; Fitzgerald's translation of *Rubaiyat of Omar Khayyam*, 33–34, 137, 305n12; Goethe's *West-östlicher Divan* (inspired by Hafez), 33–34, 89–90, 137, 251; the Islamic Republic and silencing of, 76–77; philosophical heritage of Iran, deep relationship to, 255–256; as untranslatable for a global audience, 79. *See also* New Persian Poetry

Persian poetry *(continued)*
(*She'r-e No*); Persian poetic imageries (*Suvar-e Khayal*); poetry collected by Kiarostami; poetry of Kiarostami; *specific poets*
Persian prose, Al-e Ahmad as revolutionizing, 79
Persian rhetoric, *Madh-e Shabih beh Zamm, or Zamm-e Shabih beh Madh*/Praise in the Form of Blame, or Blame in the Form of Praise, 14–15
philosophy. *See* agonistic philosophical heritage; European and Eurocentric film-philosophy; European and Eurocentric philosophy; Islamic philosophy; postcolonial film-philosophy
photography: of Bahman Jalali, 79, 267–268; Iranian filmmakers with serious interest in, 257
photography by Kiarostami: overview, 35, 256–257; allegorical vs. categorical reading of, 104–105; and films of Kiarostami, mutual memories of, 257; *Regardez-moi/Look at Me* (series), 71; retrospective exhibition in Locarno (1995, Museo Casa Rusca), 192–193; and social and intellectual context of Iran, 257–258; the spectator as part of the frame in, 71; *24 Frames* and use of, 209. *See also Roads and Rain* (landscape photo series)
Piazzo, Philippe, 177
Picasso, Pablo, *Guernica*, 276
Pilaram, Faramarz, 273, 277
pilgrimage, Kiarostami's interest in writing poetry as, 251, 252–253, 255. *See also* nomadic un/knowing subject—as pilgrim
Plato: allegory of the cave, 25–26, 33, 102, 198, 239, 282; European philosophy claiming exclusivity to, 57–58, 102, 155; the illusion of arts as suspect, 227; Islamic and Iranian philosophies rooted in, 102, 156; World of Ideas/World of Forms, 102
poetic ontology of the un/real: and post-Islamist liberation theology, 85; *Traveler* as staging, 77; and Verfremdungseffekt from of form and fact, 74, 291. *See also* fictive transparency of the real; foreign familiarity of the un/real
poetry. *See* Persian poetry; poetry by Kiarostami; poetry collected by Kiarostami
poetry by Kiarostami: as act of pious pilgrimage to Persian poetry, 255; collections published, 35, 253; lack of ability as poet, 250, 253–255; and poetic disposition to cinema of Kiarostami, 255–256; as take on New Persian Poetry, 253–255; vacuous praise for, 254, 317n9. Works: *Walking with the Wind/Hamrah ba bad*, 253, 317n9; *The Wind and the Leaf/Bad-o Barg*, 253–254; *A Wolf in Hiding/Gorgi dar Kamin*, 253

poetry collected by Kiarostami: as acts of piety and pilgrimage to Persian poetry, 251, 252–253; and nod to New Persian Poetry, 251; publishing of, as abuse of his branded name, 252–253; as violating classical prosody, 55–56, 251–253. Works: *Atash dar Bad/Fire in the Wind: A Selection of Rumi's Ghazals*, 251, 252–253, 255; *Dad az Gham-e Tanha'i/Alas the Sorrow of Loneliness*, 35–36; *Hafez beh Revayat Abbas Kiarostami/Hafez as Told by Abbas Kiarostami*, 251–253, 255; Nima Yushij, *Ab/Water* (Kiarostami's anthology of poems of), 55–56, 57; *Sa'di az dast Khishtan Faryad/Sa'di, Woe Unto Thee*, 251, 252–253, 255
Ponzanesi, Sandra, 30
Positif (magazine), 175–176
post-anthropocentrism, 217–221, 284
postcolonial aesthetic judgment: overview, 198–200, 221, 292–294; the beautiful and sublime and, 221; the beautiful as the true, 88–89, 157–158; as engaging with but not possessed by the "the West," 207–208, 210, 212–213, 215, 216, 217–218, 220, 220–221; fabling the world, 208–212, 220, 292; inclusivity of, 220–221; miasmatic text of films and, 213; the nomadic un/knowing subject as author of, 293–294; as not a nativist project, 208, 220; ontology of *Mumkin al-Wujud* (Contingent Being) and, 213–214; particularity of, becoming universal, 221; as reversing the colonial gaze, 210. *See also* humanism—and postcolonial Iranian cinema; knowing European subject—exclusion of non-Europeans from; nomadic un/knowing subject; postcolonial film-philosophy; semblance of subjectivity; semblant subject
postcolonial cinema studies, and condition of coloniality, overcoming of, 30
postcolonial film-philosophy: overview, 198–200; Alexander Lighthouse metaphor,

32–33; and alterity vs. identity, 30–31, 295; Attar's metaphor of the birds, 25–26, 33, *162*, 163, 208, 211, 243–244, 282, 285; Avicenna's *al-Hikmah al-Mashriqiyah* (Oriental Philosophy), 210–212, 294; and condition of coloniality, liberation from, 29–30, 119; as decolonial project, 39–40, 224–225, 291–295; double vision and, 28, 29–30; and European postmodernist debate, 136, 308n15; Persian poetic imageries and, 54; and "postcolonial" as term, 40; as post-European film-philosophy, 294–295; as provincializing Europe and questioning Eurocentricity, 28–29, 41, 89, 134–136, 212, 216, 242, 249, 294, 295–296, 317n6. *See also* actual realism of Kiarostami; agonistic philosophical heritage; alternative theories *to* modernity; avian allegories; factasy; film-philosophy; interstitial space; intuition of transcendence; nomadic un/knowing subject; Persian poetic imageries (*Suvar-e Khayal*); postcolonial aesthetic judgment; post-Islamist liberation theology; Saqqa-khaneh art movement; semblance of subjectivity; semblant subject; Shabih-khani ("Persian Passion Play"); tertiary space

postcolonialism, 109

postcolonial studies, rejection by Farhadpour and Eslami, 128–129

postcolonial subject. *See* nomadic un/knowing subject

post-European film-philosophy. *See* agonistic philosophical heritage; postcolonial film-philosophy

posthuman agency, 217–220

post-Islamist aesthetics, Ta'zieh ritual performances and the post-Islamist dramaturgical transition to Shabih-khani, 225, 226, 315n5

post-Islamist liberation theology: overview, 78; Al-e Ahmad as harbinger of, 78–79, 80; cinema of Kiarostami as, 287, 292; and the poetic "Now," 112, 291; and the poetics of Divine in/visibility, 80–85, 291; the Saqqa-khaneh art movement and, 264, 276–278, 280–281, 292; soteriological conception of worldly salvation, 79–80; tongue-in-cheek filmic prose and, 80

postmodernism, 135–136, 308n15

postnational cinema: as anthropology, 13; as catering to European film festivals, 11, 21; conditions of coloniality as placing national cinemas in, 18; definition of, 11; degeneration into the "Oriental" art industry, 22, 62–63; as emerging out of global traumas, 21–22; filmmakers emerging directly into, 22; in-person screening of films not required for, 12; Islamic censorial policies as factor in the rise of, 13–14; Kiarostami as harbinger of, 23; and Kurdish filmmaker Yilmaz Güney, 14; national cinemas as yielding to, 21–22; national viewership not required for, 12; as overriding national traumas, 11; politicking and, 11–12, 13, 21. *See also* "Borromean rings" of national, postnational, and world cinemas

post-postmodernism, 147

Pournamdarian, Taqi, 104, 306n19

pre-Islamic literature: *Kelilah and Dimnah*, 210–211, 294; Kiarostami's first and last film and, 211; Shahnameh, 123, 225–226; *Sug-e Seyavash*/Mourning for Seyavash practice, 225–226

Premier, 166–167

Protestant Reformation, 108

public sphere (*Vatan*/Homeland): cultural origins of, 74–75; the Iranian Revolution and internal exile of, 75; as parapublic sphere, 161, 310n63; Persian poetry and, 69; the work of art articulating the postcolonial subject, 161. *See also* transnational public sphere

Puccini, *Turandot*, 229

Qajar period, 64, 69, 275, 288

Qazvini, Aref, 69

Qobadi, Bahman, 76–77, 302n40

Qukasian, Zaven, 193

Qur'an: the Prophet's Mi'raj, 81, 83–84; repressed visuality and, 285; Surah Al-Zalzalah/The Earthquake, Kiarostami reciting, 150, 283–284, 285; the Unseen Seer in, 286

racism: denial of visas to Kiarostami as, 228–229, 230, 315n15; Farhadpour and Islami's dismissal of Africa, 129, 131. *See also* European and Eurocentric philosophy—racism

Radi, Akbar, 79

Rahimian, Behzad, 174

Ray, Satyajit: overview, 127; and the agonistic philosophical heritage, 158; Apu Trilogy, 9; film-philosophy ignoring immediate provenance of, 134; and global cinema, 62; as influence, 17, 34, 68, 163; Kiarostami hailed as a "new," 167; and postcolonial cinema, 30, 41, 224; and simplicity, 266
Razi, Shaykh Abu al-Futuh al, 283–284
realism: European binary of modernism and, 101, 102; habitual assimilation backward of Iranian cinema to Italian "neorealism," 101, 163; mythic, 57, 61–62, 67; virtual, 61–62; visual, 20, 61–62. *See also* actual realism of Kiarostami
reception theory, 5
reciprocity, dialectic of, 22
Regardez-moi/Look at Me (photo series), 71
Rekabtalaei, Golbarg, 40
Rendi (Hafez), 250
Renoir, Pierre-Auguste, 174
Resaleh al-Tayr/Bird Treatises, 210–212; Attar, Farid al-Din, *Mantiq al-Tayr/Conference of the Birds*, 25–26, 33, *162*, 163, 208, 211, 243–244, 282, 285
revisioning the world anew: and the early films of Kiarostami, 56–57; in Iranian culture, generally, 67; Persian poetic imageries (*Suvar-e Khayal*) and, 53–55. *See also* actual realism of Kiarostami
Reza'i, Hossein, 181
Reza Shah: abdication of, 64; military coup by, 64
Richard, Frederic, 177
Rilke, Rainer Maria, 256
Rimbaud, Arthur, 251
Roads and Rain (landscape photo series), 265; and allegorical readings of reality, 104–105; and the nomadic un/knowing subject as pilgrim, 256–257, 260, 264, 265; roads and cars as independent character in, 214; and the Saqqa-Khaneh art movement, 260, 264, 266–267, 269, 273, 274, 281; travel as central motif in, 266; zigzag roads as motif, 43, 266. *See also* travel (*Safar*) as central motif in Kiarostami
Roads of Kiarostami (film), 104–105
Roberto Rossellini's award, 174
Rokh-Sefat, Mostafa, 75
Rosenbaum, Jonathan, 90–91
Rossellini, Roberto: Cannes award in name of, 174; critics comparing Kiarostami to, 174

Rostamabad Trilogy. *See* Koker Trilogy (Earthquake Trilogy)
Rudaki Samarqandi, 53, 54
Ruhani, Omid, 171
Ruhi, Mohammad Hosain, 171
Rumi, Maulana Jalal al-din: on the eternal Now, 111; European reception of, 90; and German Romanticism and American Transcendentalism, 90; as influence, 94; Kiarostami's volume on (*Atash dar Bad/Fire in the Wind: A Selection of Rumi's Ghazals*), 251, 252–253, 255, 287; *Masnavi*, 218–220; philosophical disposition of, 255; proverbial elephant in a dark room, 37; and *Sama'*/Dance, 206
Russia, colonial heritage of, 64, 198

Sabzian, Hossein, 140, *141*, 151, 161, 163
Sa'di, Shirazi: Emerson's tribute to ("Saadi"), 137; European reception of, 90; in Kiarostami's collection of lines from Persian poets, 35; Kiarostami's volume on (*Sa'di az dast Khishtan Faryad/Sa'di, Woe Unto Thee*), 251, 252–253, 255, 287; philosophical disposition of, 255
Sa'edi, Gholamhossein, 8, 66, 67, 76, 78, 79
Safarian, Robert, 170
Safar. *See* travel (*Safar*) as central motif
Safavid period, 59, 74–75, 273, 275
Said, Edward: Al-e Ahmad and the spirit of, 78; cited in self-hating text by Farhadpour and Eslami, 128–129; contrapuntal reading, 39, 158; death of, 47; double vision, 28, 29; as possessed by the West, 208. Works: *After the Last Sky*, 29; *Orientalism*, 128, 211
Saint Peter's Basilica (Rome), 319n42
Salih, Tayeb, *Season of Migration to the North*, 17
Samini, Naghmeh, 172
Sanai, Hakim, *Seyr al-Ibad ila al-Ma'ad/The Journey of Many to Eternity*, 266
Saqqa-khaneh art movement: overview, 260–261; and the aesthetic intuition of transcendence, 269; and aesthetic of emancipation, 277; allegorical iconography of, 261, 273–274, 277, 281; the artists as Shi'ite Muslims, 264, 272, 281; clerical figures of power and authority staged in subversive versions, 277; as contemporary art movement, 259, 260–261, 270, 273–274; as crafting a new iconography, 264; cultural authenticity questions, 258,

260, 263; and the "decorative," 270, 281; Karim Emami as recognizing the movement and coining the term, 259, 264, 269, 271–272, 273, 280, 281; as "event" (Badiou), 261–262; as exceeding appropriation by the Islamic Republic, 261, 264–265, 268–269, 272, 273, 276, 278; as exceeding appropriation by the Pahlavi state-sponsored modernism, 260, 261, 264–265, 268–269, 272, 273, 275–276, 278; as exceeding the modernist narrative of Eurocentric art histories, 262, 264, 275, 278; expansion of aesthetic boundaries of, 261, 263, 266–269, 276–278; as exposing political lies, 262; and exteriority of the pilgrimage route, 267–268, 269, 280–281; factasy and, 268; folk and vernacular culture as inspiration for, 274; as formally and aesthetically caught between modernists and reactionaries, 263–264, 271; and frame of reference going back to the Qajar and Safavid periods, 274, 275; historical moment of, postcolonial, 272, 273–274, 281; intentions of the artworks of (*intentio operis*), 318n27, 363–364; and interiority of the sacred, 269, 280–281; Jalali and, 263, 267–268, 269, 277, 280–281; Kalantari and, 267–268, 269, 277, 280–281; martyrdom and sacrifice in, 276; minimalist imagery and, 267–268; "modern art" and connection to "modernity" as misnomer for, 259–260, 262–263, 264, 269–272, 274–275, 280; as national artistic expression, 258, 261, 276, 278; as "neo-traditionalist" (Keshmirshekan), 258; and the nomadic un/knowing subject as pilgrim, 263, 264, 265, 268, 274, 277–278, 280–281; Oveissi and, 269, 277, 280–281; parables (as *Tamsil*), 268; Pilaram and, 273, 277; as post-Islamist liberation theology, 264, 276–278, 280–281, 292; redemptive suffering and battle for justice in, 276; and the relevance of the beautiful, 279, 281; religious sublimity and, 273; and sacred certitude, register of, 264, 272; and the sacred, return of, 280–281, 284–285; as "sacrilegious," 263, 264; *Saqqa-khaneh* as water station decorated with talismanic sacred iconography of Shi'ism, 259, 260–261, 263, 267, 274, 278, 280; and semblance of subjectivity, 278; Tabrizi and, 269, 280–281; Tanavoli and, 273, 274, 277; touching and kissing the talismanic objects, 269, 279–280, 281, 319n42; "traditional" as misnomer for, 259, 260, 264; and urban life, 277; "votive" practices and, 270, 272–273; Zenderoudi and, 272, 273, 274; and *Ziarat* (sacred journeys), 266–267, 278

—Kiarostami and: asceticism of Kiarostami's lenswork and, 265–266, 292; and extension of boundaries of the movement, 261; and the global recognition of Kiarostami, 261, 262; landscape photography and (*Roads and Rain*), 260, 264, 266–267, 269, 273, 274, 281

Sarmadi moment, 114
Sartre, Jean-Paul, 68–69, 302n40
Scorsese, Martin, 127; *Shutter Island*, 239–240
Scott, A. O., 150
the secular and secularism: alienation, 86 (*see also* aesthetic alienation); Christianity concealed as, 271; as ideological subterfuge for colonialism, 93; lack of Persian or Arabic word for, 259; opposition to Islamist "religious intellectuals," secularist/modernist cadre, 75–76; "the religions" not the opposite of, 95. *See also* European (capitalist) modernity
Seiter, William, *Belle of the Yukon*, 240
the self, the cinema redirecting attention from, 30–31
Sembène, Ousmane, 127, 134, 224
semblance of subjectivity: Adorno's project as critique of, 227–228; and the arts as critiquing illusion, including their own, 227–228, 231; for audiences, the semblance of truth as positing, 226; as contrapuntally generated via European reception, 225; and counterfeit, staging, 234–235, 239–240, 292; and darkness, strategic, 234–235, 240, 292; and mirroring effect, truth as, 243–244; Ozu and Kiarostami as positing, for each other, 225, 230; and reversing the camera angle, 236–239, 240, 244, 292; Saqqa-khaneh art and, 278; simulation and semblance, 239–241; and the surface, mystery of, 244. *See also* semblant subject
semblant subject: overview, 224–225, 244, 256; condition of coloniality of, as overcome through that coloniality, 226; interstitial space and formation of, 292;

semblant subject *(continued)*
  Kiarostami himself as, 229–230, 233; meditation on the in/visibility of the transcendental signifier and formation of, 285–286; nomadic un/knowing subject, formation of, 256, 292; the semblance of subjectivity for audiences as philosophical predicate of, 226. *See also* semblance of subjectivity
semblant truth. *See* Shabih (semblant truth) as Persianate theory of mimesis
Sepanta, Abdolhossein, *Dokhtar-e Lor/Lor Girl*, 8
Sepehri, Sohrab: overview, 187–188; and aesthetic alienation, overcoming, 291; and death, 73; and Dionysian celebration of life, 188–189; and the fictive transparency of the real, 142, 143, 154–155; and the hyperrealized signifier, 105; as influence, 39, 248–249; internalized alterity in, 31; Kiarostami's cinema as the visual sublimation of poetry of, 152–155; in New Persian Poetry/Nimaic tradition, 188, 253, 254; and the Now, 121–122; as painter, 189; and poetics of the self-evident, 153; and politics/ideologies, distaste for, 188; and the sacred, return of, 284–285; and simplicity, 188–189, 248–249, 268; and subversive redefinition of reality, 189. Works: "Lahzeh-ye Gomshodeh/The Lost Moment," 86; "Neshani/Address," 119–120, 121–122, 256; "Seda-ye Pa-ye Ab/The Sound of the Footsteps of Water," 124, 152–155, 187–189, 248–249, 284–285
sexuality, and culture of inhibition, 182, 183–184
Shabestari, Mohamad, 75
Shabih (semblant truth) as Persianate theory of mimesis: overview, 226–227, 242; cinema of Kiarostami and, 240–241; cinema of Kiarostami as similar but not identical with Ozu's, 233–234; as cognate of *Tashbih* (simile), 226, 242; as independent of Aristotelian origins, 227; *shabih-khani* (reciting similarities), 233; *shabih-nama'i* (showing similarities), 233; and *Ta'biyeh* (staging or mise en scene), 226; as transition from resemblance to semblance, 226–227, 228
Shabih-khani ("Persian Passion Play"): aesthetic alienation not needed in, 3; and fusion of tragedy and comedy, 226; and Kiarostami as semblant subject, 229–230; Kiarostami's staging of Ta'ziyeh, 3, 71, 228, 229–230, 237, 278; mobile performances, 226–227; nonprofessional actors of, 226–227, 229; and the pre-Islamic practice of *Sug-e Seyavash*/Mourning for Seyavash, 225–226; as semblance of subjectivity, 244; Ta'zieh ritual performances and the post-Islamist dramaturgical transition to, 225, 226, 315n5
Shafi'i-Kadkani, Mohammad Reza: overview, 131; aesthetic interpretation of Sufi texts, 157–158; *An-su-ye Harf-o-Sut*, 157–158; Kiarostami's praise for, 132–133; "My Pigeons" (poem for Kiarostami), 131–133; in New Persian Poetry/Nimaic tradition, 254; and proposed inclusiveness of film-philosophy, 249; *Suvar-e Khayal*, 51–54, 149–150, 294
Shahid Sales, Sohrab, 22, 35, 57, 76, 276
Shamlou, Ahmad, 65, 76, 252, 253, 254; "Ebrahim dar Atash/Abraham in Fire," 284
Shams al-Va'zin, Mashallah, 75
Shariati, Ali, 75
Shariati, Susan, 110
Shi'ism: Dissimulation (*Taqiyya*, *Kitman*), 240–241; as guilt-ridden, 190–191; militant, and asceticism, 75, 272; and split between revolutionary politics and its repressed aesthetic imagination, 272, 285; touching of icons as necessary, 279–280, 319n42. *See also* Saqqa-khaneh art movement
Shirdel, Kamran, 24, 61, 62
Shirin, 71, 112–115, 224–225, 234, 236–238
Shishegaran, Koorosh, 79
Shiva, Zarifeh, 181, 191–192
Shklovsky, Viktor: "Art as Device," 54; *Ostranenie*, 3, 164, 292. *See also* aesthetic alienation
simplicity: as cinematic virtue of Kiarostami, 248, 266; and Parviz Kalantari's paintings, 268; moral authority and sacred provenance of, 266; Ozu and, 232, 248, 266; Ray and, 266; Sepehri and, 188–189, 248–249, 268; as strategy of subversion in Kiarostami, 188, 191–192
Singer, Irving, 121
Sirjani, Ali-Akbar Sa'idi: as dissident political activist, 115; *Sima-ye Do Zan/The Portrait of Two Women*, 114–115, 238

Sissako, Abderrahmane, 127
Slaymaker, James, 297
Sobchack, Vivian, 319-320n6
Soja, Edward, 6
Sontag, Susan, *Against Interpretation*, 192
Sorfa, David, *What Is Film-Philosophy?*, 28
Soroush, Abdolkarim, 75
Sotoudeh, Nasrin, 13
Sousa Santos, Boaventura de, 30
sovereign subject. *See* knowing European subject
sovereignty. *See* aesthetic sovereignty of the unknowing subject; aesthetic sovereignty of the work of art
Soviet Union, 191; occupation of Iran, 16, 64
spectators: as mirror image of themselves, 163; as part of the frame, 71-72, 288, *289*, 290; semblance of subjectivity of, 226
Spinoza, Baruch, monism, 216, 217-218, 220
Spivak, Gayatri, 128, 134, 190
Stone, Oliver, *Any Given Sunday*, 23
subversion in Kiarostami's cinema: of absolutist terms of certitude, 165, 176-177, 188; of all "intensities," 177; of the culture of guilt, death, and denial, 190-192; of culture of inhibition, 182-184; of ideological forces involved in Iran/US hostilities, 166; of interpretation, 192; relentless gaze of Kiarostami, as angering his critics, 189; seeking visual and poetic ways to redefine reality, 189; simplicity as strategy of, 188, 191-192; the strategically counter-essentializing camera and, 190; uncodability and, 192; "weak thought" (*il pensiero debole*) as opposition to violent thinking, 188
Sufi saint mausoleums, 267
Sufism: aesthetic interpretation of texts (Shafi'i-Kadkani), 157-158; and the eternal Now (*Ibn al-Waqt*), 111; *fana* as opposed to *baqa* (dying while still alive), 73; God as Friend, 287; heteroglossia and, 106; and *Sama'*/Dance, 206
Sug-e Seyavash/Mourning for Seyavash practice, 225-226
al-Suhrawardi, Shahab a-Din Yahya: *Alam al-Mithal*/Mundus Imaginalis, 101-102, 185; *Aql-e Sorkh*/*The Red Intellect*, 122-123, 211; and European philosophy cast as Philosophy, 200, 249; fusion of fiction and philosophy, 106-107, 122-123; Illuminationist Philosophy (*Falsafah Ishraq*), 102-103, 156; *Na-Koja-abad* ("Nowhereville"), 101-103, 294; and Oriental Philosophy/avian allegories, 211-212; and reading of Kiarostami as allegory, 103-104, 105-107; speculative metaphysics, 102; and the tertiary space, 109-110; visionary recitals of, 106-107, 122-123
the surface, aesthetics of: Kiarostami and motion/exterior, 232; as opposed to the illusion of the depth, 224, 228, 244; Ozu and presence/interior, 232
Suvar-e Khayal. *See* Persian poetic imageries (*Suvar-e Khayal*)

Tabar, Alireza Alavi, 75
Tabataba'i, Allamah, 103
Ta'biyeh (staging or mise en scene), 226
Tabrizi, Sadegh, 269, 280-281
Taghazzol/Lovemaking, 237-239
Taghva'i, Nasser: and the Iranian New Wave, 35; as photographer, 257
Tajaddod, 259-260
Tajrobeh/The Experience, 56-57
Tajvar, Behruz, "Why Did Ms. Teacher Cry?," 120
Take Me Home, 94-95
Takhti, Gholamreza, 276
Talebi-nezhad, Ahmad, 172
Tanavoli, Parviz, 273, 274, 277
Taqiyya or *Kitman* (Dissimulation), 240-241
Tarkovsky, Andrei, 34, 41, 121, 127
Tartaglione, Nancy, 12
Tasawwuf, 157, 250
Tashbih (simile), 226
Taste of Cherry/Ta'm-e Gilas, 27, 50, 197, *214*; and alienation/Verfremdungseffekt, 72-74, 164, 291; in BBC Culture's 100 greatest foreign-language films, 6; the camera as visible to itself, 84-85; Cannes Palme d'Or (1997), 23, 27, 31, 34, 37, 128, 148, 196; as Khayyamesque fear of death turned upside down, 72; long shot in, 72; mobile vision of reality and, 214-215; and Mulla Sudra as philosophical context, 118; and the nomadic un/knowing subject, 213, 217; rumors of unacknowledged sources used in, 120; as search for the Unseen Seer in guise of a search for death, 287; suicide as subject of, 1-2; as thematically in the Koker Trilogy, 115; winding roads as motif, 287
al-Tawhidi, Abu Hayyan, 53

Ta'ziyeh. *See* Shabih-khani ("Persian Passion Play")
Ta'ziyeh staged by Kiarostami, 3, 71, 228, 229-230, 237, 278
temporal tenor of the sacred, 250, 254-256, 281, 292
Ten/Dah: overview, 13; Kiarostami on, 14; mobile vision of reality and, 213-214; and New York Film Festival, 44; and the nomadic un/knowing subject, 213, 217; reviews of, 195-196, 197
tertiary space: overview, 295; as "both/and" accommodation, 98-99, 105; factasy as, 97, 107, 235; form and fact morphing into, 77; hybridity distinguished from, 295; as liberation from aesthetic alienation, 109-110, 165; modernity's tyranny of Reason cannot hold in, 97; traumatic national events standing next to art the nation produces, 92; the un/knowing subject and, 71. *See also* interstitial space
textual authenticity, 73
theater. *See* opera; Persian dramatists and the theater; Shabih-khani
Third World-ism, 97, 115, 199
Through the Olive Trees, 108, 180, 184; overview, 80, 115, 165, 167-168; and aesthetic alienation, liberation from, 164-165; on *Cahiers du Cinema* cover, 193; and the culture of inhibition, 182-184; factasy and, 177, 178-179, 181, 185; and fictive transparency of the real, 182-187, 292; and fusion between cast and crew, 107; long shot of concluding scene of, 172, 185-187, 235; New York Film Festival and release in the US, 166; peace quiet of the set, 187; and Persian poetic imageries of Sepehri, 187-189; poststructural method of storytelling, 180-181; reception of, global, 165-167, 186; reception of, Iranian, 165-166, 167-168, 172-174; release of, 31, 176; staircase shot, repeated takes of, 189-190; as subversive of absolutist terms of certitude, 165. *See also* Koker Trilogy (Earthquake Trilogy)
Tlatli, Moufida, 127
Tobin, Yann, 176
tongue-in-cheek filmic prose: in *Close-Up*, 67, 161; in Koker Trilogy, 80; in *Traveler*, 56. *See also* factasy; fictive transparency of the real

tradition: European capitalist modernity's invention of, 95, 98-99, 100, 104; not the "opposite" of modernity, 260
Transcendental Philosophy (*al-Hikmah al-Muta'aliyah*), 117-118, 156
Transcendental Signified: the camera of Kiarostami as Unseen Seer, 84-85, 282-288, 290; Derridean, 81, 83, 286; and Ghaffari's "Untitled" (painting), 288, *289*; as *Wajib al-Wujud*/Necessary Being, 83, 213, 285-287
transnational public sphere: cosmopolitanism of Kiarostami and, 68; European capitalist modernity and, 93-94; and global triangulation of Kiarostami's cinema, 61-63; humanism of Iranian cinema and, 69; Iranian cinema as formed in, 7-10, 68; the nomadic un/knowing subject as rooted in, 293-294; and the postcolonial disposition, 212-213, 282. *See also* global recognition of Kiarostami as visionary filmmaker
trauma: Iranian cinema, defining national trauma of, 17, 45; national cinemas as predicated on national trauma, 11, 15, 16-18, 21; postnational cinema as predicated on global traumas, 21-22; and the Saqqa-khaneh art movement, 272, 273-274, 276-277
travel (*Safar*) as central motif in Kiarostami: camera point of view, 266; car shots, 266; as fading into infinity, 266, 269; minimalist prose of, 267; and the nomadic un/knowing subject, at home in Safar/Travel and Hazar/Home, 268, 274, 278, 281, 292; sacred journeys (*Ziarat*), and Persian poetry/Islamic philosophy, 266-267; sound design and, 266; and the surface, aesthetics of, 232; zigzag/winding road motif, 43, 266, *267*, 287
Traveler/Mosafer, 56, 77
travel narratives, 214-215
Truffaut, François: critics comparing Kiarostami to, 166, 174; *Day for Night*, 166; *Fahrenheit 451*, 24; prize in his name given to *And Life Goes On*, 174
Trump, Donald, 44
truth: art as both illusion and, 244; the beautiful as the true, 88-89, 157-158, 285; European and Eurocentric philosophy and partition between the beautiful and, 88-89, 92, 224, 256; as illusion, 242-243; as mirroring effect, 243-244; and

the relevance of the beautiful, 279, 281; simulacrum as having supplanted, 243. *See also* semblance of subjectivity; semblant subject
Tunisia: and coloniality, conditions of, 15–17; national cinema and, 15–17
Türkiye, and Kurdish filmmaker Yilmaz Güney, 14
Tusi, Javad, 169–170, 172
24 Frames, 297; as animal (and also human) fable, 208–209, 210–212, 220; framing citation in, 5; on the nature of the cinema in post-filmic era, 297; and the nomadic un/knowing subject, 220–221; posthumous completion of, 240; reception of, 209–210, 297; and the zigzag road motif, 266, *267*
Tyler-Hall, Elaine, 229

uncodability of Kiarostami's cinema, 192, 193–194
United Kingdom: aid to military coup of Reza Khan, 64; coup of 1953 (staged by CIA-MI6), 45, 64, 257–258, 272, 274; occupation of Iran, 16, 198; opera, Kiarostami as director in absentia of Mozart's *Così fan Tutte*, 228–230, 315nn14–15; visa denied to Kiarostami as "prospective terrorist," 228–229, 230, 315n15
United Nations, Kiarostami project for Women's Effort to Save Orphans (UWESO) (Uganda), 235
United States: coup of 1953 (staged by CIA-MI6), 45, 64, 257–258, 272, 274; hostility with Iran (Islamic Republic), 166, 198; Iran hostage crisis (1979–1980), 45, 91–92; *Through the Olive Trees* released in, 166; visa denied to Kiarostami as "prospective terrorist," 44–46, 216–217, 230, 302–303n42
universalities: embrace of non-European, 95, 97, 249–250; as emerging from the ordinary, 63; as emerging from the particularity of postcolonial aesthetic judgment, 221
universalizing claims by Eurocentric philosophy, as false: overview, 58; and aesthetic alienation, 116–117; anthropocentrism as Eurocentrism in, 216, 220; in Blanchot's *Friendship*, 313n15; cast as all and only Philosophy, 57–60, 102, 116–117, 155–156, 199–200, 224; comparative modernity as project, 95; Europe taken for the world, 108; humanism as Eurocentrism in, 216; not present in colonial modernity, 125; of the particular, 204, 313n15; partition between truth and the beautiful, 88–89; periodization of cinema, 135–136
unknowing nomadic subject. *See* nomadic un/knowing subject
unknowing subject: definition of, 124–125; the postcolonial semblant subject as modus operandi of, 227–228

Vali, Shah Ne'amatollah, 35
Van Heusen, Jimmy, 240
Varda, Agnès, 127
Variety, 15
Vattimo, Gianni, 188
Venice Film Festival: Mehrjui's *Gav/The Cow* (prize), 8; Panahi's *Dayereh/Circle* (prize), 9; as vacation destination, 70; *The Wind Will Carry Us/Bad Ma Ra Khahad Bord* (Golden Lion), 196. *See also* European film festivals
Verfremdungseffekt (Bertolt Brecht's alienation effect): Iranian performing arts as not requiring, 2–3; Ozu's camera and, 233; as restoring the strangeness of things, 105; in *Taste of Cherry*, as being-toward-death, 72–74, 164, 291. *See also* aesthetic alienation
Vertov, Dziga, *Man with a Movie Camera*, 84
Village Voice, 186
Visconti, Luchino, 62
visual idiomaticity of Kiarostami's work: as enduring beyond death, 73; as overcoming language barriers, 150
Vivaldi, 170
Von Trotta, Margarethe, 127
voyeurism, cinematic, 214

Walking with the Wind/Hamrah ba bad, 253, 317n9
Waller, Marguerite, 30
Weber, Max, 89, 92, 270; disenchantment, 125
Weir, Peter, 127
"Western Modernity," "the West." *See* European (capitalist) modernity
Western philosophy, construction of Christian philosophy as, 58. *See also* European and Eurocentric philosophy
Where Is My Romeo?, 238

Where Is the Friend's House?/Khaneh-ye Dust Kojast, 193; overview, 80, 115, 167; and allusion to God as Friend, 287; in BBC Culture's top 100 greatest foreign-language films, 6; and central normativity of form, 46; claims on origin of the script for, 119–120; as composite or "ur" text, 120–121; Locarno Film Festival (Bronze Leopard), 9, 175, 192; and "the Now," 119–122; poster for, in *And Life Goes On*, 171, 172; reception of, Iranian, 170, 175; and search for the Unseen Seer, 287; and semblance, 287; Sepehri's "Address" and, 119–120, 121–122, 256; and visionary recitals of Suhrawardi, 122–123; the zigzag road motif, 266. *See also* Koker Trilogy (Earthquake Trilogy)

Wilcox, Paul, 109

Wilde, Oscar, 192

The Wind and the Leaf/Bad-o Barg, 253–254

The Wind Will Carry Us/Bad Ma Ra Khahad Bord, 236; and global recognition of Kiarostami, 34; long shots/long takes and the stable scene, 24, 235; mobile vision of reality and, 214–215; and the nomadic un/knowing subject, 213, 217; and the Persian poetic disposition of Kiarostami, 256; Venice Film Festival (Golden Lion), 196

Wittgenstein, Ludwig, 43, 199, 249, 256

A Wolf in Hiding/Gorgi dar Kamin, 253

women: culture of inhibition and, 182–184; "Islamic dress" of, 180, 237; non-European, and exclusion from human agency, 204; subjectivity of, and *Shirin*, 237–239

Women's Effort to Save Orphans (UWESO) (Uganda), film project, 238

wonder in the ordinary, and early films of Kiarostami, 60–61

Wong Kar-wai, 127

world cinema: and cosmopolitanism of Kiarostami, 68; as disguise for hegemony of Hollywood, 231; European film festivals and construction of, 6–7, 18–19; Iranian cinema and, 6–7, 9, 10, 19, 290; as paradoxical site of colonial modernity, 231; pedagogical promise of, 40–41; scholarly works on, 18; worldly cinema distinguished from, 18, 230–231. *See also* "Borromean rings" of national, postnational, and world cinemas; worldly cinema

worldly cinema: distinguished from "world cinema," 18, 230–231; of Kiarostami, 104–105, 230–231, 233, 241, 293, 296; of Naderi, 19–20, 21; of Ozu, 230–231, 233; three interrelated worlds of, as dismantling the hegemony of Hollywood, 231

World War I, occupation of Iran, 16

World War II: atomic bombings, 96; the Holocaust as modernity come home to roost, 96, 97, 99, 135, 136; occupation of Iran, 16, 64

Yazdi, Farrokhi, 69

Yimou, Zhang, 127

Yousefi-Eshkevari, Hasan 75

Yousef, Surah (The Qur'an), 285

Zarathustra: as central figure in Akhavan-e Sales, 284; *Gathas* of, 103; Mozart and figure of, 89, 90; as Nietzsche's dramatic persona, 89, 90, 137

Zeffirelli, Franco: production of Puccini's *Turandot*, 229; *Romeo and Juliet*, 238

Zeinab, 276

Zen Buddhism, 121

Zenderoudi, Hossein, 272, 273, 274

Ziarat (sacred journeys), 266–267, 278

Zoroastrian symbolism, 123

Zuidervaart, Lambert, ed., *The Semblance of Subjectivity: Essays in Adorno's Aesthetic Theory*, 227–228

Zwingli, Huldrych, 108

Founded in 1893,
UNIVERSITY OF CALIFORNIA PRESS
publishes bold, progressive books and journals
on topics in the arts, humanities, social sciences,
and natural sciences—with a focus on social
justice issues—that inspire thought and action
among readers worldwide.

The UC PRESS FOUNDATION
raises funds to uphold the press's vital role
as an independent, nonprofit publisher, and
receives philanthropic support from a wide
range of individuals and institutions—and from
committed readers like you. To learn more, visit
ucpress.edu/supportus.